CONTROL AND DYNAMIC SYSTEMS

Advances in Theory and Applications

Volume 27

CONTROL AND DYNAMIC SYSTEMS

ADVANCES IN THEORY AND APPLICATIONS

Edited by
C. T. LEONDES

School of Engineering and Applied Science
University of California, Los Angeles
Los Angeles, California

VOLUME 27: SYSTEM IDENTIFICATION AND ADAPTIVE CONTROL
Part 3 of 3

ACADEMIC PRESS, INC.
Harcourt Brace Jovanovich, Publishers
San Diego New York Berkeley Boston
London Sydney Tokyo Toronto

ACADEMIC PRESS RAPID MANUSCRIPT REPRODUCTION

ACADEMIC PRESS, INC.
1250 Sixth Avenue, San Diego, California 92101

United Kingdom Edition published by
ACADEMIC PRESS INC. (LONDON) LTD.
24–28 Oval Road, London NW1 7DX

LIBRARY OF CONGRESS CATALOG CARD NUMBER: 64-8027

ISBN 0–12–012727–X (alk. paper)

PRINTED IN THE UNITED STATES OF AMERICA
88 89 90 91   9 8 7 6 5 4 3 2 1

CONTENTS

Optimal Control for Air Conditioning Systems:
Large-Scale Systems Hierarchy

Charl E. Janeke

A Linear Programming Approach to Constrained
Multivariable Process Control

C. Brosilow and G. Q. Zhao

Techniques for the Identification of Distributed Systems
Using the Finite Element Approximation

K. Y. Lee

An Identification Scheme for Linear Control Systems
with Waveform-Type Disturbances

Joseph Chen

Realizations for Generalized State Space Singular Systems

Manolis A. Christodoulou

Discrete Systems with Multiple Time Scales

Magdi S. Mahmoud

PREFACE

Volume 27 of *Control and Dynamic Systems* is the third volume in a trilogy whose theme is advances in the theory and application of system parameter identification and adaptive control. System parameter identification and adaptive control techniques have now matured to the point where such a trilogy is useful for practitioners in the field who need a comprehensive reference source of techniques having significant applied implications.

The first contribution in this volume, "A New Approach to Adaptive Control," by C. D. Johnson, presents a powerful new approach to multivariable model reference adaptive control based on the ideas and techniques of disturbance-accommodating control theory, which Professor Johnson also originated. The remarkable degree of adaptive performance that these new controllers can achieve is demonstrated by numerous computer simulation results. The chapter begins with a significant discussion noting the distinction between "robust controllers" and "adaptive controllers."

Certainly one of the most important areas of research over the past two or three decades is the modeling of biological systems, and among the most important researchers on the international scene are G. G. Jaros and his colleagues at the University of Cape Town. In the second chapter, "Biological Systems: A General Approach," Jaros, Belonje, and Breuer present a generalized methodology and terminology for modeling biological systems based on a top-down systems approach. The powerful results presented make this an important reference source for research workers in this significant field.

Among the large-scale complex systems applications benefiting from the large knowledge base developed in system identification and adaptive control is that of optimal environmental control of large buildings. This is becoming increasingly more important with the clear trend toward "megastructures" on the international scene. The third contribution, "Optimal Control for Air Conditioning Systems: Large-Scale Systems Hierarchy," by C. E. Janeke, one of the major international contributors in this area, is a comprehensive treatment of the essential techniques in this extremely important and complex area. The next contribution, "A Linear Programming Approach to Constrained Multivariable Process Control," by C. Brosilow and G. Q. Zhao, presents significant new results for the efficient operation of a process operating at or near constraints on the control efforts and/or process output variables in order to prevent an often inevitable, and possibly severe, degradation in performance. Starting with the control structure used by inferential and internal model controllers, design methods which present significantly less computational burden on the controller (and, therefore, are capable of being implemented with microprocessor-based hardware) are developed and illustrated by computer simulations.

The next contribution, "Techniques for the Identification of Distributed Systems Using the Finite Element Approximation," by K. Y. Lee, is a remarkably comprehensive treatment of this subject of broad applied significance. Many engineering physical systems as well as environmental and ecological systems are distributed systems and, therefore, are described by partial differential equations. Their modeling and parameter identification, for the purposes of an implementable control, present formidable problems. Two rather powerful approaches to this problem are presented in this contribution: one is to approximate the distributed system as a finite-dimensional (lumped) system and then to develop a parameter identification scheme; the other is first to develop an infinite-dimensional parameter estimation scheme and then to approximate the solution algorithm using the finite-element method. Both approaches for distributed system modeling and parameter identification are demonstrated numerically and, by numerical example, shown to be highly efficient and effective. In the next chapter, "An Identification Scheme for Linear Control Systems with Waveform-Type Disturbances," by J. Chen, a powerful method is presented for system parameter identification in the presence of system environmental disturbances which cannot be measured. An identification technique is developed that utilizes the disturbance-accommodation control technique of C. D. Johnson to counteract waveform disturbances and applies the maximum likelihood method to identify unknown parameters. Noiselike disturbances are shown to be included as a special case. Numerical examples included in this contribution illustrate the satisfactory convergence of this technique.

"Realizations for Generalized State Space Singular Systems," by M. A. Christodoulou, deals with the fundamentally significant problem of developing irreducible state space realizations or equations for systems from their transfer function representation. The requirement for state space representations of multivariable systems in irreducible or lowest order state vector form deals exactly with the issue of system models of a most efficient form or description. This contribution, which includes significant extensions to the current literature, presents a comprehensive treatment of this fundamentally important subject. The final chapter, "Discrete Systems with Multiple Time Scales," by M. S. Mahmoud, notes that many physical and engineering problems are described by large-scale dynamic models that, as a result, require computational efforts for control analysis and optimization which can be quite excessive. Fundamental techniques for the use of multiple time scales to develop reduced order models which approximate the dynamic behavior of large-scale systems are developed. Interesting adaptive control problems for dominant and nondominant time scale elements of large-scale systems are also developed.

When the theme for this trilogy of volumes was decided upon, there seemed little doubt that it was most timely. The field has been quite active for nearly three decades and has now reached a level of maturity calling for such a trilogy. Because of the substantially important contributions of the authors of this volume and the two previous volumes, however, all three volumes promise to be not only timely but also of lasting fundamental value.

A NEW APPROACH
TO ADAPTIVE CONTROL

C. D. JOHNSON

Electrical and Computer Engineering Department
University of Alabama in Huntsville
Huntsville, Alabama 35899

I.   INTRODUCTION

In practical applications of control engineering it is common to find that the physical plant (system) one is attempting to control is subject to a range P of plant uncertainties. These plant uncertainties can take the form of uncontrollable changes in plant parameters that occur during operation of the system and/or can arise from the inevitable modeling errors and modeling approximations associated with controller designs for complex systems. In addition, controlled plants typically must operate over a range E of uncertain environmental conditions involving a variety of measurable and unmeasurable external input disturbances which are uncontrollable and have uncertain behavior. It follows that an effective controller must be capable of achieving *and maintaining* system closed-loop performance specifications in the face of all anticipated plant uncertainties P and environment uncertainties E.

If the range P of plant uncertainty is sufficiently "small," and the effects of environment uncertainty E are sufficiently "mild," a satisfactory controller can usually be designed by elementary control engineering procedures. However, as the effects of P and/or E become increasingly more severe, the design procedures of elementary control engineering become ineffective and one must then resort to a more advanced form of controller design. Controllers of this advanced type belong to a broad category generally referred to as "adaptive controllers" [1]. It should be mentioned, however, that in recent years some researchers have proposed introducing an intermediate category of advanced controllers called "robust controllers" [2], which lie somewhere between elementary controllers and adaptive controllers. There may be a useful purpose served by the concept of a robust (but nonadaptive) controller. Unfortunately, the essential scientific distinction(s) between "nonlinear robust controllers" and "nonlinear adaptive controllers" has never been made clear in the literature and, consequently, it is difficult to distinguish between robust and adaptive controllers in general; see remarks at the end of Section V,B. The recent introduction of the new term "Robust adaptive controller" [59, 60] has not helped to clarify this issue.

A.   DEFINITION OF AN ADAPTIVE CONTROLLER

The precise, universal definition of an adaptive controller is a topic which has been argued among control researchers for many years and the issue still remains unsettled. Our own researches have led us to propose the following definition of an adaptive controller.

Proposed Definition of an Adaptive Controller. Let $x_m(t; x_{m0})$ be the ideal (desired) closed-loop state-trajectory motion for a controlled plant, and let $x(t, u(t); x_0)$ denote the plant's actual state-trajectory motion under control action $u(t)$. Suppose the plant must operate in the presence of major plant uncertainties P and environment uncertainties E. Further, let the adaptation error state $e_a(t)$ be defined as

$$e_a(t) = x_m(t; x_{m0}) - x(t, u(t); x_0).$$

Then, an adaptive controller is defined as any controller that can consistently regulate $e_a(t) \to 0$ with satisfactorily small settling time, for *all* anticipated plant initial conditions x_0, *all* anticipated plant uncertainties P, and *all* anticipated environment uncertainties E. The geometric interpretation of this definition of adaptive control is shown in Fig. 1. It should be noted in Fig. 1 that the space (domain) X_m on which x_m is defined need not be the same as that for x, in general; see Section I,B.

Remarks on the Proposed Definition. The "ideal" state-trajectory motion $x_m(t; x_{m0})$ is commonly called the "ideal model" of behavior $\mathscr{M}$ and reflects the desired quality of plant behavior in response to plant setpoints, servocommands, etc. The ideal model $\mathscr{M}$ can be defined either explicitly or implicitly. In the explicit case the definition takes the form of either a given vector function $x_m(t; x_{m0}) = \mu(t)$ or a given ideal state-evolution equation $\dot{x}_m = F_m(x_m, t)$, $x_m(0) = \mu(0) = x_{m0} \in X_m$, for the plant, where X_m is invariant for all $x_m(t)$. In the implicit case, the ideal model $x_m(t; x_{m0})$ is defined as the plant trajectory which minimizes some given functional J on $x(t, u(t); x_0)$ and/or $u(t)$, subject to specified constraints and boundary conditions. When $x_m(t; x_{m0})$ is defined explicitly, the controller is called a model-reference adaptive controller. When $x_m(t; x_{m0})$ is defined implicitly, the controller is called a self-optimizing adaptive controller. Note that, in general, the definition of $x_m(t; x_{m0})$ can be either independent of the plant characteristics, dependent on only (known) nominal plant characteristics, or dependent on the actual (real-time) perturbed plant characteristics. The latter often arises, for instance, when $x_m(t; x_{m0})$ is defined implicitly.

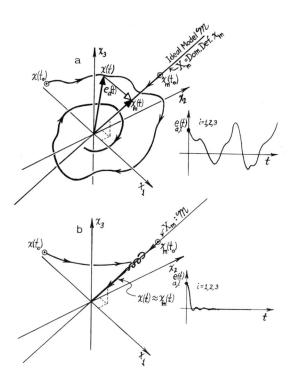

Fig. 1. Proposed definition of an adaptive controller, (a) without and (b) with adaptive control.

The two nebulous terms "major uncertainties" and "satisfactorily small settling time" are admittedly a weakness in our definition of an adaptive controller – but it appears such a weakness is unavoidable. For instance, if the definition allowed "minor" uncertainties and/or "arbitrarily large" settling times for $e_a(t) \to 0$, then almost any well-designed elementary controller would qualify as an adaptive controller. Thus, any definition of adaptive control must impose thresholds on the extent of uncertainty and limits on the $e_a(t)$ settling time to avoid such degeneracy. Otherwise, one must introduce equally nebulous qualifying terms such as weakly adaptive, strongly adaptive, etc.

Our definition of an adaptive controller is based on the time behavior of the adaptation error state $e_a(t)$ and imposes no restrictions or requirements on the mathematical, algorithmic, or physical structure of the controller itself. Indeed, adaptive controller definitions which impose controller structural requirements such as: an adaptive controller must always be "nonlinear," or an adaptive controller must always have "adjustable controller gains," appear to have no rational scientific basis, in our opinion, and such structural requirements have no precedent in control engineering, i.e., compare with the commonly accepted structure-free definitions of a stabilizing controller, setpoint controller, servocontroller, optimal controller, etc.

B.   PLANT MODELS VERSUS IDEAL MODELS:
      RELATIVE ORDERS

In practical applications of adaptive control the "ideal model" $x_m(t; x_{m0}) = \mu(t)$, or $\dot{x}_m = F_m(x_m, t)$, $x_{m0} \in X_m$, may correspond to an ideal system whose dynamical order n_m is: higher than, equal to, or lower than the order n of the actual plant being controlled. For instance, Fig. 1 illustrates the case $n > n_m$ where the actual plant is third order, but the ideal model is only first order (and linear). In Section V,C, a family of examples of the case $n < n_m$ is presented, consisting of a family of linear and nonlinear first-order plants with a common (fixed) linear second-order ideal model; see end of Section V,C and Fig. 11. Thus, the appropriate dimension of the underlying space of Fig. 1, in which to view such cases, consists of the largest dimension $\max(n, n_m)$ plus one additonal dimenison for $x_{n+1} = t$, if appropriate. In that underlying space, the lower-order system is represented by an embedded lower-dimensional linear subspace, affine space, or nonlinear manifold as discussed and illustrated in Refs. [3–6].

C.   CONVERSION FROM IMPLICIT
      TO EXPLICIT IDEAL MODELS

Implicit ideal models are specified only in an indirect manner, as the trajectory family $x_m(t; x_{m0})$ which minimizes some given functional (optimization criterion) J on $x(t)$ and/or $u(t)$. However, in some cases it is possible to explicitly identify the implicit ideal model $x_m(t; x_{m0})$ from the form of the functional J. For example, it has been shown in [7, 8] that the implicit ideal model associated with the n-th-order, time-invariant plant $\dot{x} = Ax + bu$ and quadratic optimization criterion $J = \int_0^\infty [x^T(t)Qx(t) + \rho u^2]\, dt$, $\rho \mapsto 0$, can be explicitly described as a certain well-defined $n_m = (m - 1)$-th order ($m \le n$) linear differential equation $\dot{x}_m = A_M x_m$ which manifests itself as a certain $(m - 1)$-dimensional hyperplane (linear subspace) in the underlying n-dimensional state space of Fig. 1. Moreover, the procedures developed [7, 8] are reversible, allowing one to go from a given $(m - 1)$-th-order ideal model $\dot{x}_m = A_M x_m$ to an n-dimensional quadratic optimization criterion J. A similar conversion result for the case $\rho \to 0$, in which case the plant and ideal model are both n-th order, is well known in linear-quadratic regulator theory [9]. An important generalization of the latter result has recently been developed [10, 11].

D. CONTRIBUTION OF THIS ARTICLE

In this article we present a new approach to multivariable model-reference adaptive control based on the ideas and techniques of disturbance-accommodating control theory [12–16]. This new approach leads to an adaptive controller design procedure that is systematic in nature and applies to a broad class of plants. Moreover, the new adaptive controllers obtained by this design procedure are strikingly simple in structure and often reduce to completely linear, time-invariant controllers. The remarkable degree of adaptive performance which these new controllers can achieve is demonstrated by numerous worked examples with computer simulation results.

II. CONCEPTUAL APPROACHES TO ADAPTIVE CONTROL: AN OVERVIEW

The idea of an "adaptive" control system has a long, colorful history and, over the years, has been the subject of numerous research efforts resulting in many technical papers [7–20] and books [1, 21–23, 50, 62]. As a result of this effort, basically two conceptual approaches to adaptive controller design have emerged.

A. THE 'ADAPTIVE-GAIN' SCHOOL OF THOUGHT

Most of the past and current research in adaptive control has focused on what we will call the "adaptive-gain" school of thought [22]. In that approach the adaptive control law is postulated in the form (linear, scalar control case shown)

$$u = k_1(\cdot)x_1 + k_2(\cdot)x_2 + \dots + k_n(\cdot)x_n, \tag{1}$$

where the control "gains" $k_i(\cdot)$ are automatically adjusted in real time, by an adaptive algorithm, in accordance with perceived perturbations in plant parameters, environmental conditions, etc. The adaptive algorithm is driven by the available plant outputs so that the $k_i(\cdot)$ in (1) are functions of (or functionals on) one or more of the plant state variables x_i. Moreover, the adaptive algorithm itself usually involves one or more nonlinear operations. As a consequence, adaptive controllers based on the adaptive-gain control law (1) are inherently nonlinear.

B. THE 'SIGNAL-SYNTHESIS' SCHOOL OF THOUGHT

Although the adaptive-gain school of thought continues to dominate most of the research in adaptive control, it is, in fact, only one of the possible conceptual approaches to adaptive controller design. Another conceptual approach to adaptive control, which received some attention in the 1950–1965 period but is rarely given more than casual mention now, is called the "signal-synthesis" (or "auxiliary-input signal") school of thought [1; pp. 13, 16–19]. This latter approach is based on the concept that expression (1) is nothing more than a particular decomposition (expansion) of the needed control action u(t) and, as such, expression (1) is only one of many possible ways to synthesize the (essentially) same adaptive control time signal u(t), $t_0 \le t \le T$. In particular, one can envision the adaptive control *signal* u(t) in (1) to be generated alternatively by a real-time weighted linear combination of "basis functions" of the form

$$u(t) = c_1 f_1(t) + c_2 f_2(t) + \ldots + c_k f_k(t), \tag{2}$$

where the set $\{f_1(t), \ldots, f_k(t)\}$ of basis functions is chosen a priori by the designer to provide a qualitative fit to the likely waveform of u(t) and the "constant" weighting coefficients c_i are automatically adjusted in real time to achieve a quantitatively good approximation to u(t). Some possible choices for the basis functions $\{f_i(t)\}$ are those associated with: power series in t, Fourier series, or any of the classical orthogonal polynomials such as Chebyshev, Legendre, Hermite, etc. The two challenges in the signal-synthesis approach to adaptive control are to determine what value u(t) should be at each t and to devise an effective real-time procedure for automatically adjusting the weighting coefficients c_i in (2) to continually realize the required adaptive control signal u(t), $t_0 \le t \le T$. Some attempts to design and implement such signal-synthesis adaptive controllers are described in Refs. [24, 25].

The fact that one can achieve essentially the same adaptive control *signals* u(t) in (1) and (2), using adaptive controllers that are very different in structure, is a point which seems to have been overlooked by many researchers and educators in the adaptive control field; see remarks at the end of Section VII.

C.   SIGNAL SYNTHESIS REVISITED

The signal-synthesis approach to model-reference adaptive control for linear plants was re-examined [26–29] using the relatively new concepts and tools of disturbance-accommodating control (DAC) theory [12–16]. The result of that effort was the development of a new, easily implemented and remarkably effective version of multivariable signal-synthesis adaptive control. These new adaptive controllers can achieve effective adaptive control for both linear and nonlinear plants and in many cases the controllers are *entirely linear* and have *constant coefficients*. The remainder of this article is a tutorial presentation of this new approach to multivariable model-reference adaptive control, including worked examples and results of computer simulation studies.

III. FORMULATION OF A GENERAL CLASS OF ADAPTIVE CONTROL PROBLEMS FOR LINEARIZED DYNAMICAL SYSTEMS

The class of adaptive control problems considered in this article is formulated around a general type of controlled, possibly nonlinear, dynamical system modeled by the state/output equations

$$\dot{x} = \mathscr{F}(x, t, u, w), \qquad x = (x_1, ..., x_n) \tag{3a}$$

$$u = (u_1, ..., u_r)$$

$$w = (w_1, ..., w_p)$$

$$y = \mathscr{G}(x, t), \qquad y = (y_1, ..., y_m), \tag{3b}$$

where x is the system state vector, y is the system output vector, and u, w are, respectively, the system control input vector and external disturbance input vector. It is assumed, for convenience only, that the operating regime $\mathscr{R}$ for (3) is sufficiently well known and the functions $\mathscr{F}(\cdot), \mathscr{G}(\cdot)$ are sufficiently smooth in $\mathscr{R}$ to permit the effective linearization of (3) in $\mathscr{R}$ so that

$$\dot{x}\Big|_{\mathscr{R}} = \mathscr{F}(x, t, u, w) = A(t)x + B(t)u + F(t)w + \eta(x, t, u, w) \tag{4a}$$

$$y\Big|_{\mathscr{R}} = \mathscr{G}(x, t) = C(t)x + v(x, t), \tag{4b}$$

where the expressions $\eta(x, t, u, w)$, $v(x, t)$ represent the collection of all higher-order (e.g., not linear) terms associated with the series expansions on the right sides of (4).

The matrices A(t), B(t), F(t), C(t) of partial derivatives $\partial \mathscr{F}_i/\partial x_j$, $\partial \mathscr{G}_s/\partial x_k$, etc., are assumed to be evaluated at a specified (given) "nominal operating point" $\pi \in \mathscr{R}$. Thus the nominal behavior (value) of each element in A(t), B(t), etc., in (4) is assumed known a priori. The expressions $\eta(\cdot)$. $v(\cdot)$ representing the higher-order terms in (4) are not assumed known but, in keeping with tradition, are assumed negligibly small in comparison with the linear terms of (4), at least in a neighborhood of the nominal operating point $\pi \in \mathscr{R}$. Actually, none of these assumptions is essential because the adaptive controller to be derived here can, in principle, accommodate even nonsmooth, unknown systems (3) and values of $\eta(\cdot)$ which are not negligibly small, as will be shown later in the examples of Section V. Thus, in a neighborhood of the specified operating point π the dynamical system (1) being controlled is represented by the linearized model

$$x = A(t)x + B(t)u + F(t)w \tag{5a}$$

$$y = C(t)x, \tag{5b}$$

where the nominal behavior of $A(t)$, $B(t)$, $F(t)$, and $C(t)$ is known. The results developed here can be generalized to the case $y = Cx + Eu + Hw$ by the techniques used in Refs. [13, Eqs. (42) and (49); 30].

A.   CHARACTERIZATION OF PLANT UNCERTAINTY

The uncertainty associated with the mathematical model (5) is presumed to be in the off-nominal behavior of $A(t)$, $B(t)$, $C(t)$, $F(t)$ and in the behavior of the external disturbance $w(t)$. In regard to the plant uncertainty, the parameter elements $a_{ij}(t)$, $b_{ik}(t)$, $c_{si}(t)$, $f_{il}(t)$ of the matrices $A(t)$, $B(t)$, $C(t)$, $F(t)$ are assumed to deviate from their known nominal behavior in a manner which is uncertain. Thus, the behavior of $A(t)$, $B(t)$, $C(t)$, $F(t)$ in (5) can be represented as

$$A(t) = A_N(t) + [\delta A(t)]; \quad C(t) = C_N(t) + [\delta C(t)]$$

$$\tag{6}$$

$$B(t) = B_N(t) + [\delta B(t)]; \quad F(t) = F_N(t) + [\delta F(t)],$$

where $A_N(t)$, $B_N(t)$, $C_N(t)$, $F_N(t)$ are known and the parameter perturbation matrices $[\delta A(t)]$, $[\delta B(t)]$, $[\delta C(t)]$, $[\delta F(t)]$ are completely unknown. In the controller design procedures to be derived below, it will be mathematically convenient to model the time behavior of the unknown perturbations $[\delta A(t)]$, $[\delta B(t)]$, $[\delta C(t)]$, $[\delta F(t)]$ as either slowly varying (time derivative ≈ 0) or as piecewise-constant with random jumps occurring in a once-in-a-while fashion. However, the final adaptive controller designs can, in fact, accommodate unknown parameter perturbations with a significant degree of nonconstant behavior, as illustrated by the worked examples presented in Section V.

B.   CHARACTERIZATION OF
DISTURBANCE UNCERTAINTY

The uncertainty associated with the behavior of measurable and unmeasurable external disturbances $w(t)$ in (5) is not modeled statistically, but rather is represented by a semideterministic waveform-model description of the generalized spline-function type. Namely, each independent element $w_i(t)$ of w is modeled as

$$w_i(t) = c_{i1}f_{i1}(t) + c_{i2}f_{i2}(t) + \ldots + c_{im_i}f_{im_i}(t), \tag{7}$$

where the "basis functions" $\{f_{i1}(t), ..., f_{im_i}(t)\}$ are completely known and the "constant" weighting coefficients $\{c_{i1}, ..., c_{im_i}\}$ are totally unknown (and may jump in value from time to time). For practical reasons, and with little loss of generality, it is further assumed that the basis functions $f_{ij}(t)$ in (7) are such that they satisfy a linear differential equation. As a consequence, there exists a linear dynamical "state model" representation of $w(t)$ having the form

$$w(t) = H(t)z; \qquad w = (w_1, ..., w_p) \qquad\qquad (8a)$$

$$\dot{z} = D(t)z + \sigma(t); \qquad z = (z_1, ..., z_\rho), \qquad\qquad (8b)$$

where $H(t)$, $D(t)$ are completely known and $\sigma = (\sigma_1, ..., \sigma_\rho)$ is a vector of impulse sequences (representing jumps in the c_{ij}) which are sparse but otherwise totally unknown.

The control engineering utility of the disturbance waveform model and state model representations (7) and (8) (and their generalizations [13, pp. 415–416]) has been exploited in a long series of papers and book chapters published over the past 20 years and has emerged as one of the central ideas in the theory of disturbance-accommodating control for uncertain disturbance inputs and plant model errors [12–16, 30–40]. In this capacity, the waveform and state models (7) and (8) have been successfully used to represent: plant model errors associated with Coulomb and other complex forms of nonlinear damping, uncertain external input disturbances, plant parameter model errors, coupling effects in reduced-order state models, etc. In some of those applications, the basis functions $f_{ij}(t)$ in (7) can be uniquely identified as naturally occurring modes of time-domain behavior; for example, as naturally occurring piecewise-constant, sinusoidal, or exponential behavior, as in Refs. [41–43]. In other applications, the diverse time-domain behavior patterns of some $w_i(t)$ are best represented synthetically by choosing Eq. (7) as an $(m_i - 1)$-degree power series in t; i.e., $f_{i1}(t) = 1$, $f_{i2}(t) = t$, $f_{i3}(t) = t^2$, ..., etc. [13, p. 413] or as one of the orthogonal polynomials commonly used in approximation theory [44, 45].

In summary, the linearized dynamical system being controlled is modeled by

$$\dot{x} = [A_N(t) + \delta A(t)]x + [B_N(t) + \delta B(t)]u + [F_N(t) + \delta F(t)]w(t) \qquad (9a)$$

$$y = [C_N(t) + \delta C(t)]x \qquad\qquad (9b)$$

$$w = H(t)z \qquad\qquad (9c)$$

$$\dot{z} = D(t)z + \sigma(t), \qquad\qquad (9d)$$

where $A_N(t)$, $B_N(t)$, $C_N(t)$, $F_N(t)$, $H(t)$, $D(t)$ are completely known and $\delta A(t)$, $\delta B(t)$, $\delta C(t)$, $\delta F(t)$, $\sigma(t)$ are unknown.

C.   INTRODUCTION OF AN EXPLICIT IDEAL MODEL $\mathcal{M}$

The given closed-loop performance specifications for (9) are assumed to be expressed in terms of an explicit ideal-model behavior for x(t). Namely, the desired behavior of x(t) is expressed by the given nth-order "ideal model" (reference model) $\mathcal{M}$.

$\mathcal{M}$: $\dot{x}_m = A_M(t)x_m$; $A_M(t)$ = specified n × n matrix.   (10)

In DAC theory one typically defines the state x in (9) in terms of "error variables" such that x = 0 corresponds to the desired plant operating condition [13, p. 450; 12, Art. VI]. In that case, the ideal model (10) defines the desired behavior of the "error state" x(t) as x(t) → 0. Thus, the task of the adaptive controller u(·) is to make the original equation of motion (9a) rapidly acquire the ideal model behavior (10) and steadily maintain that ideal behavior in the face of arbitrary initial conditions $x(t_0)$, uncertain parameter perturbations $\delta A(t)$, $\delta B(t)$, etc., and all input disturbances w(t) which can be generated by (9c and d) (see Fig. 1). Moreover, the adaptive controller must accomplish this task using only the on-line, real-time measurements of the system output vector $y(t) = (y_1(t), y_2(t), ..., y_m(t))$ in (9b). Note that when x in (9) corresponds to the "error state," the system output y in (9b) will embody both the plant measurements *and* the system commands (setpoints, servo commands, etc.). This feature is illustrated in the worked examples presented in Section V.

IV.   SOLUTION OF THE ADAPTIVE CONTROL PROBLEM OF EQS. (9) AND (10) FOR THE CASE $\{[\delta B(t)], [\delta C(t)], [\delta F(t)]\} = 0$

In this section we will show how the principles and techniques of DAC theory can be used to address the model-reference adaptive control problem formulated in Section III. For simplicity, we will first consider the special case of the general problem (9) and (10) corresponding to $\{[\delta B(t)], [\delta C(t)], [\delta F(t)]\} = 0$; i.e., uncertain perturbations occur *only* in the plant matrix $A(t) = A_N(t) + [\delta A(t)]$. The controller developed in this section will, in fact, adapt to a moderate range of [δB], [δF] as a byproduct of accommodating [δA] and w(t). However, the formal consideration of perturbations in B(t), F(t), and C(t) is presented later in Section VI, where a general class of [δB], [δF], and one particular class of [δC], are treated. Accommodation of the most general case of [δC] is a problem which is not completely solved at this time.

A.   APPLICATION OF DAC PRINCIPLES

The analytical design of an adaptive controller $u(\cdot)$ which will make (9a) mimic the reference model (10), in the face of uncertain parameter perturbations $\delta A(t)$ and uncertain external disturbances $w(t)$, can be derived by applying the principles of disturbance-accommodating control theory [26–28]. For this purpose, one first agrees to split the total control effort $u(\cdot)$ into three "parts," each having its own specific task. Thus, the control vector $u(\cdot)$ in (9a) is written in the form

$$u = u_d + u_a + u_p, \tag{11}$$

where the individual control tasks are assigned as follows:

u_d –   responsible for cancelling out the effects of
              $w(t)$ on the motion of $x(t)$ in (9a)

u_a –   responsible for cancelling out the effects of   (12)
              $\delta A(t)$ on the motion of $x(t)$ in (9a)

u_p –   responsible for achieving the condition
              $A_N(t)x(t) + B(t)u_p = A_M(t)x(t)$, for all $x(t)$.

It turns out that these three control tasks are essentially independent of each other (the "design separation principle" of DAC theory [32, p. 517]), so that one can proceed to design u_d, u_a, u_p in any order. This also means that u_d., u_a, u_p will be implemented as three *separate* feedback-control loops, operating simultaneously, with each performing its own independent task (i.e., a "decentralized" controller structure will result).

To proceed, Eqs. (11) and (9c) are substituted into (9a) to obtain

$$\dot{x} = A_N(t)x + B(t)u_p + [\delta A(t)]x + B(t)u_a \tag{13}$$

$$+ B(t)u_d + F(t)H(t)z$$

where $B = B_N$, $F = F_N$, $C = C_N$. In light of (13), the three control tasks (12) can now be stated more precisely in the following idealized form:

u_d must satisfy the condition

$$B(t)u_d(t) = -F(t)H(t)z(t), \quad \text{for all } z(t) \tag{14a}$$

u_a must satisfy the condition

$$B(t)u_a(t) = -[\delta A(t)]x(t), \quad \text{for all } \delta A(t) \text{ and } x(t) \tag{14b}$$

u_p must satisfy the condition

$$B(t)u_p(t) = -[A_N(t) - A_M(t)]x(t), \quad \text{for all } x(t). \tag{14c}$$

The necessary and sufficient conditions for the existence of solutions (u_d, u_a, u_p) to (14) are as follows [13]:

for u_d:

$$\text{rank}[B(t)|F(t)H(t)] \equiv \text{rank}[B(t)] \tag{15a}$$

$$\Rightarrow F(t)H(t) \equiv B(t)\Gamma_d(t), \quad \text{for some matrix } \Gamma_d(t) \tag{15b}$$

for u_a:

$$\text{rank}[B(t)|\delta A(t)] \equiv \text{rank}[B(t)] \tag{16a}$$

$$\Rightarrow \delta A(t) \equiv B(t)\Gamma_A(t), \quad \text{for some matrix } \Gamma_A(t) \tag{16b}$$

for u_p:

$$\text{rank}[B(t)|A_N(t) - A_M(t)] \equiv \text{rank}[B(t)] \tag{17a}$$

$$\Rightarrow [A_N(t) - A_M(t)] \equiv B(t)\Gamma_p(t) \text{ for some matrix } \Gamma_p(t). \tag{17b}$$

In some applications, the ideal model matrix A_M in (10) is specified *only* in terms of its required eigenvalues λ_i or characteristic polynomial $\mathscr{P}(\lambda)$. That is, one only specifies that A_M be constant and satisfy

$$\mathscr{P}(\lambda) = \det[\lambda I - A_M] = \lambda^n + \beta_n\lambda^{n-1} + \ldots + \beta_2\lambda + \beta_1 = 0 \tag{18}$$

where the "ideal" ($\beta_1, \ldots, \beta_n$) in (18) are precisely specified. In that event, one chooses (ideally)

$$u_p = K_px \tag{19a}$$

and the necessary and sufficient condition for the existence of u_p becomes

$$\det[\lambda I - (A_N + BK_p)] = \lambda^n + \beta_n\lambda^{n-1} + \ldots + \beta_2\lambda + \beta_1, \text{ for some } K_p. \tag{19b}$$

The design of K_p in (19), for specified $(\beta_1, \ldots, \beta_n)$, is a standard problem in modern control theory for which there is a variety of algorithms [46, Articles 6, 8; 47].

Assuming the conditions (15b), (16b), and (17b) are satisfied, the decentralized control terms (14) can be expressed ideally as

$$u_d = -\Gamma_d(t)z(t) \tag{20a}$$

$$u_a = -\Gamma_A(t)x(t) \tag{20b}$$

$$u_p = -\Gamma_p x(t), \quad [\text{or } K_p x(t)]. \tag{20c}$$

Expressions (20) are said to be idealized because, in reality, the state vectors $(z(t), x(t))$ in (20) cannot be directly measured in real time. However, if one can somehow generate reliable real-time estimates $z(t)$, $x(t)$ of $z(t)$, $x(t)$, then at least the u_d and u_p terms (20a) and (20c) can be physically implemented as

$$u_d = -\Gamma_d(t)\hat{z}(t) \tag{21a}$$

$$u_p = -\Gamma_p(t)\hat{x}(t), [\text{or } K_p\hat{x}(t)] \tag{21b}$$

B.   MODELING AND ESTIMATION OF $[\delta A(t)]x(t)$

Controller implementations of the form (21) are standard procedure in DAC theory [13]. The practical implementation of the u_a term (20b) is *not* standard procedure and is somewhat challenging because, in view of (16b), the matrix $\Gamma_A(t)$ is itself unknown and, in fact, changes in an uncertain manner. The main contribution of the new adaptive theory presented here, from the DAC-theoretic point of view, is in the unique way we model and generate reliable real-time estimates of the plant parameter perturbation effect $[\delta A(t)]x(t)$ in (13), so that (20b) can be effectively implemented.

It is remarked that in practical applications some of the elements of $[\delta A(t)]$ may be known *a priori* to be always zero, or to be functionally related in some fashion. For instance, if A(t) occurs naturally in the "companion form"

$$A(t) = \begin{bmatrix} 0 & 1 & 0 & 0 & . & . & . & 0 \\ 0 & 0 & 1 & 0 & . & . & . & 0 \\ 0 & 0 & 0 & 1 & . & . & . & 0 \\ & & & & . & & & \\ & & & & & . & & \\ 0 & 0 & 0 & 0 & . & . & . & 1 \\ a_1 & a_2 & & . & . & . & & a_n \end{bmatrix} \tag{22}$$

it may turn out that only the elements in the last row of $A(t)$ suffer nonzero parameter perturbations $\delta a_i(t)$. However, for the time being we will treat $[\delta A(t)]$ as an $n \times n$ perturbation matrix, with independent elements δa_{ij}, in order to preserve the generality of our results (see Section IV,I).

The key to the successful implementation of the parameter adaptive control term u_a in (20b) is the development of a practical means for modeling and on-line estimating the behavior of the uncertain parameter disturbance term $[\delta A(t)]x(t)$ in (13). For this purpose we propose the following technique. First, suppose one can somehow generate reliable on-line estimates of $\hat{x}(t)$, $\hat{z}(t)$ $x(t)$, $z(t)$ and set

$$\varepsilon_x = x - \hat{x} \tag{23a}$$

$$\varepsilon_z = z - \hat{z} \tag{23b}$$

where presumably $\varepsilon_x(t) \to 0$, $\varepsilon_z(t) \to 0$ rapidly. Then, substituting (21) and (23) into (13), using (15d) and (17b), one obtains

$$\dot{x} = A_M(t)x + [\delta A(t)]x + B(t)u_a + B(t)[\Gamma_p(t)\varepsilon_x + \Gamma_d(t)\varepsilon_z]. \tag{24}$$

Assuming $\varepsilon_x \approx 0$, $\varepsilon_z \approx 0$ in (24), one obtains the "almost ideal" equation of motion

$$x = A_M(t)x + [\delta A(t)]x + B(t)u_a. \tag{25}$$

If $[\delta A(t)] \equiv 0$ in (25), one can set $u_a(t) \equiv 0$ to immediately obtain the desired "ideal model behavior" (10). Thus, the problem is to model and estimate the term $[\delta A(t)]x(t)$ in (25), and then design $u_a(t)$ to automatically cancel that term, in real time. Note that $[\delta A(t)]$ in (25) can also represent perturbations in Γ_p (or K_p).

Since the behavior of the parameter perturbations $\delta A(t)$ are assumed essentially totally unknown, it would appear that the only feasible approach would be to proceed as in Ref. [13, p. 413] and treat each element of the vector $[\delta A(t)]x(t)$ in (25) as having "unfamiliar" dynamics and model its dynamic behavior as some M-th-degree polynomial in time, with uncertain piecewise constant coefficients c_0, c_1, ..., c_m; that is, invoke the polynomial spline approximation

$$[\delta A(t)]x(t)|_{\text{i-th element}} \approx c_{i0} + c_{i1}t + c_{i2}t^2 + \ldots + c_{iM_i}t^{M_i}, \tag{26}$$

for some appropriate degree M_i, $i = 1, 2, \ldots, n$.

The simplicity of (26) and of its corresponding state differential equation model (8) {an $(M_i + 1)$-th-order integrator model [13]} is very appealing from the practical implementation point of view, and adaptive controllers designed on that basis have been proposed and studied for more than 10 years [13, 44, 45]. However, the power-series basis functions $\{1, t, t^2, \ldots, t^{M_i}\}$ in (26) are synthetic representations of the actual waveform models of $[\delta A(t)]x(t)$ and, therefore, are not necessarily the most efficient ones to use in terms of the number of basis functions (e.g., value of M_i) needed to obtain a specified degree of approximation accuracy. With this in mind, we now turn to a novel alternative approach to modeling the dynamic behavior of $[\delta A(t)]x(t)$ in (25), using natural basis functions for $[\delta A(t)]x(t)$.

Up to this point, we have not invoked any special assumptions regarding the waveform behavior of $A_M(t)$ or the parameter perturbation matrix $[\delta A(t)]$. However, from the practical applications point of view it seems reasonable to assume that $A_M(t)$ and the parameter perturbations $\delta A(t)$ change either relatively slowly, so that

$$\frac{dA_M(t)}{dt} \approx 0 \text{ and } \frac{d[\delta A(t)]}{dt} \approx 0 \tag{27a}$$

or else behave as essentially piecewise constant matrices (which "jump" in value every once in a while), in which case

$$\frac{dA_M(t)}{dt} = 0 \text{ and } \frac{d[\delta A(t)]}{dt} = 0, \tag{27b}$$

almost everywhere. Thus, we hereafter invoke the assumption that conditions (27) are valid for the class of $A_M(t)$ and parameter perturbation $\delta A(t)$ being considered. As indicated below (6), our final controller design will, in fact, accommodate a significant degree (but not arbitrary degree) of time variation in $[\delta A]$. To proceed, we write the plant parameter "disturbance" n-vector $[\delta A]x(t)$ in (25) as

$$w_a = [\delta A]x(t) = \begin{bmatrix} p_1 \\ p_2 \\ \cdot \\ \cdot \\ \cdot \\ p_n \end{bmatrix} x(t) = \begin{bmatrix} w_{a1} \\ w_{a2} \\ \cdot \\ \cdot \\ \cdot \\ w_{an} \end{bmatrix}, \tag{28}$$

where p_i denotes the i-th row of $[\delta A]$ and

$$w_{ai} = \langle p_i, x \rangle, \tag{29}$$

where the angle brackets denote an inner product. Expression (29) can be viewed as representing a time-domain waveform model of the type (7) where, in this case, the basis functions $\{f_{ij}\}$ for (29) are implicitly defined as those associated with the perturbed, closed-loop controlled motions $x(t)$ of the system (25). Since $[\delta A]$ in (25) is unknown, and the control law $u_a = u_a$ (?) in (25) has not yet been selected, the basis functions for (29) appear ill-defined and hopelessly elusive, in general. However, recall that the objective of $u_a(\cdot)$ in (25) is to completely cancel (counteract) the plant parameter disturbance $[\delta A]x(t)$. Thus it follows that u_a should ideally satisfy the relation

$$Bu_a = -[\delta A]x = -w_a. \tag{30}$$

At this point, it will be tacitly assumed that the final, physically realizable design of $u_a(\cdot)$ will reflect the qualitative structure indicated in (30). In particular, Bu_a will be assumed to have the form

$$Bu_a = -\hat{w}_a(t), \tag{31}$$

where $w_a(t)$ represents an accurate, physically realizable, on-line estimate of $w_a(t) = [\delta A]x$ in (30). Under assumption (31), accurate estimates of the basis functions associated with (29) can be easily computed – which in turn allows assumption (31) to be realized! To see this, we proceed to examine the higher time derivatives of each of the scalar elements w_{ai} in (29), using (27) and (31). Thus, the first derivative yields

$$\dot{w}_{ai} = \langle p_i, A_M x \rangle + \langle p_i, [\delta A]x \rangle - \langle p_i, \hat{w}_a \rangle. \tag{32}$$

The important features to notice about (32) are: 1) the last two terms on the right of (32) are, respectively, quadratic functions of the perturbation elements δa_{ij} and cross-product functions of δa_{ij} and the estimates $\hat{\delta a}_{kl}$, and 2) the last term on the right of (32) is (presumably) an accurate estimate of the next-to-last term. Thus, if the δa_{ij} and their estimates $\hat{\delta a}_{ij}$ are all sufficiently "small," each of the last two terms on the right of (32) is, by itself, negligible with respect to the linear (first) terms, provided $\langle p_i, A_M x \rangle \neq 0$. Note, however, that even if δa_{ij} and $\hat{\delta a}_{ij}$ are *not* that small, the sum of the last two terms is negligible if the estimate $\hat{w}_a$ is sufficiently accurate. If the δa_{ij}, $\hat{\delta a}_{ij}$ are indeed small and, in addition, $\hat{w}_a$ is sufficiently accurate, then the negligibility is compounded and the sum of the last two terms is extraordinarily small compared to the (nonzero) linear term, i.e., the difference of two higher-order terms which are approximately equal. This compounding effect will enable our adaptive controller to accommodate parameter perturbations δa_{ij} which are relatively large compared to nominal values. Thus, if one assumes that the $\hat{\delta a}_{ij}$, δa_{ij} are sufficiently small and/or $\hat{w}_a$ is sufficiently accurate, then (32) is closely approximated by

$$\dot{w}_{ai} \cong \langle p_i, A_M x \rangle; \quad \langle p_i, A_M x(t) \rangle \neq 0. \tag{33}$$

Employing a similar line of reasoning to the higher time derivatives of w_a, one obtains the close approximations

$$\ddot{w}_{ai} \cong \langle p_i, A^2_M x \rangle$$

$$\dddot{w}_{ai} \cong \langle p_i, A^3_M x \rangle$$

etc., assuming $\langle p_i, A^k_M x(t) \rangle \neq 0, k \geq 1.$ \hfill (34)

It follows from the Cayley–Hamilton theorem that, for arbitrary values of i, p_i, and x, the sequence in (29), (33), and (34) always satisfies the linear, homogeneous expression (differential equation)

$$\overset{(n)}{w}_{ai} + \beta_n \overset{(n-1)}{w}_{ai} + \dots + \beta_2 \dot{w}_{ai} + \beta_1 w_{ai} = 0, \tag{35}$$

where $(\beta_1, \beta_2, \dots, \beta_n)$ are the known coefficients of the characteristic polynomial of A_M.

$$\det[\gamma I - A_M] = \lambda^n + \beta_n \lambda^{n-1} + \dots + \beta_2 \lambda + \beta_1 = 0. \tag{36}$$

Thus, under the assumptions stated [and approximations (33), (34), etc.], and for "arbitrary" $[\delta A]$, *each* component w_{ai} of w_a in (28) satisfies the *same* n-th-order linear differential equation (35) along solutions of (25), (27), and (31). In other words, the n eigenmodes of (35) are the "natural" basis functions $\{f_i(t)\}$ for each $w_{ai}(t)$; compare with the synthetic basis set in (26). Note that a separate model (35) is required to represent *each* independent component w_{ai}. It is remarked that for particular numerical values of p_i, the associated $w_{ai}(t)$ may also satisfy a linear differential equation (35) having lower order than n. However, since the p_i in practice are completley unknown (and may change randomly from time to time), the nth-order equation (35) is the only equation which is guaranteed to govern (model) the behavior of $w_{ai}(t)$ for arbitrary perturbations p_i. Each scalar expression (35) can be put in the standard DAC state-model format (8) by choosing state variables as $w_{ai} = z_{i1}$, $\dot{w}_{ai} = z_{i2}$, etc., so that one obtains (8) as

$$w_{ai} = (1, 0, 0, \dots, 0) \begin{pmatrix} z_{i1} \\ z_{i2} \\ \cdot \\ \cdot \\ \cdot \\ z_{in} \end{pmatrix} \tag{37a}$$

$$
\begin{pmatrix} \dot{z}_{i1} \\ \dot{z}_{i2} \\ \cdot \\ \cdot \\ \cdot \\ \dot{z}_{in} \end{pmatrix}
=
\begin{bmatrix} 0 & 1 & 0 & \cdots & 0 \\ 0 & 0 & 1 & \cdots & 0 \\ \cdot & & & & \cdot \\ \cdot & & & \cdots & \cdot \\ 0 & 0 & & & 1 \\ -\beta_1 & -\beta_2 & & \cdots & -\beta_n \end{bmatrix}
\begin{pmatrix} z_{i1} \\ z_{i2} \\ \cdot \\ \cdot \\ \cdot \\ z_{in} \end{pmatrix}
+
\begin{pmatrix} \sigma_{i1} \\ \sigma_{i2} \\ \cdot \\ \cdot \\ \cdot \\ \sigma_{in} \end{pmatrix}
\tag{37b}
$$

where $i = 1, 2, \ldots, n$, and the sparse impulse sequences σ_{ij} symbolically model the unknown once-in-a-while changes in p_i = the i-th row of $[\delta A]$. The set of n identical nth-order state models (37) can be collectively represented as one composite n^2-order state model (8) by setting $z_a = (z_a^{(1)}|z_a^{(2)}|\cdots|z_a^{(n)})^T$, where the superscript T denotes the transpose, and where $z_a^{(i)} = (z_{i1}, z_{i2}, \ldots, z_{in})^T$, so that the n vector w_a in (28) has the state model.[1]

$$w_a = H_a z_a \tag{38a}$$

$$\dot{z}_a = D_a z_a + \sigma_a, \tag{38b}$$

where H_a, D_a are, respectively, $n \times n^2$ and $n^2 \times n^2$ matrices of the "repeating block" form

$$
H_a = \begin{bmatrix} h_0 & 0 & \cdots & 0 \\ 0 & h_0 & & 0 \\ \cdot & & \cdot & \cdot \\ \cdot & & & \cdot \cdot \\ 0 & 0 & \cdots & h_0 \end{bmatrix} ; \quad h_0 = (1, 0, \ldots, 0)
\tag{39a}
$$

$$
D_a = \begin{bmatrix} D_0 & 0 & \cdots & 0 \\ 0 & D_0 & \cdots & 0 \\ \cdot & & \cdot & \cdot \\ \cdot & & \cdot & \cdot \\ 0 & 0 & \cdots & D_0 \end{bmatrix} ,
\tag{39b}
$$

---

[1] The model (38) presumes that *each element* w_{ai} (each row of $[\delta A]$) is independent. If the elements w_{ai} are *not* all independent, the dimension of z_a in (38) is reduced accordingly.

where there are n terms in h_0 and where each block D_0 is the (same) completely known $n \times n$ companion matrix in (37b). The natural basis functions for each element w_{ai} of $w_a(t)$ are thus imbedded in the model (38) as the n^2 eigenmodes of D_a. This feature will allow our adaptive controller to automatically generate the signal-synthesis format (2) in a new and highly efficient manner, using a real-time observer based on (38).

C.   IDEAL AND PRACTICAL FORMS OF $u_a(t)$

Incorporating (28) and (38) into (25), the basic state model (25) can be closely approximated as the enlarged (and now unperturbed) system

$$\dot{x} = A_M x + B u_a + H_a z_a \tag{40a}$$

$$\dot{z}_a = D_a z_a + \sigma_a \tag{40b}$$

$$y = Cx; \quad C = C_N, \tag{40c}$$

where u_a and each of the p_i are presumed to satisfy (31) and the "nonsingular condition" $\langle p_i, A^k_M x(t) \rangle \neq 0$, $k = 1, \ldots, n$, in (34). The rare circumstances under which this singular condition can occur, and its consequences to our adaptive controller, are analyzed in detail in Appendix A of this article. In view of (40a), the ideal design relation (30) for u_a can be rewritten as

$$B u_a = -H_a z_a, \tag{41}$$

where z_a is "arbitrary."[1] The necessary and sufficient condition for existence of a solution u_a to (41) is

$$H_a = B \Gamma_a, \quad \text{for some matrix } \Gamma_a, \tag{42}$$

in which case the ideal solution for the parameter adaptive control u_a in (41) is given as [compare with (20b); note that $\Gamma_A \neq \Gamma_a$]

$$u_a = -\Gamma_a z_a. \tag{43}$$

Owing to the special structure (39a) of H_a, which is a consequence of the assumed arbitrary nature of $[\delta A]$, it turns out that

$$\text{rank } H_a = n, \tag{44}$$

and, therefore, (42) can be satisfied if and only if

$$\text{rank } B = n, \tag{45a}$$

in which case

$$\Gamma_a = B^{-1}H_a. \tag{45b}$$

Condition (45a) simply means that if $[\delta A]$ is completley arbitrary, the control vector u_a *must* be n-dimensional ($r = n$) in order to completely cancel the n^2-parameter "disturbance" term $[\delta A]x$, for arbitrary x. On the other hand, the requirement that $r = n$ can be significantly relaxed if the perturbations in $[\delta A]$ are confined to only a few rows. In particular, the control dimension r must equal the number of nonzero rows of $[\delta A]$, in general. For example, in the "companion" case (22) only a scalar control u_a is required ($r = 1$) to accommodate all perturbations in the last row of A. In that particular case, $D_a = D_0$ and H_a in (39a) would reduce to an $n \times n$ matrix with the first $n - 1$ rows all zero. Therefore, the requirements (41) and (42) on B would be relaxed. Some of the examples presented later will illustrate this case.

The main advantage of introducing the enlarged model (40) is the fact that the uncertain parameter disturbance term $[\delta A]x(t)$ in (25) is then represented by a "state vector" $z_a(t)$ which is known to obey the known differential equation (40b). By this means, the practical implementation of the ideal parameter adaptive control term (43) can be realized in the state-feedback form

$$u_a = -\Gamma_a \hat{z}_a(t), \tag{46}$$

where $\hat{z}_a(t)$ is an on-line, real-time estimate of $z_a(t)$ generated by an "observer" or Kalman filter device which will be described below. Note that $u_a(t)$ produced by (46) and (40b) will have the (vector) signal synthesis form (2), where the f_i are the eigenmodes of D_a.

D.   SUMMARY OF THE COMPLETE ADAPTIVE CONTROL LAW

It is recalled from (11) that at the outset our adaptive controller u for (13) was decomposed (decentralized) into three separate terms: u_d, u_a, and u_p. The individual designs for each of those control terms have been given in (21a), (21b) and (46). Thus, the final expression for the complete adaptive control law (11), in practical form, is

$$u = -[\Gamma_d(t)\hat{z} + \Gamma_a(t)\hat{z}_a + \Gamma_p(t)\hat{x}], \tag{47}$$

where the matrices Γ_d, Γ_a, Γ_p (or K_p) are defined, respectively, by (15b), (42), and (17b) [or (19b)]. Provided that the real-time estimates $\hat{z}$, $\hat{z}_a$, $\hat{x}$ in (47) are reliable, the linear adaptive control law (47) applied to (9a) (with $\delta B = 0$, $\delta F = 0$, $\delta C = 0$)

will automatically: 1) cancel the effects of the uncertain external disturbance w(t), 2) cancel the effects of the uncertain parameter perturbations [δA], and 3) cause the remaining dynamics of (9a) to mimic the ideal model equation (10). Thus, (47) is a new form of "model reference adaptive control law" using signal synthesis adaptation (auxiliary input signals) as described in Section II,B of this article. It is important to note that the gain matrices $\Gamma_d(t)$, $\Gamma_a(t)$, $\Gamma_p(t)$ in our adaptive control law (47) are not "time-varying adaptive gains" in the sense of (1). In fact it is easy to see from (15b), (42), and (17b) [or (19b)] that Γ_d, Γ_a, Γ_p will be *constant* matrices when {B, F, H, A_N, A_M} are constant. Nevertheless, the controller (47) generates essentially the *same* control *signal* u(t) as would a traditional nonlinear "adaptive-gain" controller (1), assuming the same plant, perturbations, disturbances, etc., appropriate for (47) (see [52]). The controller (47) will, in fact, adapt to a moderate range of [δB], [δF]; however, formal consideration of this topic is postponed until Section VI.

E. DESIGN OF COMPOSITE STATE-OBSERVERS
   FOR THE ADAPTIVE CONTROL LAW (47)

The effectiveness of the adaptive control law (47) is determined mainly by the quality of the real-time state estimates $\hat{z}(t)$, $\hat{z}_a(t)$, $\hat{x}(t)$ In DAC theory such estimates are generated by "composite" state observers [13, p. 430; 30] which reflect the combined dynamical models of z(t), $z_a(t)$, and x(t). To develop such an observer for the adaptive control law (47), we proceed as follows. First, one combines the individual dynamical models in (9), (28), and (38) to obtain the (n + ρ + n^2)-th-order composite model (recall the assumption B = B_N, F = F_N, C = C_N in this section)

$$\begin{pmatrix} \dot{x} \\ \dot{z} \\ \dot{z}_a \end{pmatrix} = \begin{bmatrix} A_N(t) & F(t)H(t) & H_a \\ 0 & D(t) & 0 \\ 0 & 0 & D_a \end{bmatrix} \begin{pmatrix} x \\ z \\ z_a \end{pmatrix} + \begin{bmatrix} B(t) \\ 0 \\ 0 \end{bmatrix} u + \begin{pmatrix} 0 \\ \sigma(t) \\ \sigma_a(t) \end{pmatrix} \qquad (48a)$$

with system output vector

$$y = [C(t)|0|0] \begin{pmatrix} x \\ z \\ z_a \end{pmatrix} \qquad (48b)$$

The problem is to generate accurate estimates $\hat{x}(t)$, $\hat{z}(t)$, $\hat{z}_a(t)$ from on-line measurements of the system output y(t) and control input u(t) in (48). For this purpose we can, in general, employ either a full-dimensional composite observer (of order n + ρ + n^2) or a reduced-dimension composite observer of order (n − m + ρ +

n^2), where m, the dimension of y, is assumed equal to the rank of $C(t)$ and, of course, the composite $\tilde{x} = (x \mid z \mid z_a)$ in (48) is tacitly assumed to be completely observable in the sense of Kalman. General design recipes for both types of composite observers are presented in Refs. [13, 30]. However, in the special "model reference" adaptive control application considered here, it turns out that a full-dimensional observer for (48) is inherently faster than a reduced-dimension observer in performing real-time identification of the plant-parameter disturbance state z_a in (48). This superiority is due to the complete "internal copy"[2] of the reference model $\dot{x} = A_M x$, which is contained in a full-dimensional observer (but not in a reduced-dimension observer) for (48). If maximum speed is not a critical factor in identifying and cancelling $[\delta A]x$ in (9), a reduced-dimension observer for (48) may be adequate. Here we will consider only the full-dimensional observer design. To proceed, we set $\tilde{x} = (x \mid z \mid z_a)$ and write (48) in the compact format

$$\dot{\tilde{x}} = \tilde{A}\tilde{x} + \tilde{B}u \tag{49a}$$

$$y = \tilde{C}\tilde{x}, \tag{49b}$$

where the sparse, unknown impulses $\sigma(t)$, $\sigma_a(t)$ have been disregarded. Next, the structure of the composite observer for (48) is chosen as the $(n + \rho + n^2)$-th-order "filter" with partially known initial conditions [29; Appendix; 48]

$$\dot{\hat{\tilde{x}}} = \tilde{A}\hat{\tilde{x}} + \tilde{B}u(t) - K_0[y(y) - \tilde{C}\hat{\tilde{x}}]; \quad \hat{\tilde{x}}(t_0) = C^\dagger y(t_0), \tag{50}$$

where $\hat{\tilde{x}}$ is the observer output, $y(t)$ and $u(t)$ are real-time inputs to the observer, K_0 is an $(n + \rho + n^2) \times m$ observer "gain" matrix to be designed, and $C^\dagger$ is the Moore–Penrose generalized inverse of C. The dynamical behavior of the composite estimation error

$$\tilde{\varepsilon} = \tilde{x} - \hat{\tilde{x}} = (\varepsilon_x \mid \varepsilon_z \mid \varepsilon_{z_a}) \tag{51}$$

is easily shown to be governed by the error dynamic equation

$$\dot{\tilde{\varepsilon}} = [\tilde{A} + K_0\tilde{C})\tilde{\varepsilon}. \tag{52}$$

Thus, one should design K_0 in (50) such that *all* solutions $\tilde{\varepsilon}(t)$ of (52) rapidly approach zero, $\tilde{\varepsilon}(t) \to 0$. Assuming the pair $(\tilde{A}, \tilde{C})$ is completely observable, the latter is a standard task in modern control theory for which there are numerous design algorithms [13, 30, 47].

---

[2] See [33, Fig. 2, and text below], and [36, Fig. 4, and last paragraph of Section 4].

If any disturbance components $w_i(t)$ of (8a) are directly measurable, one can design a separate observer to estimate the associated disturbance state [13].

F. CONTINUOUS INJECTION OF OBSERVER INITIAL CONDITION DATA

The incorporation of the "partially known initial condition" data $\hat{x}(t_0) = C^{\dagger}y(t_0)$ in (50) is a relatively new idea in general observer theory [29, Appendix; 48] and is explained in more detail in Appendix B of this article. In the special adaptive controller applications considered here, we take that idea one step further (see the examples in Section V) by using the real-time system measurements $y(t)$ in (49b) to continually inject running-time "initial conditions" on the observer output $\hat{x}(t)$ in (50). In particular, the observer (50) is implemented in such a way that the continuous output measurements $y(t) = Cx(t)$ are used to continuously upgrade the accuracy of the estimate $\hat{x}(t)$ in the face of abrupt setpoint changes, etc. As a consequence of this special running-time "initial-condition" injection feature, the composite observer (50) is continually provided with available real-time information from which the complete estimate $\hat{x}(t)$ and the real-time estimate $\hat{z}_a(t)$ of the "parameter perturbation state" in (48) can be more quickly identified. Without this special "initial-condition" injection feature in (50), the adaptive controller (47) and (50) will still perform correctly, qualitatively speaking, but larger transient deviations from the ideal-model response (10) will occur due to increased delays in identifying $\hat{x}(t), \hat{z}(t), \hat{z}_a(t)$ and cancelling $[\delta A]x = H_a z_a$ in (48).

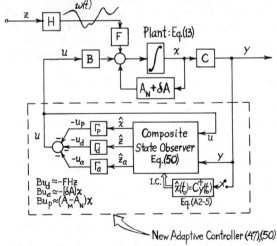

Fig. 2. Block diagram of new adaptive controller (47) and (50) (for the case $\{[\delta B], [\delta F], [\delta C]\} = 0$).

G.   SUMMARY OF THE NEW ADAPTIVE CONTROLLER

In summary, the overall adaptive controller for the system (9a), (9b) (with $\delta B = 0$, $\delta F = 0$, $\delta C = 0$) consists of the $(n + \rho + n^2)$-th-order linear composite observer (50), having on-line, real-time vector inputs $y(t)$, $u(t)$, and generating the three vector outputs $\hat{x}(t)$, $\hat{z}(t)$, $\hat{z}_a(t)$, followed by the linear adaptive control law (47). Note that $u(t)$ generated by (47) must be fed back into the observer (50) as well as to the system (9a). Provided that the "nonsingular condition" in (34) is satisfied (see Appendix A), the linear adaptive controller (47) and (50) will automatically detect, identify, and cancel an "arbitrary" uncertain parameter term $[\delta A]x(t)$ and an arbitrary uncertain external disturbance term $w(t)$ [obeying (9c), (9d)], in real time. Moreover, the subsequent motion of $x(t)$ in (9a) will then closely follow (mimic) the ideal-model motion $x_m(t)$ in (10), in accordance with Eq. (25). Thus, the controller (47) and (50) is a completely linear form of a multivariable "signal-synthesis, model-reference adaptive controller" [1, pp. 13, 16–19], where the signal-synthesis basis functions $\{f_1(t), ..., f_M(t)\}$ in (2) are the natural eigenmodes associated with the models (8) and (38). A generic block diagram of this new all-linear adaptive controller is shown in Fig. 2.

H.   CLOSED-LOOP DYNAMICS WITH THE
NEW ADAPTIVE CONTROLLER OF EQS. (47) AND (50)

The closed-loop performance of the original system (9a) with the new adaptive controller (47) and (50) installed can be studied analytically by consolidating (9), (47), and (50) into one large composite linear system. There are several different ways to perform this consolidation, and the final results are not equally illuminating. One of the more informative ways of expressing the overall closed-loop performance of (9), (47), and (50) appears to be as follows. First, one augments the error variables ε_x, ε_z defined in (23) by the additional error variable

$$\varepsilon_a = H_a^T[\delta A]x - \hat{z}_a. \tag{53}$$

The unusual structure of (53) is motivated by the fact that our dynamical model (38) is only an approximate representation of the actual dynamical behavior of $[\delta A]x(t)$; see comments above (33). Thus, to study the actual behavior of the closed-loop system, one must examine how $H_a\hat{z}_a(t)$ compares with $[\delta A]x(t)$ rather than how $\hat{z}_a(t)$ compares with the "fictitious" variable $z_a(t)$ governed by (38). Note from (53) that $H_a\varepsilon_a = [\delta A]x - H_a\hat{z}_a$ thanks to the fact that $H_aH_a^T = I$. If one now introduces the error variables (23) and (53) into (47) and (50), the closed-loop consolidation of (9), (47), and (50) can be expressed as the following composite vector matrix differential equation of dimension $(2n + \rho + n^2)$:

$$\begin{pmatrix} \dot{x} \\ \dot{\varepsilon}_x \\ \dot{\varepsilon}_z \\ \dot{\varepsilon}_a \end{pmatrix} = \begin{bmatrix} A_M & B\Gamma_p & B\Gamma_d & H_a \\ 0 & A_N + K_\alpha C & B\Gamma_d & H_a \\ 0 & K_\alpha C & D & 0 \\ e_{41} & e_{42} + K_\beta C & e_{43} & e_{44} + D_a \end{bmatrix} \begin{pmatrix} x \\ \varepsilon_x \\ \varepsilon_z \\ \varepsilon_a \end{pmatrix}, \tag{54a}$$

where $(e_{41}, e_{42}, e_{43}, e_{44})$ are perturbation-related matrices defined as

$$e_{41} = H_a^T[\delta A]A_M - D_a H_a^T[\delta A]; \quad e_{42} = H_a^T[\delta A]B\Gamma_p \tag{54b}$$

$$e_{43} = H_a^T[\delta A]B\Gamma_d; \quad e_{44} = H_a^T[\delta A]H_a \tag{54c}$$

Thus, to study the dynamics of the overall closed-loop system analytically, with the linear adaptive controller (47) and (50), one need only study the motions $x(t)$ generated by the consolidated system (54). For this purpose, one can introduce representative parameter perturbations $[\delta A]$ via (54b), (54c) and initial conditions on ε_a. Representative external disturbances $w(t)$ are introduced via initial conditions on ε_z.

If all matrices in (54a) are constant, one can study the closed-loop eigenvalues (poles) associated with the block matrix on the right side of (54a). For instance, when $[\delta A] = 0$, one has $e_{41} = e_{42} = e_{43} = e_{44} = 0$, in which case (54a) is upper-triangular and therefore its eigenvalues are seen to consist of the n eigenvalues of the ideal model A_M plus the $(n + \rho + n^2)$ eigenvalues of the observer error dynamics (52). The latter eigenvalues are presumably set deep enough in the left half-plane to cause rapid decay of the observer estimation errors $(\varepsilon_x, \varepsilon_z, \varepsilon_{za})$ so that $x(t)$ is essentially governed by the ideal eigenvalues of A_M. When $[\delta A]$ is nonzero, the matrices $e_{41}, e_{42}, e_{43}, e_{44}$ in (54) become nonzero, in general, and the closed-loop eigenvalues of (54) are caused to "shift" to some extent. The amount of that shift is determined by the size and location of the parameter perturbations (elements of $[\delta A]$) which are nonzero.

An analytical analysis of the closed-loop performance of (9), (47), and (50) can also be made using classical root-locus techniques. For this purpose, the "arbitrary" elements δa_{ij} of $[\delta A]$ are treated as root-locus gain parameters and the associated plant + controller "open-loop transfer functions" are computed. The migration paths of the closed-loop roots of (9), (47), and (50) as the "gains" δa_{ij} are varied can then be developed using standard root-locus construction rules. Application of this procedure to a specific example is illustrated in Ref. [27, p. 208].

I.   COMMENTS ON THE DIMENSION AND ORDER
      OF ADAPTIVE CONTROLLER OF EQS. (47) AND (50)

As indicated below (45), it is essential to assign an independent control action (independent element of u_a) to cancel each nonzero row of $[\delta A]$. This explains why in (45) one needs an n-dimensional vector control $u = (u_1, ..., u_r)$, $r = n$, and a full-rank matrix B in (25) in order to accommodate a completely arbitrary $[\delta A]$. On the other hand, in practical applications the given structure of A is usually such that only a few rows of A are capable of experiencing parameter perturbations δa_{ij}. For example, in many practical applications, the given matrix A consists of a block-triangular structure with the diagonal blocks having the companion structure (22) and with all other nonzero blocks being relatively sparse. Such cases may require a relatively low-dimensional vector control u_a to accommodate "arbitrary" $[\delta A]$.

The dynamical order of the full-dimensional composite observer (50) is (n + ρ + n^2), where the n^2 part arises from the presumed n^2 dimension of z_a in (38). If only k($<$n) rows of A can experience perturbations δa_{ij}, then z_a reduces to kn dimension, and the order of the observer (50) is reduced accordingly. In other words, each row of A which can experience perturbations δa_{ij} contributes an independent n-th-order dynamical subsystem to the observer (50); see comments below (36). For instance, in the special case of (22), the full-dimensional observer (50) would reduce to (n + ρ + n) order.

J.   INCLUSION OF POLYNOMIAL BASIS FUNCTIONS
      TO ACCOMMODATE RESIDUAL MODELING ERRORS
      IN $w_a(t)$ AND/OR $w(t)$

The practical effectiveness of the adaptive controller (47) and (50) is determined by the accuracy of the dynamic models for $w_a(t)$ and $w(t)$. In this regard, the "natural" dynamic model (35)–(39) of the parameter perturbation disturbance $w_a = \langle p_i, x \rangle$ is a significant improvement over the "synthetic" polynomial-spline approach of (26). However, even (35)–(39) are an approximation to reality, as can be seen by recalling (27) and comparing (32) with (33) and (34). To enhance the adaptive performance of (47) and (50) even more, one can enlarge the differential equation model (35) to include, say, a particular solution of the first-order or second-order polynomial type $w_{ai}(t) = c_0 + c_1 t$, etc. The inclusion of such an extra mode of behavior of $w_{ai}(t)$ in (35) would help to model and accommodate the case where $\delta A(t)$ and/or $A_M(t)$ are not "essentially constant" and to "check" the small residual errors which inevitably occur when (33) is used to approximate (32), etc., and when (5) is used to approximate (3); see remarks below (4). Similar comments apply to the inclusion of a polynomial mode in the external disturbance model (7) and (8) to accommodate residual errors in modeling $w(t)$. However, to avoid loss of (Z_a, Z) observability these polynomial modes should *not* be duplicated in any common element of $[\delta A]x$ and FHz in (13).

V.   SOME WORKED EXAMPLES USING THE NEW ADAPTIVE CONTROLLER, (47) AND (50)

The simplicity and systematic nature of the design procedure for the new adaptive controller (47) and (50), and the degree of adaptive performance which that controller can achieve, are best demonstrated by the study and simulation of specific numerical examples. With this in mind, we will now work out several simple examples and show their adaptive performance as obtained from computer simulations of the closed-loop systems. An additional example will be considered in Section VI.

A.   A FIRST-ORDER EXAMPLE

As an example of the simplest possible case of (9a), consider a setpoint regulator problem for the first-order plant

$$\dot{y} = (a_N + \delta a)y + u + w(t) \tag{55a}$$

where $w(t)$ is an uncertain "constant" disturbance and y is the plant output measurement with given setpoint

$$y_{desired} = y_{sp} \tag{55b}$$

where y_{sp} is a given real number. Following standard DAC techniques [13, p. 450], we define the setpoint "error state" x as

$$x = (y_{sp} - y), \tag{56}$$

so that the objective of control is to achieve $x(t) \to 0$ promptly; see remarks below (10). It is readily determined that x in (56) obeys a dynamic state equation (9a) of the form

$$\dot{x} = a_N x + (\delta a)x - a_N y_{sp} - (\delta a)y_{sp} - u - w(t) \tag{57}$$

where $(\delta a)y_{sp}$ is an unknown constant disturbance, and the term $a_N y_{sp}$ is a completely measurable constant "disturbance." For simplicity, we will assume the ideal model (10) for this example is simply $\dot{x}_m = a_N x_m$; i.e., $a_M = a_N < 0$. Then, setting

$$w_a = (\delta a)x = z_a; \quad w_d = (\delta a)y_{sp} + w(t) = z \tag{58}$$

and decentralizing the control u as in (11)

$$u = u_a + u_s + u_d,$$ (59)

one can write (57) in the form of (13)

$$\dot{x} = a_M x + (z_a - u_a) - (a_N y_{sp} + u_s) - (z + u_d)$$ (60a)

where (8b) and (38b) for this example have the form

$$\dot{z} = 0$$ (60b)

$$\dot{z}_a \cong a_M z_a; \quad \text{i.e.,} \quad \dot{w}_a \cong a_M w_a \quad [\text{in (35)}].$$ (60c)

It is clear from (60a) that the control terms u_a, u_s, u_d should be designed as

$$u_a = z_a; \quad u_s = -a_N y_{sp}; \quad u_d = -z.$$ (61)

A full-dimensional composite observer for (60) which generates $\hat{x}, \hat{z}, \hat{z}_a$ is given by (50), where (56) is the "observer input" and

$$\tilde{A} = \begin{bmatrix} a_M & -1 & 1 \\ 0 & 0 & 0 \\ 0 & 0 & a_M \end{bmatrix}; \quad \tilde{B}u = \begin{pmatrix} -1 \\ 0 \\ 0 \end{pmatrix} (u_a + u_d); \quad K_0 = \begin{pmatrix} k_{01} \\ k_{02} \\ k_{03} \end{pmatrix}$$ (62)

and where $u_s = -a_N y_{sp}$ is assumed installed. The associated error dynamics (52) for the observer is thus

$$\dot{\tilde{\varepsilon}} = \begin{bmatrix} (a_M + k_{01}) & -1 & 1 \\ k_{02} & 0 & 0 \\ k_{03} & 0 & a_M \end{bmatrix} \tilde{\varepsilon}.$$ (63)

Although $\hat{x}(t)$ is not needed in the implementation of (61) (because $a_M = a_N$), it is automatically generated by the full-dimensional observer. The desired eigenvalues λ_{oi} of (63) will be taken as $\lambda_{01} = \lambda_{02} = \lambda_{03} = l$, where $l < 0$ is chosen sufficiently "large" to make $\tilde{\varepsilon}(t) \to 0$ promptly. Constraining (63) to have such eigenvalues, by means of an expression similar to (19b), one obtains the required observer gains k_{01}, k_{02}, k_{03} to be

$$k_{01} = -2a_M + 3l; \quad k_{02} = l^3/a_M \tag{64a}$$

$$k_{03} = -a_M^2 + 3a_M l - 3l^2 + l^3/a_M. \tag{64b}$$

The fact that k_{02}, k_{03} in (64) become infinite as $a_M \to 0$ is a consequence of the unobservability (indistinguishability) of z and z_a as $a_M \to 0$; see (60). The adaptive control terms u_a and u_d do not exist in that latter case.

The individual observer equations (50), after installing $u_a + u_d$, become

$$\dot{\hat{x}} = a_M \hat{x} - k_{01}(x - \hat{x}); \, \hat{x}(0) = y_{sp} - y(0) \tag{65a}$$

$$\dot{\hat{z}} = -k_{02}(x - \hat{x}); \, \hat{z}(0) = 0 \tag{65b}$$

$$\dot{\hat{z}}_a = a_M \hat{z}_a - k_{03}(x - \hat{x}); \, \hat{z}_a(0) = 0, \tag{65c}$$

where, by (56)

$$x = \text{observer "input"} = (y_{sp} - y). \tag{65d}$$

During normal operation of the observer (65), the "constant" setpoint y_{sp} can experience abrupt once-in-a-while jumps in value. As a consequence, the error state $x(t)$ in (56) experiences similar jumps, and this causes abrupt differences to develop between the observer estimate $\hat{x}(t)$ and the true value of $x(t)$. Of course, the observer (65) will eventually drive $\hat{x}(t) \to x(t)$ and thereby eliminate that observer error. However, the step increase in observer error ε_x caused by jumps in y_{sp}, and the subsequent corrective action within the observer (65), sends a rippling transient disturbance throughout the observer (65) and may induce excessive error ripples in $\varepsilon_z(t)$ and/or $\varepsilon_{z_a}(t)$. This entire effect of observer errors induced by jumps in y_{sp} can be essentially eliminated if one allows the observer estimate $\hat{x}(t)$ in (65a) to be "corrected," in real time, by automatic injection of the available real-time "initial condition" data

$$x(t) = y_{sp} - y(t), \quad t_0 \le t. \tag{66}$$

To see the benefit of imposing (66) on the output $\hat{x}(t)$ of (65a), note that the observer error ε_x associated with (65a) can be expressed as

$$\varepsilon_x = x - \hat{x} = y_{sp} - y - (\widehat{y_{sp} - y}). \tag{67a}$$

Thus, if the actual y_{sp} experiences a jump change Δy_{sp} at the time t_1, the value of $\varepsilon_x(t)$ immediately after that jump (at time $t = t_1^+$) will be

$$\varepsilon_x(t_1^+) = y_{sp} + \Delta y_{sp} - y - (\widehat{y_{sp} - y}) \tag{67b}$$
$$= \varepsilon_x(t_1^-) + \Delta y_{sp},$$

which shows that $\varepsilon_x(t)$ will suffer an abrupt jump of amount Δy_{sp}. However, if the observer equation (65a) is implemented in an alternative way such that

$$\hat{x}(t) = y_{sp} - \hat{y}(t), \tag{68a}$$

where y_{sp} is the true value, then

$$\varepsilon_x = x - \hat{x} = y_{sp} - y - (y_{sp} - \hat{y}) = -(y - \hat{y}). \tag{68b}$$

It follows from (68b) that $\varepsilon_x(t)$ will now be continuous across all jumps in y_{sp}.

The modification of (65) to produce $\hat{x}(t)$ in the improved format (68a) can be accomplished by introducing the simple change of variable

$$\xi = \hat{x} - y_{sp} \tag{69}$$

in the observer equations. Thus, substituting (69) into (65), one immediately obtains the modified observer equations as

$$\dot{\xi} = a_M \xi + a_M y_{sp} + k_{01}(y + \xi); \quad \xi(0) = -y(0) \tag{70a}$$

$$\dot{\hat{z}} = k_{02}(y + \xi); \hat{z}(0) = 0 \tag{70b}$$

$$\dot{\hat{z}}_a = a_M \hat{z}_a + k_{03}(y + \xi); \hat{z}_a(0) = 0, \tag{70c}$$

where now $\hat{x}(t)$ is obtained by "injecting" y_{sp} as follows:

$$\hat{x}(t) = \xi(t) + y_{sp}. \tag{70d}$$

Note that the new variable ξ has the physical significance $\xi(t) = -\hat{y}(t)$. In summary, the complete adaptive controller (59) and (61) for the setpoint regulator problem (55) with ideal model $\dot{x} = a_N x$, $x = y_{sp} - y$, is a third-order linear, constant coefficient controller with

$$u = \hat{z}_a - a_N y_{sp} - \hat{z}, \tag{71}$$

where $\hat{z}_a, \hat{z}$ are generated by the modified observer (70).

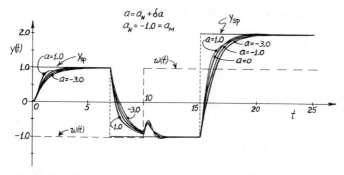

Fig. 3. Simulation results for the first-order example of Section V,A.

The plant (55a) with linear adaptive controller (70) and (71) installed (with $a_M = a_N = -1$ and $l = -5$) was simulated on a digital computer and exercised with a variety of plant-parameter perturbations δa, setpoint values y_{sp}, and "constant" disturbances $w(t)$. Some representative plots of the closed-loop plant response $y(t)$ are shown in Fig. 3, where it can be seen that $y(t)$ closely mimics the ideal-model response over a wide range of plant parameter perturbations δa (including large "destabilizing" values of δa) and external disturbances $w(t)$. The results of a further study of the first-order plant (55), using a second-order ideal model, are presented in Section V,C and Fig. 11.

B. A SECOND-ORDER EXAMPLE

In this setpoint regulator example, the plant is second order and is modeled by

$$\ddot{y} = a_2\dot{y} - a_1y = u + w; \quad y(t) = \text{plant output}, \tag{72}$$

where $a_2 = -1.4 + \delta a_2$, $a_1 = -1.0 + \delta a_1$; δa_1, δa_2, are unknown "constant" parameter perturbations; w is an unknown time-varying disturbance modeled by (7), where $w = c_1 + c_2 t$ and c_1, c_2 are piecewise constant and unknown, and y_{sp} is a given setpoint for $y(t)$. Following the procedure outlined below (10), the setpoint error state $x = (x_1, x_2)$ is defined as $x_1 = y_{sp} - y$, $x_2 = \dot{x}_1$, and the ideal behavior of $x_1(t)$ is expressed by the explicit "ideal model" $\ddot{x}_{1m} + 1.4\dot{x}_{1m} + x_{1m} = 0$. The system state equations (9a) for this example are

$$\dot{x}_1 = x_2 \tag{73a}$$

$$\dot{x}_2 = -x_1 - 1.4x_2 + \delta a_1 x_1 + \delta a_2 x_2 + y_{sp} - (\delta a_1)y_{sp} - u - w, \tag{73b}$$

and the state model (8) of the consolidated disturbance $\overline{w}(t) = (\delta a_1)y_{sp} + w(t)$ is

$$\overline{w} = z_1 \tag{74a}$$

$$\dot{z}_1 = z_2 \tag{74b}$$

$$\dot{z}_2 = 0 + \sigma(t). \tag{74c}$$

Following (28)–(38), we set

$$w_{a1} = 0 \tag{75a}$$

$$w_{a2} = (\delta a_1)x_1 + (\delta a_2)x_2 = z_{21} \tag{75b}$$

$$\dot{z}_{21} = z_{22} + \sigma_{21} \tag{75c}$$

$$\dot{z}_{22} = -z_{21} - 1.4z_{22} + \sigma_{22}. \tag{75d}$$

Setting $u = u_a + u_s + u_d$ in (73b), it follows that one should design

$$u_a = \hat{z}_{21}; \quad u_s = y_{sp}; \quad u_d = -\hat{z}_1. \tag{76}$$

Note that for this example A has the companion form (22) and also $A_M = A_N$ so that u_p in (14c) is zero.

The composite system model (48) can now be developed using (73)–(75). The associated composite observer (50) is then easily computed and the final result, after introducing the "initial-condition injection" variable $\xi = \hat{x}_1 - y_{sp}$, is the sixth-order observer

$$\dot{\xi} = \hat{x}_2 + k_{01}(y + \xi); \quad \xi(0) = -y(0) \tag{77a}$$

$$\dot{\hat{x}}_2 = -(\xi + y_{sp}) - 1.4\hat{x}_2 + k_{02}(y + \xi) \tag{77b}$$

$$\dot{\hat{z}}_1 + \dot{\hat{z}}_2 + k_{03}(y + \xi) \tag{77c}$$

$$\dot{\hat{z}}_2 = k_{04}(y + \xi) \tag{77d}$$

$$\dot{\hat{z}}_{21} = \hat{z}_{22} + k_{05}(y + \xi) \tag{77e}$$

$$\dot{\hat{z}}_{22} = -\hat{z}_{21} - 1.4\hat{z}_{22} + k_{06}(y + \xi). \tag{77f}$$

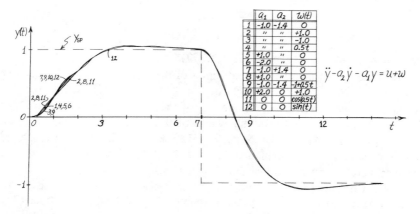

	a_1	a_2	$w(t)$
1	-1.0	-1.4	0
2	"	"	+1.0
3	"	"	-1.0
4	"	"	0.5t
5	+1.0	"	0
6	-2.0	"	0
7	-1.0	+1.4	0
8	+1.0	"	0
9	-1.0	-1.4	-1+0.5t
10	+2.0	0	+1.0
11	0	0	cos(0.5t)
12	0	0	sin(t)

$$\ddot{y} - a_2\dot{y} - a_1 y = u + w$$

Fig. 4. Simulation results for the second-order example of Section V,B: the case of constant parameter perturbations [δA].

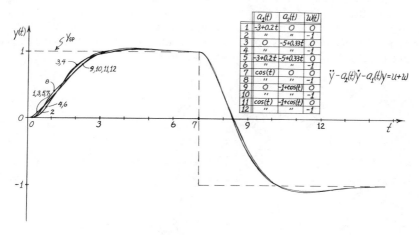

	$a_1(t)$	$a_2(t)$	$w(t)$
1	-3+0.2t	0	0
2	"	"	-1
3	0	-5+0.33t	0
4	"	"	-1
5	-3+0.2t	-5+0.33t	0
6	"	"	-1
7	cos(t)	0	0
8	"	"	-1
9	0	-1+cos(t)	0
10	"	"	-1
11	cos(t)	-1+cos(t)	0
12	"	"	-1

$$\ddot{y} - a_2(t)\dot{y} - a_1(t)y = u + w$$

Fig. 5. Simulation results for the second-order example of Section V,B; the case of time-varying perturbations [$\delta A(t)$].

where $\hat{x}_1 = \xi + y_{sp}$, y in (77) is the plant output in (72), and k_{oi}, $i = 1, 2, ..., 6$, are fixed observer gains to be designed. All initial conditions in (77b)–(77f) are set to zero at $t = 0$.

In summary, the complete adaptive controller for this example is the linear, constant coefficient, sixth-order controller

$$u = y_{sp} + \hat{z}_{21} - \hat{z}_1, \tag{78}$$

where $\hat{z}_{21}, \hat{z}_1$ are obtained from the observer (77).

For the closed-loop simulation studies of the plant (72), with the adaptive controller (77) and (78) installed, the observer gains k_{oi} in (77) were designed to place all six observer-error eigenvalues λ_{oi} of (52) at the common location $\lambda_{oi} = -5.0$, $i = 1, 2, ..., 6$. The resulting values of the k_{oi} are $k_{01} = -27.2$, $k_{02} = -294.9$, $k_{03} = -3125$, $k_{04} = 15,625$, $k_{05} = -5129$, $k_{06} = +9389.4$. The results of exercising the closed-loop simulation for a variety of disturbances and rather large "constant" parameter perturbations δa_1, δa_2 are shown in Fig. 4.

Introduction of Time-Varying Perturbations. It was stated below (6) [see also remarks below (27)] that in spite of the technical assumptions (27), the final adaptive controller (47) and (50) can, in fact, accommodate a significant degree of nonconstant behavior of $[\delta A]$. To demonstrate this feature the plant parameter perturbations δa_1, δa_2 in this example were next allowed to vary with time in various linear and sinusoidal fashions using the same linear, time-invariant adaptive controller (77) and (78) with the same numerical gains k_{oi} used in Fig. 4. The resulting closed-loop simulation responses for $y(t)$ are shown in Fig. 5, where it can be seen that the adaptive performance obtained is virtually the same as that obtained in Fig. 4 for "constant" parameter perturbations.

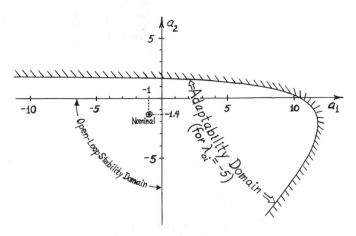

Fig. 6. Adaptability domain for plant (72) with adaptive controller (77) and (78) and $\lambda_{oi} = -5$, $i = 1, 2, ... , 6$.

Adaptability Domains in Parameter Space. For sufficiently large parameter perturbations δa_i (constant or time varying), the general adaptive controller (47) and (50) (with a fixed gain K_0) will eventually be "overpowered" and a serious loss of performance (or instability) will then result. A redesign of K_o to set the observer error eigenvalues λ_{oi} deeper in the left half-plane will forestall the onset of this loss of performance but will not prevent its eventual occurrence for a sufficiently large $[\delta A]$, in general. This situation appears to be characteristic of all forms of adaptive controllers [1, 22]. In this regard, a unique feature of our linear, time-invariant adaptive controller (47) and (50) is that the domain of system closed-loop stability, in the perturbed parameter space $a_{ij} = a_{N,ij} + \delta a_{ij}$, $\delta a_{ij} =$ "constant," can be calculated exactly using linear stability criteria (Routh–Hurwitz, root–locus, etc.). We call such a parameter domain the "adaptability domain" for the closed-loop system. The adaptability domain for the plant (72) and adaptive controller (77) and (78), with $\lambda_{oi} = -5$, $i = 1, 2, ..., 6$, is shown in Fig. 6.

The effectiveness of a (model-reference) adaptive controller, with respect to δA perturbations in linear plants, is measured by: 1) the extent of the adaptability domain, and 2) the degree to which actual response mimics ideal-model response within the adaptability domain; see Fig. 1-b and the proposed definition in Section I,A. The latter consideration is particularly important because it appears to be the only rational basis on which one might distinguish between adaptive control and so-called robust control for linear plants; see remarks preceding Section I,A. The responses $y(t)$ shown in Fig. 4 are representative of those corresponding to a large subset of operating points within the adaptability domain shown in Fig. 6. Of course, as the operating point (a_1, a_2) approaches the boundary of the adaptability domain in Fig. 6, the idealness of the time-response $y(t)$ will gradually deteriorate, exhibiting the characteristic oscillations associated with a system operating near its boundary of stability.

C.   A 'UNIVERSAL ADAPTIVE CONTROLLER' FOR A
      BROAD CLASS OF LINEAR AND NONLINEAR
      SECOND- AND FIRST-ORDER PLANTS

The effectiveness of the adaptive controller (77) and (78) in accommodating unknown, unmeasurable time-varying parameter perturbations $\delta a_1(t)$, $\delta a_2(t)$ for the linear plant (72), as illustrated in Fig. 5, suggests that the controller (77) and (78) might also be effective in accommodating "time-varying perturbations" $\partial a_1(t)$, $\partial a_2(t)$ caused by state-dependent parameters a_1, a_2 in (72); i.e., effective in accommodating a nonlinear plant (72). For example, suppose $a_1 = a_1(y, y)$, $a_2 = a_2(y, y)$ in (72). Then the left side of (72) can be written as

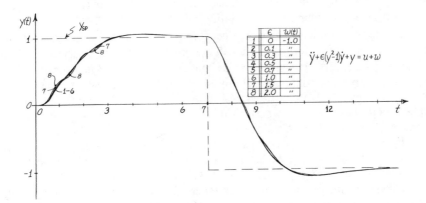

Fig. 7. Simulation results for the Van der Pol plant example of Section V,C.

$$\ddot{y} - a_2(y, \dot{y})\dot{y} - a_1(y, \dot{y})y = \ddot{y} + 1.4y$$

$$- [a_2(y, \dot{y}) + 1.4]\dot{y} + y - [a_1(y, \dot{y}) + 1]y, \tag{79}$$

so that along solutions of (72) and (79) one can imagine the time-varying terms

$$[a_1(y(t), \dot{y}(t)) + 1] = \partial a_1(t) \tag{80a}$$

$$[a_2(y(t), \dot{y}(t)) + 1.4] = \partial a_2(t) \tag{80b}$$

to behave as "time-varying parameter perturbations" (pseudoperturbations) with respect to the ideal (reference) model parameter values $a_1 = -1.0$, $a_2 = -1.4$. Thus, an interesting question is: Can the adaptive controller (77) and (78) accommodate the time-varying pseudoperturbations $\partial a_i(t)$ in (80) as well as it accommodates the time-varying genuine parameter perturbations $\delta a_i(t)$ in Fig. 5? To investigate this question, the $a_1(y, \dot{y})$, $a_2(y, \dot{y})$ in (79) were chosen to yield the classical Van der Pol equation so that

$$a_1 = -1.0; \quad a_2 = -\epsilon(y^2 - 1); \quad \epsilon \geq 0. \tag{81}$$

The controller equations (77) and (78), observer gains k_{oi}, and all other considerations were kept the same as before. The results of exercising a computer simulation of the Van der Pol plant (72) and (81) using the same linear adaptive controller

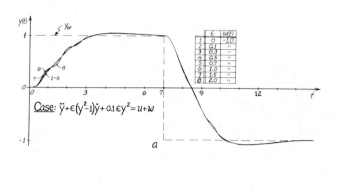

	ε	w(t)
1	0	-1.0
2	0.1	,,
3	0.3	,,
4	0.5	,,
5	0.7	,,
6	1.0	,,
7	1.5	,,
8	2.0	,,

$\underline{Case}:\ \ddot{y}+\epsilon(y^2-1)\dot{y}+0.1\epsilon y^2 = u+w$

a

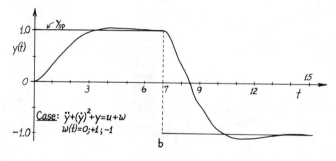

$\underline{Case}:\ \ddot{y}+(\dot{y})^2+y=u+w$
$\qquad w(t)=0;+1;-1$

b

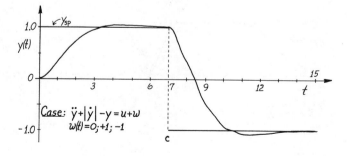

$\underline{Case}:\ \ddot{y}+|\dot{y}|-y=u+w$
$\qquad w(t)=0;+1;-1$

c

Fig. 8. Simulation results for other nonlinear plants in the example of Section V,C.

C. D. JOHNSON

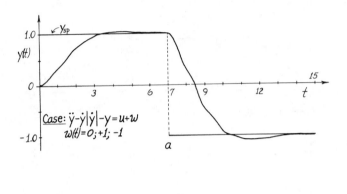

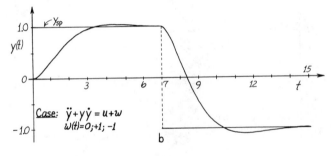

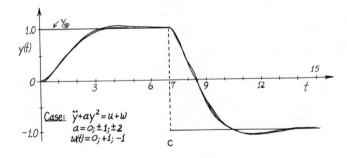

Fig. 9. Simulation results for other nonlinear plants in the example of Section V,C.

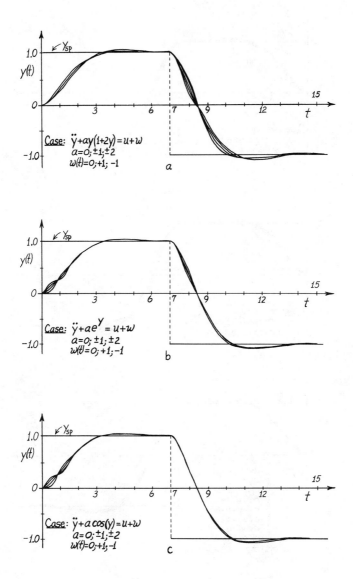

Fig. 10. Simulation results for other nonlinear plants in the example of Section V,C.

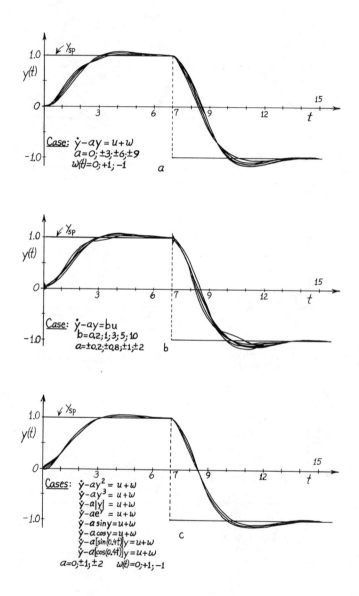

Fig. 11. Simulation results for some first-order plants using the "universal" adaptive controller (77) and (78).

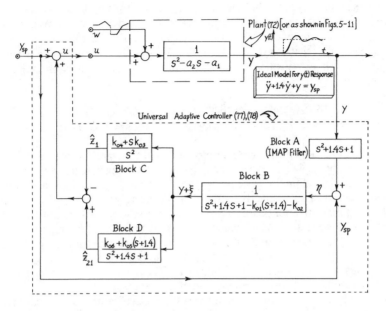

Fig. 12. Transfer function interpretation of the universal adaptive controller (77) and (78).

(77) and (78) are shown in Fig. 7, which is seen to compare closely with the previous results in Figs. 4 and 5.

The similarity of Figs. 4, 5, 7 suggests that the controller (77) and (78) might be able to accommodate a variety of different linear and nonlinear plants of general second-order form

$$\ddot{y} + f(y, \dot{y}) = u + w. \tag{82}$$

To investigate this possibility, the same controller (77) and (78) with the same numerical gains k_{oi} was installed on a wide variety of nonlinear plants having the generic form (82), and the closed-loop systems were exercised on a computer simulation. The results are shown in Figs. 8–10. Comparing those results with Figs. 4, 5, 7 indicates that the one linear adaptive controller (77) and (78) with the fixed gain values k_{oi} listed below (78) can indeed achieve the same second-order linear ideal-model behavior from a wide variety of nonlinear plants. This remarkable result suggests that, with respect to the "ideal model" specified, the controller (77) and (78) can be called a "universal adaptive controller" for a broad class of linear and nonlinear plants having the form (82). This surprising capability of an all-linear observer (77) and control law (78) to accommodate a broad class of nonlinear plants suggests that the practical "need" for nonlinear observer design procedures may not be as great as many researchers and designers have imagined.

The universality of (77) and (78) does not carry over to plants of order $n \geq 3$, in general, for reasons explained in [58]. However, (77) and (78) do behave as a universal adaptive controller for plants of order $n = 1$, as can be seen in the typical responses in Fig. 11.

D. TRANSFER-FUNCTION INTERPRETATION OF THE
    UNIVERSAL ADAPTIVE CONTROLLER (77) AND (78)

The time-domain state equations (47) and (50) are the natural format for representing the new multivariable adaptive controller developed in Section IV, and use of that time-domain format for the synthesis, simulation, and practical implementation of such adaptive controllers is strongly recommended in all cases – including time-invariant cases. Nevertheless, in the time-invariant case of (47) and (50), it is interesting to calculate and examine the controller "transfer-function" structure implied by (47) and (50), to see if any novel structural properties or interpretations emerge. For this purpose, the results are easier to see if one examines various particular cases of (47) and (50). The one case examined below yields structural results which are representative of the general case.

In the particular case of the universal adaptive controller (77) and (78), as used for all 22 different plants associated with Figs. 4–11, it is easy to show [53] that the controller transfer-function structure implied by (77) and (78) consists of the 4-block network shown in Fig. 12. The most striking feature of Fig. 12 is the fact that in block A the controller equations (77) and (78) have, in effect, physically realized an "all-numerator" ideal-model annihilating polynomial (IMAP) filter which would ordinarily be regarded as unrealizable. This unique IMAP filter acts as a notch filter (blocking or rejection filter) for the homogeneous part of the "ideal" plant response model $\ddot{y} + 1.4\dot{y} + y = y_{sp}$. In other words, when $y(t)$ is correctly approaching y_{sp} in accordance with the specified ideal model $\ddot{x}_{1m} + 1.4\dot{x}_{1m} + x_{1m} = 0$, $x_{1m} = y_{sp} - y$, the output of the IMAP filter is simply y_{sp}. Otherwise, the output of the IMAP filter can be written as $y_{sp} + \eta$, where η is defined as the collective result of IMAP action on all nonideal properties of $y(t)$ due to $\{\delta a_i, w(t),$ observer transients, $y(t) \to y_{sp}\}$, etc.

The propagation of the composite error signal η through blocks B, C automatically synthesizes the adaptive control signal "$\hat{z}_1$" needed to cancel the nonideal effect of $\overline{w}(t)$ on $y(t)$; see Eq. (74). Likewise, the propagation of η through blocks B, D automatically synthesizes the adaptive control signal "$\hat{z}_{21}$" needed to cancel the combined effect (75b) of δa_1 and δa_2 [or the combined effect

(79) and (80) of $\partial a_1(t)$, $\partial a_2(t)$ in the case of nonlinear plants in Figs. 7–11. The ideal-model polynomial $s^2 + 1.4s + 1$ comprising the denominator of block D allows the adaptive control signal $\hat{z}_{21}(t)$ to be generated in the signal-synthesis form (2) where the basis functions $\{f_1(t), f_2(t)\}$ are the natural ideal-model eigenmodes of $s^2 + 1.4s + 1$. A similar interpretation applies to the denominator of block C, where $\hat{z}_1(t) = \hat{\bar{w}}(t) = c_1 + c_2 t$, as in (7). The main function of block B and the numerators of blocks C and D is to provide the additional controller structure and design parameters required for physical realizability and to achieve sufficiently rapid settling time for $\hat{z}_1(t) \rightarrow z_1(t)$ and $\hat{z}_{21}(t) \rightarrow z_{21}(t)$.

In summary, the transfer-function interpretation, Fig. 12, of the universal adaptive controller (77) and (78) exhibits a novel "exact realization" of an all-numerator, ideal-model annihilating polynomial filter, block A, which automatically "blocks" ("rejects") all plant responses $y(t)$ satisfying $\ddot{y} + 1.4\dot{y} + y = 0$. As a result of this IMAP prefilter action, all nonideal behavior of $y(t)$, including $y(t) \not\rightarrow y_{sp}$, is quickly detected, quantified, and embodied in the composite error signal $\eta(t)$. Finally, the composite error signal η is then propagated through blocks B, C and blocks B, D to rapidly synthesize the adaptive control signals $\hat{z}_1(t)$ and $\hat{z}_{21}(t)$ needed to cancel (correct for) all nonideal behavior of $y(t)$. This disturbance-accommodating signal-synthesis adaptive control action, and the unique IMAP controller structure shown in Fig. 12, are distinctly different from the controllers traditionally used in model-reference control system design [1]. For instance, the IMAP filter in Fig. 12 generates a model-reference corrective signal η even when $y_{sp} = 0$ and/or the plant has unmeasurable nonzero initial conditions $\dot{y}(0)$, etc. Further discussion of the transfer-function interpretation of these new adaptive controllers may be found in [27, 28, 53].

E.   GENERALIZATION OF THE 'UNIVERSAL
      ADAPTIVE CONTROLLER' IDEA

The preceding experimental results concerning the universality of (77) and (78) for first- and second-order plants suggests that one might be able to develop similar "universal" controllers for each of the plant cases $n = 3, 4, 5$, etc. This intriguing idea is currently being investigated [58] using similar experimental means. An interesting area for further research is to see if one can establish the universal nature of various cases of (47) and (50) using purely analytical means based on generic mathematical descriptions of the type (82). Another research area is to investigate the adaptive performance benefits obtained by using a higher-order (≥ 3) polynomial spline model $w = c_1 + c_2 t + c_3 t^2 + \ldots$ to represent general uncertain disturbances in "universal adaptive controllers."

VI.   GENERALIZATION OF THE NEW APPROACH: CONSIDERATION OF NONZERO [δB], [δF], [δC]

The adaptive controller (47) and (50) was derived under the assumptions [δB] = 0, [δF] = 0, [δC] = 0 in (9). However, as stated earlier, the controller (47), (50) will, in fact, tolerate a moderate range of [δF], [δB]. In this section we will show how the same DAC techniques used to derive (47) and (50) can be generalized to accommodate the cases of nonzero [δB], [δF]. In the case of [δB] this will require a mild nonlinearity (multiplier) in the controller. Accommodation of the case of nonzero [δC] is also discussed and illustrated by solving a class of problems with a special form of [δC]. However, the case of a general form of [δC] is a more difficult problem whose general solution is not available at this time.

To begin, we enlarge the decentralization of control (11) to include two new "parts"

$$u = u_d + u_a + u_p + u_b + u_f, \tag{83}$$

where u_b, u_f are responsible for cancelling the effects of [δB], [δF], respectively, in (9). Since the design of u_a has already been covered in Section IV, we will assume that (9) has the simplified form

$$x = A_N(t)x + [B_N(t) + \delta B(t)]u + [F_N(t) + \delta F(t)]w(t) \tag{84a}$$

$$y = [C_N(t) + \delta C(t)]x, \tag{84b}$$

where

$$u = u_d + u_p + u_b + u_f, \tag{84c}$$

and w(t) obeys (9c), (9d). Accommodation of the effects of [δC] will be approached by modifying the composite observer design to account for the uncertain term [δC]x in (84b); see (110)–(123) to follow.

A.   ACCOMMODATION OF NONZERO [δB], [δF]

The accommodation of [δB], [δF] will require a composite observer similar to (50) to identify [δB], [δF]w in real time. Thus, it will be necessary to tacitly assume a complete-observability condition for those perturbations, similar to the one assumed for (48). In this regard it is important to note that [δB] and [δF] are totally unobservable whenever u(t) ≡ 0, w(t) ≡ 0. Thus, the on-line identification of [δB] and [δF] will require that u(t) ≢ 0, w(t) ≡ 0 during appropriate intervals of time. Moreover, the special perturbations $[\delta B] = -B_N$ and $[\delta F] = -F_N$ will present singularities in *any* identification procedure.

Substituting (84c) into (84a) yields the counterpart of (13) as

$$\dot{x} = A_N(t)x + B_N(t)u_p + B_N(t)u_b + [\delta B(t)]u$$
$$+ B_N(t)\,(u_d + u_f) + [F_N(t) + \delta F(t)]H(t)z.$$

(85)

It follows from (85) that u_b and $(u_d + u_f)$ should ideally satisfy the cancellation conditions

$$B_N(t)u_b \equiv -[\delta B(t)]u$$

(86a)

$$B_N(t)\,(u_d + u_f) \equiv -[F_N(t) + \delta F(t)]H(t)z.$$

(86b)

An approximate method for satisfying (86) is to model the right sides of (86) by polynomial splines, as in (26), and use the technique of (7), (8), (14). We will now present a more exact method for satisfying (86).

The necessary and sufficient condition for satisfaction of (86a) is

$$\text{rank}[B_N(t)|\delta B(t)] = \text{rank}[B_N(t)],$$

(87a)

which implies

$$[\delta B(t)] = B_N(t)\Gamma_b(t)$$

(87b)

for some matrix $\Gamma_b(t)$. In light of (87b), the condition (86a) becomes

$$B_N(t)\,[u_b + \Gamma_b(t)u] \equiv 0,$$

(88a)

and thus it suffices to design u_b ideally as

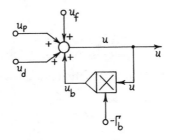

Fig. 13. Control synthesis circuit for the idealized expression (88b).

$$u_b = -\Gamma_b(t)u, \tag{88b}$$

which implies the mildly nonlinear[3] synthesis circuit shown in Fig. 13.
The necessary and sufficient condition for satisfaction of (86b) is

$$\text{rank}[B_N(t)|[F_N(t)] + \delta F(t)]H(t) = \text{rank}[B_N(t)], \tag{89a}$$

which implies

$$[F_N(t) + \delta F(t)]H(t) = B_N(t)\Gamma_F(t) \tag{89b}$$

for some matrix $\Gamma_F(t)$. At this point, it is convenient to separate $F(t) = F_N(t) + \delta F(t)$ into the sum of another two matrices, as follows:

$$F(t) = F_1(t) + F_2(t), \tag{90}$$

where the i-th row of F_1 equals the i-th row of F, *if* for all t that row has *no* uncertain perturbations δF_{ij} associated with it, and otherwise equals zero. Likewise, the i-th row of F_2 equals the i-th row of F, if for any t that row has *any* uncertain perturbations δF_{ij} associated with it, and otherwise equals zero. Thus, $F_2 = \delta F$ plus those rows of F_N corresponding to nonidentically zero rows of $[\delta F]$.

In light of (90), one can write

$$F(t)H(t)z = F_1(t)H(t)z + F_2(t)H(t)z \tag{91}$$

and rewrite (86b) as

$$B_N(t)u_d + B_N(t)u_f \equiv -F_1(t)H(t)z - F_2(t)H(t)z. \tag{92}$$

Since the first term on the right side of (92) has no parameter uncertainty associated with it, one can proceed to design u_d to (ideally) satisfy

$$B_N(t)u_d \equiv -F_1(t)H(t)z \tag{93}$$

just as in (14a) and (20a). Note that F_1 will always contain some zero rows (if $\delta F \neq 0$) and thus the expression for F_1Hz in (93) can be simplified. The second term on the right of (91) is accommodated by defining the new disturbance variable $\overline{w}$ as

$$\overline{w} = F_2(t)H(t)z = \overline{z} \tag{94}$$

---

[3] The polynomial spline method mentioned below (86) does not require a nonlinear synthesis circuit.

and designing u_f to (ideally) satisfy

$$B_N(t)u_f \equiv -\overline{z}. \tag{95}$$

To establish the state equation (8b) for $\overline{z}(t)$, observe that each scalar element $\overline{z}_i$ of $\overline{z}$ is related to z by an expression of the form

$$\overline{z} = \langle \varphi^{(i)}, z \rangle, \tag{96}$$

where $\varphi^{(i)}$ denotes the i-th row of $F_2(t)H(t)$. Note that when $\varphi^{(i)} = 0$, for some i, then $\overline{z}_i(t) \equiv 0$, and the requirement on (95) is thereby relaxed; see (106) and (108) in the following. At this point we will proceed as in (27) and invoke the assumption/approximation

$$\frac{dD}{dt} = 0 \text{ and } \frac{d\varphi^{(i)}}{dt} = 0, \text{ almost everywhere.} \tag{97}$$

As a consequence of (97), the successive time derivatives of (96) along solutions of (8) are

$$\dot{\overline{z}}_i = \langle \varphi^{(i)}, Dz \rangle$$

$$\ddot{\overline{z}}_i = \langle \varphi^{(i)}, D^2z \rangle \tag{98}$$

$$\vdots$$

$$\overset{(k)}{\overline{z}} = \langle \varphi^{(i)}, D^k z \rangle.$$

It follows from (98) and the Cayley–Hamilton theorem that if $\varphi^{(i)} \neq 0$ the associated z_i obeys (at least) the ρ-th-order linear, constant coefficient differential equation

$$\overset{(\rho)}{\overline{z}}_i + \alpha_\rho \overset{(\rho-1)}{\overline{z}}_i + \ldots + \alpha_2\dot{\overline{z}}_i + \alpha_1\overline{z}_i = 0. \tag{99}$$

where

$$\det(\lambda I - D) = \lambda^\rho + \alpha_\rho\lambda^{\rho-1} + \ldots + \alpha_2\lambda + \alpha_1 = 0. \tag{100}$$

Now, for each nonzero $\varphi^{(i)}$, $i = 1, \ldots, \rho$, one can convert (99) to a state model of the type (8), just as was done in (35) and (37). Then, the collection of such state models can be consolidated into one large state model

$$\dot{\overline{z}} = \overline{D}\overline{z} + \overline{\sigma}, \tag{101}$$

just as was done in (37)–(39). Thus, (95), (94), and (101) can now be treated just as in (15) and (8).

Practical Implementation of (88b) and (95). The practical implementation of (88b) and (95) involves the use of a composite observer, of the type (50), to generate reliable real-time estimates $\hat{\Gamma}_b$, $\hat{z}$ of Γ_b, $\bar{z}$. For this purpose it is convenient to rewrite the term $\Gamma_b u$ in (88b) as

$$\Gamma_b u = U\gamma_b, \tag{102a}$$

where

$$U = \begin{bmatrix} u^T & & \mathbf{O} \\ & u^T & \\ \mathbf{O} & & u^T \end{bmatrix} = \text{an } r \times r^2 \text{ matrix}, \tag{102b}$$

$$\gamma_b = (\gamma_b^{(1)}|\gamma_b^{(2)}| \cdots |\gamma_b^{(r)})^T; \ (\bullet) = \text{transpose} \tag{102c}$$

and

$$\gamma_b^{(i)} = \text{the i-th row of } \Gamma_b. \tag{102d}$$

Using (87b) and (102), the perturbation term $[\delta B(t)]u$ in (86a) can be written

$$[\delta B(t)]u = B_N(t)U\gamma_b(t). \tag{103}$$

Now, in the spirit of (27) we assume $\delta B(t)$ varies sufficiently slowly, or is piecewise constant, so one can invoke the approximation

$$\frac{d\gamma_b(t)}{dt} \approx 0, \quad \text{almost everywhere.} \tag{104}$$

In this way, γ_b in (103) becomes an uncertain "constant" vector which embodies all the uncertainty of $[\delta B]$. Thus, to practically implement (88b) one can write

$$u_b = -U\hat{\gamma}_b, \tag{105}$$

where $\hat{\gamma}_b$ is an estimate of γ_b obtained from a composite observer. The synthesis circuit in Fig. 13 is applicable also to (105).

To implement (95) it is convenient to first reduce the dimension of $\bar{z}$ by eliminating (purging) all elements of z which are identically zero. In this way $\bar{z} \rightarrow \tilde{z}$ and (95) can be written

$$B_N(t)u_f = -\overline{H}\tilde{z} \tag{106}$$

where the i-th row of $\overline{H}$ is zero, if the i-th row of F_2 is zero, and is otherwise of the form $(0, ..., 0, 1, 0, ..., 0)$, where the placement of the element 1 depends on the location of the zero elements of $\bar{z}$. The state model for $\tilde{z}$ is obtained from (101) by purging the zero elements of $\bar{z}$ and removing the associated rows and columns of $\overline{D}$ so that $\overline{D} \rightarrow \tilde{D}$. From (106) it follows that u_f can be implemented as

$$u_f = -\Gamma_f \hat{\tilde{z}}, \tag{107}$$

where Γ_f is defined by

$$B_N\Gamma_f = \overline{H}, \tag{108}$$

and it is assumed that $rank[B_N|\overline{H}] = rank[B_N]$.

In summary, the practical implementation of (88b) and (95) is given by (105) and (107), where the estimates $\hat{\gamma}_b$, $\hat{\tilde{z}}$ are obtained from a composite observer. In terms of (85), that composite observer would be based on the composite dynamic model

$$\dot{x} = A_Nx + B_Nu_p + B_Nu_b + B_NU\gamma_b + B_Nu_d + B_Nu_f + F_1Hz + \overline{H}\tilde{z} \tag{109a}$$

$$\dot{\gamma}_b = 0 \tag{109b}$$

$$\dot{z} = Dz + \sigma \tag{109c}$$

$$\dot{\tilde{z}} = \tilde{D}\tilde{z} + \tilde{\sigma} \tag{109d}$$

However, in practice one would consolidate (109) with (48) to avoid redundancy (and unobservability) in the observer. If $[\delta C] = 0$ in (84b), the composite observer design proceeds just as in (48)–(50). On the other hand, if $[\delta C] \neq 0$, the observer design is more complicated since then one must account for and model the dynamic effects of the uncertain term $[\delta C]x$ in the measurement vector (observer input) y. The most effective way to accomplish this latter step, in the general case of $[\delta C]$, is an issue which is not completely resolved at this time. The following is an outline and demonstration of the basic principles for accommodating $[\delta C] \neq 0$.

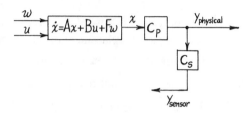

Fig. 14. Correct interpretation (111) of the traditional output expression (110).

B. ACCOMMODATION OF NONZERO [δC]: BASIC PRINCIPLES

The appearance of perturbations [δC] in the system output expression (84) raises several new issues which are subtle in nature but are fundamentally important from the adaptive control point of view. First, it is important to realize that the traditional "output" expression

$$y = Cx = [C_N + \delta C]x \tag{110}$$

as used in (5) and (9) and virtually all modern control literature [9, 47] is actually the concatenation of two essentially different things: 1) the set of system physical quantities y_{phy} which are accessible for measurement (such as relative motions, temperature differences, etc.) and 2) the outputs of the set of sensors (instruments) y_{sen} which actually detect and measure those physical quantities. Thus, it is more correct to replace (110) by the two expressions

$$y_{phy} = C_p x \tag{111a}$$

$$y_{sen} = C_s y_{phy} = C_s C_p x, \tag{111b}$$

where y in (110) usually corresponds to y_{sen}; i.e., $C = C_s C_p$, as shown in Fig. 14. However, the reader is cautioned that the control literature is curiously vague on this point.

The subtle distinction in (111) has (apparently) not been given much attention in any of the control engineering literature. However, that distinction becomes highly important when the parameter uncertainty [δC] arises in (110) because, then, to properly accommodate [δC] in the control design, it is absolutely essential to know if [δC] is due to: a perturbation [δC_p] in (111a); a perturbation [δC_s] in (111b); or perturbations in both [C_p] and [C_s]. For example, referring to Fig. 14, if the primary control task is to regulate $y_{phy}(t)$ to a specified setpoint y_{sp}, a perturbation [δC] caused by [δC_p] leads to one set of control design considerations. On the other hand, if [δC] is due entirely to sensor perturbations [δC_s], then a *different* set of control design considerations must be invoked. In other words, one must be careful to avoid the pitfall of regulating $y_{sen}(t) \to y_{sp}$ when, in fact, y_{sen} is an unreliable indication of y_{phy}! This kind of subtlety becomes even more complicated when [δC] is due to simultaneous perturbations [δC_p] and [δC_s], or when the primary control task is to regulate a specific state variable $x_i(t)$ which is *not* accessible for direct measurement.

In the following, it will be assumed that y in (110) corresponds to the "sensor output" y_{sen} in (111b), and thus C in (110) has the interpretation

$$C = C_s C_p. \tag{112}$$

We have just shown how the proper accommodation of a [δC] in (112), in an adaptive control law design, will depend critically on whether [δC] is due to [δC_s] or [δC_p] (or both). On the other hand, the proper accommodation of a [δC] in the design of a composite state observer of the type (50) does not depend on whether [δC] is due to [δC_s] or [δC_p]. Thus, we will now focus our attention on the latter issue, writing (110) in the form

$$y = y_{sen} = Cx = [C_N + \delta C]x, \tag{113a}$$

where

$$C = C_s C_p = [C_{sN} + \delta C_s][C_{pN} + \delta C_p] \tag{113b}$$

$$C_N = C_{sN} C_{pN} \tag{113c}$$

$$\delta C = [\delta C_s]C_{pN} + C_{sN}[\delta C_p] + [\delta C_s][\delta C_p]. \tag{113d}$$

Two Approaches to Modeling [δC] Effects. The problem is to find a way of modeling and accommodating [δC] in (113) in the design of a composite state observer of the type (50). For this purpose there are essentially two ways to model the effect of [δC]. The first method, called the "additive model" approach, consists of writing (113a) in the form

$$y = C_N x + [\delta C]x, \tag{114a}$$

where

$$v = [\delta C]x \tag{114b}$$

is viewed as a "disturbance" added to the nominal output

$$y_N = C_N x. \tag{115}$$

Then, in principle, an appropriate dynamical (state) model for the disturbance $v(t)$ can be developed along the lines of (8) using, say, the assumption $d[\delta C]/dt \approx 0$ and the polynomial spline approximation (26), and a composite state observer of the form (50) can then be designed to produce reliable estimates $\hat{x}, \hat{2}, \hat{2}_a, \ldots$, etc., *and* $\hat{v}$. In this regard, note that it is imperative that $[\delta C]$ not destroy the (nominal) composite complete-observability condition for the consolidated system. A convenient sufficient condition for assuring this is to require that $[C_N + \delta C]$ preserves the row range space of C_N. That is, restrict $[\delta C]$ to be of the form

$$[\delta C] = \Gamma_c C_N, \text{ where } \Gamma_c \text{ is such that det } (I + \Gamma_c) \neq 0. \tag{116}$$

The second modeling method, called the "multiplier model" approach, consists of writing (113a) in the alternative form

$$y = [C_N + \delta C]x = \Psi C_N x, \tag{117}$$

where the "uncertain" multiplying matrix Ψ embodies the effects of $[\delta C]$. In particular,

$$\Psi = \Psi_N + [\delta\Psi] = I + [\delta\Psi], \tag{118a}$$

where

$$[\delta C] = [\delta\Psi]C_N. \tag{118b}$$

The format (117) automatically preserves the row range space of C_N provided det $\Psi \neq 0$; compare (116) and (118b). Now, one can develop an appropriate dynamical model for the uncertain matrix Ψ in (117) and, in principle, proceed to design a composite observer which will produce reliable estimates $\hat{x}, \hat{2}, \hat{2}_a, \ldots$, etc. *and* $\hat{\Psi}$. For this purpose, it is convenient to follow the spirit of (27) and assume $d[\Psi]/dt \approx 0$.

C. ACCOMMODATION OF [δC]
    IN CONTROL LAW DESIGNS

The preceding remarks indicate, in principle, how one might approach the modeling and accommodation of [δC] in the design of a composite state observer of the type (50). This accounting for the [δC] effects in the observer design permits the generation of reliable estimates $\hat{x}$, $\hat{z}$, $\hat{z}_a$, ..., etc. *and* $\hat{v}$ or $\hat{\Psi}$, in the face of [δC]. What the designer then does with the estimates $\hat{v}$ or $\hat{\Psi}$ depends on the nature of the primary control task and on whether [δC] is caused by [δC_s] or [δC_p], or both. For example, if a "compensating signal" $u_c(t)$ is added to (113a) to yield

$$y = C_N x + [\delta C]x + u_c(t), \tag{119}$$

and if $u_c(t)$ is chosen as

$$u_c(t) = -\hat{v}(t), \tag{120}$$

then the effect of [δC] on y is approximately cancelled, so that

$$y \approx C_N x, \quad \text{for "all" } [\delta C]. \tag{121}$$

Likewise, if Ψ is nonsingular and the output y(t) in (113a) is multiplied by $[\hat{\Psi}]^{-1} \approx \Psi^{-1}$ to produce the "new" output

$$y_{new} = [\hat{\Psi}]^{-1} y, \tag{122}$$

then, by (117),

$$y_{new} \approx C_N x, \quad \text{for "all" } [\delta C]. \tag{123}$$

However, as explained above, the "cancellation" operations (119), (120), and (122) might not be the appropriate actions to accommodate [δC], from the primary control point of view.

The detailed design of state models and composite observers for generating estimates $\hat{v}$ or $\hat{\Psi}$, using the principles outlined above, turns out to be somewhat complicated and not totally free of pitfalls, in the general case. Consequently, the most effective general procedure for accomplishing such designs is still in the development stage. On the other hand, it is easy to demonstrate the principles we are advocating by working a particular class of problems, which we will now do.

D. A DESIGN METHOD FOR ACCOMMODATING [δC] IN A PARTICULAR CLASS OF PROBLEMS

To demonstrate the principle of accommodating [δC] by the multiplier modeling approach (117), we will now consider the following particular class of problems. The plant is assumed to have the general scalar-control, scalar-output form

$$\dot{x} = Ax + bu, \quad u = \text{scalar} \tag{124a}$$
$$x = (x_1, x_2, ..., x_n)$$
$$y = cx, \quad y = \text{scalar}, \tag{124b}$$

where the pair (A, b) is assumed constant, completely known, and completely controllable. The only uncertainty in (124) is in the uncertain value of the row vector c. Following the approach (117) it is assumed that c can be written as

$$c = (c_N + \delta c) = \Psi c_N, \tag{125}$$

where $c_N = $ a known constant vector, and where the uncertain "constant" scalar $\Psi \neq 0$ embodies all uncertainty in the n-vector c [see remarks above (116)], and the pair (A, c_N) is completely observable.

The problem is to design a "smart" observer which can generate reliable state estimates $\hat{x}_1(t), \hat{x}_2(t), ..., \hat{x}_n(t)$ in the face of arbitrary uncertain ($\approx$piecewise constant) nonzero values of Ψ in (124b) and (125). For this purpose it is convenient to first transform the original x-state space of (124) to a new ξ-state space according to the recently developed nonsingular linear transformation [49]

$$\Psi = \begin{bmatrix} c_N \\ c_N A \\ c_N A^2 \\ \cdot \\ \cdot \\ \cdot \\ c_N A^{n-1} \end{bmatrix} \begin{pmatrix} x_1 \\ x_2 \\ x_3 \\ \cdot \\ \cdot \\ \cdot \\ x_n \end{pmatrix} \begin{bmatrix} 1 & 0 & 0 & ... & 0 & 0 \\ \alpha_n & 1 & 0 & ... & 0 & 0 \\ (\alpha_n^2 + \alpha_{n-1}) & \alpha_n & 1 & ... & 0 & 0 \\ (\alpha_n^3 + 2\alpha_n\alpha_{n-1} + ... + \alpha_{n-2}) & (\alpha_n^2 + \alpha_{n-1}) & \alpha_n & ... & 0 & 0 \\ \cdot & & & & & \cdot \\ \cdot & & & & & \cdot \\ (\alpha_n^{(n-1)} + ... + \alpha_2) & & & ... & \alpha_n & 1 \end{bmatrix} \begin{pmatrix} \xi \\ \xi \\ \xi \\ \\ \\ \\ \xi \end{pmatrix}$$

where $(-\alpha_1, -\alpha_2, ..., -\alpha_n)$ are the coefficients of the characteristic polynomial of A

$$\det(\lambda I - A) = \lambda^n - \alpha_n\lambda^{n-1} - ... - \alpha_2\lambda - \alpha_1. \tag{127}$$

Under the special canonical transformation (126) the original state equation (124), together with the appended equation $\dot{\Psi} = 0$, can be written in the consolidated homogeneous-like form

$$\begin{pmatrix} \dot{\xi} \\ \dot{\Psi} \end{pmatrix} = \begin{bmatrix} \bar{A} \end{bmatrix} \begin{pmatrix} \xi \\ \Psi \end{pmatrix}$$

$$y = (1, 0, ..., 0|0)\begin{pmatrix} \xi \\ \Psi \end{pmatrix}, \tag{128b}$$

where

$$\bar{A} = \begin{bmatrix}
\alpha_n & 1 & 0 & ... & 0 & c_N bu \\
\alpha_{n-1} & 0 & 1 & & 0 & c_N(A - \alpha_n I)bu \\
\alpha_{n-2} & 0 & 0 & ... & 0 & c_N(A^2 - \alpha_n A - \alpha_{n-1}I)bu \\
\cdot & & & & & \cdot \\
\cdot & & & & & \cdot \\
\cdot & & & & & \cdot \\
\alpha_1 & 0 & 0 & ... & 0 & c_N(A^{n-1} - \alpha_n A^{n-2} - ... - \alpha_2 I)bu \\
0 & 0 & 0 & ... & 0 & 0
\end{bmatrix} \tag{128c}$$

It is readily verified [49] that the consolidated $(n + 1)$-order system (128) is completely observable, for any "constant" $u(t)$, if and only if

$$c_N(A^{n-1} - \alpha_n A^{n-2} - ... - \alpha_2 I)bu \neq 0. \tag{129}$$

Satisfaction of (129) thus requires two simultaneous conditions:

$$u(t) \neq 0 \tag{130a}$$

and

$$c_N(A^{n-1} - \alpha_n A^{n-2} - \ldots - \alpha_2 I)b \neq 0 \qquad (130b)$$

It can be shown [49] that condition (130b) is simply a requirement that the numerator polynomial of the transfer function $y(s)/u(s) = G(s)$ of (124) does not have a zero factor; i.e., the plant (124) does not have an open-loop "zero" at the origin.

The canonical system (128) is a very special type of bilinear dynamical system for which a novel full-order observer design has recently been developed [49]. That new observer is completely linear in structure, as far as $\hat{\xi}$, $\hat{\Psi}$ is concerned, and utilizes a rather mild form of saturation nonlinear element [on $u_-^{-1}(t)$ only] to synthesize certain of the "observer gains." Using that observer, one can generate reliably accurate real-time estimates $\hat{\xi}_1(t)$, $\hat{\xi}_2(t)$, ..., $\hat{\xi}_n(t)$, $\hat{\Psi}$ for (128) by processing the real-time control input $u(t)$ and measurement $y(t)$ from (124), assuming $\Psi \neq 0$, $u(t) \not\equiv 0$. A concrete demonstration of this new observer design is given in the specific example presented below.

The corresponding observer for the original state variables $(x_1, x_2, ..., x_n)$ in (124) can then be obtained by invoking the inverse transformation $\hat{\xi} \to \hat{x}$ from (126). That is,

$$\hat{x}(t) = (\hat{\Psi})^{-1} \begin{bmatrix} c_N \\ c_N A \\ \cdot \\ \cdot \\ \cdot \\ \cdot \\ c_N A^{n-1} \end{bmatrix}^{-1} \begin{bmatrix} 1 & 0 & \ldots & 0 & 0 \\ \alpha_n & 1 & \ldots & 0 & 0 \\ (\alpha_n^2 + \alpha_{n-1}) & \alpha_n & \ldots & 0 & 0 \\ & & & \cdot & \\ & & & \cdot & \\ \cdot & & \ldots & \alpha_n & 1 \end{bmatrix} (\hat{\xi}) \qquad (131)$$

In summary, the uncertain piecewise-constant nonzero vector c in the plant model (124) and (125) can be accommodated by first invoking the new canonical transformation (126) and then designing a special form of observer [49] for the enlarged canonical bilinear system (128). The outputs of that observer are the $(n + 1)$ estimates $\hat{\xi}_1(t)$, $\hat{\xi}_2(t)$, ..., $\hat{\xi}_n(t)$, $\hat{\Psi}$. Then the desired estimates $(\hat{x}_1(t), \hat{x}_2(t), ...,$

$\hat{x}_n(t)$) for (124) are obtained by applying the inverse canonical transformation (131). Note that the estimate $\hat{\Psi}$ of the nonzero "unknown" Ψ is used in (131).

The estimate $\hat{\Psi}$ may also play a role in expressions like (122) and (123), or appear as a term in the primary control law, depending on the specific nature of the primary control task(s) [see remarks below (123)].

The details of the procedure just outlined are illustrated by the following concrete example.

E.   SPECIFIC EXAMPLE OF THE [δC] ACCOMMODATION DESIGN METHOD (124)–(131)

As a specific example of the [δC] accommodation method (124)–(131), we will consider the general second-order case

$$\begin{pmatrix} x_1 \\ x_2 \end{pmatrix} = [A] \begin{pmatrix} x_1 \\ x_2 \end{pmatrix} + bu \tag{132a}$$

$$y = \Psi c_N \begin{pmatrix} x_1 \\ x_2 \end{pmatrix}, \tag{132b}$$

where (A, c_N) = completely observable; $c_N = (c_1, c_2)$; Ψ = unknown, piecewise constant, $\neq 0$. For (132) the canonical transformation (126) reduces to

$$\begin{pmatrix} x_1 \\ x_2 \end{pmatrix} = \Psi^{-1} \begin{bmatrix} c_N \\ c_N A \end{bmatrix}^{-1} \begin{bmatrix} 1 & 0 \\ \alpha_2 & 1 \end{bmatrix} \begin{pmatrix} \xi_1 \\ \xi_2 \end{pmatrix}, \tag{133}$$

and the corresponding enlarged canonical system (128) becomes

$$
\begin{pmatrix} \dot{\xi}_1 \\ \dot{\xi}_2 \\ \dot{\Psi} \end{pmatrix} = \begin{bmatrix} \alpha_2 & 1 & c_N bu \\ \alpha_1 & 0 & c_N(A - \alpha_2 I)bu \\ 0 & 0 & 0 \end{bmatrix} \begin{pmatrix} \xi_1 \\ \xi_2 \\ \Psi \end{pmatrix} \tag{134a}
$$

$$
y = (1, 0, 0) \begin{pmatrix} \xi_1 \\ \xi_2 \\ \Psi \end{pmatrix}. \tag{134b}
$$

To check the complete observability of (134), for $u(t) = $ constant $\neq 0$, we compute Kalman's well-known observability determinant

$$
\det[c^T | A^T c^T | A^{T^2} c^T] = \det \begin{bmatrix} 1 & \alpha_2 & \alpha_2^2 + \alpha_1 \\ 0 & 1 & \alpha_2 \\ 0 & c_N bu & c_N Abu \end{bmatrix} = c_N(A - \alpha_2 I)bu. \tag{135}
$$

Thus, in addition to requiring $u(t) \neq 0$, we need to assume

$$
c_N(A - \alpha_2 I)b \neq 0, \tag{136}
$$

which simply means the plant transfer function $y(s)/u(s) = G(s)$ of (132) has no "zero" (numerator root) at the origin. Under the assumption (136), we can proceed to design a special form of full-order bilinear observer [49] which can generate reliable estimates $(\hat{\xi}_1, \hat{\xi}_2, \hat{\Psi})$ of (134). For this specific example, that observer is [here, K_0 in (50) is written as $-K_0$]

$$
\begin{pmatrix} \dot{\hat{\xi}}_1 \\ \dot{\hat{\xi}}_2 \\ \dot{\hat{\Psi}} \end{pmatrix} = \begin{bmatrix} \alpha_2 & 1 & c_N bu \\ \alpha_1 & 0 & c_N[A - \alpha_2 I]bu \\ 0 & 0 & 0 \end{bmatrix} \begin{pmatrix} \hat{\xi}_1 \\ \hat{\xi}_2 \\ \hat{\Psi} \end{pmatrix} + \begin{pmatrix} k_{01} \\ k_{02} \\ k_{03} \end{pmatrix} (y - \hat{\xi}_1) \tag{137}
$$

and the dynamical equation for the observer's estimation error

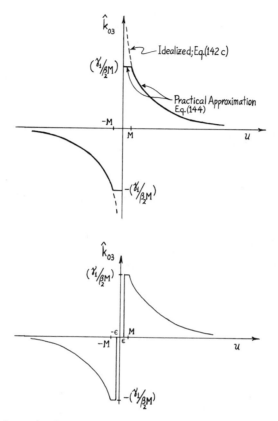

Fig. 15. Approximation of the idealized expression (142c) for k_{03}: (a) for $u \neq 0$; (b) for $u \cong 0$.

$$e = \left(\frac{\xi}{\Psi}\right) - \left(\frac{\hat{\xi}}{\hat{\Psi}}\right) \qquad (138)$$

is

$$\dot{e} = \begin{bmatrix} \alpha_2 - k_{01} & 1 & c_N bu \\ \alpha_1 - k_{02} & 0 & c_N(A - \alpha_2 I)bu \\ -k_{03} & 0 & 0 \end{bmatrix} e \qquad (139)$$

The "characteristic polynomial" of (139), assuming u = constant, is computed to be

$$P(\lambda) = \lambda^3 + \lambda^2(k_{01} - \alpha_2) + \lambda(k_{02} - \alpha_1 + k_{03}c_N bu) \tag{140}$$
$$+ k_{03}c_N(A - \alpha_2 I)bu = 0.$$

Suppose the desired roots of (140) are $(\lambda_{01}, \lambda_{02}, \lambda_{03})$. Then, by equating (140) to the desired polynomial

$$P_d(\lambda) = (\lambda - \lambda_{01})(\lambda - \lambda_{02})(\lambda - \lambda_{03}), \tag{141}$$

we obtain the required values of k_{01}, k_{02}, k_{03} as

$$k_{01} = \gamma_3 + \alpha_2 \tag{142a}$$

$$k_{02} = \gamma_2 + \alpha_1 - (\beta_1/\beta_2)\gamma_1 \tag{142b}$$

$$k_{03} = (\gamma_1/\beta_2 u), \tag{142c}$$

where

$$\gamma_1 = -\lambda_{01}\lambda_{02}\lambda_{03} \tag{143a}$$

$$\gamma_2 = \lambda_{01}\lambda_{02} + \lambda_{01}\lambda_{03} + \lambda_{02}\lambda_{03} \tag{143b}$$

$$\gamma_3 = -(\lambda_{01} + \lambda_{02} + \lambda_{03}) \tag{143c}$$

$$\beta_1 = c_N b \tag{143d}$$

$$\beta_2 = c_N(A - \alpha_2 I)b. \tag{143e}$$

The expression (142c) must be considered idealized because, in practice, the magnitude of u(t) may become quite small (once in a while), or pass through zero at isolated points in time. Therefore, to implement (142c) in practical applications, it is recommended [49] that the idealized k_{03} be approximated as (see Fig. 15a)

$$\hat{k}_{03} = (\gamma_1/\beta_2)M^{-1} \operatorname{sat}(M/u) \tag{144}$$

where M is a suitably small positive constant so that

$$\hat{k}_{03}u = (\gamma_1/\beta_2), \qquad \text{if } |u| \geq M; \tag{145}$$

$$= (\gamma_1/\beta_2)M^{-1}|u|, \quad \text{if } |u| < M.$$

The appropriate value of M depends on the particular application, but values in the range $0.01 \leq M \leq 0.1$ are typical.

In summary, the special observer for the bilinear canonical system (134) is given as (137), where the three gains k_{0i} are given by (142a), (142b), (143), and (144). Assuming $\Psi \neq 0$, and providing $u(t) \not\equiv 0$ for a sufficient period of time, that observer will generate reliable estimates $(\hat{\xi}_1(t), \hat{\xi}_2(t), \hat{\Psi}(t))$. Then, by invoking (133), one can generate the desired estimates $\hat{x}_1(t), \hat{x}_2(t)$. When $u(t) \equiv 0$, the observer (137) cannot produce reliable estimates due to the onset of unobservability in (135). Thus, it is recommended that $\hat{k}_{03}$ in (144) be set to $\hat{k}_{03} = 0$ while $u(t) \equiv 0$; see Fig. 15b.

A Numerical Example. In order to demonstrate the performance capability of the solution procedure (133)–(144), using simulation techniques, the following numerical values were chosen:

$$A = \begin{bmatrix} 0 & 1 \\ -1.0 & -1.4 \end{bmatrix}; \quad b = \begin{pmatrix} 1.0 \\ 0.6 \end{pmatrix}; \tag{146}$$

$$c_N = (1, 0);$$

$$\lambda_{01} = \lambda_{02} = \lambda_{03} = -5.$$

The results of a digital simulation study of (132) and (146), using the observer (137), (142a), (142b), (143), and (144) with $M = 0.01$ and several unknown perturbations in c, are shown in Fig. 16.

The procedures for accommodating $[\delta B]$, $[\delta F]$, $[\delta C]$, presented in this section, are recent extensions of the original theory developed in Refs. [26–29]. Further development and refinement of these procedures is an active area of current research.

VII. RAPPROCHEMENT WITH TRADITIONAL ADAPTIVE CONTROL DESIGNS

As pointed out in Section II,A, most of the past and current research in adaptive control has been focused on the "adaptive-gain" approach as typified by expression (1). The nature of that classical approach is such that the resulting adaptive controller is always inherently nonlinear (even when $[\delta A]$ is the only plant parameter perturbation, as we considered in Section IV). This nonlinear form

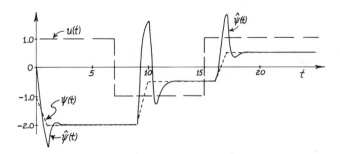

Fig. 16. Simulation results for the numerical case (146); the example of Section VI,E.

of controller structure allows the classical "adaptive-gain" approach to be applied to a much broader class of: 1) nonlinear plants; 2) complex parameter/structural perturbations and noises/disturbances; and 3) generalized performance criteria J and explicit ideal models $\mathcal{M}$. Moreover, the current state of the art in "adaptive-gain" type controllers, as reflected in Refs. [50, 51, 62], indicates that major advances in the theory and application of the classical "adaptive-gain" approach (1) have been achieved in recent years.

Thus, it must be admitted that the new DAC-based approach to adaptive control described in this article is, in principle: 1) not as general in nature and, 2) not capable of accommodating the same degree (extent) of structural and parameter perturbation excursions as the traditional (nonlinear) "adaptive-gain" approach (1). On the other hand, the new approach presented here leads to an essentially new class of multivariable adaptive controllers which: 1) are strikingly simple in nature (in many cases all linear with constant coefficients!), 2) deliver a surprisingly high degree of adaptive performance (Figs. 3–5) – even for nonlinear plants (Figs. 7–11), and 3) are based on elementary principles of modern linear control engineering, and 4) admit unique transfer function interpretations (Fig. 12). These features may make our new approach to adaptive control an attractive design option for the class of practical applications where the nature of the plant perturbations and structure uncertainties does not warrant the full generality and capability of a classical nonlinear "adaptive-gain" controller (1). The examples presented in this article give some idea of what constitutes that class of applications; however, this new approach to adaptive control is still in its infancy, and further generalization and enhancement of the theory is currently an active area of research.

Remarks on the Structure of Adaptive Controllers. Today, it is often argued that a controller cannot be "adaptive" unless it has variable gains or other nonfixed parameters which can be adaptively adjusted in real time. This attitude fails to recognize the fact that in adaptive control problems the fundamental requirement is that the control signal (control action) u(t) properly "adapt."

It is not a fundamental requirement that the controller parameters or controller structure itself change, although such a controller may be a convenient form of implementation and may become "necessary" if, for instance, the range of plant perturbations becomes extremely large. The early attempts to implement adaptive control, in the 1950s, just happened to choose the adjustable-gain approach to generate the needed adaptive control signal u(t) [similarly, the earliest forms of "optimal" controllers had a bang-bang (relay) structure, but today that early structure is, fortunately, *not* a requirement for *all* optimal controllers]. Is it possible that a fixed controller structure with fixed parameters can generate a family of adaptive control signals? The answer is yes, and the particular all-linear, constant-coefficient controller (77) and (78) is a vivid example of that fact. In particular, a nonlinear "variable-gain" adaptive controller (1) designed for the same plant, ideal model, range of perturbations, disturbances, etc., as (77) and (78) will generate essentially the same adaptive control signal u(t) as (77) and (78). The numerical example data and range of perturbations, disturbances, etc., associated with Figs. 4 and 5, provide a convenient basis for making such a comparison of adaptive control *signals* [52]. A more extensive performance comparison of contemporary adaptive-controllers and the new controller presented here may be found in [61].

VIII. SUMMARY AND CONCLUSIONS

In this article we have described and illustrated a new approach to multivariable adaptive control, based on the ideas and techniques of disturbance-accommodating control theory. This new approach can be viewed as a novel form of multivariable "signal-synthesis" ("auxiliary input signal") model-reference adaptive control [1, pp. 13, 16–19], in which the required adaptive control signals u(t) are automatically synthesized as linear combinations (2) of "natural basis functions," using a special form of full-order observer. This approach leads to a new class of adaptive controllers which are based on elementary principles of modern linear control theory, are relatively easy to analyze and implement, do not use adaptive gains, and, in many cases, turn out to be completely linear, time-invariant controllers. Although not as general in scope as the more conventional "adaptive-gain" controllers (1), these new adaptive controllers are appropriate for a broad class of realistic industrial applications.

The degree of adaptive performance which can be achieved by these new controllers has been illustrated here by numerous worked examples and computer simulation results. These experimental results suggest that, for the intended class of applications, the new approach presented here is a major breakthrough in achieving a practical, simple, and reliable form of adaptive control implementation. Moreover, it has been shown in Section V,C that this new approach leads to controller designs which bear the features of "universal adaptive controllers"; i.e., *one* controller design yields adaptive performance for a wide range of linear and nonlinear plants; see Figs. 4–11. This aspect of these new adaptive controllers opens up an exciting area for further research.

Epilogue. Traditionally, the "theory and design of adaptive controllers" has been viewed academically as an advanced graduate-level subject, requiring specialized prerequisite training in nonlinear and stochastic control ideas. The new approach to adaptive control developed in this article is based on elementary principles of linear, deterministic disturbance-accommodating control theory and, therefore, much of that approach can be effectively taught in the first undergraduate course in control engineering, and can be interpreted in terms of classical transfer-function ideas, Fig. 12 and Refs. [27, 28, 53]. The ability to teach beginning control engineering students how to design (linear) adaptive controllers that can deliver adaptive performance such as that typified in Figs. 3–5 is an exciting new opportunity which, we believe, will result in some major changes in the way elementary and advanced control engineering is taught [54] and practiced [55].

IX. APPENDIX A:
ANALYSIS OF THE SINGULAR CONDITION ASSOCIATED WITH EQ. (34)

In the derivation of (38), it was assumed that a certain singular condition in (34) did not occur. In this appendix we examine that singular condition in detail and derive the necessary and sufficient condition for its occurrence.

In connection with the definitions (28) and (29), the sequence of time derivatives $\{\dot{w}_{ai}, \ddot{w}_{ai}, \ldots, \overset{(n)}{w}_{ai}\}$ of $w_{ai} = \langle p_i, x \rangle$ along arbitrary solutions of (25) can be written for each $i = 1, 2, \ldots, n$ as

$$\dot{w}_{ai} = \langle p_i, A_M x \rangle + \langle p_i, (\delta A x + B u_a) \rangle$$

$$\ddot{w}_{ai} = \langle p_i, A_M^2 x \rangle + \langle p_i, A_M(\delta A x + B u_a) \rangle + \langle p_i, \overline{(\delta A x + B u_a)}^{\,\cdot} \rangle,$$

$$\text{etc.,} \quad i = 1, 2, \ldots, n. \tag{A1}$$

At this point in the derivation leading to (34), the assumption is made that the terms in (A1) which are linear in the "small" perturbations δa_{ij} [i.e., the first terms on the right side of (A1)] dominate the terms which are quadratic or higher order in the δa_{ij} – assuming that u_a itself will be some linear function of δA as indicated in (31). However, linear terms in small perturbations δa_{ij} will dominate higher-order terms in δa_{ij} only if the linear terms themselves are present. Thus, one can raise a technical question about what special (singular) conditions would make the linear terms fail to appear in (A1) and thereby invalidate the assumption that the higher-order terms in (A1) are negligible.

1. Investigation of the Singular Condition in (A1)

The singular condition related to (A1), as just described, can be defined more precisely as follows.

Definition. Let the terms $\langle p_i, A^s_M x \rangle$, $s = 1, 2, \ldots, n$, appearing on the right side of (A1), be denoted as the "linear terms." Then, the singular condition in (A1) is defined as the condition in which one or more of the derivative expressions in (A1) has no linear terms appearing.

The mathematical relations which will allow this singular condition to occur will now be investigated.

A Fundamental Result. A fundamental result regarding the singular condition in (A1) is:

Theorem A1. Suppose p_i is a fixed (row) n-vector, and set $u_a(t) \equiv 0$ in (25). Let k be the smallest positive integer, such that

$$\langle p_i, A^k_M x(t) \rangle \equiv 0, \tag{A2}$$

along some particular solution of (25). Then, along that same particular solution of (25) all derivative expressions in (A1) corresponding to the subsequence $\{w_{ai}^{(s)}\}$, s = k, (k + 1), ..., n, are void of all linear terms.

Proof of Theorem A1. The proof follows immediately from setting to zero the successively higher time derivatives of $\langle p_i, A^k_M x(t) \rangle$ along the solutions of (25).

Remarks. 1) The disappearance of linear terms in the subset of derivative expressions $\{w_{ai}^{(s)}\}$, s = k, (k + 1), ..., n, in (A1) does *not* necessarily imply the identical vanishing $\langle p_i, A^s_M x(t) \rangle \equiv 0$ of the linear terms themselves, except for s = k. 2) If k = 1 in (A2), then *all* derivatives in (A1) are void of linear terms.

The Main Result. It follows from Theorem A1 that the singular condition related to (A1) has an "avalanche" characteristic, triggered by the lowest indexed identical vanishing in (A2). Thus, the crux of the singular problem is to discover what conditions are necessary and sufficient for the occurrence of (A2). The answer is provided by:

Theorem A2. Suppose $u_a(t) \equiv 0$ in (25), and let p_i be fixed. Then, the identical vanishing in (A2) can occur if and only if the pair $(A_M + \delta A, p_i A^k_M)$ is unobservable in the sense of Kalman.

Proof of Theorem A2. It is clear that the necessary and sufficient conditions for occurrence of (A2) are

$$\frac{d^m}{dt^m}\langle p_i, A_M^k x\rangle = 0, \quad m = 0, 1, 2, \ldots, (n-1), \tag{A3}$$

along some non-null solution $x(t)$ of (25). Using (25), the Lie derivatives (A3) are computed to be

$$\frac{d^m}{dt^m}\langle p_i, A_M^k x\rangle = \langle p_i, A_M^k(A_M + \delta A)^m x\rangle = 0,$$
$$m = 0, 1, \ldots, (n-1), \tag{A4}$$

which can be arranged as

$$\begin{bmatrix} p_i A_M^k \\ p_i A_M^{k.}(A_M + \delta A) \\ \cdot \\ \cdot \\ \cdot \\ p_i A_M^k(A_M + \delta A)^{n-1} \end{bmatrix}^{(x)} = 0, \quad x \neq 0. \tag{A5}$$

It follows that (A5) can be realized for some $x \neq 0$ if and only if

$$\det[c^T|(A_M + \delta A)^T c^T| \ldots |(A_M + \delta A)^{T(n-1)}c^T] = 0, \tag{A6a}$$

where

$$c = p_i A_M^k. \tag{A6b}$$

Expression (A6) is recognized as Kalman's necessary and sufficient condition for unobservability of the pair $(A_M + \delta A, c)$.

Remark. In light of the essential structure revealed in (A6), one should refer to the singular condition in (A1) more precisely as: "the row perturbation p_i is k singular with respect to the *overall* perturbation matrix δA," or, more concisely, "the pair $(\delta A, p_i)$ is k-singular."

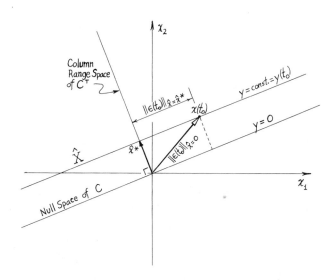

Fig. 17. State space geometry for the observer "optimal" initial condition $\hat{x}^*$ in (B5).

Corollary. It follows from (A6) that the necessary and sufficient condition for nonsingularity in (A1) is the nonvanishing of the determinant (A6) for each $(\delta A, p_i)$ and all $k = 1, 2, ..., n$.

2. Likelihood of Satisfying the Singularity Criterion (A6) in Practical Applications

It is well known in the theory of controllability and observability [3, 56, 57] that the condition (A6) can occur if and only if the row vector $c = p_i A^k_M$ is precisely aligned along certain "critical" directions determined by the matrix $(A_M + \delta A)$. If the singularity condition (A6) *is* initially satisfied, and c and/or $(A_M + \delta A)$ are given "almost any" small perturbation away from their initial values, the determinant in (A6) will become nonzero and the pair $(\delta A, p_i)$ will no longer be singular in (A1). Since the elements δa_{ij} which create $\delta A = [\delta a_{ij}]$ and its i-th row $p_i = (\delta a_{i1}, \delta a_{i2}, ..., \delta a_{in})$ in (25), (28), and (A1) are themselves uncertain, random-like piecewise-constant perturbations, it follows that the likelihood of (A6) occurring in practical applications is very small.

X.   APPENDIX B:
OPTIMAL INITIAL CONDITIONS
FOR FULL-ORDER OBSERVERS

A conventional full-order observer for the linear dynamical system

$$\dot{x} = Ax + Bu \tag{B1}$$

$$y = Cx \tag{B2}$$

has the form

$$\dot{\hat{x}} = A\hat{x} + Bu - K_0(y - C\hat{x}), \tag{B3}$$

where the observer gain matrix K_0 is designed to give sufficiently small settling time to the observer error $\varepsilon(t) = x(t) - x(t)$, which is known to be governed by

$$\dot{\varepsilon} = (A + K_0 C)\varepsilon, \quad \varepsilon(0) = x(0) - \hat{x}(0). \tag{B4}$$

In practical applications of observers the value of $x(0)$ is not known or measurable, but $y(0)$ is directly measurable. The question of how to best "set" the observer initial condition $x(0)$ in (B3) has recently been studied [48], where it was shown that the initial measurement $y(0)$ in (B2) provides a rational basis for choosing the "optimum" setting of $x(0)$ as

$$\hat{x}(0) = \hat{x}* = C^{\dagger}y(0), \tag{B5}$$

where $C^{\dagger}$ is the classical Moore–Penrose generalized inverse of C. In particular, it is established [48] that

Theorem B1. Suppose $\{A, B, C\}$ in (B1) and (B2) are given, and suppose the initial output measurement $y(0)$ is the *only* information known about the plant initial state $x(0)$. Then the set $\hat{X}$ of all observer initial conditions $\hat{x}(0)$ in (B3), which are compatible with the measurement value $y(0)$, is given by

$$\hat{X} = \{\hat{x}(0) | \hat{x}(0) = C^{\dagger}y(0) + Nq\}, \tag{B6}$$

where N is any $n \times p$ matrix whose columns span the null space of C, $p = n -$ rank C, and q is a completely arbitrary (real) p-vector. Moreover, the particular choice (B5) of observer initial condition $\hat{x}(0)$ is the "optimal" rational choice in the following sense:

(1)   All information embodied in y(0), about the unknown x(0), is reflected in (B5).

(2)   The norm $\|\hat{x}^*\|$ of (B5) is minimal among all $\hat{x} \in \hat{X}$.

(3)   The initial condition of observer-error norm $\|\epsilon(0)\|$ in (B4), associated with the choice (B5), is: (a) consistently smaller than the value $\|\epsilon(0)\| = \|x(0)\|$ associated with the default choice $\hat{x}(0) = 0$ – for all x(0) such that y(0) $\neq$ 0 – and (b) is equal to the value $\|\epsilon(0)\| = \|x(0)\|$ for all x(0) such that y(0) = 0.

This result is illustrated in Fig. 17.

When the initial condition $\hat{x}(0)$ in (B3) is set to the "optimal" value (B5), rather than to $\hat{x} = 0$, a significant reduction in observer-error transient deviations may result [48]. An alternative way of deriving the optimum $\hat{x}(0)$ in (B5), using a special state-space transformation introduced in [12, Appendix 1], is presented in [29, Appendix]. The latter derivation shows that the choice (B5) essentially reduces the performance of (B3) to that of a reduced-order observer.

ACKNOWLEDGMENTS

       The author would like to acknowledge the valuable assistance of Jelel Ezzine, Jianchao Zhu, Xiaohong Fan, Jian-Zhong You, and Daniel Hahs, who provided numerous analog and digital simulation studies in support of the development of the new adaptive control theory presented here.
       The author is also deeply indebted to John E. Givson and James S. Meditch for originally stirring his interest in adaptive control theory, and the signal-synthesis approach in particular, in the early 1960s at Purdue University's Control and Information Systems Laboratory, School of Electrical Engineering.

REFERENCES

1.   I. D. LANDAU, "Adaptive Control; The Model Reference Approach," Dekker, New York, 1979.
2.   IEEE Proc., "Special Issue on Sensitivity and Robustness," *Proc. IEEE, Control Theor.*, Part D (1982).
3.   C. D. JOHNSON, "Invariant Hyperplanes for Linear Dynamical Systems," *IEEE Trans. Autom. Control, AC-11*, 113-116 (1966).
4.   C. D. JOHNSON, "Stabilization of Linear Dynamical Systems with Respect to Arbitrary Linear Subspaces," *J. Math. Anal. Appl., 44*, 175-186, October (1973).
5.   C. D. JOHNSON, "State Overdescription and Uncontrollability of Dynamical Systems: Part I, Nonlinear Systems," *Int. J. Control, 19*, 225-242, February (1974).
6.   C. D. JOHNSON, "State Overdescription and Uncontrollability of Dynamical Systems; Part II, Linear Systems," *Int. J. Control, 19*, 1087–1100, June (1974).

7.   W. M. WONHAM and C. D. JOHNSON, "Optimal Bang-Bang Control with Quadratic Performance Index," *Proc. 4th JACC, Univ. Minn.*, 101, June (1963); see also *ASME Trans., J. Basic Eng., 86*, 107, March (1964).

8.   C. D. JOHNSON, "The Fundamental Cost Decomposition for Linear Quadratic Control Problems; Part I, The Case of Scalar Control," *Int. J. Control, 44*, 625 (1986).

9.   H. KWAKERNAAK and R. SIVAN, "Linear Optimal Control Systems," Wiley (Interscience), New York, 1972.

10. C. D. JOHNSON, "Limits of Propriety for Linear-Quadratic Regulator Problems," *Int. J. Control, 45*, No. 5, p. 1835 (1987).

11. C. D. JOHNSON, "The 'Unreachable Poles' Defect in LQR Theory; Analysis and Remedy," *Proc. Southeast. Symp. Syst. Theory, 19th, Clemson Univ., Clemson, S. C.*, p. 263, March (1987); see also *Int. J. Control* (1988).

12. C. D. JOHNSON, "Accommodation of Disturbances in Linear Regulator and Servo-Mechanism Problems," *IEEE Trans. Autom. Control (Special Issue Linear-Quadratic-Gaussian Problem), AC-16*, 635-644, Dec. (1971).

13. C. D. JOHNSON, Theory of Disturbance-Accommodating Controllers, in: "Advances in Control and Dynamic Systems," (C. T. Leondes, ed.), Vol. 12, Ch. 7, Academic Press, New York, 1976.

14. "Special Issue on Disturbance-Accommodating Control Theory," *J. Interdiscipl. Model. Simul., 3*, No. 1 (1980).

15. C. D. JOHNSON, Discrete-Time Disturbance-Accommodating Control Theory, in: Control and Dynamic Systems; Advances in Theory and Applications," Vol. 18, Academic Press, New York, 1982.

16. C. D. JOHNSON, "Disturbance-Accommodating Control; An Overview," *Proc. Am. Control Conf., Seattle, Wash.* (, p. 526 1986).

17. J. A. ASELTINE, A. R. MANCHINI, and C. W. SARTURE, "A Survey of Adaptive Control Systems," *IRE Trans. Autom. Control, 3*, 102 (1958).

18. I. D. LANDAU, "A Survey of Model Reference Adaptive Techniques; Theory and Applications," *Automatica, 10*, 353 (1974).

19. R. B. ASHER, D. ANDRISANI, II, and P. DORATO, "Bibliography on Adaptive Control Systems," *Proc. IIEEE, 64*, 1226 (1976).

20. C. E. ROHS, L. VALAVANI, M. ATHANS, and G. STEIN, "Robustness of Continuous-Time Adaptive Control Algorithms in the Presence of Unmodeled Dynamics," *IEEE Trans. Autom. Control, AC-30*, 881 (1985).

21. YA. Z. TSYPKIN, "Adaptation and Learning in Automatic Systems," Academic Press, New York, 1971.

22. H. UNBEHAUEN (ed.), "Methods and Applications in Adaptive Control," Springer-Verlag, Berlin, 1980.

23. K. S. NARENDRA and R. V. MONOPOLI (eds.), "Applications of Adaptive Control," Acadmic Press, New York, 1980.

24. L. BRAUN, Jr., "On Adaptive Control Systems," *IRE Trans. Autom. Control, AC-4*, 30 (1959).

25. J. S. MEDITCH and J. E. GIBSON, "On the Real-Time Control of Time-Varying Linear Systems," *IRE Trans. Autom. Control, AC-7*, 3 (1962).

26. C. D. JOHNSON, "A New Approach to Adaptive Controller Design," *Proc. 16th Southeast. Symp. Syst. Theor., Miss. State Univ.*, 16 (1984).

27. C. D. JOHNSON, "Adaptive Controller Design Using Disturbance-Accommodation Techniques," *Int. J. Control, 42*, 193 (1985).

28. C. D. JOHNSON, "Linear Adaptive Control; A New Result in Model-Error Compensation Design," *Proc. 1st IFAC Workshop Model-Error Concepts Compensation, Boston*, June, p. 21, 1985; Pergamon, Oxford, 1986.

29. C. D. JOHNSON, "Linear Adaptive Control via Disturbance-Accommodation; Some Case Studies," *Proc. Am. Control Conf., Seattle, Wash.* (, p. 5421986).

30. C. D. JOHNSON, "On Observers for Systems with Unknown Inaccessible Inputs," *Int. J. Control, 21*, 825-831 (1975).

31. C. D. JOHNSON, "Optimal Control of the Linear Regulator with Constant Disturbances," *IEEE Trans. Autom. Control, AC-13,* 416-421 (1968).

32. C. D. JOHNSON, "Comments on 'Optimal Control of the Linear Regulator with Constant Disturbances'," *IEEE Trans. Autom. Control, AC-15,* 516-518 (1970).

33. C. D. JOHNSON, "Further Study of the Linear Regulator with Disturbances; The Case of Vector Disturbances Satisfying a Linear Differential Equation," *IIEEE Trans. Autom. Control, AC-15,* 222-228 (1970).

34. C. D. JOHNSON, "Accommodation of Disturbances in Optimal Control Problems," *3rd Southeast. Symp. Syst. Theor., Atlanta, 1971; P. A4-1; Int. J. Control, 15,* 209-231 (1972).

35. C. D. JOHNSON, Control of Dynamical Systems in the Face of Uncertain Disturbances, *in:* "Stochastic Problems in Mechanics," S. M. Series, Univ. of Waterloo Press, Waterloo, Ontario, Canada, 1974.

36. C. D. JOHNSON, "Algebraic Solution of the Servomechanism Problem with External Distrubances," *ASME Trans. J. Dyn. Syst., Measure., Control, 96, Ser. G,* 25-35 (1974); also, *97,* 161 (1975).

37. C. D. JOHNSON, "Disturbance-Accommodating Control; A History of Its Development," *Proc. 15th Annu. Meet. Soc. Eng. Sci., Gainesville, Fla.,* Dec. (1978).

38. C. D. JOHNSON, "Utility of Disturbances in Disturbance-Accommodating Control Problems," *Proc. 15th Annu. Meet. Soc. Eng. Sci., Gainesville, Fla.,* p. 331, Dec.

39. C. D. JOHNSON, "Disturbance-Utilizing Control for Noisy Measurements and Disturbances, Part I, The Continuous-Time Case," *Int. J. Control, 39,* 859-868 (1984).

40. C. D. JOHNSON, "Disturbance-Utilizing Control for Noisy Measurements and Disturbances, Part II, The Discrete-Time Case," *Int. J. Control, 39,* 869-877 (1984).

41. C. D. JOHNSON and G. A. MILLER, "Design of a Disturbance -Accommodating Controller for an Airborne Pointing Device," *Proc. Conf. Decision Control, Clearwater Beach, FL,* 1171-1179 (1976).

42. C. D. JOHNSON and R. E. SKELTON, "Optimal Desaturation of Momentum Exchange Control Systems," *11th Joint Autom. Control Conf., Atlanta* (1970); also *J. AIAA, 9,* 12-22 (1971).

43. N. K. LOH, D. H. CHUNG, N. COLEMAN, R. J. RADKIEWICZ, and R. E. KASTEN, "Design and Implementation of an Optimal Helicopter Turret Control System," *J. Interdisc. Model. Simul., 3,* 31 (1980).

44. R. E. SKELTON AND P. W. LIKINS, "Orthogonal Filters for Model-Error Compensation in the Control of Nonrigid Spacecraft," *AIAA J. Guidance Control, _1,* 41–49 (1978).

45. R. E. SKELTON, "Application of Disturbance-Accommodating Control in the Model-Error Problem," *J. Interdisc. Model. Simul., 3,* 47-62 (1980).

46. C. D. JOHNSON, "A Unified Canonical Form for Controllable and Uncontrollable Linear Dynamical Systems," *Proc. 10th Joint Autom. Control Conf., Boulder, Colo.,* August (1969); also *Int. J. Control, 13,* 497-517 (1971).

47. W. L. BROGAN, "Modern Control Theory," Quantum Publ., New York, 1974.

48. C. D. JOHNSON, "Optimal Initial Conditions for Full-Order Observers," *Proc. 19th Southeast. Symp. Syst. Theor., Clemson Univ., Clemson, S. C.,* p. 289, March, 1987. Also to appear in *Int. J. Control.*

49. C. D. JOHNSON, "A New Canonical Form and Observer Design for Accommodation of Uncertain Plant Parameters," submitted to *Int. J. Control* (1987).

50. K. S. NARENDRA (ed.), "Adaptive and Learning Systems; Theory and Applications," Plenum, New York, 1986.

51. Session of Papers on Adaptive Control, *Proc. Am. Control Conf., Seattle, Washington,* June (1986), Ibid, Minneapolis, Minn., June (1987).

52. C. D. JOHNSON, "Equivalence of Control Signals in a Nonlinear 'Adaptive-Gain' and an 'All-Linear' Adaptive Controllers," submitted to *Int. J. Control* (1987.)

53. C. D. JOHNSON, "Transfer Function Interpretation of a New All-Linear, Constant-Coefficient Adaptive Controller," submitted to *Int. J. Control* (1987).

54. C. D. JOHNSON, "Teaching a New 'Linear Adaptive Control Theory' In The First Undergraduate Control Course; Lecture Notes and Experiments," to appear 1988.

55.   C. D. JOHNSON, "Practical Applications of a New Adaptive Control Theory," ito appear, 1988.

56.   E. B. LEE and L. MARKUS, "Foundations of Optimal Control Theory," Wiley, New York, 1967.

57.   D. A. FORD and C. D. JOHNSON, "Invariant Subspaces and the Controllability and Observability of Linear Dynamical Systems," *SIAM J. Control, 6,* 553-558 (1968).

58.   C. D. JOHNSON, "A Family of Universal Adaptive Controllers for Linear and Nonlinear Plants," submitted to *Int. J. Control* (1987).

59.   P. A. IOANNOU and K. S. TSAKALIS, "A Robust Direct Adaptive Controller," *IEEE Trans. Autom. Control, AC-31,* 1033–1043 (1986).

60.   J. KRAUSE and G. STEIN, "Structural Limitations of Model Reference Adaptive Controllers," *Proc. 1987 American Control Conference,* pp. 230–237, Minneapolis, Minn., June, 1987.

61.   C. D. JOHNSON, "Contemporary Adaptive Controllers vs. a New Linear Adaptive Controller; Some Performance Comparisons," to appear, 1988.

62.   V. V. CHALAM, "Adaptive Control Systems; Techniques and Applications," Dekker, New York (1987).

BIOLOGICAL SYSTEMS: A GENERAL APPROACH

G. G. JAROS,* P. C. BELONJE,† and H. BREUER‡

Departments of *Biomedical Engineering, †Physiology, and ‡Cardiac Surgery
Medical School, University of Cape Town and Groote Schuur Hospital
Observatory 7925, Cape Town, Republic of South Africa

I. INTRODUCTION

A. MODELING AND SIMULATION

The words modeling and simulation are often used as though they were synonymous [1, 2]. However, we propose that the term "modeling" should be reserved for the construction of a model, while "simulation" should be used for the running of the model. It must be clear that building a complex and validated model, such as that of the circulatory system designed by Guyton *et al.* [3], requires many man-years, whereas learning how to use the model for simulation can often be achieved in a few minutes. An analogy to illustrate this point could be to compare the complexity of constructing a motor car (modeling) and the relative ease of driving it (simulation).

Physiological mechanisms are very complex, and therefore one has to attempt to approach reality through various levels of approximation. So, for instance, in zero approximation one attempts to present only a rough outline of the system while the subsequent approximations describe the real system in closer detail.

The main goal in constructing a model is to be able to use a vast amount of data in a properly coordinated way to predict the behavior of a system. In every field of human endeavor there has been such an explosion of knowledge that without the use of a modeling approach and the power of the computer it is practically impossible to comprehend it all. Through modeling we can derive models of importance in medicine and use them in teaching, diagnosis, and patient management. However, a most important spinoff of the modeling process is generally overlooked. As one collates and arranges the data, one comes to understand more fully the organization and functional aspects of the system. The quantitative data which are necessary for the process allow one to stratify the levels of importance of various functions and to expose gaps in the knowledge about the system being modeled.

As mentioned previously, the modeling of complex physiological systems is intellectually demanding and time consuming. The modeler should therefore make every attempt to provide clear and concise documentation about the model and make it available to others. This would enable others to learn about the system by either studying the model directly or using it for simulation purposes. Unfortunately, this is rarely done, and consequently many models become buried in dusty archives and the knowledge gained during the modeling process is taken by the modeler to the grave.

Some of the above-mentioned problems can be avoided by using a top-down systems approach. We shall show that biological systems can be analyzed in this way, and because the various subsystems are similar, we have been able to develop a generalized method and terminology. The article ends with specific examples of how to formulate a model. Although models do not have to be computer-based, the real test of a complex model can only be handled by the computer. Therefore, a method for formulating computer programs will also be described.

B.   REASONS FOR MODELING COMPLEX SYSTEMS

There is a tremendous amount of largely uncoordinated data on physiological systems in the literature, and we believe that researchers should incorporate extensive systems analyses into their modeling techniques to coordinate it. It is surprising that so few integrated models have been constructed to date. The reason may be that it is the vast amount of detail itself which makes the construction of a satisfactory model a daunting task. Considerable insight into the system is essential for the modeler to be able to evaluate the data critically and perhaps even to eliminate such data that appear to be irrelevant to the envisaged approximation of the system. So, for instance, a parameter which changes the system only slightly is clearly unimportant in a zero-approximation model.

De Greene [4], discussing the field of ergonomics, pointed out that there was a "mismatch between operational data needs and research outputs [due to the] lack of transferability of laboratory results to the real world, fragmentation of and poor communication between scientific disciplines, preoccupation with outmoded concepts of 'basic' research, continued dependence on obsolete paradigms stemming from earlier eras of scientific research, the nature of the basic unit of analysis, lack of a systems approach and lack of integrating theory." These conclusions are probably equally valid in medical and biological research, as no major shift from "component"-type thinking has occurred despite many books that have been written about modeling biological systems [5–11].

It must be re-emphasized that traditional component research explores small areas of a particular subject in depth. This usually gives one a momentary glimpse of a small section of a complex system, often biased by "leaders" in the field. Seldom is a total perspective given. In our opinion, one can only obtain this perspective and attempt not only to comprehend the body's multidimensional functions, but also absorb new developments by making use of systems analysis and modeling techniques.

As models should be used to frame data into meaningful interrelationships (facilitating the understanding of and pointing out the gaps in the existing knowledge), it is essential that researchers have access to an up-to-date model of the system they are investigating. Using the top-down approach, a simple zero-approximation model can be constructed initially and later refined where necessary.

Unfortunately, the health-care professions appear to be generally unconvinced of the value of the systems approach, even though they are intimately involved in diagnosing and treating a malfunction or breakdown of a particular system in the body. The reasons for this are complex. To quote De Greene [4] again, "[funding] agencies may select research on the basis of 'scientific merit.' But the interpretation of scientific merit almost always suffers from disciplinary bias and from methodological orientations which have proved 'successful' or have been accepted in the past. An unhealthy positive feedback loop is established among the discipline-based divisions of sponsoring agencies, the peer reviewers of proposed research, and the research and researchers eventually supported. The result may be a time lag of years between the kinds of basic research that should be undertaken in order to anticipate future applied needs and what is actually encouraged and supported based on past arbitrary criteria for success. The cumulative time lag between recognition of basic research requirements and 'problem solved' may approach two decades.... Yet the results [in this type of research] may apply only to the specific laboratory environment of the research. Even if the results are generalizable, they may not be integrable with other research findings. Systems research and advanced exploratory research are notoriously hard to sell. Pressures to produce immediate results, whether hypotheses-tested and verified or programs-supported, are immense.... The peer review process discriminates against new interdisciplinary science even though it may be ripe with breakthrough potential."

C.   ERGONOMICS OF MODELING

A knowledge of the principles of ergonomics is most useful in the development of models, particularly if these models are to be used by others. Ergonomics is the science of examining the way in which a "tool" enhances the efficiency of the user by analyzing the combined system of user and tool. In this "ergosystem" the interrelationships between the various components of each of the subsystems are optimized in order to obtain maximum efficiency of the combined system. In the context of this article the tool is the resultant model and this must be designed to be easily understood and used, i.e., "user-friendly." On the other hand, the user must be well disposed toward the model, i.e., "model-friendly."

Both of these aspects depend on the original modeler, on his dexterity in constructing the model, and on his expertise in presenting a comprehensible model acceptable to prospective users.

One of the reasons why modeling has been unsuccessful in medical science might be that, although the models are mathematically sound, they are invariably unacceptably complex [12]. It is therefore essential that models be constructed with the user in mind and then "sold" to him. The first target group should be educators and researchers. Once this group has been convinced, the use of models will naturally spread to a wider group of people. In "selling" the model the modeler must not hide the fact that anyone who wishes to use a model must learn a certain amount of flow-charting, block diagram construction, use of symbols, and both algebraical and mathematical techniques. But the modeler must at the same time point out the large dividends that will accrue from a relatively modest intellectual investment; the cost/benefit ratio is favorable.

It is essential that any model has the capability of expansion, change, and refinement in order to incorporate new information. But, and this is practically the definition of a useful model, those alterations must be merely further approximations and must be absorbed without basic changes to the model.

D.   CONSTRUCTION OF MODELS

There are two basic ways to construct models of systems. The first is the "bottom-up" approach, which starts with a large amount of detail and attempts to structure it into a model. The second is the "top-down" approach, which begins with an overall systems concept and progressively moves down the levels of organization ultimately to incorporate all the details. The former approach has been largely unsuccessful [4], as there are inherent difficulties in integrating component research and in aggregating task elements to predict systems performance. The modeler is swamped with detailed information about the system but has no yardstick by which to sort out the essential from the peripheral features.

The top-down approach confronts the modeler with the formidable problem of having initially neither structure nor data. However, the modeler has a set of conservation laws at his disposal and thus an accepted framework into which data can be incorporated. This is a base from which new strategies can be planned. Moreover, this approach allows the modeler to construct his model in steps of increasing complexity. The initial (or zero) approximation of the model can later be refined into a first approximation covering more detail, and so on, until the model is a satisfactory reflection of the system. Following this approach, it must be understood that any refinement of the model, e.g., progressing toward a further approximation, should leave the previous approximate model intact. In short, the n-th approximation incorporates fully the (n − 1)-th approximation.

There are a large number of constructs available in the literature on the behavioral and social sciences, which may be of value to modeling by the top-down approach in the biological sciences. One of the frustrations in the top-down approach has been that modelers in several fields have expected to find off-the-shelf submodels in the literature which could be immediately plugged into an all-encompassing systems model [12]. Unfortunately, there are no readily available off-the-shelf submodels, and thus we need patience and perseverance to construct them ourselves.

In the top-down approach, modeling must always commence with a thorough systems analysis. This involves the establishment of a framework into which information can be cataloged in an ordered way. Strictly speaking, all well-planned and ordered learning processes should involve systems analysis, but unfortunately this is seldom the case. Usually information is accumulated in a rather haphazard fashion without real regard to its position and interactions within a general framework. This is especially true in the biological sciences. As mentioned previously, we believe that by designing appropriate frameworks in which to catalog information, the learning process will be enhanced and the deficiencies in current knowledge would be identified.

An important thing to remember when analyzing a physiological system is that one is dealing with time-dependent functions not confined to single anatomical structures. As an example, the subsystems of the "functional oxygen supply system" include the airways, lungs, red blood cells, heart, blood vessels, capillary wall, interstitial fluid, cell membrane, cytoplasm, and finally the points of oxidation within the mitochondria. Each of the subsystems has its own time constant. For example, the average life span of a red blood cell, which transports the oxygen, is of the order of 120 days, while blood circulation time is of the order of seconds. Impeding blood flow will thus have immediate consequences, whereas an impairment in the development of the blood cells may take some time to manifest itself. Expressed differently: if the oxygen supply system is modeled for a short time span, the circulation time is a first-order effect, while the finite life of a normal red blood cell is not even a second-order effect and can be neglected. It is therefore most important to take the various time constants of the individual subsystems into account. In the behavior of the entire oxygen supply system a malfunction in any one of the subsystems will affect the whole system, but this will be within the time constant of the affected subsystem. This view of the body as the integration of functional and time-dependent systems is often neglected [13].

Although functional physiological systems and their subsystems have been stressed, it is conceded that structural anatomical organization can be of great help in the design of a model. The reason for this is that the anatomical structures are well documented and easily depicted in a spatial representation. Once having grouped the anatomical structures into functional subsystems, it is important to consider carefully both the "within subsystem" as well as the "between subsystem" relationships, keeping in mind that each subsystem must be modeled to the same approximation.

When commencing systems analysis, the first easy step is the use of block diagrams and the tabulation of known interrelationships. The former identifies the subsystems and their interconnections, while the latter are useful to record their quantitative details. The result of this initial systems analysis is a conceptual or schematic model which represents the basic knowledge. Now, by using the "top-down" approach, the model can be refined step by step by incorporating more and more detail. The model therefore progresses from zero level to higher levels of approximation of the system. The construction of the model is thus an iterative process leading to increasing refinement approaching that of the real system.

E.   TESTING OF KNOWLEDGE

As soon as information can be derived from the model, its validity should be tested. To assess the degree of correspondence between the model and the real system, quantiative experimental data from real systems are naturally indispensable. In order to extract quantitative information from a model, accurate and reliable mathematical formulas must be developed. Techniques on how to do this are described comprehensively by Carson et al. [14]. These authors propose that the first step in modeling is the definition of the purpose of the model; only then can mathematical techniques enter. Once the mathematical formulations have been completed, the model can be compared with the real system.

Those who have constructed models of complex systems will testify that their models were usually modified during the mathematical formulation process. The purpose of a zero approximation is only to test the model against basic knowledge. After this, the interrelationships and interconnections within and between subsystems are described in such a way as to make them easily usable for mathematical analysis. It is at this stage when basic assumptions are formulated and the limitations of the model are determined. By this time the physical and spatial organization of the system must be sorted out.

The next step is to attach numerical values and time constants to the relationships, thus establishing their relative importance within the system. This rigorous mathematical process requires unambiguous statements which will often expose deficiencies in the available data. This will necessitate an in-depth search of the literature or laboratory experimentation on the real systems under investigation. One of the problems, however, is that much of the potentially useful data are often hidden in a mass of information seemingly irrelevant to the system. Also, some parameters, variables, and relationships are not measurable with current techniques and certain details will have to be assumed. But with the development of new techniques, more relevant and usable data will become available, and this will lead to better and more reliable models.

The translation of a detailed mathematical model into a computer model is the next major step. Fortunately, various "simulation packages" are available which reduce the extent and difficulty of the task considerably. Examples of such programs are: SAAM [15], ISL [16], CSMP [17], DRIVER [18], and SIM2 [19]. Using any of the simulation packages, the modeler only needs a rudimentary command of computer programming to transcribe the systems equations into FORTRAN, PASCAL, or BASIC.

Once the system has been computerized, the model must be validated. If data extracted from the model match (within given limits) data from experiments performed on the real system, then one has a quantitatively validated model. This, however, usually does not happen with complex models due to the incompleteness of quantitative data, and in these cases the best one can hope for is a qualitative validation. If neither quantitative nor qualitative validation can be achieved, then either 1) the zero-approximation model is incorrect, 2) data or assumed relationships are incorrect, 3) the mathematical formulation is wrong, or 4) the computational programming is at fault. One should check the last two first. If they are found to be correct, the only way out is to go back to the learning process, obtaining additional data and re-evaluating the concepts on which the zero-approximation model was based.

F.   DOCUMENTATION OF THE MODEL

If one has constructed a quantitatively or qualitatively validated model, it is necessary to document it in such a way that it is user-friendly. This is done by describing the details of the model including its time dependence, the way it fits into a larger organization, the external influences, subsystems and their interconnections, the numerical range of parameters, constants and variables, details of the computer program, and the results of the validation experiments. Most of this can, in fact, be achieved by means of a profusely annotated computer model.

When one has a validated and documented model, it is possible to adapt it for various purposes. It could be used as a predictive model for patient management, as a diagnostic tool, or as a teaching aid. In each adaptation, the original model can probably be simplified to suit the specific purpose, but all new assumptions must be within the stated limits of the parameters of the original model.

II.   GENERAL FRAMEWORK
FOR ENDODYNAMIC PROCESSES

No living organism operates in isolation; it is part of a living network arranged in a hierarchical fashion. Miller [20] proposed a general approach to the analysis of living systems in which the presence of seven hierarchical levels was postulated, viz., supranational, national, organization, group, organism, organ, and cell. The level at which we study physiological systems is the level of the *organism*. We have eliminated the organ as a distinct level in the hierarchy and selected the *cell* as the level below the *organism*. Further, we combined Miller's four levels above the organism in a single level, simply referred to as the *environment*. Therefore, our model of a living system is composed of three levels interconnected hierarchically in the following order from top to bottom: 1) environment, 2) organism, 3) cell.

In addition to dividing living systems horizontally into levels, Miller [20] also divided them vertically into two groups, viz., matter/energy and information processing systems. We believe that such a division cannot be made at the organism level for at least two reasons. First, all matter/energy processing sys-

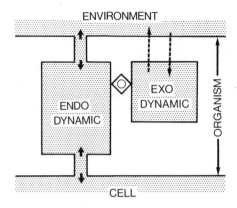

Fig. 1. The relationship between the three hierarchical levels and the endo- and exodynamic processes.

tems have information processing subsystems incorporated in them for control purposes. Therefore, separating the two types of systems on this level is practically impossible, although it is possible on a subsystem level, as will be shown later. Second, information processing in itself is often achieved by the handling of matter/energy. A good example of this is the endocrine system, in which hormones are physically circulated through the body for control purposes.

We propose to divide the organism vertically into two major groups of processes, viz., *endodynamic processes* and *exodynamic processes* (see Fig. 1). We must point out at this stage that, although such a grouping is made, none of these processes can proceed in isolation. In fact, they interact with one another at various levels. The division simply signifies that the interactions *within* the groups are much stronger than *between* the groups. However, the main reason for dividing the processes into two groups is the similarity in the way they function and in which their purposes are aimed.

Endodynamic processes are directed toward a lower level of the hierarchy. On the level of the organism, which is the focus of the present paper, endodynamic processes are directed toward the maintenance of the "cell." Obviously, as cells are the building blocks of the organism, the latter will also benefit from the proper functioning of the endodynamic processes. The processes in this category are mainly concerned with the transfer of matter/energy between the environment and the cells or vice versa. The kind of substances involved are, for example, nutrients, vitamins, minerals, and waste products. It must be pointed out that the matter/energy transfer can take place in both an upward and a downward direction through the organism. Nutrients, for example, move from environment to the cells, whereas waste products move in the opposite direction. Nevertheless, the purpose of both these processes is directed toward the maintenance of the cells.

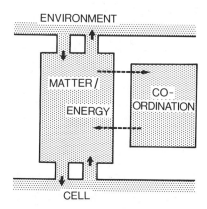

Fig. 2. A zero-order framework for endodynamic processes.

Exodynamic processes are aimed toward the external environment of the hierarchical level under observation. The reason for the existence of these processes is to ensure the continued existence of the organism within its environment and include bodily movement, thinking, feeling, communication, and reproduction.

The subdivision of the whole system into endodynamic and exodynamic processes helps to sort available knowledge into smaller compartments. The processes which belong to the endodynamic group have much in common, which means that a general approach can be used to study them. The same applies to exodynamic processes. However, we must sound a warning again. Although each of the processes can be looked at separately, their relationship to the whole organism must be identified right at the onset. A systematic analysis of interactions between the system being studied and the rest of the organism is therefore mandatory.

In the present section we shall describe the general properties of endodynamic processes. A similar approach could be developed for exodynamic processes, but this is beyond the scope of the present article.

A. ENDODYNAMICS

At the level of the organism, endodynamics can be defined as the study of processes involved in the conservation of optimal cellular function. Although these processes are concerned primarily with the processing of matter and energy, each of them needs a considerable amount of information processing for control purposes. As we mentioned earlier, we believe that the similarities between the various endodynamic processes are so great that a generalized method of analysis using a standard framework is possible. The proposed framework (Fig. 2) is based

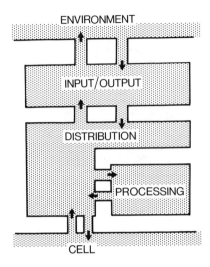

Fig. 3. A schematic diagram of matter/energy processing subsystems.

on a model developed by Jaros *et al.* [21], which in turn evolved from the work of Bronner [22].

The framework divides endodynamic processes into two major types of subsystems, viz., matter/energy handling subsystems and coordination (information processing) subsystems. The matter/energy handling subsystems fulfill the endodynamic purpose of providing a link between the environment and the cells, while the coordination processes can be regarded as accessory to ensure their optimal functioning.

1. Matter/Energy Handling Subsystems

There are obvious similarities between the various matter/energy handling and coordination processes to execute their functions. Both the matter/energy handling and coordination processes can be divided into three types of subsystems: 1) input/output subsystems, 2) distribution subsystems, and 3) processing subsystems. (See Fig. 3.)

a. Input/Output Subsystems. In general, matter/energy needed by the cells is obtained from the environment, which is also the destination of the waste products coming from the cells. The input/output subsystems are situated across the dividing line between the environment and the organism, and are involved in the exchange of matter/energy between the two levels in both directions. The most important subsystems in this group are the following:

(1)   The alimentary canal (al) is the subsystem in which nutrients, vitamins, electrolytes, minerals, and water are taken up from the environment.

It is also responsible for the excretion of a few substances such as bile pigments and the reabsorption of digestive secretions such as bile salts.

(2)   The kidneys (ki) are responsible for the excretion of most of the water-soluble waste products.

(3)   The skin (sk) is a site where heat is exchanged and some substances such as water and certain electrolytes are lost.

(4)   The lungs (lu) are responsible for the uptake of oxygen and elimination of carbon dioxide. A certain amount of water and heat is also lost via this route.

(5)   The uterus (ut) is a subsystem which provides the site of interaction between the mother and the fetus for the exchange of metabolites during pregnancy.

(6)   The mammary gland (ma) provides an output route for milk during lactation. As milk consists of several substances such as water, proteins, fats, carbohydrates, and minerals, the mammary gland plays a role in the endodynamics of all these substances.

b.   Distribution Subsystems. The function of these subsystems is to transport substances between the various parts of the organism. There are several ways that transport can take place: some substances are transported by cells (e.g., oxygen); some attached to carrier proteins (e.g., iron); and some are carried in solution (e.g., glucose). In many cases more than one method of transport is utilized.

(1)   The circulatory (ci) subsystem is the most important distribution subsystem. It consists of three main components. The heart provides the power for the circulation of blood, which acts as the distributing medium, while the blood vessels are the conduits. Although the circulatory subsystem acts as a closed loop, matter/energy to be transported enters and leaves it via the capillary vessels in the organs.

(2)   The interstitial fluid (if) is found between the cells in the tissues and acts as a medium to transport substances between the capillaries and the cells. This transport is achieved by means of concentration gradients and hydrostatic pressure differences.

(3)   The lymphatic (ly) subsystem conducts excess interstitial fluid from the intercellular spaces back to the great blood vessels. The power needed to propel the lymph is provided mainly by the contraction of the muscles surrounding the lymphatic vessels.

c. Processing (and Storage) Subsystems. Substances taken up by the input/output subsystems cannot always be utilized immediately or in the same form as they entered the organism. In some cases they are stored (e.g., glucose in the form of glycogen); in other cases they are changed into another compound (e.g., proteins to glucose); in still other cases they are produced from other components within the organism (e.g., amino acids to protein). Examples of processing and storage subsystems are as follows:

(1)   The liver (li) is the most important single processing subsystem, and its position in series with the alimentary canal bears witness to its importance. It is the major organ where chemical transformations take place. In addition, it serves as a storage organ for different substances such as glycogen, iron, and various vitamins.

(2)   The bone (bo) is a storage place for calcium, phosphate, and magnesium.

(3)   The bone marrow (bm) produces red blood cells as well as certain white blood cells.

(4)   The reticuloendothelial system (re) produces antibodies.

(5)   The adipose tissue (ad) stores and converts fats.

2.   Coordination Process

Endodynamic processes are complex and depend on contributions from many organs and tissues. For example, the effective supply of oxygen to the tissues depends on the proper functioning of the lungs, the unhindered movement of oxygen from the alveoli to the blood, the efficient binding of oxygen to the hemoglobin in the red blood cells, the proper circulation of blood, the effective diffusion of oxygen from the blood to the cells, as well as the normal intracellular transport of oxygen. This is, in fact, a simplified picture, as there are many more details to consider in the whole process. The main point to remember, however, is that there is a complex, interlocking, and continuous sequence of reactions, flows, and time constants, all of which contributed to the process. Each of the components must function properly in order to ensure efficiency of the entire process. A malfunction in any one of the components, or a change in one of the time constants, can cause a breakdown of the complete process; therefore, a stringent control must be exercised over the components.

There are two major ways in which endodynamic processes can be controlled, viz., through autoregulation and through remote control via the endocrine subsystem and the autonomic nervous subsystem. In both cases regulation is based on negative feedback processes, viz., that a deviation from "normal" initiates a series of events which oppose the change in order to regain the "normal" state. For example, a change in blood pressure is opposed by several mechanisms in an attempt to keep it constant. A detuning or a break in the feedback loop destabilizes the subsystem, leading to malfunction and, in severe cases, to death.

 a. Autoregulation. This is generally the simplest but at the same time the most immediate and important form of control within endodynamic subsystems. Examples are the regulation of local blood flow, the maintenance of a constant blood pH by chemical buffers, and the regulation of oxygen association and dissociation within the red blood cells.

 b. Remote Control. Two main subsystems are involved:

(1)   The endocrine subsystem exercises control through hormones. A summary of this subsystem has been compiled by Rasmussen [23]. Although several new facts have emerged since then, the structural organization of the subsystem as described by Rasmussen is still valid.

(2)   The autonomic nervous subsystem complements the endocrine subsystem. Its activity can be localized or diffused, and its time constant is generally smaller than that of the endocrine subsystem. There is a direct interaction between the endocrine subsystem and the autonomic nervous subsystem in the hypothalamus, which therefore can be considered to be part of both subsystems.

The above-mentioned coordination subsystems are in fact information processing subsystems which either carry information by hormones or by trains of nerve impulses. As in the case of matter/energy handling processes, the information handling processes are performed mainly by three kinds of subsystems, viz., input/output, distribution, and processing subsystems, as described previously. Although this is true for the endocrine subsystem, it is slightly different in the case of the autonomic nervous subsystem. In the latter case, the input/output subsystems transmit information through input or output transducers called receptors and effectors; the distribution subsystems are the nervous pathways connecting the various parts of the organism; and the processing subsystems store, convert, and manipulate information in complex neuronal networks.

B.   INTERACTIONS BETWEEN PROCESSES

An endodynamic process does not proceed in isolation, as it is related to other endodynamic and exodynamic processes. Generally the affinity between various endodynamic processes is stronger than between endodynamic and exodynamic processes; but some relationships between endodynamic processes are stronger than others, resulting in the formation of process clusters. The following groups of substances are handled by the various clusters:

(1) nutrients, e.g., carbohydrates, fats, and proteins,

(2) minerals, e.g., calcium, magnesium, and phosphate,

(3) energy, heat, and oxygen,

(4) electrolytes and water, e.g., sodium, potassium, and water,

(5) acid-base substances, e.g., hydrogen ions, chloride, carbon dioxide, and bicarbonate,

(6) waste products, e.g., bilirubin, urea, uric acid, and

(7) miscellaneous substances, e.g., vitamins, trace elements.

Processes within a cluster can influence one another in different ways and at different locations. The three most important ways are 1) matter/energy transfer between processes, 2) information transfer between processes, and 3) the sharing of coordinating processes.

(1)   Matter/energy transfer between processes takes place mainly in the processing subsystems. One can take the cluster in which nutrient processing takes place as an example. In the liver, carbohydrates and proteins can be converted into fats and fats and proteins into carbohydrates through the intermingling of their metabolic pathways.

(2)   Information transfer is achieved by an event or substance within one process influencing another process. For example, in the kidneys sodium transport influences calcium transport; thus sodium endodynamics influences calcium endodynamics. Another example is that the carbon dioxide concentration in the blood influences oxygen endodynamics not only by its action on the rate of respiration, but also by its effect on oxygen dissociation in the red blood cell.

(3)   The most important reason for grouping processes into clusters is that they share coordination subsystems. For example, the cluster dealing with nutrients is "serviced" by a group of hormones consisting of insulin, glucagon, cortisol, growth hormone, adrenalin, and thyroxine, among others; the "mineral cluster" is controlled by parathyroid hormone, calcitonin, and dihydroxycholecalciferol; and the "water/electrolyte cluster" depends on aldosterone and antidiuretic hormone for its control.

The usual way of interaction between processes belonging to different clusters is generally achieved through information transfer. The existence of clusters necessitates that all processes within a cluster should be considered together even when only one of them needs to be analyzed. If this is not possible, the interrelationships between the processes should at least be documented. One must be aware that there is often a two-way interaction between processes, in which case the modeling of all processes within the cluster becomes mandatory.

It must be remembered that exodynamic processes and environmental factors also influence endodynamic processes. We believe that the identification of these, even simply on a qualitative or descriptive basis, can be very useful and, therefore, a formal approach to evaluate these influences needs to be developed.

III. GENERAL METHOD FOR THE MATHEMATICAL FORMULATION OF ENDODYNAMIC MODELS

Once a general framework for a given system has been determined and the information provided by the literature review has been incorporated within it, the mathematical formulation can commence. In the present section we shall be looking at ways this formulation can be done. First we shall introduce a general modeling terminology to help with the procedure. After that we shall be looking at matter/energy handling, viz., flows (F), quantities (Q), and rates of change of quantities ($R = dQ/dt$) in the main endodynamic subsystems and their compartments. This will be followed by a description of the way some of the fluxes arise and how they can be represented in the model.

A. A GENERAL MODELING TERMINOLOGY FOR ENDODYNAMIC PROCESSES

It should be obvious from what has been said before that there are similarities between the various endodynamic processes, and that these similarities are important enough to warrant the creation of a generalized approach to the study of these processes. Formalized models of the processes can be described in terms of parameters which recur in the various processes. Therefore, the creation of a general modeling terminology (GMT) seems to be feasible. Such a terminology will help to tie each process under discussion into the general framework. It will also enable researchers to understand systems with which they are not entirely familiar. In the present section only endodynamic processes are considered. However, exodynamic processes can also be analyzed in a similar fashion.

There are three main characteristics which the general terminology describes: 1) the type of variable or parameter, 2) the location of the part of the process in question, and 3) the matter/energy being studied. We are using a single character symbol to represent a variable or a parameter, and a subscript consisting of 4 to 6 letters to represent the location and the matter/energy components.

Table I. Examples of Subscripts Indicating Location

ac	Adrenal cortex	ex	External
ad	Adipose tissue	gd	Gland
al	Alimentary canal	gl	Glomerulus
am	Adrenal medulla	if	Interstitial fluid
bf	Bone fluid	io	Input/output
bl	Blood	ki	kidney
bm	Bone marrow	lh	Loop of Henle
bo	Bone	li	Liver
bs	Bone solid	lu	Lung
bx	Bone crystal	ly	Lymph
cb	Capsule of Bowman	ma	Mammary gland
ce	Cell	mo	Mouth
cf	Cellular fluid	pg	Parathyroid gland
ci	Circulatory system	pl	Plasma
co	Colon	pr	Processing
cp	Compartment	pt	Proximal tubule
ct	Collecting tubule	re	Reticuloendothelial
di	Distribution	si	Small intestine
dt	Distal tubule	sk	Skin
du	Duodenum	st	Stomach
dy	Decay	tg	Thyroid gland
ec	Extracellular fluid	ut	Uterus
en	Environment		

1. Variable or Parameter

The type of variable or parameter indicates the nature of the process taking place. There are 11 variables important in endodynamic processes. They are listed together with applicable units: A, activity (appropriate units); C, concentration (mmol/liter); E, energy expended per second (W); F, flow (mmol/s); K, factor of proportionality (generally constant); L, distance (m); N, relative neuronal activity (no activity = 0, normal = 1); P, pressure (kilopascal); Q, quantity (mmol); R = dQ/dt, rate of change of Q inside a compartment (mmol/s); T, time or time span (s); V, volume (liter). The remaining 15 letters of the alphabet can be used to extend the system.

2. Location

The location is identified by the initial part of the subscript to the variable or parameter. Although an endodynamic process usually spans several anatomical organs, its components occur in identifiable single anatomical or histological structures. For most of the above-mentioned variables or parameters (except for F, L, and K), it is generally sufficient to define the location by a single compartment. The first two positions in the subscript are allocated to indicate the location. For

Table II. Examples of the Subscripts Indicating Matter/Energy

act	ACTH	k	Potassium
adh	ADH	mg	Magnesium
adr	Adrenalin	na	Sodium
alb	Albumin	oxy	Oxytocin
ald	Aldosterone	o2	Oxygen
atp	Adenosine triphosphate	po4	Phosphate
bil	Biliribin	pro	Protein
ca	Calcium	pth	Parathyroid hormone
cl	Chlorine	rbc	Red blood cells
co2	Carbon dioxide	sth	Growth hormone
cor	Cortisol	sst	Somatostatin
dhc	Dihydroxycholecalciferol	tct	(Thyro)calcitonin
fat	Fat (lipid)	th3	Tri-iodothyronine
fe	Iron	th4	Thyroxine
glu	Glucose	ura	Uric acid
h	Hydrogen	ure	Urea
hcl	Hydrochloric acid	vb1	Vitamin B1
hco	Bicarbonate	vc	Vitamin C
h2o	Water	vd1	Vitamin D
ins	Insulin	wbc	White blood cells

example, C_{pl} = concentration in the plasma; V_{ec} = volume of fluid in the extracellular compartment. Table I shows examples of two-letter subscripts which are used to indicate different locations in the body.

It is obvious that two of the variables, viz., F and L, cannot be expressed in terms of a single location, because both the origin and the destination of the processes must be indicated. Therefore, a four-letter subscript is used in these cases. For example: F_{plki} = flow *from* plasma *to* kidney, e.g., glomerular filtration; F_{kipl} = flow *from* kidney *to* plasma, e.g., tubular reabsorption.

This first part of the subscript – either two or four characters long – is separated from the second part by a slash.

3. Matter/Energy

Matter/energy is identified by the last part of the subscript to the variable or parameter. Because of the great number of substances which are involved in endodynamics, it is necessary to use three letters of the subscript for this purpose. However, if a one- or two-letter symbol or abbreviation already exists for a substance, this must be used. For example: $C_{ec/ca}$ = concentration *in* the extracellular component *of* calcium; $C_{pl/na}$ = concentration *in* the plasma *of* sodium; or $V_{ec/h2o}$ = volume *in* extracellular space *of* water. But $F_{plki/glu}$ = flow *from* plasma *to* kidney *of* glucose; $F_{kipl/na}$ = flow *from* kidney *to* plasma of sodium. Table II shows examples of the most common subscripts for substances in general endodynamic processes. Note that some subscripts coincide with the chemical symbols.

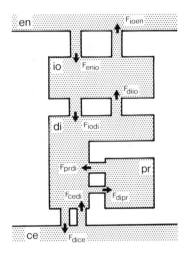

Fig. 4. The main matter/energy processing subsystems.   io, Input/output; di, distribution; pr, processing; f, flow; en, environment; ce, cell.

It must be pointed out that it is in conjunction with the computer that our standardized system really becomes useful. The automatic sorting, classification, and retrieval of data in a large model is difficult without such a general system.

B.   DESCRIPTION OF THE MAIN MATTER/ENERGY PROCESSING SUBSYSTEMS

It was shown in the previous section that there are three major matter/energy handling subsystems. These are the distribution (di), input/output (io), and processing (pr) subsystems (Fig. 4). The input/output subsystems make contact with the environment (en) and the distribution subsystem with the cells (ce).

When analyzing a process, one should look at the dynamics in each of the subsystems which, at the first level of approximation, can be considered as single compartments. In this discussion we are dealing with matter/energy in general. This, of course, allows us to omit the matter/energy section of the subscript. If we refer to a specific substance, the appropriate subscript will be used.

(1) The distribution system (di) (Fig. 4). The analysis of any compartment can be described in four steps.

(i) One begins by totaling all the flows entering the compartment (F_{exdi}), and then all those which leave it (F_{diex}).

$$F_{exdi} = F_{iodi} + F_{prdi} + F_{cedi}$$
$$F_{diex} = F_{diio} + F_{dipr} + F_{dice}.$$

Generally, there are several input/output and processing compartments. The flows to and from these must, of course, all be included in the above two equations.

It is also possible to add a flow to the model which accounts for the introduction of matter/energy directly into or out of a compartment which normally does not make contact with the environment. Such a flow could, for example, be a blood transfusion, F_{endi}, and blood loss, F_{dien}.

The loss of substances such as hormones and drugs from a compartment could also be due to decay processes. The decay rate inside the (distribution) subsystem (F_{didy}) is proportional to the quantity of the substance (Q_{di}) as follows:

$$F_{didy} = K_{didy} \times Q_{di},$$

where K_{didy} is the decay constant for the particular process which is related to the half-life ($T_{1/2}$) of the process:

$$K_{didy} = 0.693/T_{1/2}.$$

If there is no decay, $K_{didy} = 0$.

(ii)   The next step calculates the rate of change of matter/energy (R) under investigation in the subsystem as follows:

$$R_{di} = F_{exdi} - F_{diex} + F_{endi} - F_{dien} - F_{didy}.$$

(iii)   From this, the amount of matter/energy in the subsystem can be calculated by integration:

$$Q_{di} = \int_{t_i}^{t_f} R_{di} \times T_{delta},$$

where $t_f - t_i$ is the time span. On the computer, this integration can be performed easily by numerical integration, as long as R_{di} is known as a function of time.

(iv)   The concentration of matter/energy in the subsystem can be computed as follows (if the volume of the subsystem is known):

$$C_{di} = Q_{di}/V_{di}.$$

(2) The input/output subsystem (io) (Fig. 4).

    (i) $F_{exio} = F_{enio} + F_{diio}$
           $F_{ioex} = F_{ioen} + F_{iodi}$

    (ii) $R_{io} = F_{exio} - F_{ioex} + F_{enio} - F_{ioen} - F_{iody}$

    (iii) $Q_{io} = \int_{t_i}^{t_f} R_{io} \times T_{delta}$

    (iv) $C_{io} = Q_{io}/V_{io}.$

(3) The processing subsystem (pr) (Fig. 4).

    (i)   As there is only one flow in each way, no initial summing is necessary.

    (ii) $R_{pr} = F_{expr} - F_{prex} + F_{enpr} - F_{pren} - F_{prdy}$

    (iii) $Q_{io} = \int_{t_i}^{t_f} R_{io_{t_i}}^{t_f} \times T_{delta}$

    (iv) $C_{pr} = Q_{pr}/V_{pr}.$

C.   EXAMPLES OF MATTER/ENERGY PROCESSING COMPARTMENTS

Each of the subsystems, which were considered as single compartments in the previous section, are generally composed of several subcompartments. Let us consider a few examples.

(1) *The alimentary canal (al).* The main compartments in the alimentary canal are the mouth (mo), the stomach (st), the small intestine (si), and the colon (co). These compartments are connected in series, as shown in Fig. 5.

Let us take the small intestine (si) as an example.

    (i)   The first step is to sum the inward and outward flows:

$F_{exsi} = F_{stsi} + F_{blsi}$
$F_{siex} = F_{sico} + F_{sibl}.$

    (ii)   An equation can be written for the rate of change of matter/energy for the subcompartment, as follows:

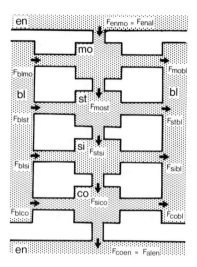

Fig. 5. The compartments in the alimentary canal subsystem: mo, mouth; st, stomach; si, small intestine; co, colon; en, environment; bl, blood.

$$R_{si} = F_{exsi} - F_{siex} + F_{ensi} - F_{sien} - F_{sidy}.$$

If one previously used a lumped diagram for the alimentary canal, i.e., if one considered it as a single compartment, one would have F_{albl} and F_{blal} as the flows between it and blood. These lumped flows, of course, represent the sum of the flows in the various subcompartments, as follows:

$$F_{albl} = F_{mobl} + F_{stbl} + F_{sibl} + F_{cobl}$$
$$F_{blal} = F_{blmo} + F_{blsi} + F_{blco}.$$

(2) *Plasma (pl).* Generally, the main distribution subsystem can be lumped into one compartment, as discussed before. However, in some cases it has to be subdivided in different ways. In oxygen homeostasis, for example, the blood subsystem has to be divided into compartments for plasma (pl) and for cellular fluid (cf) within the blood cells (Fig. 6). In this case the red blood cell, although part of the distribution system, acts as if it were part of a storage system.

The total of the systems in plasma are:

$$F_{expl} = F_{iopl} + F_{cfpl} + F_{cepl}$$
$$F_{plex} = F_{plio} + F_{plcf} + F_{plce}.$$

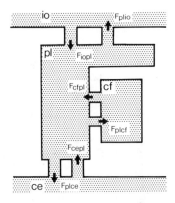

Fig. 6. Compartments in the blood: pl, plasma; cf, cellular fluid; ce, body cell; io, input/output subsystem.

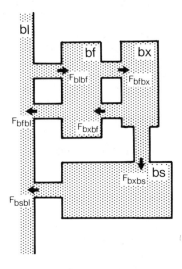

Fig. 7. Compartments in the bone subsystem: bf, bone "fluid"; bx, bone crystals; bs, solid bone; bl, blood.

(3) *Bone (bo)*. The structural arrangement of the different processing systems shows a wide range of variability. It is therefore important to draw up a block diagram complete with flows for each case. As an example of a processing subsystem we shall use the role of the bone in calcium endodynamics (Fig. 7).

For the bone fluid compartment (bf):

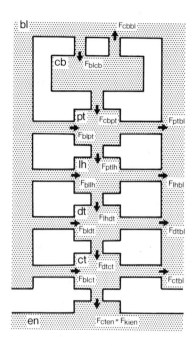

Fig. 8. The compartments of the kidney subsystem: bl, blood; cb, capsule of Bowman; pt, proximal tubule; lh, loop of Henle; dt, distal tubule; ct, collecting tubule; en, environment.

$$F_{exbf} = F_{blbf} + F_{bxbf}$$
$$F_{bfex} = F_{bfbl} + F_{bfbx}.$$

For the solid bone compartment (bs):

$$F_{exbs} = F_{bxbs}$$
$$F_{bsex} = F_{bsbl}.$$

D. SUBSYSTEMS AND COMPARTMENTS CONTINUOUSLY IN A STEADY STATE

In certain cases a compartment in a process can be considered to be continuously in a steady state; thus the total amount of matter/energy entering the compartment (cp) in unit time (F_{excp}) is equal to the total amount leaving it (F_{cpex}); i.e., $R_{cp} = F_{excp} - F_{cpex} = 0$, all the time.

The proximal tubule (pt) of the kidney will be used to illustrate a compartment in steady state (Fig. 8).

(1) $F_{expt} = F_{cbpt} + F_{blpt}$
     $F_{ptex} = F_{ptbl} + F_{ptlh}.$

(2) $R_{pt} = F_{expt} - F_{ptex} = 0.$

The same procedure can be used for other compartments when they are considered to be in the steady state.

E.   NATURE OF FLOWS IN ENDODYNAMIC PROCESSES

There are various ways flows can arise in endodynamic systems. They can be the result of pressure differences, concentration or electrical gradients, active transport phenomena, or decay of matter/energy. Let us examine some of these flows.

(1) *Bulk flow*. Bulk flow is generally produced if there is a pressure difference between two compartments, C_1 and C_2. According to Ohm's law, the flow (F_{c1c2}) is given by:

$$F_{c1c2} = K_{c1c2} \times (P_{c1} - P_{c2}),$$

where K_{c1c2} is the conductance of the channel between the two compartments.

(2) *Diffusion*. The diffusion of a substance between the two compartments, C_3 and C_4, can be described by the equation:

$$F_{c3c4} = K_{c3c4} \times (C_{c3} - C_{c4}),$$

where K_{c3c4} is the diffusion coefficient for the channel between the two compartments and C_{c3} and C_{c4} are the concentrations of the substance in the two compartments.

(3) *Facilitated diffusion*. In this case, the diffusion coefficient is not a constant, but a function of another factor. For example, the flow of glucose from blood into the cells ($F_{blce/glu}$) is a function of the concentration difference as well as the insulin concentration in blood ($C_{bl/ins}$), as follows:

$$F_{blce/glu} = K_{blce/glu} \times (C_{bl/glu} - C_{ce/glu}) \times f(C_{bl/ins}),$$

where f denotes "function of."
    The actual nature of $f(C_{bl/ins})$ is not yet determined. In general, these functions are nonlinear and in many cases they are not even expressible in a simple mathematical form. However, often provision is made in simula-

tion packages for entering the function into a coordinate grid, point by point, or by using a best-fit approximation for $f(C_{bl/ins})$.

(4) *Active transport.* This term is used for flows which do not depend on gradients. These active processes usually require an energy input and other factors for their functioning. The functional relationship between the flow and its governing factors is not always known. Example: sodium (na) re-absorption in the distal tubules (dt) of the kidney can be described as

$$F_{dtbl/na} = f(E_{dt/atp}, C_{dt/na}, C_{bl/ald}).$$

where $E_{dt/atp}$ is the energy produced by the cells in the distal tubule, $C_{dt/na}$ is the sodium concentration in the distal tubule, and $C_{bl/ald}$ is the aldosterone concentration in the blood. For computation empirical functions are used.

(5) *Decay.* As mentioned previously, this process can be considered to be a flow originating in and leaving a compartment, thus:

$$F_{didy} = K_{didy} \times Q_{di}.$$

F. COORDINATION SYSTEMS

Local coordination of endodynamic processes varies from case to case; at present there are no general descriptions available.

Neuronal coordination through the autonomic nervous system is largely unknown, and thus we have simply incorporated its influence by the factor N into the model. N represents the relative neuronal activity on a location described by the first part of the subscript. The second part of the subscript indicates the division of the analyzed autonomic system. For example: $N_{si/par}$ is the relative neuronal activity of the parasympathetic nerves in the small intestine (si).

Endocrine coordination systems can either be single or multiple compartment systems. As they handle matter in the form of hormones, they can be represented by a model similar to the other matter/energy processing systems described above. However, there are major differences.

(1) Generally there are no natural input/output systems from the environment, except in some multicompartmental endocrine systems. For example, one compartment of the dihydroxycholecalciferol (dhc) subsystem relies on the intake of a precursor of dhc.

(2) The endocrine gland (gl) can be considered to be a processing system producing a hormone at the rate of F_{glbl}.

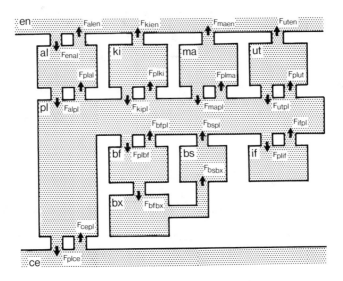

Fig. 9. The matter/energy subsystems of calcium endodynamics.

(3) Hormones generally decay within the various compartments.

IV.   AN EXAMPLE OF THE FORMATION
OF A SPECIFIC MODEL

Our aim has been to show that a standard method can be used for the modeling of biological systems. We have chosen endodynamic processes to illustrate this point, and we are using data from various sources, which have been extrapolated to model processes in a 70-kg adult human.

The extent of the overlap between various endodynamic processes and the usefulness of a general modeling terminology in setting up the mathematical formulation for these processes has been demonstrated. In the present section, GMT is put into practice using calcium endodynamics as the example. We shall utilize the general analysis to define the system, GMT to describe its parts mathematically, and also provide a few examples of actual computer programs. Data summarized in an earlier publication [21] are used for this purpose. However, no attempt will be made either to set up a complete computer model for calcium endodynamics or to validate the model.

In our example, we are only going to deal with calcium endodynamics; but it must be remembered that it forms a part of the "mineral cluster" with magnesium (mg) and phosphate (po$_4$). Therefore, all the interactions between these three endodynamic systems should always be kept in mind.

A. GENERAL SYSTEMS ANALYSIS:
    ZERO APPROXIMATION

The first step in setting up the model is to find a general structure consisting of both the matter/energy processing subsystems and the coordination subsystems.

(1) Matter/energy subsystems (Fig. 9).

(a) Input/output (io);

(i) Alimentary canal (al);
(ii) Kidney (ki);
(iii) Mammary gland (ma) (lactating);
(iv) Uterus (ut) (pregnant and menstruating).

(b) Distribution (di).

(i) Plasma (pl);
(ii) Interstitial fluid (if);

(c) Processing (pr).

(i) Bone fluid (bf);
(ii) Bone solid (bs);
(iii) Bone crystal (bx).

(2) Coordination subsystems. These include parathyroid hormone (pth), calcitonin (tct), and dihydroxycholecalciferol (dhc). Although each of these subsystems is multicompartmental, in the zero approximation they can be considered to be single compartment hormonal systems.

B. MATHEMATICAL FORMULATION OF SUBSYSTEMS

1. General Approach

Having established the main framework (zero-approximation model) for calcium endodynamics, we can proceed to define each compartment (or subsystem) mathematically. It is advisable to deal with the peripheral compartments first, viz., input/output and processing compartments; this is where the flows can best be defined. A suitable symbol for the compartment should be chosen from Table II.

As pointed out previously, when one is dealing with only one endodynamic system, the final subscript which indicates the subsystem can be omitted; thus $F_{alpl/ca}$ becomes F_{alpl}.

As there is a great deal of similarity between the functioning of the various compartments, it is possible to follow a rigorous procedure step by step:

a. Flows. Define each flow and indicate its initial value. These values will have to be obtained from the literature. As data for humans are incomplete, extrapolation has to be made from results obtained in animal experiments. When there are no data available at all, experiments have to be performed to obtain these. Estimated values can be used temporarily, in which case this has to be indicated clearly.

b. The Total Flows. Write an expression for the total flow into the compartment (cp) (F_{excp}) and the total flow out of the compartment (F_{cpex}).

c. Compartmental Dynamics. Indicate whether the compartment is assumed to be in a dynamic state or continuously in a steady state. In the latter case the sum of flows into the compartment minus the sum of flows out of the compartment equals zero and remains zero all the time; i.e., $R_{cp} = F_{excp} - F_{cpex} = 0$, all the time.

d. Initial Values and Parameters. Obtain the initial values of the compartmental variables (i.e., Q_{cp} and C_{cp}) and of the compartmental parameters (i.e., V_{cp}, T_{delta}, and K_{cpdy}). If $R_{cp} = 0$, these values are not needed.

e. External Factors. Define all external factors under the following headings:

(i) Endodynamic influences within cluster;

(ii) Endodynamic influences outside cluster;

(iii) Exodynamic influences;

(iv) Environmental influences.

Then indicate the source and the target of these influences and whether they can be described mathematically. These influences should be noted even if a mathematical description of their effects does not exist. This is important when experiments are set up to predict the behavior of a system. In this case, the influences must either be controlled at a constant level or at least constantly monitored.

f. Delays. Establish the delay for each flow.

g. Computer Program. Set up the computer program. This is done by first selecting a suitable simulation package which will define the rules for setting up the program for the model and then entering it together with the package into the computer. The simulation package performs the routine operations which are generally required when a model is run. These include precompilation, tabulation, drawing graphs, changing proportionality factors, incrementation, and timing, among others. The use of a simulation package speeds up the setting up of the simulation process considerably.

2. Model of the Alimentary Canal (al)

The above-mentioned steps from *a* to *g* will now be used in each of the examples.

a. Flows.

(1) F_{enal} = dietary calcium intake. This can be considered to be constant, i.e., equal to 1 mmol/hour or 24 mmol/day. Alternatively, it can be assumed to be three lots of 8 mmol/hour for 1 hour after each meal.

(2) $F_{alpl} = f(C_{pl/dhc}, F_{enal}, E_{al/atp})$, where atp = adenosine triphosphate. In the present model we assume constant energy ($E_{al/atp}$ is constant) and linearity of the other factors, viz.,

$$F_{alpl} = K_{alpl} \times C_{pl/dhc} \times F_{enal}.$$

(3)

$$F_{plal} = K_{plal} \times C_{pl}$$
$$= \text{calcium present in secretions.}$$

(4)

$$F_{alen} = F_{enal} + F_{plal} - F_{alpl},$$

since $R_{al} = 0$ (see *c* below).

b. Total Flows.

$$F_{exal} = F_{enal} + F_{plal};$$
$$F_{alex} = F_{alen} + F_{alpl}.$$

c. Compartmental Dynamics.

$$R_{al} = 0,$$

i.e., $F_{enal} + F_{plal} = F_{alen} + F_{alpl}.$

d. Initial Conditions and Parameters. Not required, since the system is assumed to be in a steady state.

e. Examples of External Influences.

(1) From within the cluster. The presence of phosphate in the diet reduces soluble calcium, and thus F_{enal}.

(2) From outside the cluster. Diarrhea may affect the rate of absorption from the gut, F_{enal}. Excessive production of digestive juices may increase the flow of calcium from the plasma to the alimentary canal, F_{plal}.

(3) Exodynamic influences. Lack of knowledge of nutrition may result in insufficient dietary intake of calcium, F_{enal}. Lack of mobility in the elderly or the severely disabled may result in insufficient intake, F_{enal}.

(4) Environmental influences. Calcium-containing products may not be available, thus reducing F_{enal}.

It is evident that F_{enal} is affected by various influences. These could either be modeled separately or they could be represented by a single factor of proportionality. K_{enal} and K_{plal}, by which F_{enal} and F_{plal}, respectively, are multiplied, have been used in the present example.

f. Delays. Processes are generally not instantaneous, but occur after a delay. The delay is characteristic of the particular situation and in the computer program this can easily be introduced by a single line of code. The following delays have been introduced:

(1) K_{moal} represents the delay which takes effect between the flow into the mouth (F_{enmo}) and the flow into the main absorbing section of the intestine (F_{enal}).

(2) K_{alpl} represents the delay between the actual changes in the dihydroxycholecalciferol concentration ($C_{pl/dhc}$) and the rate of calcium absorption (F_{alpl}). To facilitate programming, the variable F_{alpl} has been introduced. Note the use of the number 1 in the subscripts of K_{alpl} and

F_{a1pl}. This arrangement enables us to enlarge the system and to avoid duplication of symbols.

g.   The Computer Program. We have chosen the simulation package SIM2 [19]. In this package FORTRAN IV or V is used within the following structure:

```
C       DYNAMICS OF ALIMENTARY CANAL (AL) CALCIUM

C       LUMPED STEADY-STATE MODEL BASED ON DATA GIVEN IN

C       JAROS ET AL. [21]

C       70 KG MAN

C       STEADY-STATE MODEL; RAL = 0

C       TO BYPASS INITIALIZATION; ZFLAG1 = 0
        IF (PZFLAG1.EQ.0.0) GO TO 1000

100     CONTINUE

C       SYMBOLS & UNITS (AL)

C       F = FLOW:MMOL/HOUR

C       T = TIME:HOUR

C       C = CONCENTRATION: MMOL/LITER

C       V = VOLUME: LITER

200     CONTINUE

C       TDELTA (AL) < 20% OF SMALLEST TIME CONSTANT

C       TDELTA < 0.5 HOURS

300     CONTINUE

C       COMPARTMENTS (AL)

C       AL = ALIMENTARY CANAL

C       PL = PLASMA

C       EN = ENVIRONMENT

C       MO = MOUTH

400     CONTINUE

C       INITIAL CONDITIONS (AL)
```

```
            FENMO      =    0.8  : DIETARY INTAKE AT MOUTH
            FENAL      =    0.8  : INTO SMALL INTESTINE [JAROS ET
                                   AL., [21]]:   EATCAL]
       C

            FALPL      =    0.7  : ABSORPTION [ALICAL]
            FA1PL      =    0.7  : TO EFFECT DELAY IN ABSORPTION
            FPLAL      =    0.6  : SECRETION [SECCAL]
            FALEN      =    0.7  : FECAL LOSS [FECCAL]
            CPL        =    1.18 : CALCIUM CONCENTRATION IN PLASMA
                                   [CONCAL]
            CPLDHC     =    1.0  : DIHYDROXYCHOLECALCIFEROL [CONDHC]

  500     CONTINUE

  C       FUNCTIONS AND SUBROUTINES (AL)

  600     CONTINUE

  C       DELAYS (AL)

            KMOAL      =    4.0  : DELAY OF 15 MINUTES TO ALLOW
       C                         : FOOD TO GET INTO THE SMALL INTESTINE

  C       KA1PL                   DELAY OF DHC – SEE IN MODEL

  700     CONTINUE

  C       PARAMETERS (AL)

            KENAL      =    1.0  : FACTOR TO ACCOUNT FOR EXTERNAL
                                   INFLUENCES ON DIETARY INTAKE

       C    KALATP     =    1.0  : NORMAL ENERGY CONDITIONS
            KPLAL      =    0.5  : SECRETORY FACTOR [SECFAC]
            KP1AL      =    1.0  : NORMAL SECRETORY CONDITIONS
                                   [SECFAC]

  800     CONTINUE

  C       EXTERNAL FACTORS (AL)

  C       KENAL REPRESENTS FACTORS INFLUENCING FENAL

  C       KPLAL REPRESENTS FACTORS INFLUENCING FPLAL

 1000     CONTINUE

  C       THE MODEL (AL)

            IF RPLDHC > 0.      : DELAY FOR THE EFFECT OF
            KA1PL = 0.5         : INCREASING DHC[ADCFAC]

            IF RPLDHC < 0.      : DELAY FOR THE EFFECT OF
            KA1PL = 0.001       : DECREASING DHC[ADCFAC]
```

$$FENAL = FENAL + (FENMO - FENAL) * KMOAL * TDELTA$$

C   DELAY – FOOD TO INTESTINE

$$FPAL\ = KPLAL * KP1AL * CPL\ :\ SECRETION$$

$$FA1PL = FENAL * KALPL * CPLDHC : LINEARITY\ ASSUMED$$

$$FALPL = FALPL + (FA1PL - FALPL) * KA1PL * TDELTA$$

C   DELAY – EFFECT OF DHC

$$FALEN = FENAL + FPLAL - FALPL : STEADY\ STATE$$

9999   STOP

        END

3. Model of the Kidney (ki)

a. *Flows.*

$$F_{kien} = f(C_{pl}, C_{pl/pth}).$$

The calculations for these functions are described in Jaros *et al.* [21]. These can be computed in a subroutine EX(CPL, APLPTH). The reason for using the activity ($A_{pl/pth}$) will be explained in Subsection *f* (Delays) below.

b. *Total Flows.*

$$F_{exki} = F_{plki};$$
$$F_{kiex} = F_{kipl} + F_{kien}.$$

c. *Compartmental Dynamics.*

$$R_{ki} = 0;$$

i.e.,

$$F_{plki} = F_{kipl} + F_{kien},$$

or

$$F_{kien} = (F_{plki} - F_{kipl}).$$

d. *Initial Conditions and Parameters.* Not required, since the system is assumed to be in a steady state.

e. Examples of External Influences. Not described here, as our focus is on examples of modeling and not on a complex model of the kidney itself. In a specific model this should, however, be done (see Section IV,B,1,*e*).

f. Delays. K_{kien} is used to account for the delay in the effect of $C_{pl/pth}$ on F_{kien}. The actual effect or activity ($A_{pl/pth}$) of the hormone can be calculated using a single line of computation.

g. The Computer Program.

```
C    DYNAMICS OF KIDNEY (KI) CALCIUM

C    LUMPED STEADY STATE MODEL BASED ON DATA GIVEN IN

C    JAROS ET AL. [21]

C    70 KG MAN

C    STEADY STATE MODEL: RKI = 0

C    FPLKI – FKIPL = FKIEN

C    TO BYPASS INITIALIZATION : ZFLAG1 = 0
     IF (ZFLAG1.Eq.0.0) GO TO 1000

100  CONTINUE

C    SYMBOLS AND UNITS (KI)

C    F = FLOW : MMOL/HOUR

C    C = CONCENTRATION : CA : MMOL/LITER

C                       : PTH : NG/LITER

C    A = ACTIVITY

200  CONTINUE

C    TDELTA (KI) < 20% SMALLEST TIME CONSTANT

C    TDELTA < 0.4 HOUR

300  CONTINUE

C    COMPARTMENTS (KI)

C    PL = PLASMA

C    KI = KIDNEY

C    EN = ENVIRONMENT
```

```
400   CONTINUE

C     INITIAL CONDITIONS (KI)

      FKIEN    = 0.1

C     CA LOSS IN URINE (JAROS ET AL. [21] : EXCAL)

      CPL      = 1.19

C     CALCIUM CONCENTRATION IN PLASMA [CONCAL]

      CPLPTH   = 138.0 :   PTH CONC IN PLASMA [CONPTH]

      APLPTH   = 138.0 :   DELAYED HORMONE CONC [ACKPTH]

500   CONTINUE

C     FUNCTIONS AND SUBROUTINES (KI)

C     EX(CPL, APLPTH) :   FROM JAROS ET AL.[21]

600   CONTINUE

C     DELAYS (KI) < 20% OF SMALLEST TIME DELAY

      KKIEN = 0.5 :   A 2 HOUR DELAY [ACKFAC]

700   CONTINUE

C     PARAMETERS (KI)

800   CONTINUE

C     EXTERNAL FACTORS (KI)

1000  CONTINUE

C     MODEL (KI)

C     DELAY - PTH EFFECT

      APLPTH = APLPTH + (CPLPTH – APLPTH) * KKIEN * TDELTA

      CALL EX(CPL, APLPTH)

9999  STOP

      END
```

4. Model of the Interstitial Fluid Compartment (if)

a. Flows. It is possible to deal with net flow, as F_{ifpl} and F_{plif} do not occur simultaneously and are governed by the same diffusion constant. In this case, $F_{ifpl} = -F_{plif}$, i.e., the direction of the flow is indicated by the positive or negative sign. Thus $(F_{plif} - F_{ifpl})$ is replaced by F_{plif}. Consider net flow, i.e.,

$$F_{plif} = K_{plif} \times (C_{pl} - C_{if}).$$

b. Total Flow.

$$F_{plex} = F_{plif}$$
$$F_{expl} = 0.$$

c. Compartmental Dynamics. $R_{if} \neq 0$. R_{if}, Q_{if}, and C_{if} can be calculated by using the equations in Section III,B,1. In the computer program these calculations are performed by a subroutine called COM(CP).

d. Parameters. K_{plif}, the diffusion constant, 0.009 (from Hurwitz [24]).

$$K_{ifdy} = 0.$$

This sets the decay to be zero.

e. Examples of External Influences. Not described here; see the explanation in Section IV,B,3,*e*.

f. Delays. Delays between the occurrence and the actual onset of the effect of the factors in *d* above should be investigated. This is not done in the present example.

g. The Computer Program.

C   DYNAMICS OF INTERSTITIAL FLUID (IF) CALCIUM

C   LUMPED STEADY STATE MODEL BASED ON DATA GIVEN IN

C   JAROS ET AL. [21]

C   70 KG MAN

C   DYNAMIC MODEL : I. E., RIF $\neq$ 0

C   TO BYPASS INITIALIZATION : ZFLAG1 = 0

       IF (ZFLAG1.EQ.0.0) GO TO 1000

100   CONTINUE

C   SYMBOLS AND UNITS (IF)

```
C     C = CONCENTRATION (MMOL/LITER)

C     F = FLOW (MMOL/HOUR)

C     Q = QUANTITY (MMOL)

C     R = DQ/DT (MMOL/LITER)

200   CONTINUE

C     TDELTA (IF) < 20% SMALLEST TIME DELAY

300   CONTINUE

C     COMPARTMENTS (IF)

C     IF = INTERSTITIAL FLUID

C     PL = PLASMA

400   CONTINUE

C     INITIAL CONDITIONS (IF)

      CPL =   1.19  : PLASMA CONCENTRATION OF CALCIUM

      CIF  =   1.19  : INTERST FLUID CALCIUM CONCENTRATION

      QIF  = 14.28  : TOTAL CALCIUM IN IF

500   CONTINUE

C     FUNCTIONS AND SUBROUTINES (IF)

C     COM (IF) :      COMPARTMENTAL DYNAMICS : RIF< QIF, AND CIF

600   CONTINUE

C     DELAYS (IF) < 20% OF SMALLEST TIME DELAY

700   CONTINUE

C     PARAMETERS (IF)

      KPLIF = 0.009 : FROM HURWITZ PERSONAL COMMUNICATION

      VIF    = 12     :  L :  INTERSTITIAL BLUID

      KIFDY = 0      : NO DECAY

800   CONTINUE

C     EXTERNAL FACTORS (IF)

1000        CONTINUE
```

```
C     MODEL (IF)

      FPLIF = KPLIF * (CPL – CIF) : DIFFUSION

      FEXPL = 0

      FPLEX = FPLIF

      CALL COM(IF)

9999  STOP

      END
```

The subroutine COM is based on the equations in Section III,B,1 as follows:

```
C     SUBROUTINE COM(CP)

C     LIST OF COMPUTATIONS ONLY

      RCP = FEXCP – FCPEX – FCPDY + FENCP – FCPEN

      QCP = QCP + RCP * TDELTA : EULER INTEGRATION

      CCP = QCP/VCP

      FCPDY = KCPDY * QCP

      RETURN
```

5. Model of the Plasma (pl)

a. Flows.

(1) For F_{alpl} and F_{plal} see alimentary canal. $F_{alpl} = 0.7$ mmol/h; $F_{plal} = 0.6$ mmol/h.

(2) For F_{plki} and F_{kipl} see kidney. F_{kien} represents $(F_{plki} - F_{kipl}) = 0.1$ mmol/h.

(3) F_{ifpl} and F_{plif} see interstitial fluid. $F_{plex} = F_{plif} = 0$.

(4) $F_{bopl} = 1.0$ [Jaros et al. [21], BONCAL + RELCAL].

(5) $F_{plbo} = 1.0$ [DEPCAL + ACRCAL].

b. Total Flows. The flow equations can be rewritten as follows:

$$F_{expl} = F_{alpl} + F_{bopl}$$
$$F_{plex} = F_{plal} + F_{kien} + F_{plbo} + F_{plif}.$$

c. *Compartmental Dynamics.* R_{pl} is variable and R_{pl}, Q_{pl}, and C_{pl} can be calculated according to the equations given in Section II,B,1. In the computer program subroutine COM(PR) performs these computations.

d. *Initial Conditions and Compartmental Parameters.*

R_{pl} = 0 (at the start of simulation);

Q_{pl} = 17.8 mmol [TOTCAL];

C_{pl} = 1.19 mmol/liter [CONCAL];

V_{pl} = 14.98 liter [ECFV];

K_{pldy} = 0 (no decay of calcium within the body).

e. *External Influences.* These have been accounted for in the peripheral subsystems.

f. *Delays.* These have been accounted for in the peripheral subsystems.

g. *The Computer Program.*

```
C    DYNAMICS OF PLASMA (PL) CALCIUM

C    LUMPED STEADY STATE MODEL BASED ON DATA GIVEN IN

C    JAROS ET AL. [21]

C    70 KG MAN

C    DYNAMIC MODEL, I. E., RIF ≠ 0

C    TO BYPASS INITIALIZATION : ZFLAG1 = 0

     IF (ZFLAG1.EQ.0.0) GO TO 1000

100  CONTINUE

C    SYMBOLS AND UNITS (PL)

C    C = CONCENTRATION (MMOL/LITER)

C    F = FLOW (MMOL/HOUR)

C    Q = QUANTITY (MMOL)
```

```
C    R = DQ/DT (MMOL/HOUR)

200  CONTINUE

C    TDELTA (PL) : HAS BEEN ACCOUNTED FOR

300  CONTINUE

C    COMPARTMENTS (PL)

C    AL = ALIMENTARY CANAL

C    BO = BONE

C    EN = ENVIRONMENT

C    IF = INTERSTITIAL FLUID

C    KI = KIDNEY

C    PL = PLASMA

400  CONTINUE

C    INITIAL CONDITIONS (PL)

         FALPL  = 0.7   : [JAROS ET AL. (21), 1979: ALICAL]

         FBOPL  = 1.0   : [BONCAL + RELCAL]

         FPLAL  = 0.6   : [SECCAL]

         FKIEN  = 0.1   : [EXCAL]

         FPLBO  = 1.0   : [DEPCAL + ACRCAL]

         FPLIF  = 0.0   : NORMALLY PL & IF ARE IN EQUILIBRIUM

         RPL    = 0.0   : START IN STEADY STATE [RATCAL]

         QPL    = 17.8 : [TOTCAL]

         CPL    = 1.18 : [CONCAL]

500      CONTINUE

C        FUNCTIONS AND SUBROUTINES (PL)

C        COM(PL) : CALCULATES RPL, QPL, AND CPL

600      CONTINUE

C        DELAYS (PL) : HAVE BEEN ACCOUNTED FOR

700      CONTINUE
```

```
C       PARAMETERS (PL)

        VPL         = 14.98 :  [ECFV]

        KPLDY       = 0.0   :  NO DECAY OF CALCIUM IN PLASMA

800     CONTINUE

C       EXTERNAL FACTORS (PL)

1000    CONTINUE
C       MODEL (PL)

        FEXPL = FALPL + FBOPL

        FPLEX = FPLAL + FKIEN + FPLBO + FPLIF

        CALL COM(PL) : CP = PL

9999    STOP

        END
```

C. GLOBAL MODEL OF CALCIUM ENDODYNAMICS

When a model of the entire calcium endodynamic process is required, it should include all the matter/energy subsystems as well as all the coordination subsystems listed at the beginning of the present section. In this section we have only analyzed a few of these subsystems as examples, but in a complete model all the subsystems will have to be analyzed. It is evident from the examples of computer programs that they follow a general pattern. This can be summarized as follows:

```
C       GLOBAL MODEL OF CALCIUM ENDODYNAMIC PROCESSES

C       GENERAL INFORMATION
        .
        .
        .

C       TO BYPASS INITIALIZATION

        IF (ZFLAG1.EQ.0.0) GO TO 1000

100     CONTINUE    : SYMBOLS AND UNITS
        .
        .
        .

200     CONTINUE    : TDELTA
        .
        .
        .
```

```
300    CONTINUE      : COMPARTMENTS
  .
  .
  .
400    CONTINUE      : INITIAL CONDITIONS
  .
  .
  .
500    CONTINUE      : FUNCTIONS AND SUBROUTINES
  .
  .
  .
600    CONTINUE      : DELAYS
  .
  .
  .
700    CONTINUE      : PARAMETERS
  .
  .
  .
800    CONTINUE      : EXTERNAL FACTORS
  .
  .
  .
1000   CONTINUE      : MODEL
  .
  .
  .

9999   STOP

       END
```

Information from the programs on the subsystems can easily be transferred to this global program by means of a text-processing package.

In conclusion, we would like to point out that this same global structure can be used to model all endodynamic processes.

ACKNOWLEDGMENTS

We wish to thank V. Sharkey for her excellent secretarial services, J. Walker for the preparation of the illustrations, and G. Hefftner for her valuable suggestions. The financial assistance provided by the South African Medical Research Council and the University of Cape Town is also gratefully appreciated.

REFERENCES

1. A. A. B. PRITSKER, *Simulation* August, 61 (1979).
2. R. BRONSON, *Byte* March, 95 (1984).
3. A. C. GUYTON, T. G. COLEMAN, and H. J. GRAINGER, *Annu. Rev. Physiol. 34*, 13 (1972).
4. K. B. DE GREENE, *Ergonomics 23*, 3 (1980).
5. D. S. RIGGS, "The Mathematical Approach to Physiological Problems," Williams & Wilkins, Baltimore, 1970.
6. R. W. JOHNES, *in* "Biological Control Mechanisms in Biological Engineering" (H. P. Schwann, Ed.), McGraw-Hill, New York, 1969.
7. D. S. RIGGS, "Control Theory and Physiological Feedback Mechanisms," Williams & Wilkins, Baltimore, 1970.
8. R. W. JONES, "Principles of Biological Regulation," Academic Press, New York, 1973.
9. B. P. ZIEGLER, "Theory of Modelling and Simulation," Wiley, New York, 1976.
10. H. J. GOLD, "Mathematical Modelling of Biological Systems – An Introductory Guide Book," Wiley, New York, 1977.
11. J. E. A. McINTOSH and R. P. McINTOSH, "Mathematical Modelling and Computers in Endocrinology," Springer-Verlag, Berlin, 1980.
12. K. E. F. WATT, *Simulation 28*, 1 (1977).
13. F. GREMY, *in* "Meeting the Challenge: Information and Medical Information" (H. C. Pages, A. H. Levy, F. Gremy, and J. Anderson, Eds.), Elsevier, Amsterdam, 1983.
14. E. R. CARSON, C. COBELLI, and L. FINKELSTEIN, "The Mathematical Modelling of Metabolic and Endocrine Systems," Wiley, New York, 1983.
15. M. BERMAN and M. F. WEISS, *SAAM Manual*, NIH PHS Publication, 1703 (1967).
16. R. B. BENHAM and G. R. TAYLOR, "Interactive Simulation Language for Hybrid Computers," Interactive Mini Systems, Kennewick, Washington, 1975.
17. F. SPECKHART and W. L. GREEN, "A Guide for Using CSMP – The Continuous System Modelling Program," Prentice-Hall, Englewood Cliffs, New Jersey, 1976.
18. P. R. FURNISS, "Description and Manual for the Use of DRIVER An Interactive Modelling Aid," South African National Scientific Programmes Report No. 17, 1977.
19. T. G. COLEMAN, *SIM2* University of Mississippi Medical Center, Jackson, 1979 (personal communication).
20. J. G. MILLER, "Living Systems," McGraw-Hill, New York, 1978.
21. G. G. JAROS, T. G. COLEMAN, and A. C. GUYTON, *Simulation* June, 193 (1979).
22. F. BRONNER, *in* "Engineering Principles in Physiology" (J. H. N. Brown and D. S. Gann, Eds.), Vol. I, p. 227. Academic Press, New York, 1973.
23. H. RASMUSSEN, *in* "Textbook of Endocrinology" (R. H. Williams, Ed.), Saunders, Philadelphia, 1974.
24. S. HURWITZ, personal communication (1984).

OPTIMAL CONTROL FOR AIR CONDITIONING SYSTEMS: LARGE-SCALE SYSTEMS HIERARCHY 11

CHARL E. JANEKE

Janeke & Cumming Consulting Engineers,
Sunnyside, 0132 Pretoria,
Republic of South Africa

I.   INTRODUCTION

Although air conditioning is commonly associated with environmental comfort, HVAC (viz., heating, ventilating, and air conditioning) in real time comprises extensive schemes of energy distribution and on-line automatic control. Prior to the early 1970s, air conditioning had a poor energy record, but the energy crisis of the mid-1970s and subsequent dawning of the microprocessor era transformed HVAC into a more efficient, competitive, and refined technology. A special ploy in air conditioning that surfaced in the early 1980s, viz., that of free-cool HVAC [2, 5] essentially obviated conventional refrigerated cooling in moderate climatic areas via a combination of passive and evaporative cooling strategies. Although the elements of free-cool HVAC (see Fig. 1) appear quite obvious and logical, real-time synthesis is substantially more complex and requires hands-on competence of various state-of-the-art computational technologies.

II.   COMPUTATIONAL COMPETENCE

State-of-the-art computational competence comprises, in short: 1) optimal designing, 2) optimal operation, and 3) optimal computational synthesis. The *large-scale* denomination of this presentation essentially conforms to the substance of the computational synthesis. Subsequent sections will, on the one hand, elaborate on the *designing* and *operation* rationale and, on the other, develop the

117

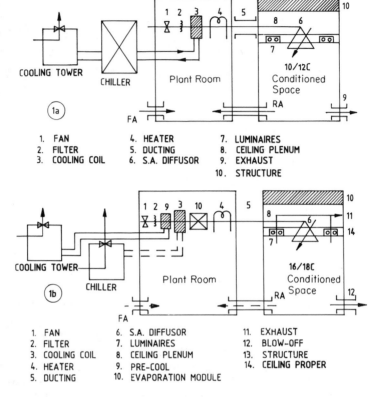

Fig. 1. HVAC schematics. a) Standard AC; b) free-cool AC.

the large-scale control model with an accent on nonautonomous (viz., *interactive*) element hierarchy.

III.   OPTIMAL DESIGNING

The optimal (HVAC) design objective is pursued via dynamic programming (DP) synthesis. In lieu of exhaustive enumeration, dynamic programming [6] comprises a systematic elimination process whereby optimal operating strategies and parameter optimization may be systematically equated. The essential DP applications relate to 1) determining the combination of HVAC parameters and building mass that will support the free-cool objective throughout a day-cycle, 2) determining the optimum precool (pull-down) cycle, and 3) equating the (optimal) operating strategies pertaining to items 1) and 2). As an extension, collective synchronization and fine tuning of the DP strategies is achieved via the TEAM-ING synthesis. Although the DP reduction processing is essentially conducted off-line, some real-time synthesis may be conducted on-line. See Appendix B on the DP exposition.

IV. OPTIMAL OPERATION

Optimal operation comprises determining the optimal control strategies on the one hand, and rationalizing the system stochastics on the other hand. The master scheme, which is being pursued [3], comprises the techniques of 1) dynamic programming and 2) Kalman filtering. Whereas dynamic programming has been introduced in the previous section, Kalman filtering is the consequence of the separation principle [7]. According to the *separation principle*, a stochastic system may be rendered *deterministic* if the state is equated as the Kalman-filtered estimate of state! The ensuing optimal (DP) strategies [and associated control response(s)] may hence be equated by simply polling the presolved DP strategies via the Kalman-filtered indices of state [4]. The DP may be resolved adaptively on-line if the system has been subjected to non-Gaussian or other deterministic per-turbations or in the even of prevailing nonlinearities in the model system. See Appendix C on Kalman filters.

The simplicity of the proposed control scheme is noted at this stage, which 1) obviates equating the usual (exhaustive) control gain and 2) offers (optimal) presolved control responses through the (n + 1)-th to terminal stages ready and available for polling in the DP look-up tables.

V. OPTIMAL COMPUTATIONAL SYNTHESIS

The optimal computational synthesis pertains essentially to 1) the room model system, 2) the large-scale postulation, and 3) the TEAM theoretic principle.

A.   HVAC MODEL SCHEME

The HVAC model scheme which is being promoted is structured around an elementary *room* system [1] which comprises *inter alia* the following features:

(1) Numerically recursive;

(2) Recurs in time and space (viz., equates vector valued variables piecewise as scalar entities);

(3) Superpositioning of *stationary* and dynamic heat load elements; and

(4) Explicitly structured (viz., enhances numerical stability).

The model has been structured around the second-order Fourier differential equation modeling the structural transients and a first-order linear differential equation modeling the *room* equilibrium. The second equation also contains the *residue* term, which encodes the time stationary room load elements. See also Appendix A.

B.   THE LARGE-SCALE POSTULATION

The large-scale postulation differentiates in real time between the trivial and nontrivial implementation schemes. The statement is very true for the HVAC scenario due to the rapidly escalating computational exhaustiveness of the DP with dimensional extensions. The computational exhaustiveness of the DP will, i.e., increase by a factor of $(10^{25}/10^5 = 10^{20})$ given $10\times$ degrees of freedom for each dimension versus $(10^{5\times5})$ computations in the event the DP may be solved individually for the respective room systems: a computational savings factor of $(10^{25}/10^5 = 10^{20}/5)$ – quite a profound gain! The name of the game hence is how to *decentralize* the DP scheme and yet conform to a common performance goal.

C.   THE TEAM SYNTHESIS

The answer to the preceding decentralization anomaly is vested in the TEAM theoretic principle [8]. According to Sinai, given a large-scale model system, the state may be decoupled into a number of independent (sub)systems and TEAMED via a common performance index which is required to be minimized both individually and collectively. According to Ref. [8], optimal control laws (via the DP or otherwise), may hence be structured for the individual subsystems and *updated adaptively* given interactive communication between the subsystems. Unintended interactions may otherwise be considered as *stochastic* perturbations (viz., random disturbances), which becomes transparent via the Kalman filter! In accordance with Sinai, the following elements are provided for in the TEAM concept:

(1) All systems comprise smaller subsystems with their own decision makers.

(2) Decision makers have only limited local data available.

(3) Individual decision makers agree to minimize the TEAM performance index, which is the sum of individual performance indices.

(4) Decision makers act individually to minimize their own performance index (via the DP).

(5) Interconnections between subsystems are considered as perturbations corrupting optimal subsystem performance (but will become transparent when treated stochastically).

(6) Decentralized (local) control proves to be more robust than centralized control.

In the HVAC scenario, real-time HVAC systems are being structured as a disjointed collection of *room* elements in accordance with the general objective of reducing the dimensional order of the modeling system. Group coherence is subsequently structured via the TEAM hierarchy. The following TEAM elements are being pursued:

(1) Disjointed (autonomous) *room* models are employed in lieu of large-scale systems integration.

(2) Solving for the elementary *room* policy sets (off-line) via the DP.

(3) Equating subsequently the general TEAM performance parameter J_i (Appendix D) in pursuit of the local control laws as:

$$J_i = E\left(\sum [x_i(t)Q_i(t)x_i(t) + U_i(t)Q_i(t)U_i(t)]\right)$$

as

$$J_i = \sum \left\{ c_i[T_b - T_b(n+1)]^2 + c_2[T_s - T_s(n+1)]^2 \right\},$$

with $J = [J_i]$, $J_i = \min$, and resolving the DP sets via the weighted DP algorithm

$$f_{in}(x_n) = \min \text{ for all D's } [f_{in}(x_{n+1}) + g_{in}(x_{n+1}) + J_i(n+1)]$$

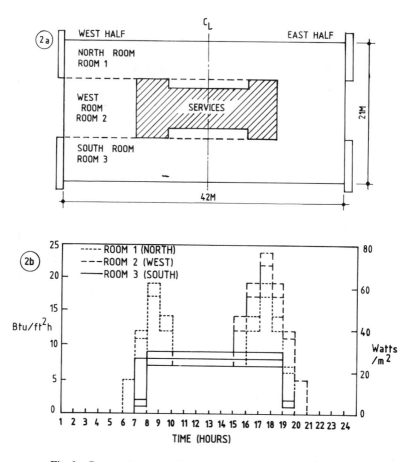

Fig. 2. Case study schematics. (a) Case study; (b) load profiles.

(4) Resolving the DP, etc., adaptively (see Section II) on-line as real-time measurements progress.

The entities c_1 and c_2 are equated as arbitrary weighting constants (viz., scaling factors), $T_b (n + 1)$ and $T_s (n + 1)$ the prevailing bulk and supply air temperatures, respectively, and T_b and T_s the bulk and supply air target temperatures, respectively. Whereas T_b may be arbitrarily allocated, T_s is equated as the collective DP mean.

The real-time implication of the foregoing is profound, viz., instead of solving the multidimensional control responses exhaustively on-line via Eqs. (D.1)–(D.8), the adaptive DP synthesis requires only real-time piecewise polling of the presolved (TEAMED) DP control laws (which may be periodically updated).

VI. UNIVERSAL CONTROL COROLLARY

An interesting lemma emanating out of the basic model equations (Appendix A) is that of the *universal storage*-cum-control *corollary*. Dedimensionalizing the equations of state in accordance with the procedures per Appendix E, and solving the DP for the dimensionless groups II_1–II_4, the universal response gains is rendered per Fig. 2. The uniqueness or *universality* is vested therein that in lieu of the results being relevant to a specific case study only, the dimensionality of the system generalizes the responses so as to be of relevance to any model system.

The corollary may be solved for the elementary rooms and by extending TEAM in accordance with the procedures outlined via the previous section. The real-time implication is profound therein that optimal control strategies for HVAC or any other process system may be synthesized easily via the proposed scheme. A further extension of the scheme is that of the *terminal control corollary*, viz., the rapid response associated with terminal missile flight, spacecraft re-entry, catalyst synthesis, anti-skid brakes, etc. Note also the relevance of this corollary to the *fuzzy*-logic concept [9] of ultrafast response schemes for robots and missiles.

VII. CASE STUDY AND CONCLUSION

A case study in HVAC has been constructed around a typical air-conditioned building with North- and South-facing rooms which are serviced by a common air handling and refrigeration plant. Refer to Fig. 3a and b. Although all three room systems have wholly different air and cooling requirements, the TEAM hierarchy has been employed in accordance with Eqs. (D.1)–(D.8) in Appendix D to rationalize the total system's instantaneous cooling requirements. It is significant how the instantaneous cooling demand and supply air temperature have been synchronized after resolving the DP in accordance with the TEAMING corollary. Normally an optimizing problem of this nature would have required equating all

CHARL E. JANEKE

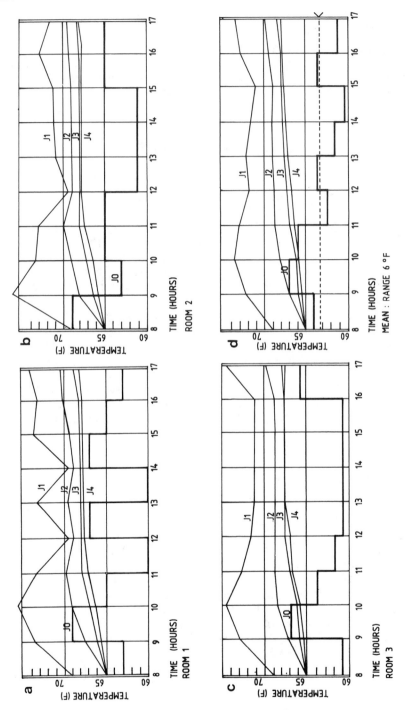

Fig. 3. Elementary DP stratgies.

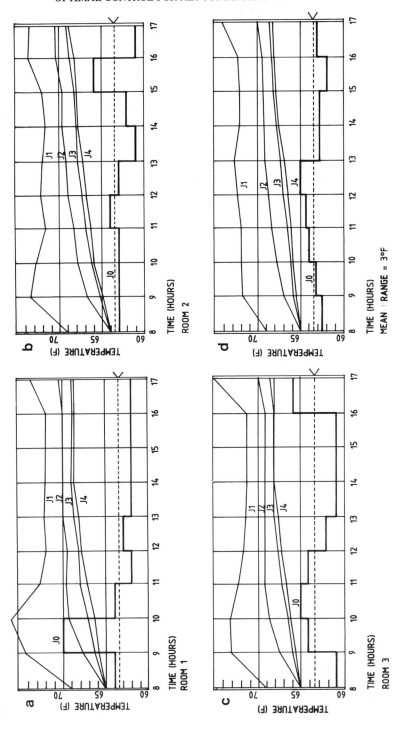

Fig. 4. Teamed strategies.

d	q_I (Btu/hft^2)	T_s (°F)	T_b (°F)	ΔT_s (°F)	II_4
4 inch (100mm)	5	69,7	71,5	1,8	2,2
4 inch (100mm)	10	67,0	72,5	5,5	1,5
4 inch (100mm)	15	–	–	–	–
8 inch (200mm)	5	69,2	70,0	1,5	2,7
8 inch (200mm)	10	70,6	74,5	3,9	2,1
8 inch (200mm)	15	66,1	74,0	7,9	1,5
12 inch (300mm)	5	69,2	70,7	1,5	2,7
12 inch (300mm)	10	70,5	74,3	3,8	2,1
12 inch (300mm)	15	61,1	74,0	7,6	1,6

(5a)

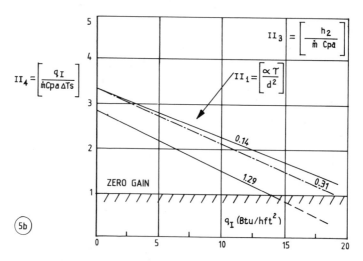

(5b)

Fig. 5. Universal control corollary.   (a) Input. data; (b) graphic representation.

the room variables simultaneously – a massive computational problem requiring supercomputer power. The TEAM corollary, however, allowed piecewise optimization of the individual *room* elements with subsequent *synchronization* with the TEAM hierarchy. Although a small penalty is incurred in this process, the computation requirements have been inhibited by a factor of several orders of magnitude. The real significance is not so much the cost of computer time, but the fact that extensive on-line control may be performed in real time with PC power (only). See figures. Appendix F reflects the computational routines.

APPENDIX A:
HVAC MODEL RECURSION

A.   SYSTEMS EQUATIONS

Heat conduction:

$$\frac{dt_w}{d\Gamma} = \alpha_w \frac{\partial^2 t}{\partial x^2} \tag{A1}$$

Equilibrium equation:

$$\frac{dt_s}{d\Gamma} = C_1 T_b + C_2 T_{w2} + C_3 T_s + C_4 q_I \tag{A2}$$

with w, b, z, z, and I denoting wall, bulk, inside wall, supply, and internal, respectively.

B.   DIFFERENCE MODEL

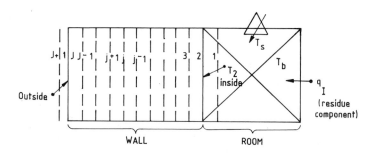

WALL   ROOM

C.   DIFFERENCE EQUATION SYSTEM

$$T_j^{n+1} = A_j^{**} T_j^{n+1} + B_j^{**} \tag{A3}$$

and

$$A_j^{**} = \frac{B_j^* B_{j-1}^{**} + C_j^*}{1 - B_j^* A_{j-1}^{**}},$$

$$B_j^* = \frac{B_j^* B_{j-1}^{**} + C_j^*}{1 - B_j^* A_{j-1}^{**}},$$

with A_j^*, B_j^*, and C_j^* modeling factorials

$$T_b^{n+1} = D^* T_2^{n+1} + B^* T_s^{n+1} + F^* q_1^{n+1} + G^* T_b^n. \tag{A4}$$

APPENDIX B:
DP SYSTEM EXPOSITION

1.   Basic DP Recursion

$$\frac{f_n(x_n)}{total} = min, \text{ all feas D's} \left(\frac{g_n(x_{n+1})}{stage} + \frac{f_n(x_{n+1})}{DP \text{ return}} \right) \tag{B1}$$

2.   DP Schematic Exposition

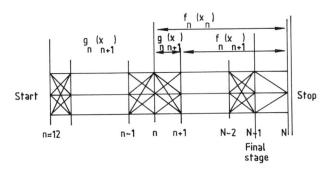

3. DP Stage Exposition

$$\frac{\text{Nth stage}}{\text{1st operation}} f_N(x_N) = \min, \text{ all feas D's } [g_N(x_{N+1}) + \text{nil}] \tag{B2}$$

$$\frac{(N-1)\text{-th stage}}{\text{2nd operation}} f_{N-1}(x_{N-1}) = \min, \text{ all feas D's } [g_{N-1}(x_N) + f_{N-1}(x_N)], \tag{B3}$$

where folding is performed on $f_{N-1}(x_N)$ in (B3) from $f_N(x_N)$ in (B2).

$$\frac{n\text{-th stage}}{(N-n)\text{-th operation}} f_n(x_n) = \min, \text{ all feas D's } [g_n(x_{n+1}) + f_n(x_{n+1})]$$

$$\frac{(n-1)\text{-th stage}}{(N-n+1)\text{-th operation}} f_{n-1}(x_{n-1})$$
$$= \min, \text{ all feas D's } [g_{n-1}(x_n) + f_{n-1}(x_n)], \tag{B4}$$

where folding in performed on $f_{n-1}(x_n)$ in (B4) from $f_n(x_n)$ in the equation above and with

$$x = \bar{x} = \begin{bmatrix} x_1 \\ x_2 \\ x_3 \end{bmatrix}.$$

In the AC scenario

$$g_n(x_{n+1}) \equiv \text{stage energy!}$$

$$f_n(x_{n+1}) \equiv \text{energy to completion!} \tag{B5}$$

$$f_n(x_n) \equiv \text{total energy!}$$

APPENDIX C:
KALMAN FILTER

A. BASIC KALMAN ALGORITHM

Equation of state:

$x(n + 1) = \varphi^{**}x(n) + \tau^{**}w(n).$

Measurement equation:

$z(n + 1) = H^*x(n + 1) + v(n + 1).$

Filter recursion:

$x(n + 1 \mid n + 1) = \varphi^{**}x(n \mid n) + K^*z(n + 1 \mid n)$ \hfill (C1)

$\varphi^*x(n \mid n) = x(n + 1 \mid n)$

$z(n + 1 \mid n) = z(n + 1) - z(n + 1 \mid n) = z(n + 1) - H^*x(n + 1 \mid n).$

$\qquad = z(n + 1) - H^*\varphi^{**}x(n \mid n).$

Gain:

$$K^* = p^{**}H^{*T}H^*p^{**}H^{*T} + \dfrac{R(n + 1)^{-1}}{\text{measurement noise CVM}} \qquad \text{(C2)}$$

CVM:

$$p^{**} = \varphi^{**}p^+\varphi^{**T} + \Gamma^{**}\dfrac{Q(n)\Gamma^{**T}}{\text{system noise CVM}} \qquad \text{(C3)}$$

$$p^+ - p^{++} = I - K^*H^*p^{**}, \qquad \text{(C4)}$$

where

$K^* = k(n + 1), \quad H^* = H(n + 1)$

$p^{**} = p(n + 1 \mid n) - p^{++} = p(n + 1 \mid n + 1)$

$\Gamma^{**} = (n + 1, n) - p^+ = p(n \mid n)$

$\varphi^{**} = \varphi(n + 1, n)$

$Q(n)$, system noise at n-th instant

$R(n + 1)$, measurement noise at $(n + 1)$-th instant.

B.   STABILIZED KALMAN ALGORITHM

$$p^{++} = (I - K*H*)p**(I - KH*)^T + K*R(n + 1)K*^T \qquad (C5)$$

C.   EXTENDED KALMAN ALGORITHM

$$K^+ = p**H^{+T}(H_L^+ p** H_L^{+T} + R^+)^{-1}. \qquad (C6)$$

APPENDIX D:
TEAM THEORETIC SYNTHESIS

A.   BASIC TEAM SYNTHESIS

According to Sinai, the linear regulator:

$$x(t + 1) = \underbrace{\frac{A(t)x(t)}{\text{state model}}}_{} + \underbrace{\frac{B(t)u(t)}{\text{control input}}}_{} + \underbrace{\frac{v(t)}{\text{disturbance}}}_{}, \qquad (D1)$$

where the disturbance is Gaussian white noise, may be decomposed some inter-connected subsystem:

$$x_i(t + 1) = A_i(t)x_i(t) + B_i(t)u_i(t) + \frac{A_{ij}(t)x(t)}{\text{intercon.}} + v_i(t). \qquad (D2)$$

A performance parameter $J = \Sigma_I J_i$ may hence be structured as:

$$J_i = E(\Sigma[x'(t)Q_{xi}(t)x_i(t) + u'(t)Q_{ui}(t)u_i(t)]) \qquad (D3)$$

with Q_x and Q_u the covariance propagation of functions [x] and [u], respectively, and E[ ] the expectation of the (random) function (·). Defining hence the performance parameter of the decomposed model system as $J = \Sigma_I J_i$, the collective TEAM objective may be rendered as:

$$\min u_{[J]} = \sum_I u_i[J_i] \qquad (D4)$$

with u_i equated via the control feedback law $u_i(t) = -L_i(t)x_i(t)$ with

$$L_i(t) = [q_{ui} + B_i(t)S_i(t + 1)B_i(t)]^{-1}B_i(t)S_i(t + 1)A_i(t)$$

$$S_i(t) = [Q_i(t) - B_i(t)L_i(t)]'S_i(t + 1)[A_i(t) - B_i(t)L_i(t)] + L_i(t)Q_{ui}(t)L_i(t) + Q_{xi}(t).$$

Although the preceding scheme offered by Sinai is perfectly valid and offers a unique and powerful solution to the large-scale control problem, the computational requirement is demanding, essentially because of the presence of the (semidefinite) Ricatti equation term $S_i(t)$ and the subsequent real-time computational context.

B.   HVAC MODEL COROLLARY

1.   Equation of State

The interactive decomposed model equation (D2) may be reduced for an autonomous system as:

$$x_i(t + 1) = A_i(t)x_i(t) + B_i(t)u_i(t) + v_i(t), \tag{D5}$$

and in terms of the HVAC model Appendix A as

$$x_{ij} = \overset{**}{A_{ij}} x_{ij} + \overset{**}{B_{ij}}$$

$$x_{i1} = C_i x_{si}(t + 1) + D_i x_{i2}(n + 1) + E_i q_{Ii}(n + 1) + F_i x_b(n) + V_i(t), \tag{D6}$$

with i and j denoting the room and space parameters, x_b, x_s, and x_2 the supply air and wall inside temperatures, respectively, and q_I the residue heat-load profile.

2.   Performance Parameter

The performance parameter equation (D3)

$$J_i \overset{\Delta}{=} \sum_I [x'(t)Q_{xi}(t)x_i(t) + u_i(t)Q_{ui}(t)u_i(y)]$$

may accordingly be restructured in terms of the HVAC parameters as

$$J_i \overset{\Delta}{=} \sum_I (Q_{xij} x_{ij}^2 + Q_{uij} u_{ij}^2), \tag{D7}$$

with Q_{xi}, Q_{ui} and x_{ij}, u_{ij} denoting the covariance and (target) variance propagation, respectively.

3.   Control Feedback Law

The control feedback law equation (D5) (see Appendix B),

$$L_i(t) = [Q_{ui} + B_i(t)S_i(t+1)B_i(t)]^{-1}B_i(t)S_i(t+1)A_i(t)$$

may be rendered for the HVAC scenario by polling of the DP (dynamic programming) critical path strategies by the TEAMED corollary $f'(x_i(t))$ as:

$$f'(x_i(t)) = \min_{\text{all feas } u_i(t+1)\text{'s}} [g(x_i(t+1)] + f'(x_i(t+1) + J_i(t+1) \tag{D8}$$

with $f'(\cdot)$ the TEAMED DP return, J_i the TEAMING term and the performance parameter per (D7) and $u_i(t+1)$ the $(t+1)$-th element of the DP critical path (viz., feasible DP strategies) law $L_i(t+1)$ of the $(t+1)$-th instant through termination.

The real-time implication of the foregoing is profound, viz., instead of solving the multidimensional control responses, Eqs. (D1)–(D5), exhaustively on-line, the adaptive (presolved) DP synthesis, Eq. (D8), is equated instead.

APPENDIX E:
DIMENSIONAL GROUPING

The HVAC equations of state, (B1) and (B2), may be dedimensionalized as follows:

A.   FOURIER EQUATION

Defining $x = T/\Delta T_s$, with $\Delta T_s = T_b - T_s$, $t' = t/\tau$, with τ the system time constant and $y = y/d$, with d the "wall" thickness, the Fourier equation may be dedimensionalized by multiplying both the left- and right-hand sides by $(\tau/\Delta T_s)$, the right-hand side by $(d/d)^2$, and taking limits, viz.,

$$\frac{\partial T_w}{\partial t} = \alpha_w \frac{\partial^2 T_w}{\partial y^2}$$

$$\left(\frac{\tau}{\Delta T_s}\right)\frac{\partial T_w}{\partial t} = \alpha_w \frac{\partial^2 T_w}{\partial t^2}\left(\frac{\tau}{\Delta t^2}\right)\left(\frac{d}{d}\right)^2$$

and hence

$$\frac{\partial x_w}{\partial t} = [II_1]\frac{\partial^2 x_w}{\partial y'^2} ,$$ (E1)

where $II_1 = NF = \alpha_w\tau/d^2$, the Fourier number!

B.   EQUILIBRIUM EQUATION

Defining again $x = T/\Delta T_s$, with $\Delta T_s = T_b - T_s$ and $t' = t/\tau$, with τ the system time constant, the equilibrium equation, Eq. (B1) may be dedimensionalized by multiplying both the left- and right-hand sides by the ratio $(\tau/\Delta T_s)$, viz.:

$$\frac{dT_b}{dt} = \frac{\dot{m}}{m}(T_s - T_b) + \frac{h_2 A_w}{mC_{pa}A_f}(T_2 - T_b) + \frac{q_I}{mC_{pa}}$$

$$\frac{\tau}{\Delta T_s}\frac{dT_b}{dt} = \left(\frac{\dot{m}}{m}(T_s - T_b) + \frac{h_2 A_w}{mC_{pa}A_f}(T_2 - T_b) + \frac{q_I}{mC_{pa}}\right)\left(\frac{\tau}{\Delta T_s}\right)$$

and hence

$$\frac{dx_b}{dt'} = II_2(x_s - x_b) + II_3(x_2 - x_b)A_R + II_4,$$ (E2)

where

$$II_2 = [m\tau/m] = [1]$$

$$II_3 = [h_2\tau/mC_{pa}] = [h_2/mC_{pa}]$$

$$II_4 = [q_I\tau/mC_{pa}\,\Delta T_s]$$

$$A_R = A_w/A_f$$

$$m = m/\tau.$$

Dimensionless groups II_3 and II_4 are unique and bear special significance toward the process substance in that the convective coefficient h_2, and the incipient heat load q_I, respectively, are equated versus the thermal flux mC_{pa}. The dimensionless group II_4 in fact gives the ratio of the instantaneous heat load against the real cooling requirement – the substance of the free-cooling "rotational" objectives!

APPENDIX F:
COMPUTATIONAL ROUTINES

A.   GENERAL INPUT DATA

```
180   M0=5                                    MASS FLOW RATE
190   M=.625                                   ROOM AIR MASS
200   C1=.25                                   SPECIFIC HEAT AIR
210   PRINT "M0 ";M0; " M " ;M; " C1 ";C1
220   A0=2400                            }     FLOOR AREA
230   A1=1400
240   D0=.5                              }     SLAB THICKNESS
250   D2=D0/2
260   K0=.5                                    CONDUCTIVITY OF RC
270   X1=.024                                  DIFFUSIVITY OF RC
280   D1=1
290   PRINT "A0";Ao;" A1";A1;"D2";D2;"K0;";K0;"X1";X1;"D1";D1
300   H4=.1
310   H2=1.4
320   PRINT 'H4";H4;"H2";H2
330   DIM Q1 (24, 6), Q2 (24)
340   INTEGER F(6,5,5,5), G(6,5,5,5), S0F(G,5,5,5), S0G(6,5,5,5)
350   REAL Fqjj(6,5,5,5),Gqji(6,6,6,6),PENALTY(30),J0array(3,30),
      Jj0m(20),Jj0(3,30)
360   B=0
370   R1=.5
371   R=.5
372   S=64
380   Z=0
391   FOR Rm=1 TO 3
392   N0=9
401   IF Rm-1 THEN RESTORE Room1
402   IF Rm-2 THEN RESTORE Room2
403   IF Rm-3 THEN RESTORE Room3
404   D1=1
```

```
405   Z=0
406   D0=.5
407   D2=D0/2
408   F0=32000
```

B. ROOM LOAD DATA

```
412   Room1:DATA  0,0,0,0,0,0,8,8,8,8,8,8,8,8,8,8,8,0,0,0,0,0,0
420          DATA  0,0,0,0,0,5,12,19,14,9,9,9,9,9,9,14,19,14,7,0,0,0,0,0
430          DATA  0,0,0,0,0,5,11,17,12,7,7,7,7,7,7,12,17,12,6,0,0,0,0,0
431          DATA 2400,1400
480   Room2:DATA  0,0,0,0,0,0,8,8,8,8,8,8,8,8,8,8,8,0,0,0,0,0,0
490          DATA  0,0,0,0,0,0,2,9,9,9,9,9,9,9,9,14,19,24,19,12,5,0,0,0,0
500          DATA  0,0,0,0,0,0,1,7,7,7,7,7,7,7,7,12,17,22,17,11,5,0,0,0,0
501          DATA 1800,1000
550   Room3:DATA  0,0,0,0,0,0,8,8,8,8,8,8,8,8,8,8,8,0,0,0,0,0,0
560          DATA  0,0,0,0,0,0,2,9,9,9,9,9,9,9,9,9,9,9,2,0,0,0,0,0
570          DATA  0,0,0,0,0,0,1,7,7,7,7,7,7,7,7,7,7,7,1,0,0,0,0,0
571          DATA 2400,1400
```

C. TEAM PREP. ROUTINE

```
792   REM START TEAM SYNTHESIS PREP
793   Yy=0
794   FOR N1=1 TO 9
795   Xx=0
796   FOR R=1 TO 3
797   Room=R
798   Jj0(R,N1)=JOarray(Room,N1)
799   Xx=Xx+Jj0(R,N1)
800   NEXT R
801   Jj0m(N1)=Xx/3
802   Yy=Yy+Jj0m(N1)
803   NEXT N1
804   J0m=Yy/9
805   REM END TEAM SYNTHESIS PREP
```

D. TEAMED DP ALGO

```
820   REM SOLVE DP ALGO 8am TO 4pm (VZ 9TH INCREMENTS)
830   FOR N1=1 TO 9
840      REM REVERSE SEQUENCE FROM 4pm (VZ 1600 h) TO 8AM
         FOR DP ROUTINE
```

```
850      N=17-N1
860      REM INDEX DATA RECORDS
870      N0=N0+1
880      OUTPUT Prt;"***** N1 ";N1;" N ";N;" *****"
890      REM START GRAD. LOOPS U1 --- U4
900      FOR U1-1 TO 6
910        I1=U1+68
920        FOR U2=1 TO 5
930          FOR U3=1 TO 5
940            FOR U4=1 TO 5
950              I4=U4+64
960              I2=U2+64
970              I3=U3+64
980              REM START FEAS. LOOPS U0
990              FOLD=32000
1000             FOR U0-1 TO 10
1010               J0=U0+60
1020               REM SOLVE AC MODEL
1030               GOSUB 1770
1040               REM COMPUTE INDEXES
1050               V4=INT((J4-64)+R1) THEN Nextt
1060               V3=INT((J3-64)+R1) THEN Nextt
1070               V2=INT((J2-64)+R1) THEN Nextt
1080               V1=INT((J1-68)+R1) THEN Nextt
1085               IF J1<65 OR J1>76 THEN Nextt
1090               IF J2<65 OR J2>70 THEN Nextt
1100               IF J3<65 OR J3>70 THEN Nextt
1110               IF J4<65 OR J4>70 THEN Nextt
1120               REM COMPUTE HEAT LOAD
1130               Q=A1*M0*Cl*((I1+J1)/2-J0)
1140               REM ADJUST FOR FREE-COOL
1141               IF J0>=64 THEN Q=Q/2
1260               IF Q<0 THEN Nextt
1280               K=Q/12000
1290               REM DO DP RETURN
1300               IF N1<=1 THEN P0=K
1310               IF N1<>1 THEN P0=K+F(V1,V2,V3,V4)
1311               REM START TEAM SYNTHESIS
1312               Dj0m=Jj0m(N1)-J0m
1313               Dj0r=Jj0(Room,N1)-J0m
1314               IF SGN9Dj0M)=SGN(Dj0r) THEN
1315                 Pen=Dj0m*Dj0m
1316                 Penratio=Dj0r/(Dj0m*3)*10
1317                 Sf=A1/12000
```

```
1318                    Penalt=Pen*Penratio*Sf
1319                    P0=P0+Penalt
1322                    END IF
1323                    REM END TEAM SYNTHESIS
1324                    If P0>=fOLD then Nextt
1330                    REM HOLD OPTIMAL RETURNS
1340                    Fold=P0
1360                    S0=J0
1370                    S1=J1
1380                    S2=J2
1390                    S3=J3
1400                    S4=J4
1410  Nextt:           REM SOLUTION INFEASIBLE ! ! FIX & CONTINUE
1420    !              OUTPUT 1;"***** SOLUTION NOT.FEASIBLE *****"
1430                    P0=32000
1440                    REM CLOSE FEAS. LOOP U0
1450                    NEXT U0
1460                    REM STORE OPTIMAL RETURNS
1470                    G(U1,U2,U3,U4)=Fold
1480                    S0g(U1,U2,U3,U4)=S0
1500                    REM CLOSE GRAD. LOOPS U1 --- U4
1510  Zzz:       NEXT U4
1520              NEXT U3
1530            NEXT U2
1540          NEXT U1
1550        REM STORE & ROTATE DEP DATA
```

SELECTED SYMBOLS

A_w — Wall area

A_s — Slab area

α_w — Wall thermal diffusivity

T_b — Bulk (room) air temperature

T_w — Wall temperature

T_s — Supply air temperature

ΔT_s — Supply air temperature differential

$T_{2,3,4}$ — Structural temperature gradient

h_2	Structural convection coefficient
C_{pa}	Specific heat of air
q_r	Residue heat load term
d	Wall/slab thickness
τ	Time parameter
t'	Dimensionless time
t	Time
II_{1-4}	Dimensionless groups
$A(t), B(t)$	Model transition matrices (linear)
φ^{**}, T^{**}	Model transition matrices (discreete)
H^*	Measurement matrix
$z(n + 1)$	Measurement
$\tilde{z}(n + 1)$	Measurement error
$x(n + 1)$	State vector
$\hat{x}(n + 1)$	(Kalman) optimal filtered estimate of state
$v(n)$	Disturbance
$u(n)$	Control input
$Q(n)$	Covariance propagation

ACKNOWLEDGMENTS

The author wishes to express his appreciation to C. T. Leondes at UCLA and Professor Roy Marcus at UwTEC/RAND (South Africa) for helping to bring this work to completion.

REFERENCES

1. C. E. JANEKE, "Thermal Swing in HVAC – A Mathematical Treatise," *7th S. A. Symp. Num. Math., Durban* July (1981).
2. C. E. JANEKE, "Free-Cool: A Total HVAC Design Concept," *ASHRAE Tech. Semin., Houston* January (1982).
3. C. E. JANEKE, "Stochastic Optimal Control: A New Concept in HVAC, *4th Int. Symp. Use of Comput. Air Cond., Tokyo* March (1983).

4.   C. E. JANEKE, Optimal Control for HVAC; The Significance of Optimal State Estima-
       tion, *NRIMS Summer Semin. Ser. Control Syst., CSIR*, January (1984).
5.   C. E. JANEKE, "Modelling Techniques, Parameter Determination and Optimal Control
       of Energy Distribution in Large Building Structures," PhD. Thesis, Rand (1985).
6.   BELLMAN and DREYFUSS, "Applied Dynamic Programming," Princeton Univ. Press,
       Princeton, New Jersey, 1962.
7.   J. S. MEDITCH, "Stochastic Optimal Linear Estimation and Control," McGraw-Hill,
       New York, 1969.
8.   M. SINAI, "Large-Scale Systems: Performance Evaluation and Decentralization," Univ.
       of California Press, Los Angeles, 1982.
9.   WATANABE and TOKAI, *Electronics*, December (1985).

A LINEAR PROGRAMMING APPROACH
TO CONSTRAINED MULTIVARIABLE
PROCESS CONTROL

C. BROSILOW and G. Q. ZHAO*

Chemical Engineering Department
Case Western Reserve University
Cleveland, Ohio 44106
and
*Automation Department
Beijing Institute of Chemical Technology
Beijing, China

I.   INTRODUCTION

Efficient operation of a process often means operation at or near constraints on the control efforts and/or process output variables. If the control system implementation does not account for such constraints, then there will be an inevitable, and possibly severe, degradation in performance over that expected from a design based on strictly linear considerations. To avoid such a performance degradation, linear controllers are often modified, after the fact, to account for the constraints on the controls. Antireset windup for PID controllers and the techniques proposed [1] for inferential controllers are typical approaches. While these methods guard against possible severe performance degradation in single input–single output control systems, they in no sense optimize the performance of such systems. Further, it is not at all obvious how to extend such methods to multiinput–multioutput systems where reaching a constraint on a control effort means a loss in degrees of freedom and a resultant need to compromise on the desired responses of the output variables.

Optimizing process performance in the presence of constraints requires the use of a mathematical model of the process to anticipate the effects of the constraints and take appropriate control action. Thus, model-based control systems such as dynamic matrix control [2], model algorithmic control [3], inferential control [4, 5], and internal model control [6] provide a natural setting for dealing with constraints. All of the foregoing have fundamentally the same structure: the model outputs are subtracted from the measured process output variables, and the model is driven only by the control effort. They differ, if at all, only in the design of the controller.

Dynamic matrix controllers are designed to minimize a quadratic performance index based on the current setpoints, a preselected time horizon, and a fixed number of allowable controller actions within that time horizon. Model algorithmic controllers also use a quadratic performance index, but minimize the distance from desired process variable trajectories rather than from the setpoints. An advantage of the latter approach is that it more readily permits specification of decoupled control. In each of the foregoing, the use of a linear process model, coupled with a quadratic performance index, results in a controller which must continuously solve a quadratic program.

The aim of this work is to present controller design methods which place significantly less computational burden on the controller and which therefore can be implemented with currently available microprocessor-based hardware. Our starting point is the control structure used by inferential and internal model controllers. This structure is then modified slightly to simplify computations by removing nonminimum phase elements of the process model from within the computational loop. Our performance criterion leads to a linear program for the controller. In some important cases this linear program can be solved *a priori* to yield a controller which can be implemented using only some simple logic and algebraic manipulations.

Section II reviews the necessary background for the design of linear inferential (internal model) controllers. Section III presents the modified controller structure for constrained control. Sections IV and V reduce the optimization problem for single input–single output and multiinput–multioutput processes to a desirable form. Section VI gives the linear programming method for solving the minimization problems and gives analytical solutions in some simple, but important, cases. Finally, Section VII presents some worked examples for single input–single output processes and two input–two output processes.

II.   REVIEW OF THE DESIGN AND PROPERTIES OF LINEAR INFERENTIAL CONTROL SYSTEMS

The aim of an inferential control system is to infer the effects of disturbances on the controlled process outputs, and to use this inference to adjust the control effort so as to counter the effects of the disturbances [4]. When the process outputs to be controlled are measured directly, then the effect of the disturbances on the outputs is obtained simply by subtracting the model output from the process output, as shown in Fig. 1. The foregoing applies whether or not there are hard constraints on the control efforts and/or process outputs. The difference between an inferential control system with or without constraints lies in how the control effort is computed to counter the effects of the disturbances on the outputs. Several of the controller design concepts developed for unconstrained systems [5, 6] carry over to the design of constrained systems and are reviewed here.

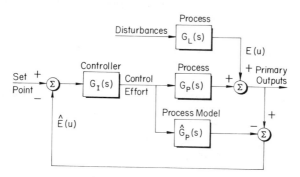

Fig. 1. Linear inferential control system with output measurements.

The inferential control system of Fig. 1 has the following loop response characteristics [5], where the controller is defined as $G_I(s) \equiv G_p^{-1}(s)F(s)$

$$y(s) = [I + (F(s) - I)T(s)]v(s) + [F(s) - I]T(s)E(s), \tag{1}$$

where

$$T(s) \equiv I + [G_p(s) - G_p(s)]G_I(s)^{-1}$$
$$G_I(s) \equiv G_p^{-1}(s)F(s)$$
$$G_p(s) = \text{process model}.$$

When there are no modeling errors, $G_p(s) = G_p(s)$, and when both $G_p(s)$ and $G_I(s)$ are stable, then the output response with a perfect model is

$$y^*(s) = F(s)v(s) + [I - F(s)]E(s). \tag{2}$$

An important property of the loop response of an inferential control system is that there is no steady-state error in the output if the steady-state gain of the filter is the identity matrix. That is,

1) $y(\infty) = v, \quad$ iff $F(0) = I.$

We call the term F(s) in Eqs. (1) and (2) the loop response filter. This terminology is used because

2) F(s) is the loop response of the output y(s) to the setpoint v(s) when the model is perfect.

3) The "filter" F(s) is used to make the controller $G_I(s)$ stable and realizable.

4) The "filter" F(s) is used to compensate for modeling errors [i.e., when $G_p(s) \neq G_p(s)$].

Qualitatively, a rapidly responding filter is used when modeling errors are small, while a more sluggish filter is used when there may be significant modeling errors.

Because the filter is chosen to make the controller $G_I(s)$ both stable and realizable, it must have the following properties:

1) F(s) must have the same dead time and right-half-plane zeros as the process *model* $G_p(s)$.

2) The order of the denominator minus the numerator of F(s) must be equal to or greater than that of the process *model*.

As an example of the above, consider a model of the form

$$G_p(s) = \frac{(s-1)}{(10s+1)^3} e^{-s\hat{T}}. \tag{3}$$

Then, since $G_I(s) = G_p^{-1}(s)F(s)$, the filter F(s) must be of the form

$$F(s) = \frac{(s-1)e^{-s\hat{T}}}{P(s)}, \tag{4}$$

where P(s) = any third-order polynomial in s such that P(s) has no roots in the right half-plane [in addition, we require that P(0) = −1 if there is to be no steady-state offset]. The choice of P(s) determines how the loop responds for either a perfect or an imperfect model. A reasonable choice for P(s) is to minimize the integral error squared performance criterion when $\hat{G}_p = G_p$. Such a P(s) is

$$P(s) = (s+1)(\varepsilon s + 1)^2, \tag{5}$$

so that

$$F(s) = \frac{s-1}{-(s+1)} \frac{e^{-s\hat{T}}}{(\varepsilon S + 1)^2}.$$

(6)

The parameter ε, above, is chosen so as to stabilize the system and yield an acceptable overall system response in spite of modeling errors [5]. Indeed, if ε is chosen sufficiently large, then the system response approximates that given by (2).

When the process model does not contain a zero in the right half of the Laplace domain, then the filer is generally chosen as

$$F(s) = \frac{e^{-s\hat{T}}}{(\varepsilon S + 1)^m},$$

(7)

where m is the order of the denominator polynomial minus the numerator polynomial of the model.

The selection of F(s) for multivariable systems follows the same rules as above, but the selection is more complicated because of the increased number of choices. As an example, consider a process described by the following model:

$$G_p(s) = \begin{bmatrix} g_{11}(s)e^{-T_{11}s} & g_{12}(s)e^{-T_{12}s} \\ g_{21}(s)e^{-T_{21}s} & g_{22}(s)e^{-T_{22}s} \end{bmatrix}.$$

.(8)

$$g_{ij}(s) \equiv N_{ij}(s)/D_{ij}(s), \quad i, j = 1, 2,$$

where $N_{ij}(s)$ and $D_{ij}(s)$ are polynomials in s, and where the order of $N_{ij}(s)$ is equal to or less than that of $D_{ij}(s)$.

In the above and in the remaining development, the caret over the model parameter will be suppressed unless there is a possibility of confusion between the process and model parameters.

Then

$$G_p^{-1}(s) = \frac{1}{\det G_p(s)} \begin{bmatrix} g_{22}(s)e^{-T_{22}s} & -g_{12}(s)e^{-T_{12}s} \\ -g_{21}(s)e^{-T_{21}s} & g_{11}(s)e^{-T_{11}s} \end{bmatrix} \tag{9}$$

$$\det G_p(s) \equiv g_{11}(s)g_{22}(s)e^{-(T_{11}+T_{22})s} - g_{12}(s)g_{21}(s)e^{-(T_{12}+T_{21})s}. \tag{10}$$

Let us assume that the det $\hat{G}_p(s)$ has no right half plane zeros and that the sum $T_{11} + T_{22}$ is less than the sum $T_{12} + T_{21}$. In this case we factor the term $g_{11}(s)g_{22}(s)e^{-(T_{11}+T_{22})s}$ out of det $\hat{G}_p(s)$. Then $\hat{G}_p^{-1}(s)$ becomes

$$G_p^{-1}(s) = \frac{1}{Q(s)} \begin{bmatrix} \dfrac{e^{T_{11}s}}{g_{11}(s)} & \dfrac{-g_{12}(s)e^{(T_{11}+T_{22}-T_{12})s}}{g_{11}(s)g_{22}(s)} \\ \dfrac{-g_{21}(s)e^{(T_{11}+T_{22}-T_{21})s}}{g_{11}(s)g_{22}(s)} & \dfrac{e^{T_{22}s}}{g_{22}(s)} \end{bmatrix} \tag{11a}$$

$$Q(s) \equiv 1 - \frac{g_{12}(s)g_{21}(s)}{g_{11}(s)g_{22}(s)}e^{-\alpha s} \tag{11b}$$

$$\alpha \equiv T_{12} + T_{21} - T_{11} - T_{22} \geq 0. \tag{11c}$$

The term $1/Q(s)$ could be realized by a feedback system with a forward transmission of unity and $(q_{12}q_{21}/q_{11}q_{22})e^{-\alpha s}$ in the feedback path. If $(q_{12}q_{21}/q_{11}q_{22})$ has no more zeros that poles, then the feedback system should have a forward transmission of $(q_{11}q_{22}/q_{12}q_{21})$ and $e^{-\alpha s}$ is in the feedback path. By assumption, $1/Q(s)$ is stable since det $G_p(s)$ has no right-half-plane zeros. The nonrealizable terms in $G_p^{-1}(s)$ are those like $(e^{T_{11}s})/g_{11}(s)$ which require prediction into the future and perhaps one or more differentiations, because the order of the numerator polynomial of $g_{11}(s)$ is generally less than the denominator polynomial in $g_{11}(s)$. To make the controller realizable, we postmultiply it by the filter. For the sake of this discussion, let us assume that we wish to have decoupled control. That is, $y_2(s)$, the second output, should not respond to a change in the setpoint for the first output $y_1(s)$, and vice versa. As can be seen from (2) (perfect model case), this specification requires a diagonal filter. [From (1), which is more representative of the real world with modeling errors, we see that we will not really have decoupled control, but that we can approach it if we choose the filter response times to be long enough.] Thus

$$F(s) = \begin{bmatrix} f_{m1}(s)e^{-a_1 s} & 0 \\ 0 & f_{m2}(s)e^{-a_2 s} \end{bmatrix}. \tag{12}$$

Now

$$G_I(s) = \frac{1}{Q(s)} \begin{bmatrix} \dfrac{f_{m1}(s)e^{-(a_1 - T_{11})s}}{g_{11}(s)} & \dfrac{-g_{12}(s)f_{m2}(s)e^{-(a_2 + T_{12} - T_{11} - T_{22})s}}{g_{11}(s)g_{22}(s)} \\ \dfrac{-f_{m1}(s)g_{21}(s)e^{-(a_1 + T_{21} - T_{11} - T_{22})s}}{g_{11}(s)g_{22}(s)} & \dfrac{f_{m2}(s)e^{-(a_2 - T_{22})s}}{g_{22}(s)} \end{bmatrix}.$$

In order for there to be no predictions in $G_I(s)$, we require that a_1 and a_2 be chosen so that

$$\min_{a_1}(a_1 - T_{11}, a_1 + T_{21} - T_{11} - T_{22}) = 0$$

$$\min_{a_2}(a_2 - T_2, a_2 + T_{12} - T_{11} - T_{22}) = 0. \tag{13}$$

That is, we choose a_1 and a_2 to be the smallest dead times possible that make $G_I(s)$ realizable. Further, we chose $f_{m1}(s)$ and $f_{m2}(s)$ so that none of the terms in $G_I(s)$ has a numerator polynomial of greater order than the denominator polynomial.

When the determinant of $G_p(s)$ has no zeros in the right half of the Laplace domain, then the terms $f_{m1}(s)$ and $f_{m2}(s)$ are usually chosen as

$$f_{mi}(s) = \frac{1}{(\varepsilon_i s + 1)^{n_i}}, \quad i = 1, 2, \tag{14}$$

where ε_i is the constant of the filter and n_i the order required to make $G_I(s)$ realizable. The time constants ε_i are chosen to compensate for modeling errors and can be calculated as shown [1, 7] when one has estimates of either the parameter variations in the process or gain and phase bounds for each of the input-output pairs.

If the determinant of $G_p(s)$ has right-half-plane zeros, then both $f_{m1}(s)$ and $f_{m2}(s)$ must have the same right-half-plane zeros in order that $G_I(s)$ be stable. Determining the *exact* location of right-half-plane zeros for determinants of the form of (10) is in general a very difficult task. Therefore, alternate approaches are needed for designing $G_I(s)$ that are beyond the scope of this article.

III.   THE STRUCTURE OF CONSTRAINED CONTROL SYSTEMS

The approach to constrained control advanced in this and the following sections is: 1) predict the effect of disturbances on the process outputs one or more sampling instances from the current time (i.e., over a preselected time horizon); 2) calculate a desired response to the predicted effect of disturbances over the selected time horizon; and 3) compute control efforts, subject to constrains on the control efforts and outputs, so as to match the desired trajectory as closely as possible. The entire computation is repeated at each sampling interval.

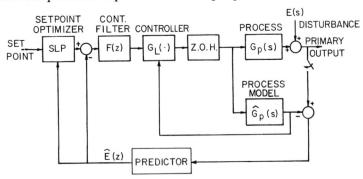

Fig. 2. Constrained inferential control system. SLP, static linear program; $G_L(\cdot)$, dynamic linear program; and Z.O.H., zero-order hold.

The control system structure which results from the above strategy is given in Fig. 2. As in the unconstrained case of Fig. 1, the current effect of the disturbances on the output is estimated by subtracting the model output from the measured process output. The observed effect of the disturbances is then projected ahead in time by the predictor (Fig. 2). The predictor can involve a very sophisticated calculation using assumed or measured statistics of the disturbances and a model of how the disturbances affect the outputs. However, we assume simply that the currently observed effect of disturbances will persist unchanged over the prediction interval. The errors introduced by such a simple prediction strategy are diminished by the fact that the prediction is updated at every sampling interval.

The computation of a desired trajectory proceeds in two steps. First, the steady-state optimizer checks to see if the desired setpoints can be achieved if the current disturbance effects persist indefinitely into the future. If the desired setpoints can indeed be achieved, then these setpoints minus the projected disturbance effects are transmitted to the desired trajectory calculation. If the desired steady state cannot be achieved, then the steady-state optimizer computes a set of achievable setpoints which are as close as possible to the desired setpoints. These achievable setpoints, minus the projected disturbance effects, are transmitted to the desired trajectory calculations.

The desired output trajectory (or trajectories in the multivariable case) is the output of the loop response filter [cf. Fig. 1 and (1) and (2)] projected ahead for the entire time horizon, where the filter input is the calculated setpoint(s) less the projected disturbance effect(s). The filter state at the end of the current sampling interval is the state used for the next sampling interval. The filter itself is designed as described in Section II, and can be implemented either as a set of linear constant coefficient equations or in impulse or step response forms. The adjustable filter parameters ε [cf. (4), (6), (7), (12), and (14)] can be obtained either by the *a priori* design methods of Chen [7] or by on-line tuning [1]. Both of the foregoing procedures select the parameters ε so as to obtain desirable loop response characteristics in spite of modeling errors.

The function of the controller in Fig. 2 is to calculate the control efforts, subject to all constraints, which forces the *model* outputs to follow the desired trajectories as closely as possible over the selected time horizon. We assume that the control effort is constant over a sampling interval. Therefore, the maximum number of degrees of freedom for each control effort is the time horizon divided by the sampling interval. Sometimes, when the time horizon is long, it may be computationally advantageous to use less than the maximum number of degrees of freedom. In this latter case, we always select the last value of the control effort to equal the steady-state control effort calculated by the setpoint optimizer. This is done so that the objective function is finite even for an infinite time horizon, and the initial portions of the trajectory are always weighted adequately. The latter is important because only the first step of the controller calculation is ever implemented, and the entire calculation is repeated at every sampling interval.

Figure 3 shows a computationally more efficient implementation of a constrained control system than that given in Fig. 2. In Fig. 3 the filter F(s) of (8), and (12) is factored into two parts, a minimum phase part F_m, and a nonminimum phase part F_R. That is,

$$F(s) \equiv F_m(s)F_R(s). \tag{15}$$

The nonminimum phase term $F_R(s)$ contains the dead times and right-half-plane zeros which were necessary to make the linear controller G_I stable and not require prediction of future events.

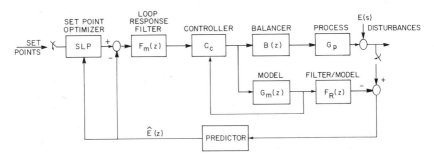

Fig. 3. Implementation version of constrained inferential control system.

The purpose of the above factorization is to reduce the computational effort of the controller by permitting use of shorter time horizons. The implementation of Fig. 2 requires that the controller use a time horizon longer than the model dead time in order that its current action will influence the model output within the time horizon. By factoring the loop response filter, and hence and the model, as shown in Fig. 3, the controller can use a time horizon which is as short as one sample period. The sample period is in turn then dependent only on the expected frequency of disturbances and the filtering imposed by the process.

An important side benefit of the implementation of Fig. 3 is that the unstable zeros of the process model are outside the inner computational feedback loop. Thus the need for exact duplication of the model right-half-plane zeros in the filter is avoided (note that, in general, G_m will be unstable if det $\hat{G}_p$ has right half-plane zeros).

For the examples in Section II, the factorization is as follows:

$$F(s) = \frac{1-s}{1+s} \frac{e^{-ST}}{(\epsilon s + 1)^2}, \quad F_m(s) \equiv \frac{1}{(\epsilon s + 1)^2}, \quad F_R(s) \equiv \frac{1-s}{1+s} e^{-ST} \tag{16}$$

$$F(s) = \frac{e^{-s\hat{T}}}{(\varepsilon s + 1)^m}; \quad F_m \equiv \frac{1}{(\varepsilon s + 1)^m}, \quad F_R(s) \equiv e^{-s\hat{T}} \tag{17}$$

$$F(s) = \text{diag}(f_{m1}(s)e^{-a_1 s}, f_{m2}(s)e^{-a_2 s})$$

$$F_m(s) \equiv \text{diag}(f_{m1}(s), f_{m2}(s)) \tag{18}$$

$$F_R(s) \equiv \text{diag}(e^{-a_1 s}, e^{-a_2 s}).$$

The balancer B of Fig. 3 acts as a zero-order hold and, for some multivariable systems, as a delay on one or more of the outputs from the controller. It is necessary to delay the controller output whenever a single control effort influences all of the model outputs through a dead time which is shorter than all other model dead times and decoupled control is desired. An alternate view of the balancer is that it makes the model factorization G_m realizable. That is,

$$G_m = F_R^{-1} G_p B^*; \quad B \equiv B^* \times \text{zero-order hold.} \tag{19}$$

For single input–single output systems, the balancer is never more than a zero-order hold, and the model G_m is always realizable.

For the two input–two output process given by (8), the delay portion of the balancer B^* is a diagonal matrix with unity steady-state gains and the least dead time required to make the G_m in (19) realizable. Substituting for F_R from (18) and G_p from (8) into (19) gives

$$G_m = \begin{bmatrix} g_{11}(s)e^{(a_1 - T_{11})s} & g_{12}(s)e^{(a_1 - T_{12})s} \\ g_{21}(s)e^{(a_2 - T_{21})s} & g_{22}(s)e^{(a_2 - T_{22})s} \end{bmatrix}. \tag{20}$$

Let us now evaluate the exponentials in (20). From (13) there are four possible cases:

1) $a_1 = T_{11}; a_2 = T_{22}; a_1 + T_{21} - T_1 - T_{22} > 0; a_2 + T_{12} - T_{11} - T_{22} > 0$

2) $a_1 = T_{11}; a_2 = T_{11} + T_{22} - T_{12}; a_1 + T_{21} - T_{11} - T_{22} > 0; a_2 - T_{22} > 0$

3) $a_1 = T_{11} + T_{22} - T_{21}, a_2 = T_{22}; a_1 - T_{11} > 0, a_2 + T_{12} - T_{11} - T_{22} > 0$

4) $a_1 = T_{11} + T_{22} - T_{21}$, $a_2 = T_{11} + T_{22} - T_{12}$; $a_1 - T_{11} > 0$; $a_2 - T_{22} > 0$.

The inequality assumed in (11c) rules out Case 4.
     In the other cases, the exponents in (20) become

1) $a_1 - T_{11} = 0$, $a_1 - T_{12} = T_{11} - T_{12} < 0$
       $a_2 - T_{21} = T_{22} - T_{21} < 0$ $a_2 - T_{22} = 0$

2) $a_1 - T_{11} = 0$ $a_1 - T_{12} = T_{11} - T_{12} > 0$

       $a_2 - T_{21} = T_{11} + T_{22} - T_{12} - T_{21} \leq 0$ $a_2 - T_{22} = T_{11} - T_{12} > 0$

3) $a_1 - T_{11} = T_{22} - T_{21} > 0$ $a_1 - T_{12} = T_{11} + T_{22}$
                                                                         $- T_{21} - T_{12} < 0$

       $a_2 - T_{21} = T_{22} - T_{21} > 0$ $a_2 - T_{22} = 0$

Case 1 presents no difficulties since all of the terms in the exponential are negative or zero. In this case, $B^* = I$ and the balancer is only a zero-order hold. The model G_m is then

$$G_m = \begin{bmatrix} g_{11}(s) & g_{12}(s)e^{-(T_{11}-T_{12})s} \\ g_{12}(s)e^{-(T_{22}-T_{21})s} & g_{22}(s) \end{bmatrix} \tag{21}$$

In Case 2), the exponents of the exponentials in the 1,2 and 2,2 elements are equal and positive. Therefore, the balancer B^* must have a dead time of $T_{11} - T_{12}$ units in order for G_m to be realizable. That is,

$$B^* = \begin{bmatrix} 1 & 0 \\ 0 & e^{-(T_{11}-T_{12})s} \end{bmatrix} \tag{22a}$$

$$G_m = \begin{bmatrix} g_{11}(s) & g_{12}(s) \\ g_{21}(s)e^{-\alpha s} & g_{22}(s) \end{bmatrix} \tag{22b}$$

Case 3 is similar to Case 2, except now control effort must be retarded by $T_{22} - T_{21}$ units of time and the balancer and model becomes

$$B^* = \begin{bmatrix} e^{-(T_{22}-T_{21})s} & 0 \\ 0 & 1 \end{bmatrix} \tag{23a}$$

$$G_m = \begin{bmatrix} g_{11}(s) & g_{12}(s)e^{-\alpha s} \\ g_{21}(s) & g_{22}(s) \end{bmatrix}. \tag{23b}$$

Notice that in each of the above cases the model G_m generally still has at least one dead-time element. However, in all cases, a different control effort affects each output instantaneously (i.e., not through a dead time).

IV. CONTROLLER FORMULATIONS FOR SINGLE INPUT–SINGLE OUTPUT SYSTEMS

A. SINGLE STEP CONTROLLERS

A single step controller computes the *constant* control effort required to make the model output (i.e., output of G_m in Fig. 3) equal to the filter output at the end of a prespecified time horizon. If the prespecified time horizon is longer than the sampling interval, and the entire calculation is repeated at each sampling interval. Time horizons which are longer than the sampling interval are useful in stabilizing the computational feedback loop of Fig. 3 when the model G_m is a second- or higher-order lag.

There is no need for setpoint optimization for single step control systems, and the balancer is merely a zero-order hold.

The control effort required to make the model output equal the filter (F_m) output after a time horizon of H is

$$m_k^*(H) - m_{k-1} + \frac{f_m(t_k + H, t_k) - y_m(t_k + H, t_k, m_{k-1})}{S_m(h)}, \tag{24}$$

where m_k^* is the control effort to be applied over the interval $t_k < t \le t_{k+1}$; m_{k-1}, the control effort applied over the previous interval $t_{k-1} < t \le t_k$; $f_m(t_k + H, t_k)$, the filter output at $t_k + H$, given its states and inputs at t_k; $y_m(t_k + H, t_k, m_{k-1})$, the model output at $t_k + H$, given its states at t_k and an input m_{k-1}; $S_m(H)$, the step response of G_m evaluated at H; H, the time horizon; and $t_{k+1} - t_k = \Delta$, the sampling interval.

An alternate form of (24) is

$$m_k^*(H) = \frac{f_m(T_k + H, t_k) - y_m(t_k + H, t_k, 0)}{S_m(H)}, \tag{25}$$

where $y_m(t_k + H, t_k, 0)$ is the model output at $t_k + H$, given its states at t_k and zero control input. The actual control effort m_k, applied over the interval $t_k < t \leq t_k + \Delta$, is

$$
\begin{aligned}
m_k &= m_k^*(H), \quad \text{if } m_L \leq m_k^*(H) \leq m_U \\
&= m_L \text{ or } m_U \quad \text{otherwise.}
\end{aligned}
\tag{26}
$$

B.   STABILITY OF SINGLE STEP CONTROLLERS

A necessary condition for the stability of constrained controllers around an *achievable* operating point is that the controller be stable for small perturbations around that operating point. This is equivalent to requiring that the unconstrained controller be stable. If, in addition to the above, none of the future controls violates constraints, then the constrained controller is guaranteed stable. The foregoing leads to the following theorem.

Theorem. The single step algorithm is stable for any finite-order linear constant coefficient model (G_m) if the time horizon H is long enough.

The proof is in two parts. First we show that the unconstrainted controller is stable if the time horizon H is long enough. Then, we show that, for a long enough horizon, the controls will not violate constraints.

1) The unconstrained single step algorithm is stable for H long enough. The process model G_m is taken as

$$
X(t) = AX(t) + bm(t)
$$
$$
y_m(t) = c^T X(t), \tag{27}
$$

where $y_m(t)$ and $m(t)$ are the scalar process output and control effort, respectively; $X(t)$, the process state vector; A, an $n \times n$ matrix whose eigenvalues have negative real parts; and b and c are n vectors. The state in (27) evolves as

$$X(t_k + \Delta, t_k) = e^{A\Delta}X(t_k) + (e^{A\Delta} - I)A^{-1}bm_k. \tag{28}$$

Substituting (25) into (28) gives

$$X(t_k + \Delta, t_k) = \Gamma(\Delta, H)X(t_k), \tag{29}$$

where

$$\Gamma(\Delta, H) \equiv e^{A\Delta} + \frac{(e^{A\Delta} - I)A^{-1}bc^{T}e^{AH}}{c^{T}(e^{AH} - I)A^{-1}B}.$$

In obtaining (29), we used the relationship

$$y_m(t_k + H, t_k, 0) = c^{T}e^{AH}X(t_k)$$
$$S_m(H) = c^{T}(e^{AH} - I)A^{-1}b \tag{30}$$

The spectral radius of $\Gamma(\Delta, H)$ approaches that of $e^{A\Delta}$ for large H since

$$\lim_{H \to \infty} e^{AH} \to 0$$

and

$$\lim_{H \to \infty} \Gamma(\Delta, H) = e^{A\Delta}.$$

Since A is a stable matrix, the spectral radius of $e^{A\Delta}$ is less than one. Hence, the spectral radius of $\Gamma(\Delta, H)$ is less than one for H/Δ large enough.

2) Future control effects will not violate constraints for a long enough time horizon.

When the time horizon H gets very long, the future control efforts approach a constant which is simply the steady-state control effort associated with the setpoint. (If the setpoint is not achievable, then the steady-state control is at the constraint.) To verify the above remark, note that substituting (30) into (25) gives

$$m_k^*(H) = \frac{f_m(t_k + H, t_k) - c^{T}e^{AH}X(t_k)}{c^{T}(e^{AH} - I)A^{-1}b} \tag{31}$$

$$\lim_{H \to \infty} m_k^*(H) = \frac{f_m(\infty)}{-c^{T}A^{-1}B}$$

which equals steady-state control, since $f_m(\infty)$ equals the setpoint when there are no disturbances and $-c^T A^{-1} b$ is the gain of the process. The behavior of the feedback law given by (26) and (25) [or (24)] for various models and different choices of H/Δ is discussed in Section VII.

C.   MULTISTEP CONTROLLERS

The constraints on the control effort can make it advantageous to use a time horizon of several sampling intervals and to explicitly account for the fact that the control effort can change at each of the several sampling instants within the time horizon. The control efforts at the sampling instants can be obtained by solving the following minimization problem.

$$\underset{\underline{m}_j}{\text{minimize}} \sum_{j=1}^{H} \gamma_j \mid y_m(t_{k+j}, t_k, \underline{m}_j) - f_m(t_{k+j}, t_k) \mid, \gamma_j \geq 0, \qquad (32)$$

where $y_m(t_{k+j}, t_k, \underline{m}_j)$ is the projected model, G_m, output starting from its state at t_k using controls $m_1, m_2, ..., m_j$; $f_m(t_{k+j}, t_k)$ is the projected filter, F_m, output starting from its state at t_k; and $\underline{m}_j$ is defined to be a vector of controls, $m_1, m_2, ..., m_j$.

The model output can be expressed as

$$y_m(t_{k+j}, t_k, \underline{m}_j) = y_m(t_{k+j}, t_k, m_{k-1})$$

$$+ \sum_{q=1}^{j} S_m((j-q+1)\Delta)(m_q - m_{q-1}), \qquad (33)$$

where $m_0 \equiv m_{k-1}$ and $y_m(t_{k+j}, t_k, m_{k-1})$ is the model output at t_{k+j} with a control effort m_{k-1}. The constraints are

$$b_L \leq c_j y_m(t_{k+j}, t_k, m_j) + m_j < b_u, \quad j = 1, ..., J \qquad (34a)$$
$$m_j = m(\infty), \quad j = R+1, R+2, ..., J \qquad (34b)$$

and m_j is the steady-state control necessary to achieve $f_m(\infty)$.

If $R = J$, then there are as many degrees of freedom for the control as there are sampling periods in the time horizon ($H = J\Delta$). When R is less than J, the last $J-R$ controls are set to their steady-state value. Also, in most practical situations, the constants c_j in (34a) are zero, so that the contraints are only on the controls m_j. If c_j is zero, then one could take $t_{k+j} = t_k + jH$, where H is the time horizon which can be longer than the sampling period. If, however, (34a) is to hold at every sampling period and $c_j \neq 0$, then taking H longer than a sampling period risks violation of (34a).

The solution to the problem given by (32)–(34) gives a set of controls m_j, $j = 1, \ldots, J$, but only the first of these is used, so that

$$m_k = m_1. \tag{35}$$

At the next sampling interval the entire problem is resolved for the next control effort.

Preparatory to solving (32)–(34), it is convenient to reformulate the problem in a standard form. We first consider the case where there are as many degrees of freedom for the control as there are sampling periods (i.e., $R = J$). For this case the standard form is

$$\underset{x_j}{\text{minimize}} \sum_{j=1}^{J} |x_j| \tag{36a}$$

Subject to

$$X_L^+ = AX + d_L \geq 0; \quad \dim d_L = \dim d_U = J$$

$$\tag{36b}$$

$$X_U^+ = -AX + d_U \geq 0,$$

where $X \equiv (x_1 \ldots x_J)^T$. To transform (32)–(34) into the form given by (36) requires the following definition and manipulations. Let

$$x_j \equiv y_m(t_{k+j}, t_k, \underline{m}_j) - f_m(t_{k+j}, t_k) \tag{37}$$

Solve (33) for m_j in terms of y_m [note that (33) is triangular in m_j]. This gives

$$m_j = m_0 + \sum_{p=1}^{j} Q_{jp}[y_m(t_{k+j}, t_k, \underline{m}_j) - y_m(t_{k+j}, t_k, m_{k-1})] \tag{38}$$

where

$$Q_{jp} = 0, \quad p > j$$

$$Q_{jj} = S_m^{-1}(\Delta)$$

$$Q_{21} = S_m^{-2}(\Delta)[S_m(2\Delta) - S_m(\Delta)]$$

$$Q_{31} = S_m^{-2}(\Delta)[S_m(3\Delta) - S_m(\Delta)] + S_m(\Delta)Q_{21}^2$$

$Q_{32} = Q_{21}$,

etc. Substituting (37) into (32) gives (36a) directly. Substituting (37) and (38) into (34a) gives (36b) with the following definitions:

$a_{jj} \equiv (c_j + Q_{jj})/\gamma_j$

$a_{jp} \equiv Q_{jp}/\gamma_p, \quad p = 1, ..., j - 1$

$\quad = 0, \quad p > j$

$(d_L)_j \equiv -b_L + r_j$ \hfill (39)

$(d_U)_j \equiv b_U - r_j$

$r_j \equiv c_j y_m(t_{k+j}, t_k, m_{k-1}) + m_0 + (c_j + Q_{jj})z_j + \sum_{p=1}^{j-1} Q_{jp}z_p$

$z_p \equiv f_m(t_{k+p}, t_k) - y_m(t_{k+p}, t_k, m_{k-1}), \quad p = 1, ..., j.$

From (39) we see that the vectors d_L and d_U must be recomputed at each sampling period from data available from the last sampling period. The solution of (36) is given in Section VI,A along with a simple example using a time horizon of two sampling periods.

Now we consider the case where the last J-R controls are set to their steady-state value. The standard form for the problem is

$$\underset{x_j}{\text{minimize}} \sum_{j=1}^{J} |x_j| \hspace{3cm} (40a)$$

subject to

$X = SW - b, \quad \dim X = J, \dim W = R$ \hfill (40b)

$X^+ = AW + d, \quad \dim X^+ = R$ \hfill (40c)

$X^+ > 0, \quad \text{for all } x_j^+$

$w_i \equiv m_i, \quad i = 1, ..., R$

The variables x_j in the objective function given by (40a) are defined by Eq. (37). Equation (40b) follows directly from (33) using the variable w_i to replace the unspecified controls m_i, $i = 1, ..., R$. The matrix S in (40b) is composed of elements which are the step response of the minimum phase portion of the model (i.e., S_m) evaluated at different times as given by (33). S is lower triangular for the first R rows. The rows between R and J are full. The vector b in (40b) is made up of elements of the form

$$b_j = \gamma_j(f_m(t_{k+j}) - y_m(t_{k+j}, \underline{m}_j))$$

Equation (40c) is obtained from (34a) by replacing $y_m(t_{k+j}, \underline{m}_j)$ in (40c) with $y_m(t_{k+j}, m_{k-1})$ and $\underline{m}_j$ using Eq. (33). Both upper and lower bounds in (40c) are rewritten as inequality bounded below by zero. Thus X^+ in (40c) plays the same role as X_L^+ and X_U^+ given in (36b). The elements of the matrix A and the vector b are obtained as a result of the foregoing manipulations. The matrix A can be partitioned into two matrices which are lower triangular for the first R rows and generally full thereafter.

V. CONTROLLER FORMATION FOR MULTIINPUT, MULTIOUTPUT SYSTEMS

A. THE SETPOINT OPTIMIZER

Whenever there are multiple outputs, there is a possibility that an operator, or a global scheduling program, will request unachievable values for the local output setpoints. It is probably a good policy to warn the operator that the current requested outputs cannot be achieved and provide him with an optimal set of achievable setpoints, which the operator could then elect to modify based on other considerations. The role of the steady-state optimizer is to provide the optimal achievable setpoints. This can be done by solving the following:

$$\underset{v_i, \overline{m}_i}{\text{minimize}} \sum_i \alpha_i \mid v_i - sp_i \mid + \beta_i \mid \overline{m}_i - m_{di} \mid \qquad (41a)$$

subject to

$$v = G_p(0)\overline{m} + E \qquad (41b)$$

$$m_{iL} \leq \overline{m}_i \leq m_{iU}, \qquad (41c)$$

where v is the vector of achievable setpoints; $\overline{m}$, the vector of steady-state controls; E, the vector of projected steady-state effects of the disturbances on the outputs; sp, the vector of desired setpoints; m_d, the vector of desired controls; $G_p(0)$, the steady-state gain matrix of the process model; and α and β, weighting coefficients. The above problem can be transformed into the standard forms given by (36) or (39) by defining x_i as follows and following the same procedures as those following (36) and (39).

$$x_i = \alpha_i(v_i - sp_i), \quad i = 1, \ldots, n$$

$$= \beta_i(m_i - m_{di}), \quad i = n + 1, \ldots, 2n. \tag{42}$$

The form given by (36) should be used when there are as many independent controls as are outputs. Otherwise, the form given by (39) is more appropriate. The suggested method of solution in either case is given in Section VI.

B.   SINGLE STEP CONTROLLERS

The controller formulation for single step controllers of multivariable processes is similar to that for ingle input–single output processes, but requires the solution of a linear program rather than a linear algebraic equation as in (24). For relatively low-dimensional systems (e.g., two input–two output), the linear program can be solved analytically, as shown in Sections VI and VII, and the resulting control law is simple and easily implemented. In this section, the programming problem is reduced to our standard form for square systems where the number of inputs and outputs is equal. Nonsquare systems can also be formulated as linear programming problems, but are not dealt with primarily because we have not yet solved example problems for such systems.

The objective functoin for square multivariable systems is taken as:

$$\text{minimize} \sum_{i=1}^{n} \gamma_i \, |y_{mi}(y_k + H, t_k, m(k)) - f_{mi}(t_k + H, t_k) | \tag{43a}$$

subject to

$$y_m(t_k + H, t_k, m(k)) = y_m(t_k + H, t_k, m(k-1)) + SM(H)[m(k) - m(k-1)] \tag{43b}$$

$$m_L \leq m(k) \leq m_U \tag{43c}$$

$$\dim y_m(\cdot, \cdot, \cdot) = \dim m(\cdot) = n, \tag{43d}$$

where $y_m(t_j, t_k, m)$ is the vector of outputs of the model G_m at time t_j, starting from t_k with a control effort vector m; $f_m(t_j, t_k)$, a vector of outputs from the filter F_m, at time t_j, starting from t_k; $SM(H)$, an $n \times n$ matrix of step responses of the outputs evaluated at $t = H$; H, the time horizon $\geq \Delta$, the sampling interval; and m_L and m_U, vectors of contraints on the controls. The objective function given by (43a) does not have a penalty on the controls because the setpoint optimizer has already accounted for such penalties at steady state and dynamic penalties for excessive control action are better treated by adjusting the filter time constant and/or the time horizon.

To transform (43) into standard form, let

$$X \equiv \Gamma[y_m(t_k + H, t_k, m(k)) - f_m(t_k + H, t_k)] \tag{44}$$

where Γ is a diagonal matrix of weights γ_i. Substituting (44) into (43a) and solving for m(k) gives

$$m(k) = AX + d^*, \tag{45}$$

where

$$d^* \equiv m(k-1) + [SM(H)]^{-1}[f(t_k + H, t_k) - y_m(t_k + H, t_k, m(k))]$$

$$A \equiv [\Gamma SM(H)]^{-1}.$$

Finally, substituting (44) and (45) into (43) gives

$$\text{minimize} \sum_i | x_i | \tag{46a}$$

subject to

$$X_L^+ = AX + d_L \geq 0 \tag{46b}$$

$$X_U^+ = -AX + d_U \geq 0, \tag{46c}$$

where

$$d_L \equiv d^* - m_L$$

$$d_U \equiv -d^* + m_U.$$

C.   MULTISTEP CONTROLLERS

The multivariable multistep controller is the generalization of the single variable multistep controller, and the development is identical except that the rules for matrix operators must be obeyed. The programming problem is

$$\underset{\underline{m}_d}{\text{minimize}} \sum_{j=1}^{J} \sum_{i=1}^{n} \gamma_i \, | \, y_{mi}(t_{k+j}, t_k, \underline{m}_j) - f_{mi}(t_{k+j}, t_k) \, | \tag{47a}$$

subject to

$$y_m(t_{k+j}, t_k, \underline{m}_j) = y_m(t_{k+j}, t_k, m(k-1))$$

$$+ \sum_{q=1}^{j} SM((j-q+1)\Delta)(m_q - m_{q-1}) \tag{47b}$$

$$B_L \le C_j y_{mi}(t_{k+j}, t_k, \underline{m}_j) + D_j m_j \le B_U, \quad j = 1, ..., J \tag{47c}$$

$$m_j = \overline{m}, \quad j = R+1, R+2, ..., J, \tag{47d}$$

where $\overline{m}$ is a vector of steady-state controls calculated by the setpoint optimizer; $\underline{m}_j$, a vector of controls at interval j in the future; $\underline{m}_j = m_1, m_2, ..., m_j$; and C_j and D_j, $n \times n$ weighting matrices.

Proceeding in a manner completely analogous to that of Section IV,B, one obtains the standard forms given by (36) and (39), except that the indicated sums are over the index i as well as j.

An important property of the constraints given by (47b) is that they are block lower triangular. Therefore, the multivariable equivalent of the matrix A in (36b) is also block lower triangular, and this property can be used to advantage in obtaining an initial feasible solution and the optimal solution of (47), as shown in the next section.

VI. CONSTRAINED CONTROLLER LINEAR PROGRAM

A. SQUARE SYSTEMS

The general form of the optimization algorithm considered in this section is

$$\text{minimize} \sum_{i=1}^{Jn} |x_i|, \tag{48a}$$

where J is the number of steps in the time horizon and n the number of outputs, which equals the inputs, subject to

$$X_L^+ = AX + d_L \ge 0$$

$$X_U^+ = -AX + d_U \ge 0. \tag{48b}$$

As shown in Section IV, any problem of the form given by (32)–(34) can be reduced to that given by (48) if the number of steps J in the time horizon is equal to the number of step changes allowed for the control effort.

The trivial solution to (48a) is $x_i = 0$ for all i, and this solution is the optimal solution provided that $d_L \geq 0$ and $d_U \geq 0$. Thus we need only consider the case where some of the d_L or d_U are less than zero. In this case, the first problem is to find a feasible solution which satisfies the constraints.

1. Obtaining a Feasible Solution

Since A in (48b) is block lower triangular, we construct a feasible solution by blocks. Let A be a matrix with square blocks A_{ij}, with $A_{ij} = 0$ for $j > 1$, and let d_{Li} and d_{Ui} be the vector partition of d_L and d_U which corresponds to "row" A_i. Starting with the first block, A_{11}, d_{L1}, d_{U1}, we look for elements of d_{L1} or d_{U1} which are less than zero [note that both $(d_{L1})_j$ and $(d_{U1})_j$ cannot both be less than zero by definition of d_L and d_U]. Starting with the first element of d_{L1} which is less than zero [say $(d_{L1})_r$], we find the largest element in magnitude in row r of A_{11} and note the X_1 variable associated with this largest element, say $(X_1)_q$. We then proceed to the next element in d_{L1}, which is less than zero, and find the element in that row of A_{11} which has the largest magnitude, exclusive of the coefficient of $(X_1)_q$ which was selected previously. We proceed in the above fashion examining all the rows of A_{11} associated with the elements of d_{L1} and d_{U1} which are less than zero and picking out elements of X_1 which have the largest coefficients, making sure not to choose any element of X_1 more than once. Having completed the first block, we proceed to the second block and choose elements of X_2 associated with those values of d_{L2} and d_{U2} which are less than zero. After having proceeded in such a fashion through all the blocks, we will finally have a number of equations (say R) equal to the number of elements in d_L and d_U which are less than zero. This set of equations can be written as

$$\hat{X}^+ = \hat{A}\hat{X} + \tilde{A}\tilde{X} + \hat{d} \geq 0 \tag{49}$$

where $\hat{d}$ is defined to be a vector of the elements of d_L and d_U which are less than zero; X^+, the subset of X_L^+ and X_U^+ associated with the elements of d_L and d_U which are less than zero; $\hat{X}$, an R vector of elements of X selected in the above procedure; $\tilde{X}$, a Jn – R vector of all of the elements of X not selected in the above procedure; $\hat{A}$, the R × R submatrix associated with $\hat{X}$; and $\tilde{A}$, the R × (Jn – R) submatrix associated with the vector X.

Because of the manner in which the elements of $\hat{X}$ have been selected, the diagonal elements of $\hat{A}$ are larger in magnitude than any other elements in their row. Thus, it is likely that $\hat{A}$ is nonsingular. Solving (49) for $\hat{X}$ gives

$$\hat{X} = \hat{A}^{-1}(\hat{X}^+ - \hat{d} - \tilde{A}\tilde{X}). \tag{50}$$

The above equation for $\hat{X}$ yields a feasible solution for our problem for any choice of $\tilde{X}$ and any $\hat{X}^+ \geq 0$. The problem now is to find out whether this partition of X into $\tilde{X}$ and $\hat{X}$ is the partition which minimized (48a) when $\tilde{X} = 0$ and $\hat{X}^+ = 0$.

2.   Test for Optimality

At this point we assume that we have a feasible solution of (48b) and we wish to see if that solution satisfies (48a). The feasible solution will be in the form given by (49) or (50), where $\hat{X}$ has dimension equal to the number of constraints which lie on the boundary. That is, the dimension of $\hat{X}$ is generally equal to the number of strict equalities in (48b). The vector $\tilde{X}$ is composed of all X variables not in $\hat{X}$. The minimization problem given by (48) can then be expressed in terms of $\hat{X}$ and $\tilde{X}$ as

$$\underset{X, \hat{X}^+}{\text{minimize}} \left(\sum_i |x_i| + \sum_j |x_j| \right) \tag{51}$$

subject to (50) and

$$X_L^{++} = \hat{A}_L^+\hat{X} + \tilde{A}_L^+\tilde{X} + d_L^+ \geq 0 \tag{52a}$$

$$X_U^{++} = -\hat{A}_U^+\hat{X} - \tilde{A}_L^+\tilde{X} + d_U^+ \geq 0 \tag{52b}$$

$$\hat{X}^+ \geq 0, \tag{52c}$$

where X_L^{++} and X_U^{++} contain all the slack variables of X^+ which are not also in $\hat{X}^+$; $\hat{A}_L^+$ and $\hat{A}_U^+$, the submatrices of A associated with the variables $\hat{X}$; $\hat{A}_L^+$ and $\hat{A}_U^+$, the submatrices of A associated with $\tilde{X}$; and d_L^+ and d_U^+ the elements of d_L and d_U associated with the vectors X_L^{++} and X_U^{++}. In standard linear programming terminology the variables X_L^{++} and X_U^{++} are called basic variables, while the $\hat{X}$ and $\tilde{X}^+$ are termed nonbasic variables. If we were to substitute (50) into (52a) and (52b), we would have the basic variables in terms of the nonbasic variables (actual substitution is not necessary).

To get the objective function (51) in terms of nonbasic variables, we substitute (50) into (51). Let

$$v_i \equiv (-\hat{A}^{-1} \hat{d})_i. \tag{53}$$

For sufficiently small changes in $\tilde{X}$ or $\hat{X}^+$, the value of x_j will be dominated by v_j. Therefore, we can replace the magnitude of x_j as follows:

$$| x_j | = (\text{sgn } v_j) \left(\sum_k b_{jk} x_k^+ + v_j + \sum_k c_{jk} \tilde{x}_k \right), \tag{54}$$

where b_{jk} are elements of the j-th row of A^{-1}, $k = 1, \ldots, R$; c_{jk}, elements of the j-th row of $A^{-1}A$, $k = 1, \ldots, Jn - R$; and R, the number of elements in $\hat{X}$. We now replace the magnitude expressions in X_i by defining

$$\tilde{x}_i \equiv x_i^+ - \tilde{x}_i,$$

where $\tilde{x}_i^+, \tilde{x}_i^- \geq 0$ and then $| \tilde{x}_i | = \tilde{x}_i^+ + \tilde{x}_i^-$, if $(\tilde{x}_i^+)(\tilde{x}_i^-) = 0$. The objective function (51) can now be written as

$$\underset{\tilde{x}_i^+, \tilde{x}_i^-, \hat{x}_j^+}{\text{minimize}} \left(\sum_i (\alpha_i \tilde{x}_i^+ + \beta_i \tilde{x}_i^-) + \sum_j \gamma_j \hat{x}_j^+ + \sum_j | v_j | \right) \tag{55}$$

subject to (52) and $(x_i^+)(x_i^-) = 0$, where

$$\alpha_i \equiv 1 + \sum_j (\text{sgn } v_j) c_{ji}$$

$$\beta_i \equiv 1 - \sum_j (\text{sgn } v_j) c_{ji} \tag{56}$$

$$\gamma_j \equiv \sum_k (\mathrm{sgn}\ v_k) b_{kj}.$$

If the coefficients α_i, β_i, and γ_j for all i and j are greater than zero, then the optimum value for the objective function is obtained when $\tilde{x}_i^+$, $\tilde{x}_i^-$, and $\hat{x}_j^+$ are all zero and the value of the objective function is given by $\sum_j |\ v_j\ |$. The criterion for optimality is then

$$\alpha_i,\ \beta_i,\ \gamma_j > 0. \tag{57}$$

If any of the α_i, β_i, γ_j are exactly zero, then we have a degenerate case, which is handled in the same manner as for a standard linear program. The probability of a degenerate case within machine accuracy is quite small.

3.   Improving the Feasibility Solution

If any of the α_i, β_i, γ_j in (55) is less than zero, then the objective function can be decreasing by increasing the values of $\tilde{x}_i^+$, $\tilde{x}_i^+$, and $\hat{x}_k^+$ associated with the negative α_i, β_j, γ_k. Notice that by the definition of α_i and β_i they cannot both be negative simultaneously; so there is no problem in maintaining the condition that $(\tilde{x}_i^+)(\tilde{x}_i^+) = 0$. Following standard linear programming practice, we now select the most negative of the α_i, β_i, γ_j coefficients and increase the value of the variable associated with that coefficient until one of the variables X_L^{++} or X_U^{++} becomes zero [cf. (52a, b)]. If none of the X_L^{++} or X_U^{++} becomes zero, then we have an unbounded problem, which in our case means that our original problem was not posed properly.) A pivot operation is performed to replace the variable which has been increased with the $(X^{++})_k$ variable which has become zero. This pivot operation is the same as that for a standard simplex algorithm and requires only that we express the variable which has been increased in terms of the new $(X^{++})_k$ variable using the equation for which $(X^{++})_k$ become zero. The coefficients α_i, β_i, and γ_j are now updated to reflect the new nonbasic variables. If the variable which was replaced in the nonbasic set was either a $\tilde{X}^+$ or $\tilde{X}^-$ variable, then the associated variable $\tilde{X}^+$ or $\tilde{X}^-$ is also removed from the nonbasic set. At this point the optimality criterion given in Section VI,B (i.e., all α_i, β_i, $\gamma_k > 0$) is checked and the procedure is repeated if the solution is nonoptimal.

4. Some Simple Examples

a. A Single-Input, Single-Output Process with a Controller Which Looks Two Steps Ahead. In this case, the optimization problem given by (48) becomes

$$\text{minimize } (|\, x_i\, | + |\, x_2\, |) \tag{58a}$$

subject to

$$x_{L1}^{+} = a_{11}x_1 + d_{L1} \geq 0 \tag{58b}$$

$$x_{L2}^{+} = a_{12}x_1 + a_{22}x_2 + d_{L2} \geq 0 \tag{58c}$$

$$x_{U1}^{+} = -a_{11}x_1 + d_{U1} \geq 0 \tag{58d}$$

$$x_{U2}^{+} = -a_{12}x_1 - a_{22}x_2 + d_{U2} \geq 0, \tag{58e}$$

where x_1 is the deviation of the process model output from the filter output at time Δ (i.e., the next time step); and x_2 is the deviation of the process model output from the filter output at time 2Δ. If either d_{L1} or d_{U1} is less than zero, then we must set $x_1 = -d_{L1}/a_{11}$ or d_{U1}/a_{11} and the control effort is obtained from

$$m(k) = m_{k-1} + [x_1 + f_m(t_{k+1}, t_k) - y_m(t_k + \Delta, t_k, m_{k-1})]/SM^*(\Delta). \tag{59}$$

Now let us assume that both d_{L1} and d_{U1} are positive, but either d_{L2} or d_{U2} is negative. For the sake of this example, say that d_{L2} is negative. In this case we need to choose either x_1 or x_2 in (58c) so as to satisfy the inequality. Since there are two time steps for this example, there are two blocks (each block is a scalar for this problem) and x_{L2}^{+} is in the second block. Therefore, by the procedure in Section VI,A, we must select x_2 so as to satisfy (58c) because only x_2 is in block 2. [Indeed, if we attempted to select x_1 to satisfy (58c), it is possible that in so doing (58b) will be violated.] Thus,

$$x_2 \equiv \hat{x}_2$$

$$= -(d_{L2} + a_{21}x_1 - x_{L2}^{+})/a_{22}. \tag{60}$$

Substituting (60) into (58) and noting that $\text{sgn}(-d_{L2}/a_{22}) = \text{sgn } a_{22}$, because $d_{L2} < 0$, gives

$$|x_1| + |x_2| = |x_1| + (\text{sgn } a_{22})\left(\frac{a_{21}}{a_{22}}x_1 + \frac{\overset{+}{x_{L2}}}{a_{22}}\right) + \left|\frac{d_{12}}{a_{22}}\right|. \tag{61}$$

The value of $|x_1| + |x_2|$ cannot be decreased by increasing $\overset{+}{x_{L2}}$ since the $(\text{sgn } a_{22})/a_{22}$ term is positive. Only if the magnitude of a_{21}/a_{22} is greater than 1 will it be possible to decrease the objective function by changing x_1. In this case, the variable x_1 should increase if a_{21} is negative and should decrease if a_{21} is positive. From (39), the values of a_{12} and a_{22} depend only on terms which can all be precomputed (i.e., they do not depend on the process operation). Thus, if $|a_{21}/a_{22}|$ is less than 1, there is no need to look at the second step in the two-step algorithm and one may use the calculated value of the control $m^*(H)$, if it lies within constraints, and use the constrained value if $m^*(H)$, as calculated by (24), lies outside the constraints.

When $|a_{21}/a_{22}|$ is greater than 1, the policy for selecting x_1 is to increase or decrease x_1 until either (58b) or (58c) becomes zero (we assumed that both were greater than zero at the start of this discussion). There are four cases, as follows: when $a_{21} < 0$ and $a_{11} < 0$, increase x_1 until $x_1 = d_{L1}/a_{11}$; when $a_{21} < 0$ and $a_{11} > 0$, increase x_1 until $x_1 = d_{U1}/a_{11}$; when $a_{21} > 0$ and $a_{11} < 0$, decrease x_1 until $x_1 = d_{U1}/a_{11}$; when $a_{21} > 0$ and $a_{11} > 0$, decrease x_1 until $x_1 = -d_{L1}/a_{11}$. Based on the value of the precomputed elements a_{21} and a_{11}, we select one of the above cases. We can go through a similar analysis for the case where $d_{L2} > 0$ but $d_{U2} < 0$.

In conclusion, then, for a SISO system, looking two steps ahead, the control system need only check the signs of d_{L2} and d_{U2} to know how to compute $m(k)$, the control effort to be applied at the current step.

   b. A Two-Input, Two-Output Process with a Controller Which Looks One Step Ahead. This problem looks formally very similar to the two-step-ahead SISO problem given above [cf. (58)] since the objective and constraints are

minimize $|x_1| + |x_2|$ $\qquad\qquad\qquad\qquad\qquad\qquad\qquad\qquad$ (62a)

subject to

$$\overset{+}{x_{L1}} = a_{11}x_1 + a_{12}x_2 + d_{L1} \geq 0 \tag{62b}$$

$$\overset{+}{x_{L2}} = a_{21}x_1 + a_{22}x_2 + d_{L2} \geq 0 \tag{62c}$$

$$\overset{+}{x_{U1}} = -a_{11}x_1 - a_{12}x_2 + d_{U1} \geq 0 \tag{62d}$$

$$\overset{+}{x_{U2}} = -a_{21}x_1 - a_{22}x_2 + d_{U2} \geq 0. \tag{62e}$$

Now, however, x_1 and x_2 are the deviations in the outputs y_1 and y_2 from the projected filter output at the next sampling time. Also, in this problem there is only one block to the matrix A in (48) since the time horizon is only one sampling interval long.

If all of the terms d_{L1}, d_{L2}, d_{U1}, d_{U2} are zero, then the minimum of (62) is zero and the control is calculated from (45) with $X = 0$. If any two of the elements of d_L and d_U are negative, then the value of X is computed by solving the appropriate subset of equations (62b)–(62e) with $X_L^+ = X_U^+ = 0$. For example, when d_{L1} and d_{U2} are less than zero:

$$a_{11}x_1 + a_{12}x_2 = -d_{L1}$$

$$a_{21}x_1 + a_{22}x_2 = d_{U2}.$$

Thus, the equation to be solved is always of the form

$$AX = \delta, \tag{63}$$

with δ made up of the appropriate elements of $-d_L$ and d_U.

The last case to be considered is when one element of d_L or d_U is negative. For the sake of example, we assume that d_{L1} is negative.

Our first problem is to find a feasible solution of (62). Following the procedure given in Section VI,A, we examine (62b) for the element of X whose coefficient has the largest magnitude. Let us assume for this example that $|a_{12}| > |a_{11}|$. Then the proposed procedures is to solve (62b) for x_2 in terms of all the other variables, giving

$$x_2 = (x_{L1}^+ - d_{L1} - a_{11}x_1)/a_{12}$$
$$\equiv \hat{x}_2. \tag{64}$$

[Note: If we had been dealing with a 3×3 system and two elements of d_L or d_U were negative (say d_{L1} and d_{L2}), then we would have proceeded to the next equation, where we would select another element of X whose coefficient has the largest magnitude (say x_3) and then solved simultaneously for x_2 and x_3 from these two equations in terms of x_{L1}^+, x_{L2}^+, d_{L1}, d_{L2}, and x_1.]

Substituting (64) into (62a) gives

$$|x_1| + |x_2| = |x_1| + (\text{sgn } a_{12})\left(\frac{x_{L1}^+}{a_{12}} - \frac{a_{11}}{a_{12}}x_1\right) + \left|\frac{d_{L1}}{a_{12}}\right| \tag{65}$$

The value of the objective function in (65) can be decreased only if the coefficient of x_{L1}^+ is negative or if the coefficient of x_1 is greater than 1 in magnitude (so that the coefficient of x_1^+ or x_1^- is less than zero, where $x_1 = x_1^+ - x_1^-$). However, by our previous assumption used to solve for x_2 [cf. (64)], the magnitude of a_{11}/a_{12} is less than 1. Thus the current solution is optimal and the control effort is found by setting $x_{L1}^+ = x_1 = 0$ and solving for x_2 in (64). These values of x_1 and x_2 are then substituted into (59) to get m(k).

The complete algorithm for calculating the single step control for a two input–two output system is to calculate d_L and d_U and use the following values for the vector X in (59):

1) If $d_L, d_U > 0, X = 0$;

2) If two elements of (d_L, d_U) are negative, then X is given by (63) and m(k) is calculated from (45);

3) If only one element of d_L or d_U is negative, then X is obtained by setting $x_j = \delta_i/a_{ij}$

$$x_k = 0, \quad k \neq j, \quad j = 1, 2, \quad k = 2, 1,$$

where $\delta_i = d_{Ui}$ or $-d_{Li}$, $i = 1, 2$, and d_{Ui} or $d_{Li} < 0$; and a_{ij} is the element in row i with the largest magnitude.

B.   NONSQUARE SYSTEMS

In this section we develop an algorithm to solve the following problem:

$$\underset{x_i}{\text{minimize}} \sum_{i=1}^{n} |x_i| \tag{66}$$

subject to

$$X = SW - b, \quad \dim X = n \tag{67}$$

$$X^+ = SW + d, \quad \dim X^+ = r, \dim W = p \tag{68}$$

$$x_i^+ \geq 0, \quad \text{for all } x_i^+. \tag{69}$$

The above problem differs from that given above in that the matrix S is not generally square with dim W < dim X.

To solve (66) we select a subset of p equations from (67) and solve for W in terms of that subset, denoted by $\tilde{X}$. That is,

$$W = \tilde{S}^{-1}(\tilde{X} + b),\tag{70}$$

where the tilde denotes that we are using only a subset of the elements of X or S. Substituting (70) into (68) gives

$$X^+ = A\tilde{S}^{-1}\tilde{X} + d + A\tilde{S}^{-1}\tilde{b}.\tag{71}$$

Defining $\hat{X}$ as all of the variables of X not included in $\tilde{X}$, and expressing $\hat{X}$ in terms of $\tilde{X}$, gives

$$\hat{X} = \hat{S}\tilde{S}^{-1}(\tilde{X} + \tilde{b}) - \hat{b}.\tag{72}$$

Let us now partition the objective function given by (66) into terms $\hat{X}$ and $\tilde{X}$. That is,

$$\text{minimize} \left(\sum |\tilde{x}_i| + \sum |x_i|\right).\tag{73}$$

As in Section VI,A, we now replace the magnitudes of the $\hat{x}_i$ as follows:

$$|\hat{x}| = [\text{sgn}(\hat{S}\tilde{S}^{-1}\tilde{b} - \hat{b})_i](\hat{S}\tilde{S}^{-1}\tilde{X} + \hat{S}\tilde{S}^{-1}\tilde{b} - \hat{b})_i.\tag{74}$$

Also, we split $\tilde{x}_i$ as

$$\tilde{x}_i = \tilde{x}_i^+ - \tilde{x}_i^-$$

$$x_i^+ \geq 0 \tag{75}$$

$$x_i^- \geq 0.$$

Then $|\tilde{x}_i| = \tilde{x}_i^+ + \tilde{x}_i^-;\ (\tilde{x}_i^+)(\tilde{x}_i^-) = 0$. Collecting terms, the optimization problem becomes

$$\underset{\tilde{x}_i}{\text{minimize}} \left(\sum \beta_i x_i^+ + \sum \gamma_i \tilde{x}_i^-\right),\tag{76}$$

where β_i and γ_i are linear combinations of the coefficients of x_i and x_i.

If all the β_i and γ_i are greater than zero, we have the optimal solution. Otherwise, select the most negative β_i or γ_i and increase the associated $\tilde{x}_i^+$ or $\tilde{x}_i^-$ until either one of the $\hat{x}_i$ or x_i^+ becomes zero. At this point the new $\hat{x}_i^+$ or $\tilde{x}_i^+$ is brought into the basis set in place of the $\tilde{x}_i^+$ or $\hat{x}_i^-$ by a pivot operation. Also, if desired, the new matrix $\tilde{S}^{-1}$ can be obtained by a rank-one update of the form

$$(\tilde{S} + \theta \varphi^T)^{-1} = \tilde{S}^{-1} - \frac{\tilde{S}^{-1} \theta \varphi^T \tilde{S}^{-1}}{1 + \varphi^T \tilde{S}^{-1} \theta},$$

where θ is a vector with elements $\delta_{ij} = 1$ if $i = j$, $= 0$ if $i \neq j$; $\varphi = \tilde{S}_r - \tilde{S}_j$; $\tilde{S}_k$, the k-th row of the matrix $\tilde{S}$; j, the index of the row of $\tilde{S}$ being replaced in the basis set; and r, the index of the row of $\tilde{S}$ coming into the basis set.

VII. EXAMPLES

In this section we demonstrate the results of applying both single and multistep methods to several example systems drawn from actual processes. The single input–single output process examples use different models of the laboratory heat exchanger shown in Fig. 4. The two input–two output example was supplied by Exxon Corporation and is an approximate, normalized model of how the desired overheat and bottom compositions of a multicomponent column respond to changes in normalized distillate flow and reboiler heat flows.

A.   SINGLE INPUT–SINGLE OUTPUT SYSTEMS

The following three models all approximate the dynamics of the heat exchanger shown in Fig. 4.

$$y/m \cong \frac{6.5e^{-19s}}{8s + 1} \tag{77a}$$

$$\cong \frac{6.5e^{-16s}}{(8s + 1)(3.1s + 1)} \tag{77b}$$

$$\cong \frac{6.5e^{-13s}}{(8s + 1)(3.1s + 1)(1.7s + 1)(1.4s + 1)}. \tag{77c}$$

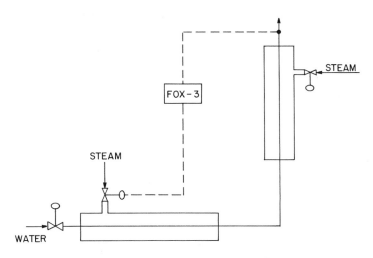

Fig. 4. Laboratory heat exchanger.

The filters used to make the controller G_I realizable for each of the above models are

$$F = \frac{e^{-19s}}{\varepsilon_1 s + 1}; \qquad F_m = \frac{1}{\varepsilon_1 s + 1}, \qquad F_R = e^{-19s} \qquad (78a)$$

$$F = \frac{e^{-16s}}{(\varepsilon_2 s + 1)^2}; \qquad F_m = \frac{1}{(\varepsilon_2 s + 1)^2}, \qquad F_R = e^{-16s} \qquad (78b)$$

$$F = \frac{e^{-13s}}{(\varepsilon_3 s + 1)^4}; \qquad F_m = \frac{1}{(\varepsilon_3 s + 1)^4}, \qquad F_R = e^{-13s} \qquad (78c)$$

The values of the filter time constants ε_1, ε_2, and ε_3 above would normally be chosen to make the control system stable and robust in spite of the anticipated modeling errors. However, since it is our purpose in this article to explore how easily and effectively the proposed algorithms deal with constraints, we will deal only with simulations where there are no modeling errors. The various algorithms have been applied to simulations with modeling errors with the expected results that the control systems are well behaved if the values of the filter time constant are properly chosen [1, 7, 8]. Indeed, the single step algorithm has been applied to the laboratory heat exchanger of Fig. 4 with good results [8].

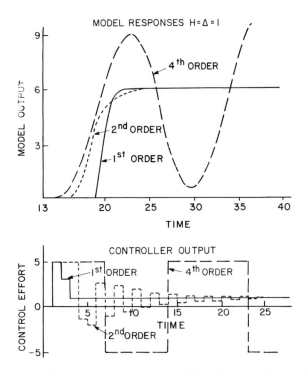

Fig. 5. Response of various heat exchanger models using a single step algorithm.

Because our aim is to compare algorithms, we select the time constants in (78) so as to yield control systems which respond in roughly the same length of time, including the dead time. Thus we choose $\varepsilon_1 = 0.5$, $\varepsilon_2 = 1.1$, and $\varepsilon_3 = 1.1$. (The selection of $\varepsilon_2 = \varepsilon_3 = 1.1$ rather than 1.0 comes about for historical rather than technical reasons.)

The results of applying the single step algorithm given by (24) and (26) with a sampling interval Δ of 1 and a time horizon $H = \Delta$ are shown in Fig. 5. [The values of $S_m(1)$ are 0.764, 0.113, and 0.00325 for the models given by (78a–c) and $m_U = 5$, $m_L = -5$.] Notice that the first- and second-order models yield exactly the expected results. However, the control effort for the second-order model is somewhat oscillatory. The algorithm *is unstable* when applied to the fourth-order model. This instability can be viewed as arising from the momentum of the process model (i.e., the derivatives of the output), which is ignored in the single step algorithm. Alternately, the instability can be looked at as arising from the fact that the z transform of the fourth-order model has zeros outside the unit circle [9], which become unstable poles when the controller attempts to force G_m to

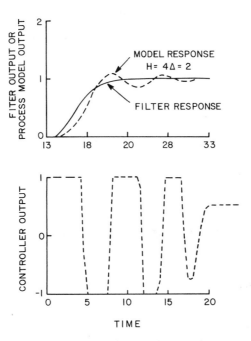

Fig. 6. Response of fourth-order heat exchanger model using a time horizon of four sampling intervals.

track F_m. In either case the only alternative for the single step algorithm is to increase the time horizon beyond the sampling interval, as shown in Fig. 6.

Figure 7 shows the results of applying a three step [cf. (32) and (34)] algorithm for the fourth-order heat exchanger model. The time horizon is the sum of the number of steps (i.e., $H = 3\Delta$ and $R = J = 3$). The algorithm is stable for all values of the filter time constant, but becomes less oscillatory as the filter time constant is increased.

Figure 8 shows how the time horizon influences the calculation for a filter time constant of zero using the configuration of Fig. 2. The problem formulation is that given by (32)–(34) with $R = 3$ and different values for J. Note that a value for J of 16 in this case corresponds to a value of J of 3 for the configuration of Fig. 3 because the dead time is 13 units. For comparison, the response shown in Fig. 7 for $\varepsilon = 1.1$ is also reproduced in Fig. 8. Again, $J = 16$ because of the 13-unit dead time. Since the amount of computation increases more than proportion-

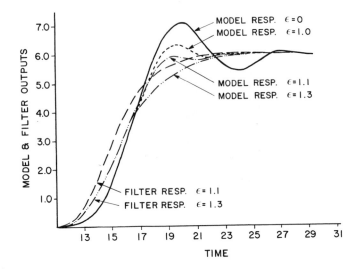

Fig. 7. Effect of filter time constant on the response of the fourth-order heat exchanger model (77c) and filter (78c).

ally with the length of the time horizon, it clearly pays to increase the filter time constant rather than the time horizon. Also, the configuration of Fig. 3 is clearly to be preferred.

B.   A TWO INPUT–TWO OUTPUT SYSTEM

A normalized version of a distillation column model supplied by Exxon is

$$\hat{G}_p(s) = \begin{bmatrix} \dfrac{240e^{-1.5s}}{1 + 2s} & \dfrac{-0.44e^{-75s}}{1 + s} \\[3mm] \dfrac{-75e^{-1.625s}}{1 + 2.5s} & \dfrac{-0.46}{1 + 1.25s} \end{bmatrix}. \tag{79}$$

The constraints on the controls are

$$-2 \le m_1(t) \le 1$$

$$-1 \le m_2(t) \le 1.$$

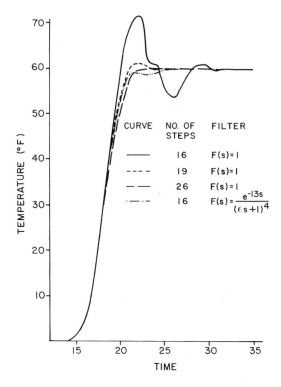

Fig. 8. Effect of time horizon and filter selection on response of fourth-order heat exchanger model using three degrees of freedom for the controller and the configuration of Fig. 2.

Following the procedure outlines in Sections II and III gives a filter of the form

$$
F = \begin{bmatrix} \dfrac{e^{-1.5s}}{\varepsilon_1 s + 1} & 0 \\[3mm] 0 & \dfrac{e^{-0.75s}}{\varepsilon_2 s + 1} \end{bmatrix}
\tag{80}
$$

$$
F_m = \mathrm{diag}\left(\frac{1}{\varepsilon_1 s + 1}, \frac{1}{\varepsilon_2 s + 1} \right)
$$

$$F_R = \text{diag}\left(e^{-1.55}, e^{-0.755}\right)$$

Multiplying (79) through by the inverse of the filter dead times to remove the time delays as outlined in Section III gives

$$F_R^{-1}\hat{G}_p(s) = \begin{bmatrix} \dfrac{240}{1 + 2s} & \dfrac{-0.44e^{0.75s}}{1 + s} \\ \\ \dfrac{-75e^{-0.875s}}{1 + 2.5s} & \dfrac{-0.46e^{0.75s}}{1 + 1.25s} \end{bmatrix}. \tag{81}$$

The model G_m is given by (19). Choosing B* to make G_m realizable gives

$$B^* = \begin{bmatrix} 1 & 0 \\ 0 & e^{-1.75s} \end{bmatrix} \tag{82}$$

$$G_m = \begin{bmatrix} \dfrac{240}{1 + 25} & \dfrac{-0.44}{185} \\ \\ \dfrac{-75e^{-0.875s}}{1 + 2.55} & \dfrac{-0.46}{1 + 1.255} \end{bmatrix}.$$

The single step algorithm is given by (45) with $\Gamma = I$. The term d* is the value of the controls m(k) if no constraints are violated.

Using a time horizon equal to the sampling time, and choosing the sampling time Δ as 0.25 units, gives the following values for the step response matrix and its inverse.

$$SM(0.25) = \begin{bmatrix} 28.2 & -0.0973 \\ 0 & -0.0834 \end{bmatrix} \tag{83a}$$

$$SM(0.25)^{-1} = \begin{bmatrix} 0.0355 & -0.0414 \\ 0 & -11.99 \end{bmatrix}. \tag{83b}$$

Following the procedure given in Section VI,B,2, the single step algorithm for this example is

1) Calculate d*, if $m_L \le d^* \le m_U$, then set m(k) = d*;

2) If only $d_1{}^*$ violates its constraints, then set $m_1(k)$ equal to the violated constraint and calculate $m_2(k)$ from

$$m_2(k) = d_2^* + \frac{11.99}{0.414}[m_1(k) - d_1^*]. \tag{84}$$

In the above case, y_2 will deviate from its desired trajectory by an amount given by

$$x_2 = \frac{m_1(k) - d_1^*}{-0.414}. \tag{85}$$

If the value of $m_2(k)$ given by (84) now violates it constraints, set $m_2(k)$ to the violated constraint. In this situation both y_1 and y_2 will deviate from their desired trajectories.

3) If only $d_2{}^*$ violates its constraints, set $m_2(k)$ equal to the violated constraints and calculate $m_1(k)$ from

$$m_1(k) = d_1^* + \frac{0.0414}{11.99}[m_2(k) - d_2^*]. \tag{86}$$

In this case $y_2{}^*$ will again violate its constraints by an amount given by x_2, where

$$x_2 = \frac{m_2(k) - d_2^*}{-11.99}. \tag{87}$$

4) If both $d_1{}^*$ and $d_2{}^*$ violate constraints, then both $m_1(k)$ and $m_2(k)$ are set to the violated constraints.

Notice that in the above algorithm it is always y_2 that deviates from its desired trajectory whenever one constraint, on either m_1 or m_2, is violated. The reason for this resides in the magnitudes of the elements of the inverse step response matrix $SM(\Delta)^{-1}$ and the weighting coefficients Γ. If we were to change Γ from the identity matrix to a diagonal matrix where x_1 is weighted sufficiently less heavily than x_2 (e.g., $\gamma_1 = 0.85$), then the (1, 1) element of $[\Gamma SM(\Delta)]^{-1}$ will have a larger magnitude than the (1, 2) elements and the output y_1 would track the filter output whenever $d_1{}^*$ violates the constraints on m_1.

The response of the single step algorithm applied to the Exxon example, for a change in setpoint in y_1 from 0 to 1, is shown in Fig. 9. Also shown in Fig. 9 is the response of a multistep algorithm with three degrees of freedom for the controller and a time horizon of 12 units using the configuration of Fig. 2.

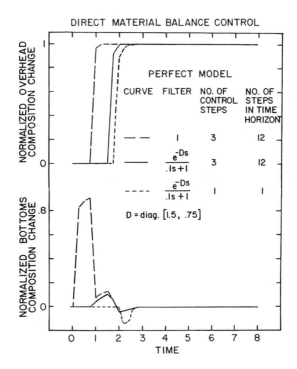

Fig. 9. Response of the distillation column model to a step change in setpoint using a single step algorithm and a multistep algorithm.

VIII. CONCLUSIONS

The control configuration given by Fig. 3 leads to controllers which are easier to implement than those of Fig. 2 and give comparable responses. The single step algorithm, developed from a linear programming perspective, is simple to implement and yields good control for the example problems. More analysis and examples are needed to see whether the single step algorithm will continue to show good performance for higher-order and/or higher-dimensional multivariable processes. In the latter cases it will probably be necessary to choose the time horizon to be longer than the sampling time.

The multistep algorithms have modest computational loads and also yield good control for appropriately chosen time horizons and sampling intervals.

REFERENCES

1. J. R. PARRISH and C. B. BROSILOW, "Inferential Control Applications," *Automatica* *21*, Sept. (1985).
2. D. B. PRETT and R. D. GILLETE, "Optimization and Constrained Multivariable Control of a Catalytic Cracking Unit," *Joint Autom. Control Conf. Proc.* San Francisco (1980).
3. R. K. MEHRA, J. ROUHANI, J. ETERNO RICHALET, and A. ROULT, "Model Algorithmic Control: Review and Recent Development," *Eng. Found. Conf. Chem. Process Control II* Sea Island, GA (1982).
4. C. B. BROSILOW *et al.*, "Inferential Control of Processes," *AIChE J.* *42*, 485-509 (1978).
5. C. B. BROSILOW, "The Structure and Design of Smith Predictors from the Viewpoint of Inferential Control," *JACC* Denver (1979).
6. M. MORARI, "Internal Model Control – Theory and Applications," *5th Int. IFAC/IMEDO Conf. Instrum. Autom. Antwerp* (1983).
7. S. C. CHEN, "Control System Design for Multivariable Uncertain Processes," Ph.D. Thesis, C.W.R.U. (1984).
8. L. POPPIEL, "Constrained Control," Control of Industrial Systems Program Sponsor's Progress Report, May 1984.
9. K. J. ÅSTRÖM, P. HAGANDER, and J. STERNBY, "Zeroes of Sampled Systems," *Automatica 20*, 31-38 (1984).

TECHNIQUES FOR THE IDENTIFICATION OF DISTRIBUTED SYSTEMS USING THE FINITE ELEMENT APPROXIMATION

K. Y. LEE

Department of Electrical Engineering
The Pennsylvania State University
University Park, Pennsylvania 16802

I. INTRODUCTION

A distributed system is a system where the variables are distributed over a spatial domain and are governed by some operations which depend on spatial variables as well as time. Many physical systems as well as environmental and ecological systems are known to be distributed systems and described by partial differential equations [1–5]. Thus for the past decade a good measure of effort has been devoted to developing the optimal control theory for such distributed systems [6–9]. The effort, however, has been limited to providing only the theoretical guidance because of the complexities involved in the computation of partial differential equations.

Toward a more practical means of controlling distributed systems, the idea of sampled-data control [10], discrete-time control [11], pointwise control [12], and a combination of these [13] have been explored. These works have proved that distributed systems can also be controlled like lumped systems using realizable controllers. Nevertheless, the computational requirements again have restricted the use of these controllers.

Apart from the complexities of the distributed systems models, the models themselves involve uncertainties, which are due to modeling assumptions and/or unknown system parameters. Here, the parameters are defined as constant or functionals of spatial variables which appear explicitly in the mathematical model for a distributed system. These parameters must be determined from the knowledge of either experimental or real data. A parameter identification problem is to determine a set of these unknown parameters which will yield the model outputs close to the system outputs from the measurements.

Most of the work on identification can be found for lumped systems that are described by ordinary differential equations. The lumped system representation can be viewed as an approximation of a distributed system under the assumption that the spatial variations can be ignored and the media can be considered homogeneous throughout the volume under consideration.

On the other hand, distributed system models are represented by partial differential equations, integral equations, or integro-differential equations. A distributed system may be approximated by spatial discretizations, such as finite-difference or finite-element methods, which then yield a set of coupled lumped systems, usually of very high dimension [14]. This high dimensionality greatly restricts the use of identification algorithms developed for a lumped system. Therefore, the parameter estimation problem for distributed systems has been the subject of recent years, which attempts to retain the distributed nature as much as possible before it is implemented numerically.

The parameter identification of distributed systems has been surveyed rather recently [15, 16]. Therefore, instead of presenting all different methods, it is planned to show the use of the most representative approximation method, the finite-element method, in the identification of distributed systems. Two different approaches will be demonstrated: one approach is to approximate the distributed system as a finite-dimensional (lumped) system and then develop a parameter identification scheme; another approach is to develop an infinite-dimensional parameter estimation scheme first and then approximate the solution algorithm using the finite-element method. The demonstration will be performed through a general class of large space structures.

II.   PARAMETER IDENTIFICATION PROBLEM

In this section we present the parameter identification problem for large space structures. The basis for the formulation is that a large space structure is a distributed system which is controlled by a few localized actuators and sensors and that the algorithm is to implement in an on-board computer of limited size. The system can be partitioned into a number of components, each of which can be modeled by a simple partial differential equation. The motivation behind this partitioning of a large space structure into localized sections is that the partial equation for a section actually describes the behavior of the spacecraft within a local neighborhood of each point. Since sensors measured and disturbances affect local variables, a reasonable job of parameter identification may be accomplished with "local" parameter identification.

A.   DISTRIBUTED SYSTEM MODEL

Large space structures are made of flexible bodies of simple structures such as strings, beams, membranes, and plates. The dynamic behavior of these flexible structures can be described by a system of partial differential equations of the form:

$$m(x)u_{tt}(x, t) + D_0u_t(x, t) + A_0u(x, t) = F(x, t),$$ (1)

where $u(x, t)$ represents instantaneous displacement of the structure on a spatial domain Ω off its equivalent position due to transient disturbances or the applied force function $F(x, t)$. The displacements can be translational and rotational, and the force can be generalized to include torque as well. The mass density $m(x)$ is positive and bounded on Ω.

The structural stiffness is determined by a time-invariant, symmetric, non-negative differential operator A_0. The domain $D(A_0)$ of A_0 contains all smooth functions satisfying the boundary conditions, and is dense in the infinite-dimensional Hilbert space $H_0 = L^2(\Omega)$, with the usual inner product $(\cdot, \cdot)_0$ and the associated norm $\| \cdot \|_0$. Examples of such operators are:

$$A_0u = \nabla \cdot k(x)\nabla u \quad \text{(membrane)},$$ (2)

where

$$\nabla u = \left(\frac{\partial u}{\partial x_1} \quad \frac{\partial u}{\partial x_2} \quad \frac{\partial u}{\partial x_3} \right)^T,$$

$$A_0u = \frac{\partial^2}{\partial x^2}\left(k(x)\frac{\partial^2 u}{\partial x^2} \right) \quad \text{(free-free beam)},$$ (3)

where $k(x)$ is the stiffness of the structure.

The damping of the structure occurs due to material properties and construction technique. It is represented by the differential operator D_0, but its actual form in a given application is much more difficult to determine than that of stiffness A_0. Some forms that D_0 might take are:

$$D_0u_t = \alpha_0u_t \quad \text{(viscous damping)},$$ (4)

$$D_0u_t = A_0^{1/2}u_t \quad \text{(viscoelastic damping)}.$$ (5)

Of course, there are other possible forms for D_0, and, in general, the damping operator might turn out not to be a differential operator at all. This is the case for some types of damping which are related to frequency in a highly nonlinear way.

The applied force distribution is

$$F(x, t) = F_C(x, t) + F_D(x, t), \tag{6}$$

where F_D represents the external disturbance forces on the system (and possible nonlinearities) and F_C represents the control forces due to M actuators

$$F_C(x, t) = B_0 f = \sum_{i=1}^{M} b_i(x) f_i(t), \tag{7}$$

where the actuator amplitudes are $f_i(t)$ and the actuator influence functions are $b_i(x)$ in H_0. These are usually localized or point devices so that $b_i(x)$ is approximated by $\delta(x - x_i)$, where x_i is a point in Ω. However, they do not need to be point sources.

The system is observed by P sensors in the form

$$y = C_0 u + E_0 u_t, \tag{8}$$

where $y_j(t) = (c_j, u)_0 + (e_j, u_t)_0$, $1 \leq j \leq P$, and c_j and e_j are influence functions of position and velocity sensors, respectively, in H_0. Again, these are usually localized or point devices.

Possible disturbance forces include thermal gradients, solar pressure, gravity gradient, aerodynamic forces due to atmospheric effects, and meteorite collisions, as well as on-board disturbacnes due to pumps and motors. Control actuators may be thrusters, control-moment gyros, momentum wheels, and interelement devices, while the sensors might be a mixture of position, velocity, and acceleration devices. In our presentation, we consider the disturbance-free force function, i.e., $F_D = 0$.

B.   BASIC PROBLEM FORMULATION

Equation (1) is a linearized system model of the large space structures, and thus the model does not represent the true model. Furthermore, parameters in the model are not known to a designer in full. Therefore, an identification methods should be developed to estimate these parameters for the best representation of the system.

Let $q(x)$ be the vector of system parameters in (1), i.e., $q(x) = [m(x), k(x), \alpha_0]$ for the translational model of (1) with a constant damping coefficient. Let Q in a compact subset of $L_\infty(\Omega) \times L_\infty(\Omega) \times R$ be an admissible set of parameters.

Then the parameter identification problem is to determine the parameter vector $q^*(x) \in Q$ which minimizes

$$J(q) = \frac{1}{2T} \int_0^T < (y - z), R(y - z) > dt, \tag{9}$$

where z is the measurement of output

$$z(x, t) = y(x, t) + e(x, t) \tag{10}$$

with a measurement error $e(x, t)$.

The symbol $\langle \cdot, \cdot \rangle$ denotes the spatial inner product in H_0 defined by

$$\langle (y - z), R(y - z) \rangle = \int_\Omega \int_\Omega [y(x, t) - z(x, t)]^T$$
$$\times R(x, s, t)[y(s, t) - z(s, t)] \, dx \, ds, \tag{11}$$

where the weighting matrix R is positive-definite and symmetric, i.e., $R(x, s, t) = R(s, x, t)^T$.

As mentioned earlier, the measurement is normally available on a set of discrete spatial points $x_1, x_2, \ldots, x_P$, where P is the total number of sensors. These measurements can be either displacement, velocity, or acceleration. If we assume only the displacement measurement, we can rewrite (8) and (10) as

$$z(x_i, t) = c_i u(x_i, t) + e(x_i, t), \tag{12}$$

where $c_i, i = 1, 2, \ldots, P$ are the influence constants. In this case the performance functional J can be written as

$$J = \int_0^T \sum_{i=1}^P [c_i u(x_i, t) - z(x_i, t)]^T R_i(t)[c_i u(x_i, t) - z(x_i, t)] \, dt \tag{13}$$

III. INFINITE-DIMENSIONAL IDENTIFICATION

There are two basic approaches to the parameter identification problem of distributed systems. One approach is to develop a parameter estimation algorithm for the partial differential equation (1), without any discrete approximation. This approach retains the distributed nature of the system in the identification algorithm and allows the discretization at the last minute for numerical calculation. An alternative approach is to discretize the partial differential equation into a set of ordinary differential equations and then reformulate an identification problem in a finite-dimensional vector space. Since the identification is based on the approximated model, this approach is viewed as less accurate compared to the first one.

A. INFINITE-DIMENSIONAL FORMULATION

The state of a lumped system (usually described by ordinary differential equations) can be viewed as a point in a finite-dimensional Euclidean vector space. However, in distributed systems governed by partial differential equations as in (1), the state is a function, at each point in time, defined on a given spatial domain, or, alternatively, the state is a point in an infinite-dimensional (function) space. Therefore, distributed systems (1) can be viewed as an abstract second-order differential equation in an infinite-dimensional (function) space. In order to formulate the corresponding infinite-dimensional identification problem, we define Hilbert spaces

$$V = H_2(\Omega), \quad H = H_0(\Omega) = L^2(\Omega), \tag{14}$$

where $H_m(\Omega)$ is the usual Sobolev space of degree m defined over the domain Ω. If we identify V to be a dense subspace of H, and H as its dual, we have the following imbeddings:

$$V \subset H \subset V', \tag{15}$$

where V' is the dual space of V.
    We can now rewrite (1) in linear operator form as

$$Mu_{tt}(t) + Du_t(t) + Au(t) = Bf(t), \quad t \in [0, T], \tag{16}$$

with initial conditions

$$u(0) = u_0 \in V \tag{17}$$

$$u_t(0) = u_1 \in H \tag{18}$$

and the output function

$$y(t) = Cu(t). \tag{19}$$

The input function is given by $f \in L_2(0, T; H)$.

The identification problem can now be formulated as an abstract problem of determining the parameter vector $q*(x) \in Q$ which minimizes

$$J(q) = \frac{1}{2T} \int_0^T [y(t) - z(t)]^T R(t)[y(t) - z(t)], \tag{20}$$

subject to $y(t)$ being the solution to (16)–(19).

B.   DEVELOPMENT OF
      INFINITE-DIMENSIONAL ALGORITHM

The identification problem defined by (16)–(20) can be viewed as an optimal control problem, where the parameter vector $q(x)$ is considered as the control. Since the parameters are in the coefficients of (16), the problem can be approached as an optimal coefficient control problem [17]. The general nonlinear control problem has been solved using the variational approach by Lions [8], and applied to a class of identification problems by Chavent [18] and Lee and Hossain [4]. The approach to be presented here will be a generalization of these developments to a broader class of second-order functional differential equations.

We first combine (16) and (20) to define an augmented cost functional

$$J_a(q) = \frac{1}{2T} \int_0^T [y(t) - z(t)]^T R(t)[y(t) - z(t)] \, dt,$$

$$+ \int_0^T p(t)^T [Mu_{tt}(t) + Du_t(t) + Au(t) - Bf(t)] \, dt, \tag{21}$$

where $p(t)$ is an adjoint state variable belonging to V. Following the variational approach, the necessary condition for the minimization of the equivalent cost functional J_a is that its first variation vanishes for an arbitrary admissible parameter variation. The variation is

$$\delta J_a = \int_0^T P^T \frac{\partial}{\partial q} [Mu_{tt} + Du_t + Au - Bf] \, \delta q \, dt$$

$$= \int_0^T [p^T M \, \delta u_{tt} + p^T D \, \delta u_t + p^T A \, \delta u + \frac{1}{T} \delta u^T C^T R(Cu - z)] \, dt. \tag{22}$$

The next step is the elimination of δu_{tt} and δu_t in (22). By the repeated use of the integration by parts,

$$\int_0^T p^T M \, \delta u_{tt} \, dt = p^T M \, \delta u_t \Big|_0^T - \int_0^T p_t^T M \, \delta u_t \, dt$$

$$\tag{23}$$

$$= p^T M \, \delta u_t \Big|_0^T - p_t^T M \, \delta u \Big|_0^T + \int_0^T p_{tt}^T M \, \delta u \, dt.$$

Since the initial conditions are given by (17) and (18), their variations are zero, i.e.,

$$\delta u(0) = \delta u_t(0) = 0. \tag{24}$$

By choosing the final conditions

$$p(T) = p_t(T) = 0, \tag{25}$$

(23) becomes

$$\int_0^T p^T M \, \delta u_{tt} \, dt = \int_0^T p_{tt}^T M \, \delta u \, dt$$

$$\tag{26}$$

$$= \int_0^T \delta u^T M^* p_{tt} \, dt,$$

where M* is the adjoint operator of M defined by

$$(u, Mv) = (M^*u, v). \tag{27}$$

Similarly,

$$\int_0^T p^T D \, \delta u_t \, dt = p^T D \, \delta u \Big|_0^T - \int_0^T p_t^T D \, \delta u \, dt$$

$$\tag{28}$$

$$= -\int_0^T p_t^T D \, \delta u \, dt = -\int_0^T \delta u^T D^* p_t \, dt.$$

Substituting (26) and (28) into (22), the variation becomes

$$\delta J_a = \int_0^T p^T \frac{\partial}{\partial q} (Mu_{tt} + Du_t + Au - Bf) \, \delta q \, dt$$

$$+ \int_0^T \partial u^T \left[M^* p_{tt} - D^* p_t + A^* p + \frac{1}{T} C^T R(Cu - z) \right] dt. \tag{29}$$

In order to obtain a direct relationship between δJ_a and δq for an arbitrary δu, it is necessary to require the second integral to be zero. This results in the adjoint differential equation

$$m^* p_{tt}(t) - D^* p_t(t) + A^* p(t) = -\frac{1}{T} C^T R(Cu - z) \tag{30}$$

with the final conditions

$$p(T) = p_t(T) = 0. \tag{31}$$

Finally, the variation in (29) becomes

$$\delta J_a = \int_0^T p^T \frac{\partial}{\partial q} (Mu_{tt} + Du_t + Au - Bf) \, \delta q \, dt, \tag{32}$$

which is a direct relationship between the parameter variation and the cost variation.

Since the necessary condition for the optimal parameter vector $q^*(x)$ requires that the first variation δJ_a is zero, an iterative algorithm can be used to choose the parameter variation δq in the direction of decreasing δJ_a.

In summary, the necessary condition for the optimal parameter vector q^* is that it satisfies the system equations (16)–(19), and the adjoint equations (30)–(31); and, moreover, the first variation in (32) is zero.

IV.   FINITE-ELEMENT APPROXIMATION

In the previous section, the necessary condition was developed for the solution of an infinite-dimensional parameter identification problem. The conditions, however, call for solving partial differential equations in the system model as well as in its adjoint system. Except for very few simple systems, closed-form solutions are not available, and one must seek some approximation schemes to solve partial differential equations.

Spatial approximation can also be performed before formulating the identification problem. This will result in a finite-dimensional identification problem, which will be presented in the next section. Whether one prefers the infinite-dimensional formulation or the finite-dimensional formulation, an approximation scheme must be utilized for numerical implementation. Lee [14] presented the finite-difference, finite-element, and integration methods to decompose distributed systems and developed coordinated control methods for distributed systems. Among these methods, the finite-element approximation scheme will be presented here because of its wide acceptance in structural analysis.

A.   THE FINITE-ELEMENT METHOD

The finite-element method is a numerical procedure for solving the differential equations of physics and engineering. The method had its birth in the aerospace industry in the early 1950s and was first published by Turner and others [19]. An important theoretical contribution was made by Melosh [20], who showed that the finite-element method was really a variation of the well-known Rayleigh–Ritz procedure.

The range of applications for the finite-element method was enlarged when other investigators [21, 22] showed that the element equations related to structural mechanics, heat transfer, and fluid mechanics could also be derived by using a weighted residual procedure such as Galerkin's method or the least-squares approach. This knowledge is a very important contribution to the theory because it allows the finite-element method to be applied to any differential equations.

The fundamental concept of the finite-element method is that any continuous quantity, such as temperature, pressure, or displacement, can be approximated by a discrete model composed of a set of piecewise continuous functions defined over a finite number of subdomains. The piecewise continuous functions are defined using the values of the continuous quantity at a finite number of points in its domain.

The more common problem occurs when the continuous quantity is unknown and one must determine the value of this quantity at certain points within the region. The construction of the discrete model is most easily explained, however, if it is assumed that the numerical value of the quantity is already known at every point within the domain. The following procedure outlines the construction of the discrete model:

1) A finite number of points in the spatial domain is determined. The points are called nodal points or nodes.

2) The value of the continuous quantity at each node is denoted as a variable which is to be determined.

3) The domain is divided into a finite number of subdomains called elements.

4) The continuous quantity is approximated over each element by a polynomial that is defined using the nodal values of the continuous quantity. A different polynomial is defined for each element, but the element polynomials are selected in such a way that continuity is maintained along the element boundaries.

The spatial domain Ω with its boundary Γ is first divided into a number of elements, and the elements and nodes are numbered. The elements are usually either m-simplex or m-rectangle of different types [23]. The simplex of type (1) is the simplex with no other nodes except vertices; type (2) is for the case when there is a node at each midpoint of the edges of the simplex. For two-dimensional space (m = 2), the 2-simplex of type (1) is a triangle with 3 nodes at vertices, and the 2-simplex of type (2) is a triangle with 3 nodes at vertices and 3 nodes at the midpoints of the edges. The m-simplex of type (1) has (m + 1) nodes, and type (2) has (m + 1)(m + 2)/2 nodes.

The labeling of the nodes should be done so that it increases the computational efficiency. The matrix equation which arises when using the finite-element method has a large number of coefficients which are zero. The nonzero elements fall between the diagonal line and the line parallel to it and separated by the bandwidth $B = (R + 1)n_x$, where R is the largest difference between the node numbers in each element and n_x is the number of state variables. A reduction in the bandwidth produces a reduction in the required computer memory space and a reduction in the computational time. The minimization of B depends on the minimizing of R, which can be partially achieved by labeling the nodes across the shortest dimension of the spatial domain.

Let $X_i = (x_{1i}, x_{2i}, \ldots, x_{mi}) \in \Omega$ be the i-th node. At each node the values of state and control variables are defined as $u_i(t) = u(X_i, t)$, $f_i(t) = f(X_i, t)$. Then the values of all variables on each element are expressed by interpolating polynomials in terms of the values defined on nodes. When the element is an m-simplex of type (1), the interpolating polynomial is linear in spatial variables and has (m + 1) coefficients. Since the number of coefficients is equal to the number of nodes on which the values of variables are defined, these coefficients can always be computed and expressed as linear polynomials in the defined variables on nodes. This results in a general representation

$$u^k(x, t) = \sum_{i \in I_k} w_i^k(x) u_i(t) = W^k(x) u^k(t), \tag{33}$$

where k denotes the k-th element, and I_k is the set of indices for nodes belonging to the k-th element E_k, i.e.,

$I_k = \{i : X_i \in E_k\}.$ (34)

The function $w_i^k(x)$ is called the shape function or interpolation function. It is a polynomial of spatial variables x_i, $i = 1, 2, \ldots, m$. The matrix $W^k(x)$ is an $n_x \times (m + 1)n_x$ matrix with $n_x \times n_x$ block matrices containing $w_i^k(x)$ in the diagonals. The vector $u^k(t)$ is made of the n_x-vectors $u_i(t)$ for all $i \in I_k$. The control vector also has the same representation as the state with the same shape function.

In our application in large space structures, we introduce an additional state variable (degree of freedom) besides the displacement at each node, i.e., the rotational variable

$$\theta_i(t) = \frac{du_i}{dx}, \quad i \in I_k,$$ (35)

is defined at node i. This will effectively double the size of the vector $u_i(t)$.

The next major step is formulating the element equation which approximates the system equation. The element equations can be derived in two different ways. One approach is the variational approach, which minimizes either potential energy or a functional formulation of the differential equation [24]. Another approach is the use of a weighted residual procedure such as Galerkin's method or the least-squares approach [21, 25]. Galerkin's method is a means of obtaining an approximate solution to a differential equation. It does this by requiring that the error between the approximate solution and the true solution be orthogonal to the functions used in the approximation.

Let us assume that the state space V is separable. Since it is infinite-dimensional, there exists a countable set $(w_1, w_2, \ldots)$ of basis which is dense in V. Let $(w_1, w_2, \ldots, w_N)$ be a finite set of linearly independent shape functions in V. Then this basis spans a regular subspace $S_h^k(\Omega)$ of V, where h is the element size and k is the order of interpolating polynomials [26]. Thus, for a single element the finite-element representation of (33) becomes

$$u^N(t) = \sum_{i-1}^{N} w_i u_i(t).$$ (36)

Substituting the finite-element approximation (36) into the system equation (16), and following Galerkin's procedure, we have

$$\left(Mu_{tt}^N(t) + Du_t^N(t) + Au^N(t) - Bf(t), w_i \right) = 0, \quad i = 1, 2, \ldots, N$$ (37)

or

$$\left(Mu_{tt}^N(t), w_i \right) + \left(Du_t^N(t), w_i \right) + \left(Au^N(t), w_i \right) = \left(Bf(t), w_i \right),$$ (38)

with initial conditions from (17) and (18),

$$u^N(0) = u_0^N = \sum_{i=1}^{N} w_i u_i(0) \tag{39}$$

$$u_t^N(0) = u_1^N = \sum_{i=1}^{N} w_i \dot{u}_i(0). \tag{40}$$

Substituting (36) into (38), we have

$$\sum_{j=1}^{N} \left[M_{ij}\ddot{u}_j(t) + D_{ij}\dot{u}_j(t) + K_{ij}u_j(t) \right] = f_i(t). \tag{41}$$

Similarly, taking the inner products of the initial conditions (39) and (40) with w_i, we have

$$\sum_{j=1}^{N} G_{ij}u_j(0) = g_i^0 \tag{42}$$

$$\sum_{j=1}^{N} G_{ij}\dot{u}_j(0) = g_i^1, \tag{43}$$

where

$$M_{ij} = (Mw_i, w_j), \qquad D_{ij} = (Dw_i, w_j)$$

$$K_{ij} = (Aw_i, w_j), \qquad G_{ij} = (w_i, w_j) \tag{44}$$

$$f_i = (f(t), w_i), \qquad g_i^0 = (u_o, w_i), \quad g_i^1 = (u_1, w_i)$$

Equations (41)–(44) can be put into matrix form

$$M\ddot{u}(t) + D\dot{u}(t) + Ku(t) = F(t) \tag{45}$$

$$Gu(0) = g^0 \tag{46}$$

$$G\dot{u}(0) = g^1 \tag{47}$$

where

$$u(t) = \left[u_1(t), u_2(t), ..., u_N(t) \right]^T$$

$$F(t) = \left[f_1(t), f_2(t), ..., f_N(t) \right]^T$$

$$g^0 = \left[g_1^0, g_2^0, ..., g_N^0 \right]^T$$

$$g^1 = \left[g_1^1, g_2^1, ..., g_N^1 \right]^T .$$

Using (44), the system matrices in (45)–(47) can be written as

$$M = \int_E W(x)^T M(x) W(x) \, dx \tag{48a}$$

$$D = \int_E W(x)^T D(x) W(x) \, dx \tag{48b}$$

$$K = \int_E W(x)^T A(x) W(x) \, dx \tag{48c}$$

$$G = \int_E W(x)^T W(x) \, dx \tag{48d}$$

$$F(t) = \int_E W(x)^T f(x, t) \, dx \tag{48e}$$

$$g^0 = \int_E W(x)^T u_0(x) \, dx \tag{49}$$

$$g^1 = \int_E W(x)^T u_1(x) \, dx \tag{50}$$

where

$$W(x) = \left[w_1(x), w_2(x), ..., w_N(t) \right]^T,$$

and E is an element in Ω.

It can be shown that solution of the finite-dimensional system (45)–(47) converges to the true solution strongly [27], i.e.,

$$u^N(t) \to u(t) = \sum_{i=1}^{\infty} w_i u_i(t) \text{ strongly in } L_2(0, T; V)$$

$$\dot{u}^N(t) \to \frac{du(t)}{dt} \text{ strongly in } L_2(0,T;V)$$

The finite-dimensional (45)–(47) are for a single element. Since distributed system will be divided into a large number of elements, the size of the system will be extremely large, and some kind of iterative solution method will be necessary in order to solve the equation element by element.

B.   FINITE-ELEMENT APPROXIMATION OF A BEAM

The finite-element method presented above will now be demonstrated by approximating a beam equation. We consider a flexible beam of length L with spatially varying stiffness EI(x) and linear mass density $\rho(x)$. The transverse vibration of the beam is described by [28]

$$\rho A(x) \frac{\partial^2 u}{\partial t^2} + \frac{\partial^2}{\partial x^2}\left(EI(x) \frac{\partial^2 u}{\partial x^2} \right) = f(t),$$

$$x \in [0, L], \quad t \geq 0. \tag{51}$$

For demonstration purpose, we assume that stiffness and density are constant, and the beam is simply supported on both ends. Then the distributed system model becomes

$$m\frac{\partial^2 u}{\partial t^2} + EI\frac{\partial^4 u}{\partial x^4} = f(t), x \in [0, L], \quad t \geq 0 \tag{52}$$

with boundary conditions

$$u(x) = \frac{\partial^2 u}{\partial x^2} = 0, \quad x \in \partial[0, L], \quad t \geq 0. \tag{53}$$

Figure 1 shows the simply supported beam divided into four elements, not necessarily of equal length. Two degrees of freedom are assumed at each node, and the transverse displacement u and the rotation θ ($\equiv \partial u/\partial x$) is defined in Fig. 1a.

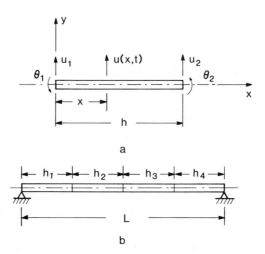

Fig. 1. Finite element of a beam. (a) Single element with four degrees of freedom; (b) simply supported beam divided into four elements.

The finite-element approximation using cubic shape functions is given in [29].

$$u(x, t) = \sum_{i=1}^{4} w_i(x)v_i(t)$$

$$= W(x)v(t),$$

(54)

where

$$v(t) = \left[u_1(t),\, \theta_1(t),\, u_2(t),\, \theta_2(t) \right]^T$$

$$W(t) = \left[w_1(x),\, w_2(x),\, w_3(x),\, w_4(x) \right]^T$$

with shape functions

$$w_1(x) = 1 - 3x^2/h^2 + 2x^3/h^3$$

$$w_2(x) = x - 2x^2/h + x^3/h^2$$

$$w_3(x) = 3x^2/h^2 - 2x^3/h^3$$

$w_4(x) = -x^2/h + x^3/h^2.$

Applying Galerkin's method to (52) for a single element, a finite-element approximation model is obtained as

$$M\ddot{u}(t) + Ku(t) = F(t), \tag{55}$$

where

$$M = \int_0^h W^T m W \, dx \tag{56}$$

$$K = \int_0^h W^T EI \frac{\partial^4 W}{\partial x^4} \, dx = \int_0^h \frac{\partial^2 W}{\partial x^2} EI \frac{\partial^2 W}{\partial x^2} \, dx \tag{57}$$

$$F = \int_0^h W^T f(x, t) \, dx. \tag{58}$$

The stiffness matrix K in (57) can be obtained by using integration by parts and neglecting boundary conditions. Performing the integrations, the mass and stiffness matrices can be obtained as

$$M = \frac{\rho A h}{420} \begin{bmatrix} 156 & 22h & 54 & -13h \\ 22h & 4h^2 & 13h & -3h^2 \\ 54 & 13h & 156 & -22h \\ -13h & -3h^2 & -22h & 4h^2 \end{bmatrix} \tag{59}$$

$$K = \frac{EI}{h^3} \begin{bmatrix} 12 & 6h & -12 & 6h \\ 6h & 4h^2 & -6h & 2h^2 \\ -12 & -6h & 12 & -6h \\ 6h & 2h^2 & -6h & 4h^2 \end{bmatrix}. \tag{60}$$

The input vector $F(t)$ to the system can also be computed using (58) when the system input function $f(x, t)$ is known. We often assume that the pointwise input is applied at a selected set of nodes. For example, let us assume that a force is applied at the midpoint of the beam in Fig. 1b. Since the midpoint is common to both the second and third elements, two input vectors need to be computed, one for each element.

For the second element the pointwise input function can be represented by

$$f(x, t) = \delta(x - h)f(t). \tag{61}$$

Thus the input vector for the second element is

$$
\begin{aligned}
F(t) &= \int_0^h W(x)^T \delta(x - h)f(t)\, dx \\
&= W(h)^T f(t) \\
&= \begin{bmatrix} 0 \\ 0 \\ 1 \\ 0 \end{bmatrix} f(t).
\end{aligned}
\tag{62}
$$

Similarly, for the third element,

$$f(x, t) = \delta(x)f(t) \tag{63}$$

and

$$
\begin{aligned}
F(t) &= \int_0^h W(x)^T \delta(x)f(t)\, dx \\
&= W(0)^T f(t) \\
&= \begin{bmatrix} 1 \\ 0 \\ 0 \\ 0 \end{bmatrix} f(t).
\end{aligned}
\tag{64}
$$

The finite-element mass and stiffness matrices have been developed without considering the boundary conditions given in (53). Since the first and fourth elements of the beam are constrained by the boundary condition, as seen in Fig. 1, only their matrices need to be modified.

The first element has no deflection at node 1, implying that $u_1 \equiv 0$. Thus the first rows and columns of its mass and stiffness matrices must be eliminated. Similarly the fourth element has no deflection at node 2, implying that $u_2 \equiv 0$, and thus the corresponding third rows and columns must be eliminated.

The last step is the formulation of the overall system matrices corresponding to total nodal variables. Since a node between any two adjacent elements is common to both elements, corresponding matrices overlap each other when they are added to form the overall matrices, i.e.,

$$
M = \begin{bmatrix}
M_1 & & & \\
& M_2 & & \\
& & M_3 & \\
& & & M_4 \\
\end{bmatrix}
\tag{65}
$$

where M_i represents the mass matrix for the i-th element. The matrix elements in each overlapping block are computed by adding corresponding entries. The stiffness matrix K is also assembled in a similar way.

One final comment is that the finite-element approximation is also used to solve the adjoint equation (30) for the infinite-dimensional identification algorithm.

V. FINITE-DIMENSIONAL IDENTIFICATION

An infinite-dimensional identification algorithm was developed in Section III, and the finite-element method was presented in Section IV for the purpose of implementing the algorithm. An alternative approach is to formulate an identification problem for the finite-element model rather than the infinite-dimensional distributed system model. The motivations behind this approach are that a large number of identification methods are available for finite-dimensional systems, and that the finite-dimensional approximation is required even for an infinite-dimensional identification algorithm. Another advantage of the approach is that the original system parameters such as EI and ρ are retained in the finite-element matrices (59) and (60), and surprisingly, the number of parameters to be estimated is not increased even though the system dimension is high.

A.   FINITE-DIMENSIONAL FORMULATION

Consider the distributed system model given in (16)–(18). We assume that it is already approximated by the finite-element method and is given by (45)–(47). Let the finite-element model be

$$M\ddot{u}(t) + D\dot{u}(t) + Ku(t) = F(t) \tag{66}$$

with initial conditions

$$Gu(0) = g^0 \tag{67}$$

$$G\dot{u}(0) = g^1 \tag{68}$$

and output equation

$$y(t) = Cu(t). \tag{69}$$

Parameters to be estimated are in matrices M, D, and K in multiplicative form as shown in (59) and (60). If the system is made of uniform material, then only one set of constant parameters (ρ, EI, and α) is in the matrices. When the material is nonuniform, then the parameters are assumed to be constant for each finite element, and (66) will have several sets of these parameters, each of which is multiplied by an element matrix in the block diagonal as shown in (65).

Let $q = [q_1, q_2, ..., q_m]$ be an unknown parameter vector in R^m, which is a collection of parameters in M, D, and K. Then the finite-dimensional parameter identification problem is to find the parameter vector $q^* \in R^m$ which minimizes

$$J(q) = \int_0^T \left[z(t) - y(t) \right]^T R \left[z(t) - y(t) \right] dt \tag{70}$$

subject to y(t) being the solution to (66)–(69), and z(t) being the measurement of the output y(t).

B.   DEVELOPMENT OF FINITE-DIMENSIONAL
ALGORITHM

The identification problem defined by (66)–(70) is a weighted least-squares formulation. A vast amount of literature is available for solving this problem, and this volume is dedicated to the theme of advances in the theory and application of system parameter identification. Therefore, it is not the intention of this section to develop a new algorithm. We have chosen here one method which has proved to be very efficient in other applications [30–32].

Since we will be using digital data in actual implementation, the cost functional can be modified to a discrete form

$$J(q) = \sum_{i=1}^{n} (z_i - y_i)^T R(z_i - y_i), \tag{71}$$

where the summation is performed over the interval of interest of recorded output data.

Linearizing the output in (69) with respect to the unknown parameter vector q, we have

$$y_i = y_{i0} + \frac{\partial y_i}{\partial q}(q - q_0), \tag{72}$$

where q_0 is a nominal value of q, y_{i0} is a nominal response corresponding to q_0, and $\partial y_i/\partial q$ is the gradient matrix of y_i with respect to q.

Substituting (72) into (71), setting the partial $\partial J/\partial q$ equal to zero, and solving for the value of q which minimizes J, we have

$$q = q_0 + \left[\sum_{i=1}^{n} \left(\frac{\partial y_i}{\partial q} \right)^T R \frac{\partial y_i}{\partial q} \right]^{-1} \left[\sum_{i=1}^{n} \left(\frac{\partial y_i}{\partial q} \right)^T R(z_i - y_{i0}) \right]. \tag{73}$$

In the Newton–Raphson sense, (73) can be written in recursive form as

$$q^{k+1} = q^k + \left[\sum_{i=1}^{n} \left(\frac{\partial y_i}{\partial q} \right)^T R \left(\frac{\partial y_i}{\partial q} \right) \right]_{q^k}^{-1} \left[\sum_{i=1}^{n} \left(\frac{\partial y_i}{\partial q} \right)^T R(z_i - y_i) \right]_{q^k}. \tag{74}$$

By taking the partial derivative of the output equation (69) with respect to the parameter vector, we have

$$\frac{\partial y}{\partial q} = C \frac{\partial u}{\partial q}. \tag{75}$$

An equation for the sensitivity vector $\partial u/\partial q$ can be obtained by taking the partial derivative of (66) with respect to q:

$$M\ddot{u}_q + D\dot{u}_q + Ku_q = F_q, \tag{76}$$

where

$$u_q = \frac{d}{dq} \frac{\partial u}{\partial q}$$

$$F_q = -\left[\left(\frac{\partial M}{\partial q}\right)\ddot{u} + \left(\frac{\partial D}{\partial q}\right)\dot{u} + \left(\frac{\partial K}{\partial q}\right)u\right]. \qquad (77)$$

The identification algorithm can now be summarized as follows:

1) Make an initial guess of the parameter vector q.

2) Update system matrices in (66) and (77).

3) Solve the state and output equations (66)–(69).

4) Solve the sensitivity equations (75)–(77).

5) Update the parameter vector using (74).

6) Return to 2) until the parameter has converged.

It should be noted that the sensitivity matrices in (77) can be easily obtained because of the multiplicative nature of parameters as seen in (59) and (60). The computation of the sensitivity equation (76) is the same as that for the state equation (66), with modified input F_q.

The solution method of these second-order system equations can be up to one's preference. The second-order equations can be converted into first-order equations and then any standard integration scheme can be applied. One can also integrate the second-order equation directly using the Newmark Beta method [33], which can be found in the NASTRAN, NASA's finite-element analysis program [34]. Of course, this solution method is also applicable to the infinite-dimensional identification algorithm in Section III.

VI. NUMERICAL RESULTS

Both approaches of parameter identification algorithms developed in this article are demonstrated here numerically using a beam equation as an example.

A.   INFINITE-DIMENSIONAL APPROACH

Consider the simply supported beam in Fig. 1. The state equation is given by

$$\rho A \frac{\partial^2 u}{\partial t^2} + EI \frac{\partial^4 u}{\partial x^4} = \delta\left(x - \frac{L}{2}\right) f(t),$$

(78)

$$x \in [0, L], \quad t > 0$$

with boundary conditions

$$u(x) = \frac{\partial^2 u}{\partial x^2}(x) = 0, \quad x = 0, L, \quad t > 0$$

(79)

and initial conditions

$$u(x, 0) = \frac{\partial u}{\partial t}(x, 0) = 0, \quad x \in [0, L].$$

(80)

The adjoint equation is, from (30) and (31),

$$\rho A \frac{\partial^2 p}{\partial t^2} + EI \frac{\partial^4 p}{\partial x^4} = -\frac{1}{T}(u - z),$$

(81)

$$x \in [0, L], \quad t \in [0, T]$$

with boundary conditions

$$p(x) = \frac{\partial^2 p}{\partial x^2}(x) = 0, \ x = 0, L, \quad t \in [0, T]$$

(82)

and final conditions

$$p(x, T) = \frac{\partial p}{\partial t}(x, T) = 0, \quad x \in [0, L].$$

(83)

The parameter vector is

$$q = [\rho A, EI] = [m, EI].$$

(84)

The first variation of the cost functional J_a with respect to a change in q is, from (32),

$$\delta J_a = \int_0^T \int_0^L P \frac{\partial^2 u}{\partial t^2} \, dx \, \delta m \, dt$$

(85)

$$+ \int_0^T \int_0^L p \frac{\partial^4 u}{\partial x^4} \, d \, \delta(EI) \, dt.$$

Integrating by parts, the spatial integral in the second term can be written as

$$\int_0^L p \frac{\partial^4 u}{\partial x^4} \, d = p \frac{\partial^3 u}{\partial x^3} \Big|_0^L - \frac{\partial p}{\partial x} \frac{\partial^2 u}{\partial x^2} \Big|_0^L + \int_0^L \frac{\partial^2 p}{\partial x^2} \frac{\partial^2 u}{\partial x^2} \, dx. \tag{86}$$

The first two terms become zero due to boundary conditions (79) and (82). Thus (85) becomes

$$\delta J_a = \int_0^T \int_0^L p \frac{\partial^2 u}{\partial t^2} \, dx \, dt \, \delta(m)$$
$$+ \int_0^T \int_0^L \frac{\partial^2 p}{\partial x^2} \frac{\partial^2 u}{\partial x^2} \, dx \, dt \, \delta(EI). \tag{87}$$

Since the objective is to decrease J_a by a choice of m and EI, we can choose

$$\delta(m) = -R_1 \int_0^T p \frac{\partial^2 u}{\partial t^2} \, dt \tag{88}$$

$$\delta(EI) = -R_2 \int_0^T \frac{\partial^2 p}{\partial x^2} \frac{\partial^2 u}{\partial x^2} \, dt, \tag{89}$$

where R_1 and R_2 are weighting or acceleration factors.

The method of steepest decent is used to iteratively compute the optimal parameters, and is summarized below:

1) Make an initial guess of m and EI.

2) Solve the state equation (78)–(80), forward in time.

3) Solve the adjoint equation (81)–(83), backward in time.

4) Compute the variations $\delta(m)$ and $\delta(EI)$ from (88) and (89).

5) Compute the cost variation δJ_a from (87).

6) Return to 2) until

$$\left(J_a^k - J_a^{k+1}\right)\Big/J_a^k \le \delta \tag{90}$$

for a small δ prescribed.

The simply supported beam was divided into four elements of equal length, and the finite-element model (55) was developed for each element to form an overall finite-element model. The finite-element model was identical for both state and adjoint equations, except the input functions.

A 4-m beam was supported at both ends, and a point force was applied at the midpoint by a 100 N/m force for a 10 ms period. A point sensor was also located at the midpoint to measure the displacement. Performance data are presented in Table I.

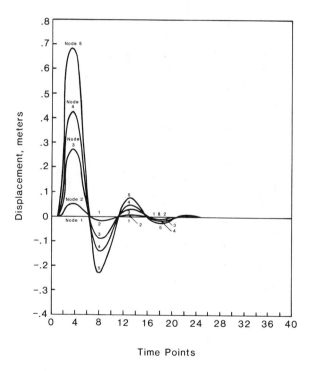

Fig. 2. Response of all node points of a cantilever.

TABLE I. Performance Data Using Infinite-Dimensional Identification

	Parameter [a]	Initial estimate	Iteration						True value
			1	2	3	4	5	6	
Case 1	E	9.1×10^4	1.067×10^5	1.108×10^5	1.186×10^5	1.309×10^5	1.291×10^5	1.309×10	1.30×10^5
	ρ	32.000	37.627	40.835	40.298	40.061	40.021	39.996	40.000
Case 2	E	1.61×10^4	1.931×10^4	2.251×10^4	2.282×10^4	2.293×10^4	2.298×10^4	2.299×10^4	2.3×10^4
	ρ	46.900	63.372	67.628	66.933	67.001	66.997	–	67.000

[a] E = Young's modulus (N/m^2), ρ = mass density (kg/m^3).

B. FINITE-DIMENSIONAL APPROACH

For a second example, we have chosen a cantilever beam which is excited at the tip of the beam. The beam is divided into four elements of equal length. Moreover, we assumed that each element is made with different materials properties. We also added a damping matrix by multiplying the stiffness matrix K by a damping coefficient α. This resulted in the finite-element model (66) as well as the sensitivity model (76) and (77).

The algorithm in Section V was implemented using the NASTRAN finite-element computer program on a UNIVAC 1100 series main-frame computer at NASA Johnson Space Center [5]. The cantilever beam was excited by a large 5000 N/m transient force. Figure 2 shows the plot of displacements of all five nodes, where node 1 is held fixed and node 5 is the end of the beam.

To estimate parameters E and ρ for all bars of the beam simultaneously, initial estimates of 70% low real values were applied as starting guesses. With the weight matrix taken as the identity matrix, the algorithm did not converge after 50 iterations even though some improvement was seen. The weight matrix was then set to reflect the different displacements of the five node points more uniformly and an acceleration factor of 3.61 was used to update parameters. Under these conditions the algorithm did converge to approximately the correct values, as can be seen in Figs. 3–6.

The elements with the greater displacement converged slightly faster; however, the convergence was not quite as smooth as the longer converging elements. If the acceleration factor is increased beyond a value greater than 4.0 to speed up convergence, the values are driven out of proportion too fast and never recover; thus these results seem to be close to optimum for this problem. Performance data are presented in Table II.

Table II. Performance Data Using Finite-Dimentsional Identification

Element	Parameter[a]	Exact	Initial	Final	No. of iterations
1	E	1.3×10^5	9.1×10^4	1.291×10^5	12
	ρ	40.0	28.0	39.72	7
2	E	2.3×10^4	1.61×10^4	2.287×10^4	8
	ρ	67.0	46.9	66.88	6
3	E	5.2×10^6	3.6×10^6	5.203×10^6	7
	ρ	25.0	17.5	25.07	6
4	E	7.6×10^6	5.32×10^6	7.594×10^6	6
	ρ	50.0	35.0	50.03	5

[a] E = Young's modulus (N/m^2), ρ = mass density (kg/m^3).

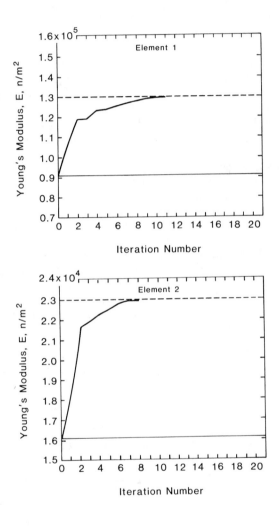

Fig. 3. Convergence rates for Young's modulus of elements 1 and 2 of a beam.

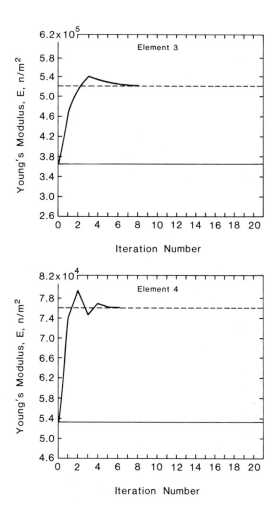

Fig. 4. Convergence rates for Young's modulus of elements 3 and 4 of a beam.

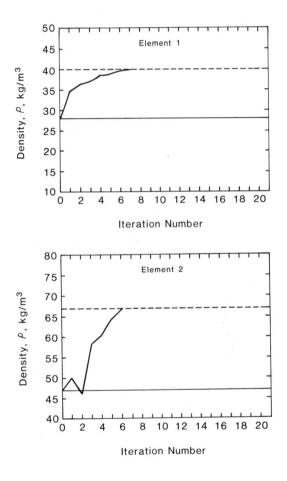

Fig. 5. Convergence rates for density of elements 1 and 2 of a beam.

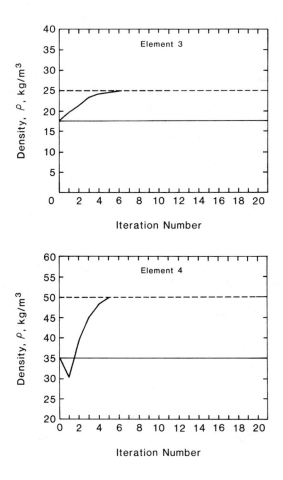

Fig. 6. Convergence rates for density of elements 3 and 4 of a beam.

214   K. Y. LEE

VII. CONCLUSION

Two approaches to parameter identification of distributed systems have been considered. One approach is the infinite-dimensional formulation of the identification problem. A necessary condition was developed in terms of an adjoint equation in infinite-dimensional function space. This approach retains the nature of distributed system until the last minute before a numerical computation is attempted, and therefore is believed to be more accurate than the other method. The finite-element method was introduced to compute both the state and adjoint equations in the approximation.

An alternative approach is the finite-dimensional formulation of the identification problem. The distributed system model is first approximated by a finite-element model and then a finite-dimensional identification problem is formulated. The accuracy of estimation depends upon the number of elements used in discretizing the spatial domain. Although the finite-dimensional model is of high order, the number of unknown parameters remains the same as that for the original distributed model, which makes this approach very practical.

Numerical results are presented to make some comparison between two methods. Both methods gave good estimates of the parameters in a reasonable number of iterations. Computational requirements are very much comparable since in both approaches two dynamic equations must be solved: the state and adjoint equations in the first approach and the state and sensitivity equations in the second approach.

Finally, the finite-element method is proved to be a very useful tool in solving the parameter identification problem. For large space structures it is almost inevitable to use the finite-element approximation, and the identification algorithms can be used on-line along with existing finite-element programs such as NASTRAN.

REFERENCES

1. K. Y. LEE, R. O. BARR, S. H. GAGE, AND A. N. KHARKAR, *J. Theor. Biol.* 59, 33–76 (1976).
2. K. Y. LEE, in "Lecture Notes in Control and Information Sciences" (A. V. Balakrishnan, Ed.), Vol. 1, pp. 325–334, Springer-Verlag, Berlin, 1978.
3. K. Y. LEE, in "Recent Developments in Variable Structure Systems, Econonomics and Biology" (R. R. Mohler and A. Ruberti, Eds.), Vol. 162, pp. 173–188, Springer-Verlag, Berlin, 1978.
4. K. Y. LEE and S. HOSSAIN, *Proc. 24th IEEE Conf. Decision Control*, 1139–1144 (1985).
5. K. Y. LEE, D. WALKER, and S. HOSSAIN, *Proc. 24th IEEE Conf. Decision Control*, 1145-1150 (1985).
6. A. G. BUTKOVSKIY, "Distributed Control Systems," Am. Elsevier, New York, 1969.
7. A. V. BALAKRISHNAN, "Applied Functional Analysis," Springer, New York, 1976.

8. J. L. LIONS, "Optimal Control of Systems Governed by Partial Differential Equations," Springer-Verlag, Berlin, 1971.

9. P. K. C. WANG, in "Advances in Control Systems" (C. T. Leondes, Ed.), Vol. 1, pp. 75–172, Academic Press, New York, 1964.

10. K. Y. LEE and R. O. BARR, *IEEE Trans. Autom. Control 17*, 806–809 (1972).

11. K. Y. LEE, S. N. CHOW, and R. O. BARR, *SIAM J. Control 10*, 361–376 (1972).

12. S. G. GREENBERG, *IEEE Trans. Autom. Control 16*, 153–159 (1971).

13. K. Y. LEE, *Proc. Milwaukee Symp. Autom. Control* 359-363 (1974).

14. K. Y. LEE, in "Distributed Parameter Control Systems" (S. A. Tzafestas, Ed.), pp. 211–238, Pergamon, New York, 1982.

15. M. P. POLIS and R. E. GOODSON, *Proc. IEEE 64*, 43–61 (1976).

16. C. S. KUBRUSLY, *Int. J. Control 26*, 509–535 (1977).

17. K. Y. LEE and J. W. CLARY, *Proc. 17th IEEE Conf. Decision Control* 886–891 (1979).

18. G. CHAVENT, *Proc. 5th IFAC Symp. Identification Syst. Parameter Estim.* 85-97 (1979).

19. M. J. TURNER, R. W. CLOUGH, H. C. MARTIN, and L. J. TOPP, *J. Aeronaut. Sci. 23*, 805–824 (1956).

20. R. J. MELOSH, *J. Am. Inst. Aeronaut. Astronaut. 1*, 1631–1637 (1965).

21. B. A. SZABO and G. C. Lee, *Int. J. Num. Methods Eng. 1*, 301–310 (1969).

22. O. C. ZIENKIEWICZ, "The Finite Element Method in Engineering Science," McGraw-Hill, London, 1971.

23. P. G. CIARLET, "The Finite Element Method for Elliptic Problems," North-Holland Publ., Amsterdam, 1978.

24. L. J. SEGERLIND, "Applied Finite Element Analysis," Wiley, New York 1976.

25. O. C. ZIENKIEWICZ and C. J. PAREKH, *Int. J. Num. Methods Eng. 2*, 61–71 (1970).

26. J. T. ODEN and J. N. REDDY, "An Introduction to the Mathematical Theory of Finite Elements," Wiley, New York, 1976.

27. H. T. BANKS and K. KUNISCH, *SIAM J. Control Optimization 20*, 815–849 (1982).

28. R. W. CLOUGH and J. PENZIEN, "Dynamics of Structures," McGraw-Hill, New York 1975.

30. G. B. WARBURTON, "The Dynamical Behaviour of Structures," Pergamon, Elmsford, New York, 1976.

31. K. Y. LEE and F. J. MEYER, *IEEE Trans. Power Appar. Syst. PAS-101*, 3303–3309 (1982).

32. F. C. TUNG, *Proc. 3rd Symp. Dyn. Control Large Flexible Spacecraft* 255–267 (1981).

33. N. M. NEWMARK, *Proc. ASCE J. Eng. Mech. Div. EM3*, 67–94 (1959).

34. H. G. SCHAEFFER, "MSC/NASTRAN Primer," Wallace Press, New York, 1982.

AN IDENTIFICATION SCHEME FOR LINEAR CONTROL SYSTEMS WITH WAVEFORM-TYPE DISTURBANCES

JOSEPH CHEN

Litton Aero Products
Moorpark, California 93021

I. INTRODUCTION

Throughout the history of automatic control, it has been known that the knowledge, which is required to design a control system, about a system and its environments is seldom available *a priori*. In practice, the environmental disturbances to be encountered by a system are usually incapable of measurement.

On the other hand, even if the system model structure described by mathematical equations which are governed by control requirements and physical laws is known in principle, it often happens that the knowledge of certain parameters is missing. Therefore, control design of such a system requires on-line determination of the uncertain parameters in the face of unmeasurable disturbances. This initiates the interest in the present study.

In this article, an identification scheme is established which utilizes disturbance accommodation control (DAC) to counteract waveform disturbances and applies the maximum likelihood (ML) method to identify the unknown parameters.

The presence of disturbances prevents an exact identification or sometimes even the possibility of identification: the identifiability problem. Therefore, any realistic treatment of such an identification problem must include certain control efforts to be made upon the disturbances.

The kind of disturbances one encounters in realistic control system design can be classified into two broad categories: noise-type disturbances and disturbances with waveform structure. Time recordings of noise-type disturbances are essentially jagged and erratic in nature, having no significant degree of smoothness or regularity in their waveforms. They are best characterized in terms of their statistical properties such as the mean, covariance, etc. On the other hand, disturbances that change slowly compared with system dynamics possess waveform structure and exhibit distinguishable waveform patterns, at least over short time periods. In the present research, the waveform-type disturbance is emphasized and, as we shall see, noise-type disturbance will be included as a special case.

In this study, a system model is assumed known for the system process as well as a model for the waveform disturbance. In other words, the corresponding "state space model structure" has been determined, and it can confidently describe the dynamic characteristics of the plant process and disturbance. Since the model structure which is described by state space equations has been determined, parameter identification is the primary problem to be solved; this is the problem of extracting the true parameter values from system input and output measurements. With the proper choice of loss function, the identification problem becomes simply one of optimization. We are then interested in reaching a minimum loss function as well as obtaining a unique solution such that parameter identification can be achieved.

During the identification process, control inputs should be designed adaptively such that the system can behave within our expectancy. In particular, with the known state model equations for the unmeasurable disturbance, a physically realizable feedback control technique called disturbance accommodation control can be employed to cope with the disturbance effects. Due to the desire to identify the system during normal operation, one also may wish to apply control of stability. Evidently the control input should be good enough for our identification usage; therefore, the perturbation signal is supplied.

Among many methods in parameter identification, the maximum likelihood method is often considered as a standard method for comparison, mainly due to its desirable statistical properties. In this study, the maximum likelihood method is applied to identify the continuous-time model parameters where the Kalman filters and sensitivity equations are computed to minimize the likelihood function.

The proposed algorithm has been implemented in digital simulations where a second-order system and two kinds of waveform disturbances are selected as examples. The convergence property of the identification method is quite satisfactory.

The algorithm may be applicable to identifying system models with certain model errors, causing a deviation from the actual system and leading to the presence of disturbance terms in corrected models.

II.   PROBLEM DESCRIPTION

In this study the problem is in the form of a linear state space representation

$$dX(t)/dt = A(\theta)X(t) + B(\theta)u(t) + Fw(t) \tag{1}$$

$$y_k = C_k X_k + v_k, \tag{2}$$

where $X(t)$ is an n-dimensional vector of state variables characterizing the system dynamic behavior, $u(t)$ an r-dimensional vector of input variables which is assumed to be measured exactly, $w(t)$ a d-dimensional vector of an unmeasurable disturbance that affects the system, y_k an m-dimensional vector of discrete-time output measurements at time instant t_k, v_k an m-dimensional vector of undesired measurement white noise with zero mean, and F an $n \times d$ matrix which is assumed known. The p-dimensional vector of known parameters θ is assumed constant. $A(\theta)$ and $B(\theta)$ are suitably dimensioned matrices whose elements constitute the unknown constant parameters in θ, while C_k is known matrix which relates y_k to the state vector X_k.

In this study a hybrid (analog-digital) structure is used where a continuous-time (analog) model describes the system dynamical behavior, and sampled output (digital) mechanization is selected for ease of working with digital computer. In the literature the unmeasurable inputs $w(t)$ are often assumed zero-mean white noise vectors for ease of analysis. However, the difficulties appear when the unmeasurable disturbances are highly structured, e.g., sinusoidal, exponential, polynomial, or dc bias. In this study we will focus our attention on a class of linear control systems with unknown constant parameters, with disturbances having waveform structures and with white output measurement noise.

The main objectives of this research are to develop an identification technique to estimate the unknown parameters such that the optimal control purpose can be achieved, to apply disturbance accommodation control to cope with unmeasurable disturbances, to model the uncancelled disturbance as stochastic noise, and to investigate the maximum likelihood method as the parameter estimator.

In this study all the elements of parameter vector θ are assumed to have certain prior information, since the step of model structure determination should be complete prior to the parameter identification. If this is not the case, the extended Kalman filter will be appropriate for this purpose.

Through the knowledge of the disturbance waveform structure, the system disturbance $w(t)$ can be represented by the state space equations

$$dz(t)/dt = Dz(t) + \sigma$$

$$w(t) = Hz(t), \tag{3}$$

where D and H are known matrices, and the elements of vector σ are sequences of completely unknown, randomly arriving, random intensity delta functions to describe any jump effects. More details will be seen in the DAC input design section.

Because the identification process is carried out during normal operation, the input signal should be carefully selected not only to ensure system stability, but also to excite the system modes of interest.

III. THE PROPOSED ALGORITHM

The proposed algorithm is depicted as in Fig. 1, and can be stated as follows:

1) Apply disturbance accommodation control u_c to counteract the unmeasurable inputs by using the current information of parameter values and assumed disturbance state space model. Apply the feedback control u_r, and the perturbation input signal u_i simultaneously to fulfill the control objective and ensure the property of persistent excitation. After a certain

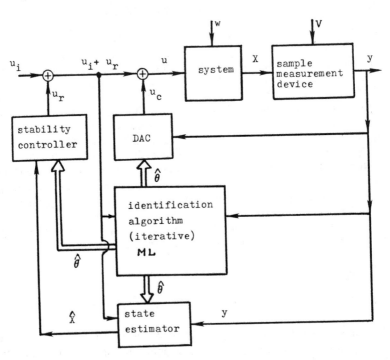

Fig. 1. The proposed algorithm.

period of pure control operation, the sampled input summation of u_r and u_i and output measurements are collected in a sufficiently long period of time for identification purposes.

2) Through modeling the effect of uncancelled disturbances as Gaussian white noise with zero mean and unknown covariance matrix. The maximum likelihood method is applied to this continuous-time process model coupled with a discrete-time output measurement.

3) Update parameter iteratively. Due to stability and accuracy reasons, the parameters are updated "iteratively." Throughout each iteration, the parameters are fixed at their estimates from previous iteration, such that the parameter update $\delta\theta$ can be obtained from the maximum likelihood algorithm. At the end of each iteration, the new parameters are computed by the scheme

$$\theta_i = \theta_{i-1} + \delta\theta_i, \tag{4}$$

where i indicates the iteration number.

Step 3) is repeated until a specified number of iterations is reached. Note that the DAC signal is applied throughout the process, and its controller is to be updated whenever the new parameters are available. In this algorithm the method of data processing is called batch processing, which is different from real-time process; i.e., the parameters are updated immediately after each sample data are received. The batch processing can be performed in on-line or off-line operation.

In Section IV, the input signal design which is threefold in disturbance canceling, regulating, and identifying is included. Certain modeling efforts on the uncancelled disturbance are discussed.

In Section V, the maximum likelihood method is stated.

IV. INPUT SIGNAL DESIGN

In order to design the system input signal properly, one has to consider the purpose of the control signal. In this study, we intend to identify the unknown parameters in a dynamic system (1) that is in the presence of waveform-type disturbances. Assume that the design of a linear regulator or servomechanism controller is required to achieve our control purpose. Then the total control effort u(t) can be split into three parts:

$$u = u_i + u_r + u_c, \tag{5}$$

where the component u_c is assigned to counteract the waveform disturbance $w(t)$, the component u_r is responsible for regulating or servomechanism, and u_i is the added perturbation signal to keep the system persistently excited.

In Section IV,A the design of u_c input is developed by using the state modeling of the waveform disturbance and is based on Johnson's work [1]. In Section IV,B the uncancelled disturbance effect is modeled as Gaussian noise. In Section IV,C the design of the regulator and servomechanism controller is briefly stated for the completeness of the theory. In Section IV,D the added perturbation signal u_i is discussed in relation to the system persistent excitation.

A. DESIGN OF DISTURBANCE ACCOMMODATION CONTROL

1. The Disturbance Model

In disturbance accommodation control design, a state space model for disturbance with waveform structure has to be determined so that a modern, state space approach to the disturbance cancellation problem can be developed.

Disturbances $w(t)$ which possess waveform structure may be mathematically modeled by a linear expression of the form

$$w(t) = c_1(t)f_1(t) + c_2(t)f_2(t) + \ldots + c_M(t)f_M(t), \tag{6}$$

where the $f_i(t)$, $i = 1, \ldots, M$, are known functions that indicate the various waveform patterns that the designer has observed in experimental recordings of $w(t)$, and the $c_i(t)$, $i = 1, \ldots, M$, are known piecewise constant weighting coefficients.

For example, if $w(t)$ is known to be composed of weighted linear combinations of steps and ramps, we can represent $w(t)$ by the analytical expression

$$w(t) = c_1 + c_2 t, \tag{7}$$

where coefficients c_1 and c_2 vary in a piecewise constant fashion and the basis functions $f_1(t)$ and $f_2(t)$ are given as

$$f_1(t) = 1, \quad f_2(t) = t. \tag{8}$$

The waveform disturbance of $w(t) = c_1 + c_2 t$ can therefore be written as

$$\begin{bmatrix} \dot{z}_1 \\ \dot{z}_2 \end{bmatrix} = \begin{bmatrix} 0 & 0 \\ 0 & 0 \end{bmatrix} \begin{bmatrix} z_1 \\ z_2 \end{bmatrix} + \begin{bmatrix} \sigma_1 \\ \sigma_2 \end{bmatrix}$$

$$w(t) = z_1(t),$$ (9)

where the disturbance states z_1 and z_2 are defined as

$$z_1 = c_2 t + c_1$$

$$z_2 = c_2.$$

The "isolated" impulse sequences σ_1 and σ_2 describe the slow and random jumps of the constants c_1 and c_2, which vary in a piecewise constant fashion. In general, the disturbance is modeled in the form of

$$dz/dt = Dz + \sigma$$

$$w = Hz,,$$ (10)

where the vector z will be called the state of disturbance w. Such a state model representation will include almost any waveform structure disturbances, such as piecewise constant, polynomial, sinusoidal, exponential, and ripple-type disturbance, etc. The detailed examples can be referred to in [1].

Other than the environmental disturbances, it is possible to have unfamiliar disturbances arising from modeling errors in system parameters. The mismatch between the real system dynamics and the corresponding mathematical model may lead to the presence of unfamiliar disturbance-like terms in the mathematical model. In the presence of unfamiliar disturbances, it can probably be approximated by some polynomial in t of the form

$$w(t) = c_1 + c_2 t + c_3 t^2 + \ldots + c_M t^{M-1},$$ (11)

where the parameter M can be selected by the designer. The state model corresponding to an unfamiliar disturbance is obtained as

$$dz_i/dt = z_{i+1} + \sigma_i, \quad i = 1, 2, \ldots, M - 1$$ (12)

.
.
.

$$dz_M/dt = \sigma_M$$

$$w = z_1.$$

2.   Design of DAC

To ease the discussion of DAC design, the parameters of dynamic system are assumed to be known exactly. The controlled system is modeled by a set of linear equations having the form

$$dX/dt = AX + Bu + FW$$
$$y = CX. \tag{13}$$

Note that the output measurement is obtained without noise. The disturbance $w(t)$ can be modeled by disturbance state equations having the form

$$dz/dt = Dz + \delta$$
$$w = Hz. \tag{14}$$

The design of a disturbance accommodation controller leads to an algebraic control law expression of the form

$$u_c(t) = \Phi\left(\overline{X}(t), \overline{z}(t), t\right), \tag{15}$$

where estimates of $X(t)$ and $z(t)$ are obtained from a composite state estimator which operatoes on the output measurement $y(t)$ and the control input $u(t)$.

A standard full-dimensional composite state estimator is

$$\begin{bmatrix} \overline{X} \\ \overline{z} \end{bmatrix} = \begin{bmatrix} A + K_1C & \dots & FH \\ \vdots & & \\ K_2C & \dots & D \end{bmatrix} \begin{bmatrix} \overline{X} \\ \overline{z} \end{bmatrix} - \begin{bmatrix} K_1 \\ K_2 \end{bmatrix} y(t) + \begin{bmatrix} B \\ 0 \end{bmatrix} u(t) \tag{16}$$

where K_1 and K_2 are gain matrices to be designed to bring the estimation errors to zero quickly. In [2] it is shown that complete observability of the pair

$$\left(\begin{bmatrix} A & \dots & FH \\ \vdots & & \\ 0 & \dots & D \end{bmatrix}, \begin{bmatrix} C & \dots & 0 \end{bmatrix} \right) \tag{17}$$

is a sufficient condition for the existence of suitable matrices K_1 and K_2.

Since disturbances $w(t)$ cause undesirable effects on system behavior, the DAC signal u_c is responsible for canceling $w(t)$ such that

$$Bu_c + Fw = 0, \text{ i.e., } Bu_c = -FHz. \tag{18}$$

The solution for DAC signal u_c is then given in [3] as

$$u_c = B^+FHz, \tag{19}$$

where B^+ is the classical Moore–Penrose generalized inverse of B having the explicit form

$$B^+ = (B^TB)^{-1}B^T. \tag{20}$$

Computing schemes for B^+ are described in [4].

In summary, the criterion for generating DAC signal u_c is given by (19), where the disturbance state estimate can be generated from the full-order observer. Note that, in discussion, we have always assumed that the system output y can be measured exactly. If the measurement device becomes noisy, the state estimators can be replaced by the stochastic state observers such as the Kalman filter and minimal-order observer. The discussion of the DAC design for more general system and disturbance models can be found in [1].

B.   MODEL OF UNCANCELLED
       DISTURBANCE EFFECT

Due to the fact that the parameter values in the system model are uncertain, the feedback DAC input has to be generated using the available prior information. In addition, the fact of the probable jumping effect in disturbance and the measurement noise in the sampled output data makes the task of complete disturbance cancellation difficult.

In order to achieve exact identification of unknown parameters, such uncancelled disturbances must be properly modeled to avoid the bias problem. In this study, those remaining effects are treated as stochastic noise and are assumed white Gaussian distributed with zero mean. This assumption is difficult to justify analytically, since it involves several factors: type of disturbance, effectiveness of DAC controller, perturbation input generating, prior information of system parameters, measurement noise, and the overall system behavior. Each element of these factors contributes a part of the uncancelled disturbance, which can be modeled as a random variable η_i.

In physical problems the Gaussian assumption may be attributed in part to the central limit theorem, which declares that the Gaussian distribution will result quite generally from the sum of a large number of independent random variables acting together. To be more specific, let $\eta_1, \eta_2, ..., \eta_l$ be mutually independent random variables whose individual distributions are not specified and may be different. The central limit theorem states that under fairly common conditions the sum random variable will be Gaussian distributed as $l \to \infty$. In practical terms, a Gaussian assumption becomes reasonable in many cases for $l > 4$ [5].

This theorem yields the result that the uncancelled disturbance is the sum of a certain number of mutually independent random elements, and it approaches a Gaussian distribution under fairly general conditions.

If the prior values of parameters are not too inaccurate and jump effects of the disturbance do not happen too frequently, the uncancelled disturbance can be assumed to be noise with zero mean. If not, the nonzero mean has to be included in the unknown parameter vector θ.

If the uncancelled disturbance is nonwhite, it is often possible to model it as the output of a dynamic system which is driven by white noise. By joining this dynamic system model to the original system equations, an augmented dynamic system with white noise input is obtained. However, the unknown parameters should be extended to include the unknown elements in whitening process. In the simulation, such an assumption is appropriate to obtain reasonably good identification results.

C. DESIGN OF REGULATOR OR SERVOMECHANISM CONTROLLER

To accomplish the control objective, we have to apply the second control effort u_r such that input u_r is responsible for regulating or servo-tracking (servomechanism). In parallel to the u_c generating, the input u_r is now implemented using the state estimates from the state observer. In the regulating problem, u_r regulates the state X to zero, and it can be written as

$$u_r = -B^T P_r \bar{X}, \tag{21}$$

where P_r is the symmetric, positive definite solution of the Riccatti equation:

$$dP_r(t)/dt = -P_r A - A^T P_r - Q_r + P_r B B^T P_r \tag{22}$$

and Q_r is an arbitrary, positive definite symmetric matrix.

In the servo-tracking problem, u_r drives the state X(t) in a desired manner r(t), and it can be given as

$$u_r = -B^T P_r \bar{X} - B^T s, \tag{23}$$

where P_r and Q_r are defined as in the regulating problem and the command signal s depends on the reference input r(t):

$$ds(t)/dt = -\left(A^T - P_r BB^T\right)s + Q_r r(t). \tag{24}$$

Detailed procedures for designing the control u_r are described in [6].

D. DESIGN OF PERTURBATION SIGNAL

As we have seen, the control inputs u_c and u_r are generated from a physically realizable "feedback" controller which is relatively insensitive to slight uncertainties in system parameter values. If the prior information of parameters is not too inaccurate, the controlled system can behave within our expectancy. It is reported [7] that identification experiments with better controls of the system gave much worse parameter estimates. To make the identification process possible to be performed during feedback control operation, an additional perturbation signal with persistent excitation is often required. It has been shown in [8] that the conditions of persistent excited stationary input are

$$\bar{u} = \lim_{N \to \infty} 1/N \sum_1^N u(k) \tag{25}$$

and that

$$\varphi_{uu}(\tau) = \lim_{N \to \infty} 1/N \sum_{k=1}^N \left[u(k) - \bar{u}\right]\left[u(k + \tau) - \bar{u}\right] \tag{26}$$

exist and with positive covariance; $\varphi_{uu}(0) > 0$. It is sufficient to supply consistent estimates for the maximum likelihood method. Astrom and Eykhoff [9] also implied that the condition of persistent excitation assures that the spectral density of the input signal does not vanish for any frequency where the spectral density is the Fourier transformation of autocorrelation function $\{\varphi_{uu}(\tau)\}$.

It can be found [10] that the persistent excitation conditions on input and also on process noise are required for the persistent excitation on system states and the innovation process, and parameter estimates are therefore consistent.

Some of the special persistently excited inputs such as white Gaussian noise and pseudorandom binary sequence (PRBS) can be easily generated. In this study only white Gaussian noise is included in the simulation as a perturbation input u_i.

V.   MAXIMUM LIKELIHOOD METHOD

In this section we will discuss the maximum likelihood (ML) method, which was mentioned in the proposed algorithm. In order to carry the idea of maximum likelihood to a linear dynamical system, an expression for the likelihood function is to be stated. Then the maximum likelihood becomes a problem of optimizing a loss function with respect to an unknown parameter subject to Kalman filter constraints. It is a nonlinear optimization problem. In Section V,A a likelihood function is stated, and the optimization of the likelihood function is discussed in Section V,B. Parameter identifiability in ML is included in Section V,C.

A.   LIKELIHOOD FUNCTION

The maximum likelihood estimate consists of choosing θ to maximize the conditional probability of a sequence of N observations given a value of θ, i.e.,

$$P(Y_N/\overline{\theta}) = \max_{\theta} P(Y_N/\theta). \tag{27}$$

In order to carry this idea over to a linear dynamic system, with process and measurement noise, an expression for the likelihood function has to be obtained. Here the system model equation is of the form

$$dX/dt = Ax + Bu + e$$

$$y_k = C_k X_k + v_k, \tag{28}$$

where u is the combination of the perturbation input u_i and feedback stability control u_r and e indicates the effect of uncancelled disturbances which can be modeled as Gaussian white noise with unknown covariance Q. The output measurement noise v_k is white Gaussian with a known covariance matrix R. θ is the vector of unknown parameter in A, B, and Q. Based on derivations in [11], the likelihood function can be written as

$$\tag{29}$$

$$J(\theta) = \log P(Y_n \mid \theta)$$

$$= -\frac{1}{2} \sum_{j=1}^{N} \left[v_j^T V^{-1}(j|j-1) v_j + \log |V(j)|j-1)| \right],$$

where v_j and $V(j/j-1)$ denote the innovations and their covariances, which can be obtained from Kalman filter equations for the system (28).

Therefore, the maximum likelihood becomes a problem of optimizing $J(\theta)$ with respect to θ subject to the Kalman filter constraints. It is a nonlinear optimization problem.

B. OPTIMIZATION OF THE LIKELIHOOD FUNCTION

In this study, the optimization will be performed by the Gauss–Newton technique, which is reported to give faster results in convergence than the nonlinear programming technique [11]. In this method, the update to the parameter estimate $\delta\theta$ is computed using the following equation:

$$\delta\theta = -M^{-1}\,\delta J^T/\delta\theta, \tag{30}$$

where M is the Fisher information matrix, M^{-1} provides the Cramer–Rao lower bound on the covariance of θ estimates, and $\delta J/\delta\theta$ is the gradient of the cost $J(\theta)$ with respect to the unknown parameters. Using (29) we can write

$$\frac{\partial J}{\partial\theta} = \sum_{j=1}^{N} v^T V^{-1}\frac{\partial n}{\partial\theta} - \frac{1}{2}v^T V^{-1}\frac{\partial V}{\partial\theta}V^{-1}v + \frac{1}{2}\,\mathrm{Tr}\!\left(V^{-1}\frac{\partial V}{\partial\theta}\right) \tag{31}$$

and

$$M_{k1} = E\left(\frac{\partial J}{\partial\theta_K}\frac{\partial J}{\partial\theta_1}^T\right) \tag{32}$$

$$= \sum_{j=1}^{N}\left[\frac{\partial v^T}{\partial\theta_K}V^{-1}\frac{\partial v}{\partial\theta_1} + \frac{1}{2}\,\mathrm{Tr}\!\left(V^{-1}\frac{\partial V}{\partial\theta_K}V^{-1}\frac{\partial V}{\partial\theta_1}\right) + \frac{1}{4}\,\mathrm{Tr}\!\left(V^{-1}\frac{\partial V}{\partial\theta_K}\right)\mathrm{Tr}\!\left(V^{-1}\frac{\partial V}{\partial\theta_1}\right)\right],$$

where the arguments of v and V are not written explicitly and the expectation in the information matrix representation is taken over the sample space. Moreover, $\delta v/\delta\theta$ and $\delta V/\delta\theta$ in (31) and (32) can be calculated by solving linear differential equations, known as "sensitivity equations," given as follows:

$$\frac{\partial v}{\partial\theta}(j) = -C_j\frac{\partial \overline{X}}{\partial\theta}(j \mid j-1) \tag{33}$$

$$\frac{\partial V}{\partial\theta}(j) = C_j\frac{\partial P}{\partial\theta}(j \ll j-1)\,C_j^T.$$

For the prediction with $(j-1) \le t \le j$,

$$\frac{\partial P}{\partial \theta}(t \mid j - 1) = \frac{\partial A}{\partial \theta}P(t \mid j - 1) + A\frac{\partial P}{\partial \theta}(t \mid j - 1)$$

$$+ \frac{\partial P}{\partial \theta}(t \mid j - 1)A^T + P(t \mid j - 1)\frac{\partial A}{\partial \theta}^T + \frac{\partial Q}{\partial \theta}.$$
(34)

For the update,

$$\frac{\partial P}{\partial \theta}(j \mid j) = [I - KC_j]\frac{\partial P}{\partial \theta}(j \mid j - 1) - \frac{\partial K}{\partial \theta}C_jP(j \mid j - 1)$$
(35)

$$\frac{\partial K}{\partial \theta} = \frac{\partial P}{\partial \theta}(j \mid j - 1)C_j\left[C_jP(j \mid j - 1)C_j^T + r \right]^{-1}$$
(36)

$$- KC_j\frac{\partial P}{\partial \theta}(j \mid j - 1)C_j^T\left[C_jP(j \mid j - 1)C_j^T + R \right]^{-1}.$$

For the prediction, $(j - 1) \le t \le j$,

$$\frac{\partial \overline{X}}{\partial \theta}(t \mid j - 1) = \frac{\partial A}{\partial \theta}\overline{X}(t \mid j - 1) + A\frac{\partial \overline{X}}{\partial \theta}(t \mid j - 1).$$
(37)

For the update,

$$\frac{\partial \overline{X}}{\partial \theta}(j \mid j) = \frac{\partial \overline{X}}{\partial \theta}(j \mid j - 1) + \frac{\partial K}{\partial \theta}v_j - KC_j\frac{\partial \overline{X}}{\partial \theta}(j \mid j - 1),$$

where all the sensitivity equations can be obtained by directly differentiating the Kalman filter equations with respect to θ. In this study the output matrix C_k and measurement covariance R are assumed to be known. If this is not the case, more general formulations can be found in [11]. In conclusion, the maximum likelihood algorithm is shown in Fig. 2.

C.   IDENTIFIABILITY IN THE ML METHOD

In [11] it is shown that under conditions of persistent excitation on input and also on the innovation process, system identifiability can be established for prediction error methods. System identifiability is the possibility of determination, on the basis of input and output measurements, of a model to which the system under test is equivalent. Equivalence here means that the model and the system give the same transfer function. By assuming all the stochastic noises to be Gaussian distributed and specifying the loss function as in the form of (29), the prediction error method becomes the maximum likelihood method. In other words, system identifiability is established upon the linear system model (28) with the use of the maximum likelihood method.

If the objective of the identification is to obtain a model that can be used to design control laws, the concept of system identifiability which gives the model with the same transfer function as the system is probably adequate.

It is known from the literature that in the maximum likelihood method local parameter identifiability can be assured from the invertibility of the information matrix M, which is mentioned in (30). If the information matrix is positive definite, a uniqueness of the minimum of the likelihood function implies parameter identifiability.

It is noteworthy that parameter identifiability depends heavily on the choice of model parametrization and does not depend on the identification method used. Generally speaking, by knowing the exact system order, restricting the form of the model matrices, and limiting the range of the unknown parameter values, we will have unique parameter identification. Note that system identifiability is a necessary condition for parameter identifiability but is not sufficient itself.

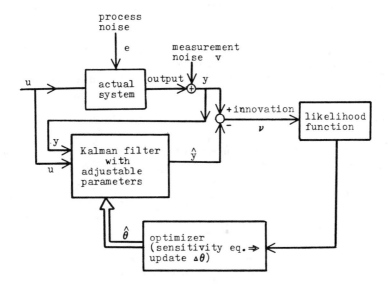

Fig. 2. Maximum likelihood algorithm.

VI. ILLUSTRATIVE EXAMPLES

In this section the application of the proposed algorithm and investigation of its accuracy performance will be illustrated. The Gaussian assumption on the effect of uncancelled disturbances will be discussed.

A.   THE SYSTEM MODEL

A second-order system is chosen, and its state space representation is of the form

$$\frac{dX(t)}{dt} = \begin{bmatrix} 0 & 1 \\ a_1 & a_2 \end{bmatrix} x(t) + \begin{bmatrix} 0 \\ 1 \end{bmatrix} u(t) + \begin{bmatrix} 0 \\ 1 \end{bmatrix} w(t) \tag{38}$$

$$y_k = [1 \ \ 0] \, X_k + v_k, \tag{39}$$

where a_1 and a_2 are unknown plant parameters, $X(t) = [X_1, X_2]^T$ is a system state vector, $w(t)$ is an unmeasurable waveform-type disturbance, y_k is the output measurement sampled at the time instant t_k, and v_k is Gaussian white noise with zero mean and known variance R. In the simulation the true parameter values are

$$a_1 = -2, \quad a_2 = -3.$$

In the simulation, we will include two kinds of waveform disturbances. In the first example, the unmeasurable disturbance is assumed constant with amplitude 2, i.e.,

$$w(t) = 2.$$

In the second example, the unmeasurable disturbance, which is composed of weighted linear combinations of steps and ramps, is in the form of

$$w(t) = 0.1 + 0.1t, \qquad 0 \le t < 50 \text{ sec}$$

$$= -4.9 + 0.2t, \quad 50 \le t \le 80 \text{ sec} \tag{40}$$

The measurement noise variance $R = \delta v^2 = 10^{-6}$, and the initial conditions $y_0 = X_{1,0} = 5$ are used in the simulation. In many practical systems the measurement matrix C_k is actually known and contains no unknown parameters. Here we have $C_k = [1 \ \ 0]$. The sampling interval is 0.1 sec.

In [12] it has been found that the continuous-time model parameters can be estimated from sample measurements with minimum bias only if the sampling interval is less than $T_c/5$, where T_c is the time constant of the dominant mode of the system. This result is also related to the accuracy of interpolation between sample points. In this simulation the input and output are sampled simultaneously and the sampled input is followed by zero-order hold, i.e.,

$$u(t) = u(k\ \delta T), \quad k\ \delta T \le t < (k + 1)\ \delta T. \tag{41}$$

Therefore, the sampling interval should be kept reasonably small to avoid a stability problem. But it cannot be so small as to increase the storage requirement and the computational complexity for the identification process.

B.   INPUT SIGNAL DESIGN

The input signal used in the simulation is divided into three parts:

$$u(t) = u_i + u_r + u_c, \tag{42}$$

where u_c is designed for counteracting $w(t)$, u_r is responsible for stabilizing the system, and u_i is the perturbation signal keeping the system persistently exciting. According to the DAC design mentioned in Section IV,A, u_c can be written as

$$u_c = -w(t). \tag{43}$$

Here the objective of control is to achieve $X = 0$, and a regulating control u_r is applied as

$$u_r = -50y - 15X_2. \tag{44}$$

The perturbation signal u_i that should be statistically independent of the measurement noise v_k is selected to be Gaussian white noise with zero mean and variance 1.

C.   IDENTIFICATION PROCESS

Since the identification algorithm is designed to operate in a stable regime, the input has to be applied for a certain period of time until the disturbance $w(t)$ is sufficiently suppressed and the system is properly oscillated.

In simulation, 150 sampling intervals (15 sec) are designated the pure control period. Hereafter, the system can be stated as:

$$\frac{dX(t)}{dt} = \begin{bmatrix} 0 & 1 \\ a_1 & a_2 \end{bmatrix} X(t) + \begin{bmatrix} 0 \\ 1 \end{bmatrix} (u_r + u_i) + \begin{bmatrix} 0 \\ u_c + w \end{bmatrix}. \tag{45}$$

The sampled input and output measurements are collected for 65 sec at a rate of 10 Hz. We assume that the data length of 650 sampling intervals is long enough to avoid a local minimum of the likelihood function.

After all the measurements have been made, the identification algorithm is started. In both examples, the effect of the uncancelled disturbance ($u_c + w$) is modeled as Gaussian white noise with zero mean and unknown variance Q.

In order to compute the likelihood function and the parameter update, all the related Kalman filter equations and sensitivity equations have to be integrated with time and updated at each sampling interval. A numerical Runge-Kutta method is used for integration interpolation.

The initial conditions of a_1, a_2, and Q are $a_{10} = -2.2$, $a_{20} = -2.8$, $Q_0 = 6 \times 10^{-6}$. The initial conditions used in the Kalman filter are

$$X(0) = 0, \quad P(0) = \begin{bmatrix} 0.1 & 0 \\ 0 & 0.1 \end{bmatrix}.$$

All the initial conditions used in the sensitivity equations are set to zero. At the end of each iteration, the parameter vector is updated. In this study, total batch iterations of 8 are selected.

In the simulation, iterative batch processing is performed on the identification experiment; nevertheless, the recursive real-time scheme can also be developed according to [13].

D.   RESULTS AND ANALYSES

Example 1. $w(t) = 2$ for all t. Figure 3 shows that an uncancelled disturbance has certain characteristics of stochastic noise. Figure 4 shows the combined input of u_i and u_r. The Kalman filter gains K_1 and K_2 are included in the

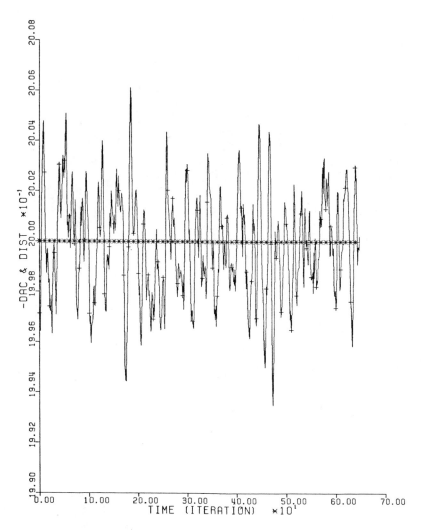

Fig. 3. Unmeasurable disturbance (*) and negative DAC input (+) versus sample intervals at 10 Hz (Example 1).

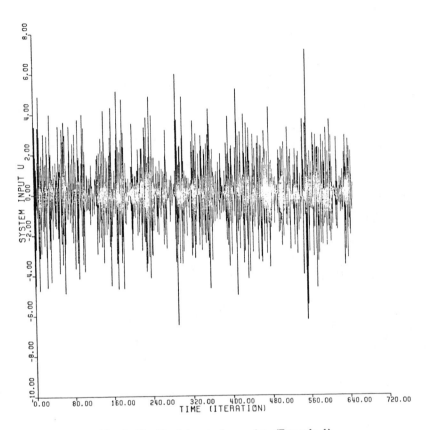

Fig. 4. Combined input of u_r and u_i (Example 1).

unknown parameter vector. The estimates and convergence results are listed in Table I (p. 247).. Figures 5 and 6 show the iterative results of simultaneously identifying the three parameters a_1, a_2, and Q. In Fig. 7 the likelihood function is computed at each iteration. Its value consistently decreases to its optimal value.

The simulation results also indicate that the Gaussian assumption of the uncancelled disturbance is appropriate for this example. Although such an as-

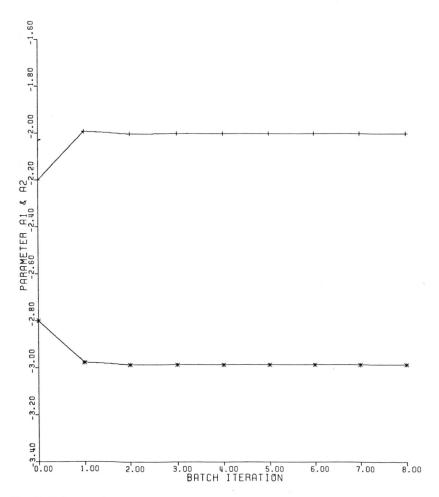

Fig. 5. Estimates of system parameters a_1 (+, true = −2) and a_2 (*, true = −3) (Example 1).

sumption is difficult to justify analytically, some statistical analyses on the collected data can be performed. In this study the autocorrelation function is computed according to the definitions of (25) and (26). The autocorrelation function is

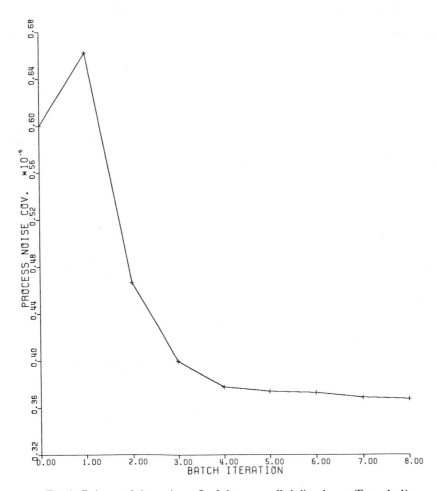

Fig. 6. Estimate of the variance Q of the uncancelled disturbance (Example 1).

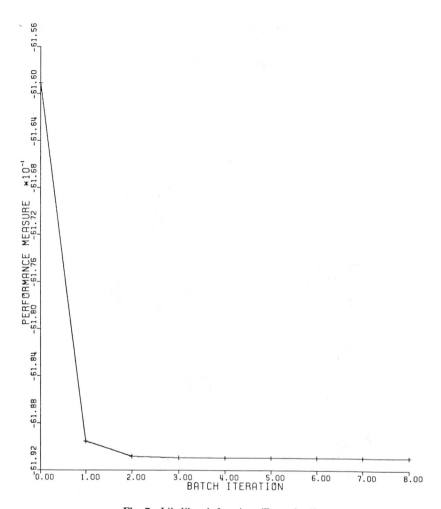

Fig. 7. Likelihood function (Example 1).

(a) Autocorrelations

```
        1- 12      .90  .72  .52  .32  .14  .01
        ST.E.      .04  .06  .08  .08  .08  .08

                  -.09 -.16 -.18 -.19 -.19 -.17
                   .08  .08  .08  .08  .08  .09

       13- 24     -.14 -.11 -.09 -.06 -.05 -.04
       ST.E.       .09  .09  .09  .09  .09  .09

                  -.04 -.05 -.05 -.06 -.06 -.06
                   .09  .09  .09  .09  .09  .09

       25- 36     -.05 -.03  0.0  .02  .06  .10
       ST.E.       .09  .09  .09  .09  .09  .09

                   .13  .14  .14  .12  .10  .08
                   .09  .09  .09  .09  .09  .09
```

(b) **PLOT OF AUTOCORRELATIONS**

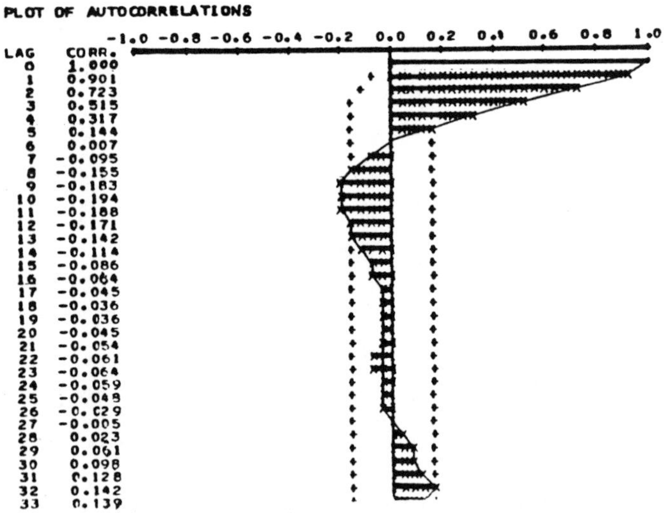

Fig. 8. Plot of autocorrelations (Example 1).

useful as a tool for detecting periodicities in random data, and the autocorrelation function might be computed as an intermediate step in the calculation of the power spectral density. Figure 8 shows the autocorrelation function of the uncancelled disturbance data in this example. First print the sample autocorrelations of the

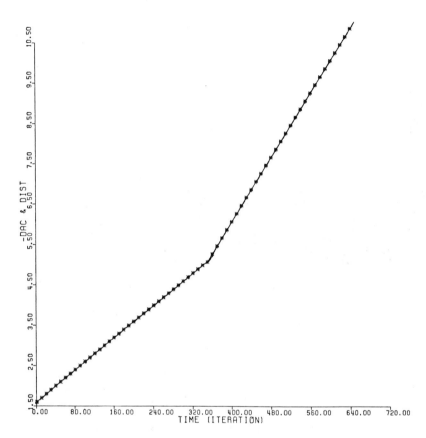

Fig. 9. Unmeasurable disturbance (*) and negative DAC input (+) versus sample intervals at 10 Hz (Example 2).

data and their standard errors. Then plot the autocorrelations and their 95% confidence intervals, which are denoted by the plus symbol on both sides of the vertical axis. The autocorrelation plot suggests that the data have autocorrelations close to an exponential cosine. Since the data are not strongly correlated, the uncancelled disturbance can be modeled as Gaussian white noise for simplicity. The simulation results indicate that the system parameter estimates are insensitive to the slight model error of the uncancelled disturbance.

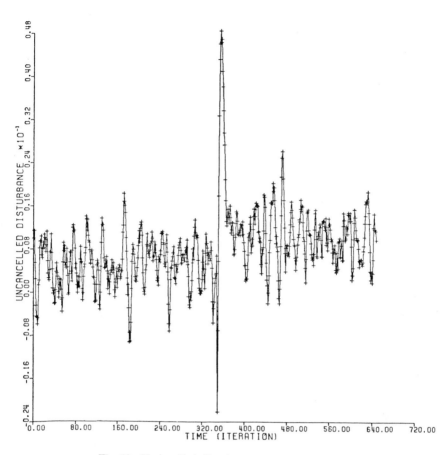

Fig. 10. Uncancelled disturbance, $u_c + w$ (Example 2).

Example 2.

$$w(t) = 0.1 + 0.1t, \qquad 0 \leq t < 50 \text{ sec}$$

$$= -4.9 + 0.2t, \quad 50 \leq t \leq 80 \text{ sec}.$$

In this example, the disturbance $w(t)$ is of the form

$$w = c_1 + c_2t,$$

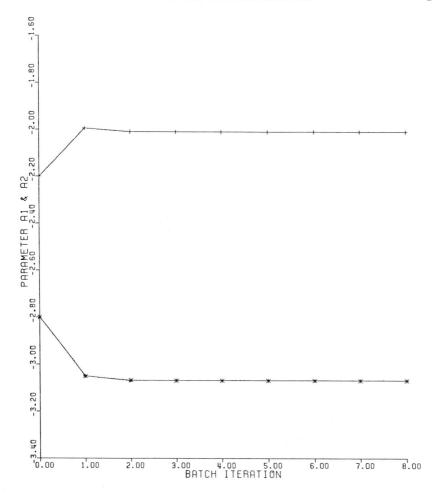

Fig. 11. Estimates of system parameters a_1 (+, true = −2) and a_2 (*, true = −3) (Example 2).

where c_1 and c_2 vary in a piecewise constant fashion. Figure 9 shows the unmeasurable disturbance and the negative DAC input. The effect of the uncancelled disturbance, $u_c + w$, is shown in Fig. 10. The jump effect of the disturbance can be seen within the plot. Similar to the results in Example 1, the convergence of system parameters a_1 and a_2 and the noise variance Q are listed in Table II. Figures 11 and 12 show the iterative results of three parameter estimates. In Fig. 13 the likelihood function decreases to its optimal value.

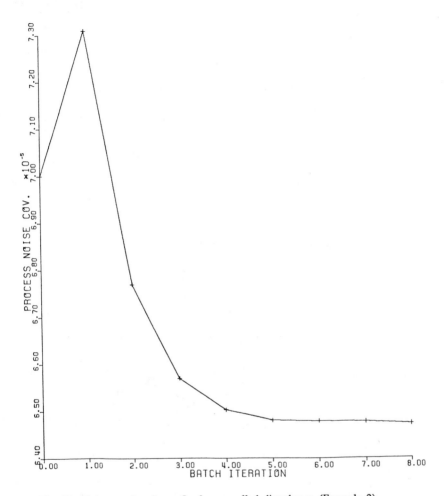

Fig. 12. Estimate of variance Q of uncancelled disturbance (Example 2).

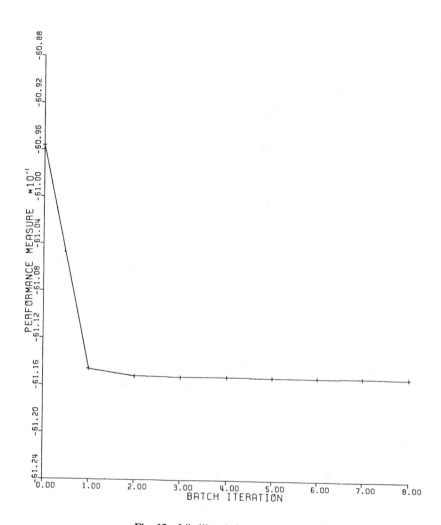

Fig. 13. Likelihood function (Example 2).

Autocorrelations

1- 12	.90	.76	.59	.44	.31	.21
ST.E.	.04	.06	.08	.08	.09	.09
	.14	.10	.07	.05	.04	.04
	.09	.09	.09	.09	.09	.09
13- 24	.06	.08	.11	.12	.13	.14
ST.E.	.09	.09	.09	.09	.09	.09
	.13	.12	.10	.10	.10	.11
	.09	.09	.09	.09	.09	.09
25- 36	.12	.13	.13	.14	.17	.19
ST.E.	.09	.09	.09	.09	.09	.09
	.21	.21	.20	.17	.14	.11
	.09	.10	.10	.10	.10	.10

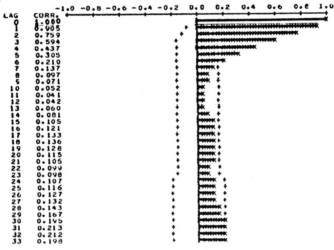

Fig. 14. Plot of autocorrelations (Example 2).

Figure 14 depicts the autocorrelation function of the uncancelled disturbance. All the specifications in the plot are the same as in Fig. 8. Again, the
uncancelled disturbance has an exponential decay in its autocorrelations. For
simplicity the uncancelled disturbance is again modeled as Gaussian white noise
without appreciable loss of accuracy in system parameter estimation. From the
analyses of two simulation examples, it is speculated that the Gaussian assumption of uncancelled disturbance may be applicable to other unmeasurable waveform
disturbances.

VII. CONCLUSIONS

The identification of plant parameters of a linear control system under the
effect of unmeasurable waveform-type disturbances has been studied. An algorithm which utilizes the DAC input design to counteract the disturbance and applies the maximum likelihood method to identify the unknown plant parameters
has been established. Throughout the study, we have demonstrated the usefulness
of this technique, where a second-order linear control system is included in two of
illustrative examples. System identifiability is assured in the prediction error
methods, which include the ML method as a special case. Parameter identifiability
that depends on the model parametrization and the range of admissible parameter
values should be treated as a problem of its own, and it does not depend on the

Table I. Parameter Estimates (Example 1)

Iteration	a_1	a_2	K_1	K_2	$Q \times 10^{-6}$	$J(\theta)$
	-2.2	-2.8	0.14963	0.12026	6.0	-6.1590
1	-1.9634	-3.0183	0.042996	0.29781	6.857	-6.0585
2	-1.9714	-2.9691	0.019271	0.49139	3.705	-5.9879
3	-1.9270	-2.9788	0.018336	0.63328	1.080	-5.9522
4	-1.9019	-2.9936	0.030690	0.71543	2.559	-5.9673
5	-1.8999	-3.0005	0.046913	0.77598	1.889	-5.9961
6	-1.8999	-3.0051	0.068954	0.75803	3.833	-6.0399
7	-1.9043	-3.0061	0.078939	0.75404	3.472	-6.0562
8	-1.9050	-3.0080	0.08440	0.73960	4.463	-6.0659
*	-2.00	-3.00	0.12329	0.08053	4.242	-6.19094

TABLE II. Parameter Estimates (Example 2)[a]

Iteration	a_1	a_2	$Q \times 10^{-6}$	$J(\theta)$
	-2.2	-2.8	7.0	-6.0960
1	-1.9946	-3.0503	7.309	-6.11462
2	-2.0086	-3.0682	6.770	-6.11520
3	-2.0089	-3.0690	6.570	-6.11526
4	-2.0088	-3.0690	6.503	-6.11526
5	-2.0088	-3.0690	6.481	-6.11527
6	-2.009	-3.0690	6.479	-6.11527
7	-2.009	-3.0690	6.477	-6.11526
8	-2.009	-3.0690	6.472	-6.11527
*	-2.00	-3.00	4.666	-6.117

$$K_1 = 0.37610, \quad K_2 = 0.86692.$$

identification method chosen. The proposed technique may be applicable to identify parameters of partially erroneous mathematical models in which such modeling errors lead to the presence of unmeasurable disturbance. Whenever the identification process is complete, optimal control can thereafter be generated based on modern, state space control technology.

REFERENCES

1. JOHNSON, C. D. Theory of Disturbance Accommodating Controllers, Chapter 7 in "Advances in Control and Dynamics System 12" (C. T. Leondes, Ed.), p. 387, Academic Press, New York, 1976.

2. C. D. JOHNSON "Accommodation of Disturbances in Optimal Control Problem," *Int. J. Control 15*, 209–231 (1972).

3. C. D. JOHNSON "Accommodation of Disturbance in Linear Regulator and and Servomechanism Problems," *IEEE Trans. Autom. Control AC-16*, 635–644 (1971).

4. L. A. ZADER and C. A. DESOER "Linear System Theory; The State Space Approach," McGraw-Hill, New York, 1963).

5. J. S. BENDAT and A. G. PIERSOL "Random Data: Analysis and Measurement Procedures," Wiley, New York, 1971.

6. D. E. KIRK "Optimal Control Theory – An Introduction," Prentice-Hall, Englewood Cliffs, New Jersey, 1970.

7. R. ISERMAN "Practical Aspects of Process Identification," *Automatica 16*, 575–587 (1980).

8. M. AOKI and R. M. STALEY "On Input Synthesis in Parameter Identification," *Automatica 6*, 431–440 (1969).

9. P. EYKHOFF and K. J. ASTROM "System Identification – A Survey," *Automatica 7*, 123–162 (1971).

10. L. LJUNG On the Consistency of Prediction Error Identification Methods, *in* "System Identification Advances and Case Studies (R. K. Mehra and D. G. Lainiotis, Eds.), p. 121. Academic Press, New York, 1976.

11. D. E. STEPNER and R. K. NEHRA "Maximum Likelihood Identification and Optimal Input Design for Identifying Aircraft Stability and Control Derivatives," NASA Rep. No. NASA CR-2200, 1973.

12. P. C. YOUNG Parameter Estimation for Continuous-Time Models – A Survey, "Identification and System Parameter Estimation," Vol. 1, p. 17, 1979.

13. M. SIDER,"Recursive Identification and Tracking of Parameters for Linear and Nonliner Multivariable Systems," *Int. J. Control 24*, 361–378 (1976).

14. J. C. CHEN "Identification of Linear Control Systems with Unmeasurable Inputs," Ph.D. Dissertation, University of California in Los Angeles,1984/

REALIZATIONS FOR GENERALIZED STATE SPACE SINGULAR SYSTEMS

MANOLIS A. CHRISTODOULOU*

Department of Computer Engineering
School of Engineering and
Computer Technology Institute
University of Patras
26500 Patras, Greece

I.   INTRODUCTION

The realization problem in linear systems is of fundamental importance as a factor in analysis as well as in feedback control loop design. The problem is the following: Given a transfer function matrix in the frequency domain, find a time domain, state space description. Normally there exist many solutions. Usually we choose specific descriptions which enjoy the desired properties.

Kalman [1] first treated the problem for regular linear systems. Then a number of papers appeared on it [2–11].

This article considers the problem of finding realization for a generalized transfer function matrix and answers questions relating minimality in singular systems and various definitions of observability and controllability. A canonical form for multivariable singular systems is derived. Furthermore, the minimality of the realization is related to the controllability and observability of singular systems (see [12–14]). The canonical form derived in this article arose in connection with the problem of obtaining an efficient state variable description for the purpose of parameter estimation, where it is desired that the number of arbitrary parameters to be estimated is minimal. In an appropriate canonical form the system is fully specified by a minimal number of independent parameters, and the parameter estimation problem reduces to finding a point in a Euclidean space of dimension equal to the above minimal number.

*Present address: Department of Electrical and Computer Engineering, Syracuse University, 111 Link Hall, Syracuse, New York 13210.

Moreover, methods are presented for the determination of a minimal realization of a singular system via the well-known Markov parameters [15, 16]. The methods can be considered as an extension of the Ho and Kalman [16] method for the realization of the regular system, which is also based on the Markov parameters. Thus any singular system described by its input–output relation may be realized.

A method is also presented for the determination of a minimal realization of a singular system via its Markov parameters and moments. In the regular systems case analogous methods are presented by the use of moments [17] and by a mixture of Markov parameters and moments [18]. The method of moments is preferred to the method of Markov parameters, especially when the data are contaminated with noise. However, the method of moments requires the computation of the inverse of a matrix. Shamash [19] and Eydgahi and Singh [20] proposed techniques for the realization of the transfer function matrix from a mixture of Markov parameters and moments. In this article the technique of Eydgahi and Singh [20] is extended to the case of singular systems.

II.   PROBLEM FORMULATION

Consider the time-invariant system of r first-order coupled linear differential equations

$$E\dot{x}(t) = Ax(t) + Bu(t) \tag{1a}$$

$$y(t) = Cx(t), \quad t \geq 0, \tag{1b}$$

where E is a singular square matrix, x is an r vector of state variables, u is an l vector of control inputs sufficiently differentiable, and y is a g vector of outputs. System (1) is the so-called *singular* or *generalized state space* or *descriptor system*. For an introduction to singular systems see [21–23].

If $Ex(0^-)$ is known and u(t) specified for $t \geq 0$, then the solution of (1) may be written in a Laplace transform (see [24]) as

$$X(s) = (sE - A)^{-1}[Ex(O^-) + BU(s)] \tag{2a}$$

$$Y(s) = CX(s). \tag{2b}$$

Here X, Y, U are the Laplace transforms of x, y, u, respectively. Assume that $(sE - A)$ is invertible, i.e., $\det(sE - A) \neq 0$. Then system (1) is solvable [21, 25, 26]. Also, it is known that under the above condition unique solutions are obtained for all $Ex(0^-)$ and U(s). The input–output relationship, under zero initial conditions, is given by the transfer function H(s) as follows:

$$Y(s) = H(s)U(s),$$

where

$$H(s) = C(sE - A)^{-1}B. \tag{3}$$

Of course, if E were nonsingular, then system (1) can readily be transformed into the usual state space description given by

$$x(t) = A^*x(t) + B^*u(t) \tag{4a}$$

$$y(t) = C^*x(t), \tag{4b}$$

where $A^* = E^{-1}A$ and $B^* = E^{-1}B$. This is called a *regular state space system*. Certain features of the regular systems that are of relevance to the material that follows with regard to the singular systems are listed below (see, for example [27–29]).

1) It can be easily seen from (2a) that knowledge of $Ex(0^-)$ is necessary and sufficient to completely determine $x(t)$ for $t \geq 0$, given $u(t)$ for $t \geq 0$. For the case of regular systems where E is nonsingular, it is evident that the r vector $Ex(0^-)$ can take r independent values. The system (1a) thus has r degrees of freedom, and this is termed the (regular) *order* of the (regular) state space system.

2) The transfer function $H(s)$ of the regular system is *strictly proper*, i.e., $H(s) \rightarrow 0$ as $s \rightarrow \infty$.

3) The free response of the regular system, i.e., $x(t)$ for $t \geq 0$ when $u(\cdot) \equiv 0$, consists of combinations of exponential motions or modes at those so-called natural frequencies $s = \lambda$ for which $(sE - A)$ is singular, namely the r finite roots of $|sE - A|$.

When E is singular, the aforementioned behavior is considerably modified. In contrast to 1–3, the following are true.

1a) The number of degrees of freedom of the singular system, i.e., the number of independent values that $Ex(0^-)$ can take, is now reduced to

$$f \overset{\Delta}{=} \text{rank } E < r. \tag{5}$$

This is the so-called generalized order [23].

2a) The transfer function $H(s)$ of the singular system may no longer be strictly proper, in which case it may be written as the sum of a strictly proper part $\bar{H}(s)$ and a polynomial part $P(s)$.

3a) For the case of singular E,

$$\deg |sE - A| = k \leq f < r. \tag{6}$$

The free response of the system in this case exhibits exponential motions, as before, at the k finite frequencies $s = \kappa$, where $sE - A$ is singular. In addition, however, it contains $f - k$ *impulsive* motions or *infinite frequency* modes [corresponding essentially to $(sE - A)$ losing rank at $s = \infty$]. Note that there is a connection between the *infinite-zero* structure of $(sE - A)$, defined via its Smith–McMillan form, and the impulsive modes mentioned previously [30, 31].

The following example illustrates 1a–3a.

Example 1. Consider system (1) with

$$
E = \begin{bmatrix} 0 & 0 & 0 & \cdots & 0 \\ 1 & 0 & 0 & \cdots & 0 \\ 0 & 1 & 0 & \cdots & 0 \\ \vdots & \vdots & \vdots & & \vdots \\ 0 & 0 & 0 & ..1 & 0 \end{bmatrix}, \quad A = I
$$

(7)

$$
b = \begin{bmatrix} 1 \\ 0 \\ 0 \\ \vdots \\ 0 \end{bmatrix}; \quad c = [0 \ 0 \ \cdots \ 0 \ -1],
$$

where I is the unity matrix.

1a) The system has generalized order

$$
f = \operatorname{rank} E = r - 1.
$$

(8)

2a) The system transfer function is

$$
H(s) = s^{r-1}.
$$

(9)

3a) The $k = \deg|\ sE - A\ |$ is equal to zero. The system's free response therefore exhibits *no* exponential motions, but does display $f - k = r - 1$ impulsive motions.

Descriptions of dynamical systems in the form (1) arise in several situations. One case is when these systems are formed from interconnected systems [32]. In fact, any system can generally be viewed as an interconnection of subsystems, and when the differential equations and algebraic constraints describing the system are first written down, they involve the internal variables of the subsystems in a description of form (1), usually with a singular coefficient matrix E. This happens, for example, when describing electrical networks using the element currents and voltages as internal variables (see [33, 34]). Even in cases where E is nonsingular, it may be of interest to relate the behavior of system (1) to that of a simplified or idealized model in which E is singular; this is characteristic of studies of singularly perturbed systems [35]. Discrete time versions of (1) also arise quite commonly [25, 37]. Applications of the above systems in economic models may be found in the Leontieff models in multisector economy [37–42], in biology in Leslie population models [21], etc.

For the generalized state space system (1), there corresponds a unique rational transfer function matrix H(s) given in (3) which will be referred to as the *generalized transfer function*. Conversely, for a given generalized transfer function matrix H(s) there is associated a whole class of singular systems of the form (1). These systems share the same input–output behavior but can differ internally. In particular, it is very easy to observe that for system (1), if H(s) is its transfer function matrix, then the system of form (1) with matrices

$$E = TET^{-1}$$

$$A = TAT^{-1}$$

$$(10)$$

$$B = TB$$

$$C = CT^{-1}$$

is associated again with the same transfer function H(s). Here T is any nonsingular $r \times r$ constant real matrix.

In this article, we consider the problem of finding a realization of a generalized transfer function matrix and answer questions relating minimality in singular systems and various definitions of observability and controllability.

In practice, the realization problem that arises is to find a canonical form for a generalized transfer function H(s).

III. MINIMAL REALIZATIONS FOR SINGLE INPUT–SINGLE OUTPUT SINGULAR SYSTEMS

The problem which will be answered in this section is stated as follows: Find a state space realization for a given scalar rational function h(s) which is not strictly proper and has the general form

$$h(s) = \frac{n(s)}{d(s)} = \frac{b_n s^n + \ldots + b_1 s + b_0}{s^m + \ldots + a_1 s + a_0}; \quad n > m. \tag{11}$$

The first step is to divide $n(s)$ by $d(s)$ so as to obtain

$$\frac{n(s)}{d(s)} = q(s) + \frac{r(s)}{d(s)}, \tag{12}$$

where

$$q(s) = q_{n-m} s^{n-m} + \ldots + q_1 s + q_0 \tag{13a}$$

is a polynomial of degree $n - m$ and

$$r(s) = r_{m-1} s^{m-1} + \ldots + r_1 s + r_0 \tag{13b}$$

is the remainder of the division such that deg $r(s) <$ deg $d(s)$. Note that $q(s)$ and $r(s)$ always exist and are unique. The form of (12) shows that the system is composed of the sum of two transfer functions, which means that the system can be realized with two subsystems connected in parallel. There are many well-known realizations for the strictly proper rational transfer function $r(s)/d(s)$. Here the most widely studied canonical form will be used, namely the so-called "phase variable" canonical form for single input systems which was first given by Kalman [1]. This canonical form is given by

$$\dot{x}_1 = A_1 x_1 + b_1 u, \quad y = c_1^T x_1, \tag{14}$$

where

$$A_1 = \begin{bmatrix} -a_{m-1} & -a_{m-2} & \cdots & -a_1 & -a_0 \\ 1 & 0 & \cdots & 0 & 0 \\ 0 & 1 & \cdots & 0 & 0 \\ \vdots & \vdots & & \vdots & \vdots \\ 0 & 0 & \cdots & 1 & 0 \end{bmatrix},$$

$$b_1 = \begin{bmatrix} 1 \\ 0 \\ 0 \\ \vdots \\ 0 \end{bmatrix}, \quad c_1^T = \begin{bmatrix} r_{m-1} & r_{m-2} & \cdots & r_0 \end{bmatrix}.$$

Clearly, A_1, b_1, and c_1 are unique in the sense that all their parameters are either prespecified or are uniquely determined by the input–output behavior of the system. In particular, the parameters a_i are the coefficients of the characteristic polynomial.

Here, a realization for the polynomial $q(s)$ is introduced. This is of the form:

$$K\dot{x}_2 = x_2 + b_2 u, \quad y = c_2^T x_2, \tag{15}$$

where

$$K = \begin{bmatrix} 0 & 0 & \cdots & 0 & 0 \\ 1 & 0 & \cdots & 0 & 0 \\ 0 & 1 & \cdots & 0 & 0 \\ \vdots & \vdots & & \vdots & \vdots \\ 0 & 0 & \cdots & 1 & 0 \end{bmatrix},$$

$$b_2 = \begin{bmatrix} 1 \\ 0 \\ 0 \\ \vdots \\ 0 \end{bmatrix}, \quad c_2^T = \begin{bmatrix} -q_0 & -q_1 & \cdots & -q_{n-m} \end{bmatrix}.$$

It is very easy to observe that the transfer function for (15), i.e.,

$$c_2^T(sK - I)^{-1}b_2, \tag{16}$$

is indeed the polynomial $q(s)$. Here, K, b_2, and c_2 are also unique. The parameters q_i are the coefficients of the polynomial. The above is a system in the generalized form, where K is a singular square matrix. It should be noted that the dimensionality of the state x_2 is $n - m + 1$ and that rank $K = n - m$, i.e., K, is rank deficient 1.

Hence the complete realization for the transfer function $h(s)$ is of the form

$$\begin{bmatrix} I & 0 \\ 0 & K \end{bmatrix}\begin{bmatrix} x_1 \\ x_2 \end{bmatrix} = \begin{bmatrix} A_1 & 0 \\ 0 & I \end{bmatrix}\begin{bmatrix} x_1 \\ x_2 \end{bmatrix} \tag{17a}$$

$$+ \begin{bmatrix} b_1 \\ b_2 \end{bmatrix} u$$

$$y = \begin{bmatrix} c_1^T & c_2^T \end{bmatrix}\begin{bmatrix} x_1 \\ x_2 \end{bmatrix} \tag{17b}$$

with order $n + 1$.

The question related to the minimality of the above realization will be answered in the following. Before going any further, two theorems concerning controllability and observability of system (17), proven in [13], are repeated here.

Theorem 1. a) The descriptor system (17) is completely controllable (c controllable) iff the augmented matrices

$$S_1 = \begin{bmatrix} b_1 & A_1 b_1 & \cdots & A_1^{m-1} b_1 \end{bmatrix}$$

and

$$S_2 = \begin{bmatrix} b_2 & K_2 & \cdots & K^{n-m} b_2 \end{bmatrix}$$

have ranks m and $n - m + 1$, respectively.

b) The descriptor system (17) is r controllable, i.e., controllable within the set of admissible initial conditions, iff the augmented matrix S_1 defined above has rank m.

Theorem 2. The descriptor system (17) is completely observable (c observable) iff the augmented matrices

$$L_1 = \begin{bmatrix} c_1 A_1^T c_1 & \cdots & (A_1^T)^{m-1} c_1 \end{bmatrix}$$

and

$$L_2 = \begin{bmatrix} c_2 K^T c_2 & \cdots & (K^T)^{n-m} c_2 \end{bmatrix}$$

are both full rank.

We say that it has finite modes observable iff only L_1 has full rank.

The following two lemmas will be useful in the sequel.

Lemma 1. If a transfer function $h(s)$ of form (11) has one $(n + 1)$-th-order c-controllable and c-observable realization, then all $(n + 1)$-th-order realizations must also be c controllable and c observable.

Proof. To prove this theorem assume that the division algorithm was used in $h(s)$ so as to obtain (13). Then any realization may be the parallel connection of one regular and one singular system. Assume that the realization which is c controllable and e observable is given by $\{(A_1, b_{11}, c_{11}), (K_1, b_{21}, c_{21})\}$, where (A_1, b_{11}, c_{11}) is the state space realization for the strictly proper part of $h(s)$ and (K_1, b_{11}, c_{21}) is the realization corresponding to the polynomial part of $h(s)$. Now if $\{(A_2, b_{12}, c_{12}), (K_2, b_{22}, c_{22})\}$ is any other $(n + 1)$-th-order realization, then by a well-known theorem for regular systems [29],

$$L_1(c_{11}, A_1) S_1(A_1, b_{11}) = L_1(c_{12}, A_2) S_1(A_2, b_{12}), \tag{18}$$

where $L_i(\cdot, \cdot)$, $S_i(\cdot, \cdot)$, $i = 1, 2$, are the observability and controllability matrices corresponding to their arguments.

Relationship (18) shows that, if its left-hand side is of full rank, then so is its right-hand side.

To proceed further, use the fact that if (K, b, c) is a realization of the form

$$K\dot{x} = x + bu \tag{19a}$$

$$y = c^T x, \tag{19b}$$

then its Hankel matrix defined by

$$M = [1, n - m] = \begin{bmatrix} c^T b & c^T Kb & \cdots & c^T K^{n-m} b \\ c^T Kb & c^T K^2 b & \cdots & c^T K^{n-m+1} b \\ \vdots & & & \\ c^T K^{n-m} b & & \cdots & c^T K^{2n-2m} b \end{bmatrix} \tag{20}$$

depends only on the transfer function

$$q(s) = c^T (sK - I)^{-1} b = -\sum_{i=1}^{\infty} \left(c^T K^{i-1} b \right) s^{i-1}. \tag{21}$$

Furthermore, it can be easily checked that

$$M[1, n - m] = L_2(c, K) S_2(K, b). \tag{22}$$

Therefore, for the two (K_1, b_{21}, c_{21}) and (K_2, b_{22}, c_{22}), $(n - m + 1)$-th-order realizations corresponding to the polynomial part of $h(s)$, the following is true:

$$L_2(c_{21}, K_1) S_2(K_1, b_{21}) = L_2(c_{22}, K_2) S_2(K_2, b_{22}). \tag{23}$$

Relationship (18) together with (23) proves the above lemma.

In view of this result, it suffices to find one case in which joint c controllability and c observability can be assured. It will be shown that form (17) will do. Before showing this, a basic lemma for polynomials will be proved.

Lemma 2. Suppose $n(s)$ and $d(s)$ are two polynomials in s, with $n = \deg n(s) > \deg d(s) = m$. Then perform the division as in (13)

$$\frac{n(s)}{d(s)} = q(s) + \frac{r(s)}{d(s)}.$$

It is true that

1) $\deg q(s) = n - m$.

2) Iff $n(s)$ and $d(s)$ are relatively prime, i.e., have no common roots, then $r(s)$ and $d(s)$ are also relatively prime.

Proof.

1) Obvious.

2) Assume that $n(s)$ and $d(s)$ are relatively prime and that $r(s)$ and $d(s)$ have a common factor. Then the quotient $r(s)/d(s)$ is equal to

$$\frac{r(s)}{d(s)} = \frac{\bar{r}(s)}{\bar{d}(s)}, \tag{24}$$

where deg $\bar{d}(s) = m - 1$. But then

$$\frac{n(s)}{d(s)} = \frac{q(s)\bar{d}(s) + \bar{r}(s)}{\bar{d}(s)}, \tag{25}$$

and this is a contradiction since deg $\bar{d}(s) = m$ and $n(s)$ and $d(s)$ are by hypothesis relatively prime.

Conversely, assume now that $r(s)$ and $d(s)$ are relatively prime and $n(s)$ and $d(s)$ are not. Then by using the same arguments as above, note that

$$\frac{\bar{n}(s) - q(s)\bar{d}(s)}{\bar{d}(s)} = \frac{r(s)}{d(s)}, \tag{26}$$

where deg $\bar{d}(s) = m - 1$. This is again a contradiction.

Lemma 3. The $(n + 1)$-th order controller form (17) which represents the c-controllable singular system will be c observable iff $n(s)$ and $d(s)$ are coprime, i.e., iff $n(s)/d(s)$ is irreducible.

Proof. Use the division algorithm for $n(s)/d(s) = q(s) + r(s)/d(s)$. Then a well-known lemma [29] for regular systems states that the strictly proper part $r(s)/d(s)$ will be observable iff $r(s)$ and $d(s)$ are coprime. This, together with Lemma 2 and the fact that L_2 is always of full rank for (15), which will be proved below, proves Lemma 3.

Lemma 4. The matrix L_2, as in Definition 1, is of full rank for the realization (15).

Proof. By constructing L_2,

$$L_2 = \begin{bmatrix} -q_0 & -q_1 & \cdots & -q_{n-m-1} & -q_{n-m} \\ -q_1 & -q_2 & \cdots & -q_{n-m} & 0 \\ \vdots & \vdots & & & \\ -q_{n-m} & 0 & & 0 & 0 \end{bmatrix} \tag{27}$$

it can be easily verified that det $(L_2) \neq 0$ since $q_{n-m} \neq 0$.

Theorem 3. A generalized scalar transfer function $h(s) = n(s)/d(s)$ is irreducible iff all $(n + 1)$-th order realizations, $n = \deg n(s)$, are c controllable and c observable.

Proof. The immediate consequence of Lemmas 1, 3, and 4.

Theorem 4. A realization $\{E, A, b, c\}$, where

$$E = \begin{bmatrix} I & 0 \\ 0 & K \end{bmatrix}, \quad A = \begin{bmatrix} A_1 & 0 \\ 0 & I \end{bmatrix} \tag{28}$$

$$b = \begin{bmatrix} b_1 \\ b_2 \end{bmatrix}, \quad c^T = \begin{bmatrix} c_1^T c_2^T \end{bmatrix}$$

as in (17), is minimal iff $n(s) = c^T$ Adj $(sE - A)b$ and $d(s) = \det(sE - A)$ are relatively prime.

Proof. Exactly as in the regular system case, [29].

Theorems 3 and 4 can be combined to obtain the following important result which provides a direct test for minimality.

Theorem 5. A generalized realization $\{E, A, B, C\}$ is minimal if it is c controllable and c observable.

Finally, note that minimal realizations are very tightly related, as indicated by the following theorem.

Theorem 6. Any two generalized minimal realizations can be connected by a *unique* similarity transformation T.

Proof. Define

$$T = \begin{bmatrix} T_1 & 0 \\ 0 & T_2 \end{bmatrix} \tag{29}$$

$$= \begin{bmatrix} L_1^{-1}(c_{11}, A_1) & L_1(c_{12}, A_2) & 0 \\ 0 & L_2^{-1}(c_{21}, K_1) & L_2(c_{22}, K_2) \end{bmatrix}$$

as in Lemma 1. From the previously noted identities (18) and (23), it is concluded that

$$T = \begin{bmatrix} S_1(A_1, b_{11}) & S_1^{-1}(A_2, b_{12}) & 0 \\ 0 & S_2(K_1, b_{21}) & S_2^{-1}(K_2, b_{22}) \end{bmatrix}. \tag{30}$$

Now it can be easily seen that

$$T^{-1}\begin{bmatrix} b_{11} \\ b_{21} \end{bmatrix} = \begin{bmatrix} b_{12} \\ b_{22} \end{bmatrix}$$

$$\begin{bmatrix} c_{11}^T & c_{21}^T \end{bmatrix} T = \begin{bmatrix} c_{12}^T & c_{22}^T \end{bmatrix}.$$

Finally, from the easily verified relations
$$L_1(c_{11}, A_1)A_1S_1(A_1, b_{11}) = L_1(c_{12}, A_2)A_2S_1(A_2, b_{12})$$

$$= (M[2, m-1])$$

and

$$L_2(c_{21}, K_1)K_1S_2(K_1, b_{21}) = L_2(c_{22}, K_2)K_2S_2(K_2, b_{22})$$

$$= (M[2, n-m])$$

it is obtained

$$\begin{bmatrix} I & 0 \\ 0 & K_2 \end{bmatrix} = T^{-1}\begin{bmatrix} I & 0 \\ 0 & K_1 \end{bmatrix} T$$

$$\begin{bmatrix} A_2 & 0 \\ 0 & I \end{bmatrix} := T^{-1}\begin{bmatrix} A_1 & 0 \\ 0 & I \end{bmatrix} T.$$

Moreover, the uniqueness is obvious.

IV. STANDARD FORMS FOR NON-c-CONTROLLABLE AND/OR NON-c-OBSERVABLE SINGULAR SYSTEMS

For some applications it will be useful to have standard forms in which non-c-controllable and/or non-c-observable systems can be represented. By using appropriate similarity transformations, it will be possible to find realizations in which the non-c-controllable and/or non-e-observable state variables can be clearly separated out.

A.   REPRESENTATION OF NON-c-CONTROLLABLE REALIZATIONS

To proceed, it is convenient to work a standard form under restricted system equivalence (following [43]). First recall from the theory of "regular pencils" [26] that there exist nonsingular M and N such that

$$M(sE - A)N = \begin{bmatrix} sI_m - A_1 & 0 \\ 0 & sK - I_{n-m+1} \end{bmatrix}, \tag{31}$$

where E and A are taken from (1) and K and A_1 are as in (17). This shows that by choosing M and N the system can be transformed to the form (17). Now let the realization $\{(A_1, b_1, c_1), (K, b_2, c_2)\}$ be such that

rank $S_1(A_1, b_1) = r_1 < m$

and

rank $S_2(K, b_2) = r_2 < n - m + 1$.

Then a transformation matrix T can always be found such that the realization

$E = T^{-1}ET, \quad A = T^{-1}AT, \quad b = T^{-1}b, \quad c = cT$

has the form

$$\bar{E} = \begin{bmatrix} 1 & 0 \\ & K_c & K_{cc} \\ 0 & 0 & K_{\bar{c}} \end{bmatrix}$$

$$\bar{A} = \begin{bmatrix} \bar{A}_c & \bar{A}_{cc} & 0 \\ 0 & A_{\bar{c}} & \\ 0 & & I \end{bmatrix}, \quad \bar{b} = \begin{bmatrix} b_{1c} \\ 0 \\ b_{2c} \\ 0 \end{bmatrix} \tag{32}$$

$$c^{-T} = \begin{bmatrix} c_{1c}^{-T} & c_{2c}^{-T} & c_{2c}^{-T} & c_{2c}^{-T} \end{bmatrix}.$$

Any realization in this form has the important properties that

1) The $(r_1 + r_2) \times (r_1 + r_2)$ subsystem $\{(A_c, b_{1c}, c_{1c}), (K_c, b_{2c}, c_{2c})\}$ is c controllable.

2) It is true that

$$\bar{c}(s\bar{E} - \bar{A})^{-1}\bar{b} = \bar{c}_c(s\bar{E}_c - \bar{A}_c)^{-1}\bar{b}_c,$$

where

$$\bar{c}_c^{-T} = \begin{bmatrix} c_{1c}^{-T} & c_{2c}^{T} \end{bmatrix}, \qquad \bar{E}_c = \begin{bmatrix} I & 0 \\ \hline 0 & K_c \end{bmatrix},$$

$$\bar{A}_c = \begin{bmatrix} \bar{A}_c & 0 \\ \hline 0 & I \end{bmatrix}, \quad \bar{b}_c = \begin{bmatrix} \bar{b}_{1c} \\ \hline \bar{b}_{2c} \end{bmatrix}.$$

(33)

Statement 2) can be proved via the well-known techniques for regular systems (see [39]). Also note that

$$S_1(\bar{A}_{1c}, \bar{b}_{1c}) = \begin{bmatrix} \bar{b}_{1c} & \bar{A}_c\bar{b}_{1c} & \cdots & \bar{A}_c^{r_1-1}\bar{b}_{1c} \\ \hline 0 & 0 & 0 \end{bmatrix} \begin{matrix} {\scriptstyle r_1} \\ \\ {\scriptstyle m-r_1} \end{matrix}$$

$$S_2(\bar{K}_c, \bar{b}_{2c}) = \begin{bmatrix} \bar{b}_{2c} & \bar{K}_c\bar{b}_{2c} & \cdots & \bar{K}_2^{r_2-1}\bar{b}_{2c} \\ \hline 0 & 0 & 0 \end{bmatrix} \begin{matrix} {\scriptstyle r_2} \\ \\ {\scriptstyle n-m+1-r_2} \end{matrix}$$

Now, since

$$S = \begin{bmatrix} S_1(\overline{A}_c, \overline{b}_{1c}) & 0 \\ 0 & S_2(\overline{K}_c, \overline{b}_{2c}) \end{bmatrix} = T^{-1} \begin{bmatrix} S_1(A_1, b_1) & 0 \\ 0 & S_2(K, b_2) \end{bmatrix} \qquad (34)$$

S has rank $(r_1 + r_2)$. Using the same arguments as for the regular state space case, the matrix T may be found [29].

B.   REPRESENTATION OF
      NON-c-OBSERVABLE REALIZATIONS

      Similar statements can be made about non-c-observable realizations. Thus, if

rank $L_1(A, c_1) = r_1 < m$

and

rank $L_2(K, c_2) = r_2 < n - m + 1,$

a nonsingular matrix T can be found such that

rank $L_2(K, c_2) = r_2 < n - m + 1,$

having the form

$$\overline{E} = \begin{bmatrix} I & 0 \\ \hline & K_0 & 0 \\ 0 & \hline & \\ & K_{00}^- & K_0^- \end{bmatrix}$$

$$\overline{A} = \begin{bmatrix} \overline{A}_0 & 0 \\ \hline \overline{A}_{00} & \overline{A}_0 & 0 \\ \hline 0 & I \end{bmatrix}, \quad \overline{b} = \begin{bmatrix} \overline{b}_{10} \\ \hline \overline{b}_{10} \\ \hline \overline{b}_{20} \\ \hline \overline{b}_{20} \end{bmatrix} \qquad (35)$$

$$\overline{c}^T = \begin{bmatrix} \overline{c}_{10} & 0 & \overline{c}_{20} & 0 \end{bmatrix}$$

and

1) The $(r_1 + r_2) \times (r_1 + r_2)$ subsystem $\{(A_0, b_{10}, c_{10}), (K_0, b_{20}, c_{20})\}$ is c observable.

2) It is true that

$$\bar{c}(s\bar{E} - \bar{A})^{-1}\bar{b} = \bar{c}_0(s\bar{E}_0 - \bar{A}_0)^{-1}\bar{b}_0,$$

where c_0, E_0, A_0, b_0 are defined as the analogous c_c, E_c, A_c, b_c in (33).

The above results suggest one way of obtaining a minimal realization from a given realization of a transfer function. Thus the following theorem, analogous to the Kalman decomposition theorem, is stated below.

Theorem 7. General decomposition theorem for generalized systems: An invertible state transformation can always be found such that to rewrite the generalized state equations (17) in the form

$$\bar{E} \ \dot{\bar{x}} = \bar{A} \ \bar{x} + \bar{b}u, \qquad y = \bar{c} \ \bar{x}$$

where

$$\bar{x}^T = \left[x_1^T \ \middle| \ x_2^T \ \cdots \ \middle| \ x_8^T \right]$$

$$\bar{E} = \begin{bmatrix} I & & & & 0 & & \\ & & \bar{K}_{c,0} & 0 & \bar{K}_{1,3} & 0 \\ 0 & & \bar{K}_{2,1} & \bar{K}_{c,0} & \bar{K}_{2,3} & \bar{K}_{2,4} \\ & & 0 & 0 & \bar{K}_{c,0} & 0 \\ & & 0 & 0 & \bar{K}_{4,3} & \bar{K}_{c,0} \end{bmatrix}$$

$$\bar{A} = \begin{bmatrix} \bar{A}_{c,0} & 0 & \bar{A}_{1,3} & 0 & \\ \bar{A}_{2,1} & \bar{A}_{c,0} & \bar{A}_{2,3} & \bar{A}_{2,4} & 0 \\ 0 & 0 & \bar{A}_{c,0} & 0 & \\ 0 & 0 & \bar{A}_{4,3} & \bar{A}_{c,0} & \\ & & 0 & & I \end{bmatrix}$$

268

MANOLIS A. CHRISTODOULOU

$$\bar{b} = \begin{bmatrix} \bar{b}_{1c,0} \\ \hline \bar{b}_{1c,0} \\ \hline 0 \\ \hline 0 \\ \hline \bar{b}_{2c,0} \\ \hline \bar{b}_{2c,0} \\ \hline 0 \\ \hline 0 \end{bmatrix},$$

(36)

$$\bar{c}^T = \begin{bmatrix} \bar{c}_{1c,0}^T & 0 & \bar{c}_{1c,0}^T & 0 & \bar{c}_{2c,0}^T & 0 & \bar{c}_{2c,0} & 0 \end{bmatrix}$$

1) The subsystem $\{(A_{c,0}, b_{1c,0}, c_{1c,0}), (K_{c,0}, b_{2c,0}, c_{2c,0})\}$ is c controllable and c observable.

2) The subsystem

$$\left\{ \left(\begin{bmatrix} \bar{A}_{c,0} & 0 \\ \bar{A}_{2,1} & \bar{A}_{c,0} \end{bmatrix}, \begin{bmatrix} \bar{b}_{1c,0} \\ \bar{b}_{1c,0} \end{bmatrix}, \begin{bmatrix} \bar{c}_{1c,0}^T & 0 \end{bmatrix} \right) \right.$$

$$\left. \left(\begin{bmatrix} \bar{K}_{c,0} & 0 \\ \bar{K}_{2,1} & \bar{K}_{c,0} \end{bmatrix}, \begin{bmatrix} \bar{b}_{2c,0} \\ \bar{b}_{2c,0} \end{bmatrix}, \begin{bmatrix} \bar{c}_{2c,0}^T & 0 \end{bmatrix} \right) \right\}$$

is c controllable.

3) The subsystem

$$
\left\{
\left(
\begin{bmatrix} \bar{A}_{c,0} & \bar{A}_{1,3} \\ 0 & \bar{A}_{\bar{c},0} \end{bmatrix},
\begin{bmatrix} \bar{b}_{1c,0} \\ 0 \end{bmatrix},
\begin{bmatrix} \bar{c}^{-T}_{1c,0} & \bar{c}^{-T}_{1\bar{c},0} \end{bmatrix}
\right)
\right.
$$

$$
\left.
\left(
\begin{bmatrix} \bar{K}_{c,0} & \bar{K}_{1,3} \\ 0 & \bar{K}_{\bar{c},0} \end{bmatrix},
\begin{bmatrix} \bar{b}_{2c,0} \\ 0 \end{bmatrix},
\begin{bmatrix} \bar{c}^{T}_{2c,0} & \bar{c}^{T}_{2\bar{c},0} \end{bmatrix}
\right)
\right\}
$$

is c observable.

4) The subsystem $\{(A_{c,0}, 0, 0), (K_{c,0}, 0, 0)\}$ is neither c controllable nor c observable. Note that the subsystem in (1) has the same transfer function as the original system.

Proof. Exactly analogous as for the regular case [29]. This general decomposition theorem was first enunciated by Gilbert [44] and Kalman [1] for the case of regular linear systems.

V.   SOME BASIC STATE SPACE REALIZATIONS FOR MULTIVARIABLE SINGULAR SYSTEMS

In this section, the realization procedures of Section III will be extended to obtain certain realizations for a generalized transfer function H(s), where H(s) is a rational matrix. However, all the problems are now more involved because, unlike the scalar case, there does not seem to be a single unique choice of realizations. A much closer analogy with the scalar results can be achieved by using the so-called matrix-fraction descriptions (MFDs) of rational matrices as the ratio of two polynomial matrices [29].

A.   A CONTROLLER FORM REALIZATION

At the beginning of this section a controller form realization is presented from a right MFD. Thus, consider a right MFD

$H(s) = N(s)D^{-1}(s),$

where $N(s)$ is a $p \times m$ polynomial matrix and $D(s)$ is a square polynomial matrix $m \times m$, with det $D(s) \neq 0$. Note that $H(s)$ does not have to be strictly proper. At this point, the following basic theorem proved in [29] will be stated.

Theorem 8. Division theorem for polynomial matrices: Let $D(s)$ be an $m \times m$ nonsingular polynomial matrix. Then for any $p \times m$ polynomial matrix $N(s)$, there exist *unique* polynomial matrices $Q(s)$, $R(s)$ such that

$$N(s) = Q(s)D(s) + R(s)$$

and $R(s)D^{-1}(s)$ is strictly proper.

Using the above theorem, $H(s)$ can be written as

$$H(s) = N(s)D^{-1}(s) = Q(s) + R(s)D^{-1}(s). \tag{37}$$

A realization for $R(s)D^{-1}(s)$ which is a strictly proper right MFD was given by Wang [45] and Wolovich [46] (see also Wolovich and Falb [47]).

Thus, given $R(s)D^{-1}(s)$, one can write for $D(s)$

$$D(s) = D_{hc}S(s) + D_{lc}\Psi(s), \tag{38}$$

where

$$S(s) = \text{diag}\{s^{k_1}, \ldots, s^{k_m}\},$$

where k_i are the column degrees of $D(s)$ and D_{hc} is the highest-column-degree coefficient matrix of $D(s)$ [29].

The term $D_{lc}\Psi(s)$ accounts for the remaining lower-column-degree terms of $D(s)$, with D_{lc} a matrix of coefficients and

$$\Psi^T(s) \triangleq \begin{bmatrix} s^{k_1-1} & \ldots & s & 1 & 0 & \ldots & & 0 \\ 0 & & s^{k_2-1} & \ldots & 1 & \ldots & & 0 \\ & & & & \ldots & & & \\ 0 & & & 0 & & \ldots & s^{k_m-1} & \ldots & 1 \end{bmatrix}. \tag{39}$$

Following the pattern of the scalar case, write for $R(s)D^{-1}(s)$

$$D(s)\xi(s) = u(s) \tag{40a}$$

$y_1(s) = N(s)\xi(s).$ (40b)

Then use (38) together with (40a) to write

$D_{hc}S(s)\xi(s) = -D_{lc}\Psi(s)\xi(s) + u(s).$ (41)

Then assuming that D_{hc} is invertible, (41) gives

$S(s)\xi = -D_{hc}^{-1}D_{lc}\Psi(s)\xi + D_{hc}^{-1}u.$ (42)

In the scalar case, $D_{hc} \neq 0$ means that the equation is indeed of the n-th order. In the matrix case, the analogous assumption with $n = \deg D(s)$ is that $D(s)$ is column reduced.

As is well known [29], $D(s)$ can always be reduced to this form without affecting the determinantal degree. Assume now that each $\xi_i^{(k_i)}$ is available and integrate each k_i times to obtain all the required lower-order derivatives. There exist m chains with k_i integrators in each chain. The outputs of the integrators are given by the entries of $\Psi(s)\xi(s)$. This gives the core realization with transfer function $\Psi(s)S^{-1}(s)$. Now assemble these integrator outputs along the input according to the prescription on the right-hand side of (42) and thus generate the left-hand side of (42). Finally, closing the loop completes the realization of (40a).

The output equation (40b) can be written as

$y_1(s) = N(s)\xi(s) = N_{lc}\Psi(s)\xi(s),$ (43)

where N_{lc} is an appropriate matrix of coefficients which shows clearly that y is obtained as weighted sums of the states.

Since now the strictly proper part is realized, it remains to realize the polynomial part $Q(s)$. This can be written as

$Q(s) = N_{hcp}\Psi_p(s),$ (44)

where N_{hcp} is an appropriate matrix of coefficients and $\Psi_p(s)$ is the following matrix:

$$\Psi_p^T(s) \triangleq \begin{bmatrix} 1 \ s \dots s^{n_1} & 0 & \dots & 0 \\ 0 & 1 \dots s^{n_2} & \dots & 0 \\ & & \ddots & \\ 0 & 0 & \dots & 1 \dots s^{n_m} \end{bmatrix},$$ (45)

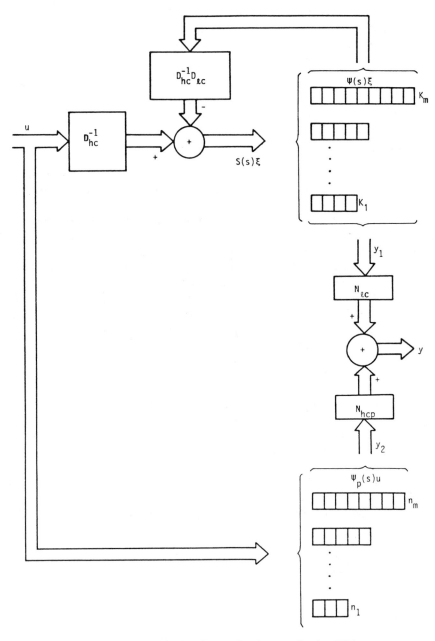

Fig. 1. Schematic of controller-form realization H(s).

where n_i are the degrees of the columns of $Q(s)$ (highest degrees of the polynomial elements of each column). Following the pattern of the scalar case as in (15) and (16), write for $Q(s)$

$$y_2(s) = Q(s)u(s). \tag{46}$$

Since each u_i is available, differentiate each n_i times to obtain all the required higher-order derivatives. There exist m chains with n_i differentiators in each chain. The outputs of the differentiators are given by the entries of $\Psi_p(s)\xi(s)$. This is the entire realization for the dynamical part of $Q(s)$. It will be shown below how it can be realized via a singular system.

The output equation here can be written as

$$y_2(s) = N_{hcp}\Psi_p(s)u(s). \tag{47}$$

The final realization for $H_p(s)$ is given as a parallel connection of the two previously studied systems. For the output it is

$$y(s) = y_1(s) + y_2(s). \tag{48}$$

The realization is shown in Fig. 1.

A description of the above procedure in the state space will be given below. Recall that for the strictly proper part $R(s)D^{-1}(s)$, the first step is to set m chains of k_i integrators each, with access to the input of the first integrator of each chain and to the outputs of every integrator of every chain. The corresponding system matrices for the realization of this core system are [29]:

$$A_c^0 = \text{block diag} \begin{bmatrix} 0 & & 0 \\ 1 & \cdot & \\ & \cdot & \\ & & \cdot \\ 0 & 1 & 0 \end{bmatrix}, \; k_i \times k_i, \; i = 1, ..., m \tag{49a}$$

$$\left[B_c^0 \right]^T = \text{block diag} [1 \quad 0 \, ... \, 0], \; 1 \times k_i, \; i = 1, ..., m \tag{49b}$$

$$C_c^0 = I_n, \; n = \deg \det D(s) = \sum_{i=1}^{m} k_i. \tag{49c}$$

It can be checked by direct calculation that

$$\left(sI - A_c^0\right)^{-1}B_c^0 = C_c^0\left(sI - A_c^0\right)^{-1}B_c^0 = \Psi(s)S^{-1}(s). \tag{50}$$

The core realization is controllable and observable, as may be seen by direct calculation; i.e., the matrices S_1 and L_1 are of full rank, where those matrices are as in Theorems 1 and 2, but now the column vectors b and c are replaced by the matrices B and C. Next, the states and the input are assembled according to the right-hand side of (42) and the loop is closed. This corresponds to state feedback through a gain $D_{hc}^{-1}D_{lc}$ and to application of an input $D_{hc}^{-1}u$. The system matrices for the realization are

$$A_1 = A_c^0 - B_c^0 D_{hc}^{-1} D_{lc}, \quad B_1 = B_c^0 D_{hc}^{-1}$$

$$C_1 = N_{lc}. \tag{51}$$

The modification is easy to carry out. Certain rows of A_c^0 are replaced by the rows of $D_{hc}^{-1}D_{lc}$ and certain rows of B_c^0 by rows of D_{hc}^{-1}.

For the polynomial part $Q(s)$ the first step is to set m chains of n_i differentiators each, with access to the input of the first differentiator of each chain and to the outputs of each differentiator of every chain. The corresponding system matrices for the realization of this core system are

$$K = \text{block diag} \begin{bmatrix} 0 & & 0 \\ 1 & \ddots & \\ 0 & 1 & 0 \end{bmatrix}, \quad (n_i + 1) \times (n_i + 1), \quad i = 1, \ldots, m \tag{52a}$$

$$B_2 = \text{block diag}[1 \quad 0 \quad \ldots \quad 0], 1 \times (n_i + 1), \quad i = 1, \ldots, m \tag{52b}$$

$$C_2 = -N_{hcp}. \tag{52c}$$

It can be checked by direct calculation that

$$C_2(sK - I)^{-1}B_2 = Q(s).$$

This realization has S_2 and L_2 of full rank, where S_2 and L_2 are as in Theorems 1 and 2. This is the final assembly for the polynomial part. The general realization as for the scalar case is

$$\begin{bmatrix} I & 0 \\ 0 & K \end{bmatrix} \begin{bmatrix} x_1 \\ x_2 \end{bmatrix} = \begin{bmatrix} A_1 & 0 \\ 0 & I \end{bmatrix} \begin{bmatrix} x_1 \\ x_2 \end{bmatrix} + \begin{bmatrix} B_1 \\ B_2 \end{bmatrix} u \tag{53a}$$

$$y = \begin{bmatrix} c_1 & c_2 \end{bmatrix} \begin{bmatrix} x_1 \\ x_2 \end{bmatrix} \tag{53b}$$

with order $n + (\Sigma_{i=1}^{m} n_i + m)$.

Note that in the scalar case there is a direct relationship between the denominator polynomial $d(s)$ and the characteristic polynomial of the controller form, viz., that $d(s) = \det (sE - A)$. A similar relation holds for the multivariable case except for the fact that $\det (sE - A)$ is monic, while $\det D(s)$ is not. Therefore, we would expect the following lemma to hold.

Lemma 5. It is true that

$$\det (sE - A) = (-1)^{\rho} (\det D_{hc})^{-1} \det D(s), \tag{54}$$

where $\rho = \Sigma_{i=1}^{m} n_i + m$

Proof. It is easy to show that

$$\det (sE - A) = \det (sI - A_1) \det (sK - I). \tag{55}$$

In [29] it is shown that

$$\det (sI - A_1) = (\det D_{hc})^{-1} \det D(s). \tag{56}$$

Also, it can be easily shown that

$$\det (sK - I) = (-1)^{\rho}. \tag{57}$$

Now (55)-(57) prove (54).

B.   AN OBSERVER FORM REALIZATION

For this case, consider a left MFD of $H(s)$ which is of the form

$$H(s) = D_L^{-1}(s) N_L(s),$$

where $D_L(s)$ and $N_L(s)$ are $p \times p$ and $p \times m$ matrices, which are different from the $m \times m$ matrix $D(s)$ and the $p \times m$ matrix $N(s)$ of the right MFD. However, for convenience, the special subscript (L) will be omitted.

The simplest way to obtain a realization is to first consider the transposed transfer function

$$H^T(s) = N^T(s)D^{-T}(s) = Q^T(s) + R^T(s)D^{-T}(s) \tag{58}$$

Here, $-T$ denotes the inverse transpose of a matrix. Then find a controller form realization as before

$$H^T(s) = \bar{c}(s\bar{E} - \bar{A})^{-1}\bar{B}. \tag{59}$$

Then a realization for H(s) is

$$H(s) = C_0(sE_0 - A_0)^{-1}B_0, \tag{60}$$

where

$$C_0 = \bar{B}^{-T}, \quad E_0 = \bar{E}^{-T}, \quad A_0 = \bar{A}^{-T}, \quad B_0 = \bar{C}^{-T}, \tag{61}$$

where the subscript zero denotes the observer-type form. The only thing remaining is to carefully identify E, A, B, C from $N^T(s)D^{-T}(s)$ because all the column-related properties of the controller realization will now depend on the rows of N(s) and D(s). Thus, the significant degrees will be l_i, the degree of the i-th row of D(s), and m_i, the degree of the i-th row of Q(s). The matrix D(s) must be row reduced, so that

$$\sum_{i=1}^{\rho} l_i = \deg \deg D(s) \tag{62}$$

and D_{hr}, the coefficient matrix of the highest-order terms in each row of D(s), is nonsingular. Also note that

$$D_{hr} = \left(D^T\right)_{hc}, \quad N_{lr} = \left(N^T\right)_{lc}, \quad N_{hrp} = \left(N^T\right)_{hcp}.$$

Following this line of thought, the core-observer realization strictly proper part $D^{-1}(s)R(s)$ is given by

$$A_0^0 = \text{block diag} \begin{bmatrix} 0 & 1 & & & 0 \\ & & \cdot & & \\ & \cdot & & \cdot & \\ & \cdot & & & 1 \\ & & \cdot & & \\ 0 & & & & 0 \end{bmatrix}, l_i \times l_i, \tag{63a}$$

$$i = 1, ..., p$$

$$C_0^0 = \text{block diag } [1 \quad 0 \quad \ldots \quad 9], \, 1 \times l_i, \tag{63b}$$

$$B_0^0 = I_n, \, n = \sum_{i=1}^{p} l_i = \deg \det D(s) \tag{63c}$$

and the observer form for $D^{-1}(s)R(s)$

$$A_1 = A_0^0 - D_{lr}D_{hr}^{-1}C_0^0 \tag{64a}$$

$$C_1 = D_{hr}^{-1}C_0^0, \quad B_1 = N_{lr}. \tag{64b}$$

For the polynomial part $Q(s)$, it is

$$K = \text{block diag } \begin{bmatrix} 0 & 1 & & 0 \\ & \cdot & \cdot & \\ & & \cdot & \cdot \\ & \cdot & & \cdot \\ 0 & & & 0 \end{bmatrix}, \, (m_i + 1) \times (m_i + 1), \tag{65a}$$

$$i = 1, \ldots, p$$

$$B_2 = -N_{hrp}$$

$$C_2 = \text{block diag } \{[1 \quad 0 \quad \ldots \quad 0], \, 1 \times (m_i + 1), \tag{65b}$$

$$i = 1, \ldots, p\}.$$

Finally, the duality should yield the schematic diagram of Fig. 2. A confirmation of the above results will be given by direct analysis. Thus, given the left MFD

$$y(s) = Q(s)u(s) + D^{-1}(s)R(s)u(s),$$

define the partial state $\xi(s)$

$$D(s)y_1(s) = \xi(s) = R(s)u(s), \tag{66}$$

and we can write

$$D(s) = S_L(s)D_{hr} + \Psi_L(s)D_{lr}, \tag{67a}$$

where

$$S_L(s) = \text{diag}\{s^{l_i}, \, i = 1, \ldots, p\} \tag{67b}$$

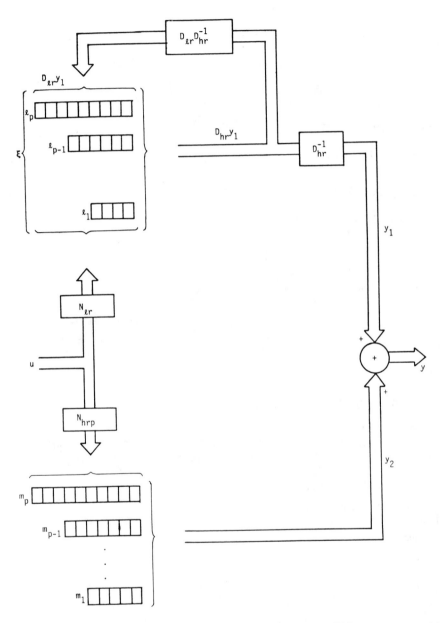

Fig. 2. Schematic of observer-form realization H(s).

$$\Psi_L(s) = \text{block diag}\left\{\left[s^{1_{i-1}}, \ldots, s, 1\right],\right.$$ (67c)

$$\left. i = 1, \ldots, p\right\}$$

and also

$$y_2(s) = Q(s)u(s),$$

where

$$Q(s) = \Psi_{LP}(s)N_{hrp}$$ (69a)

and

$$\Psi_{LP}(s) = \text{block diag}\left\{[1, 2, \ldots, s^{m_i}],\right.$$ (69b)

$$\left. i = 1, \ldots, p\right\}$$

and, therefore, using the assumption that $D(s)$ is row reduced, we have

$$y_1(s) = D_{hr}^{-1}S_L^{-1}\left[\xi(s) - \Psi_L(s)D_h\,y_1(s)\right].$$ (70)

This equation can be implemented as shown in Fig. 2, where the integrator chains for the strictly proper part realize what may be called the core-observer form. The realization for the strictly proper part is completed by feeding the input into the integrator chains according to

$$\xi(s) = R(s)u(s) = \Psi_L(s)N_{lr}u(s).$$ (71)

For the polynomial part, using (68) and (69), it is true that

$$y_2(s) = \Psi_{LP}(s)N_{hrp}u(s).$$ (72)

Thus, (72) can be implemented as shown in Fig. 2, where the differentiator chains for the polynomial part realize the polynomial part of the system.

In general, it is true that the controller- and observer-form realizations given above present an approach on how to realize a generalized transfer function. These results may be useful in finding other realizations which satisfy certain given requirements.

It has been shown how to generalize the scalar procedures of Section III to obtain controller and observer form realizations of a matrix transfer function. While the basic concepts of Section III have been extended, there is one feature still missing. With any $(n + 1)$-th order controllable realization of a scalar transfer function

$$H(s) = \frac{n(s)}{d(s)}, \quad \deg n(s) = n,$$

there can be associated a *unique* state space realization of order $n + 1$, called the controller canonical form. For the matrix case, however, this has not been achieved. Given a right MFD

$$H(s) = N(s)D^{-1}(s),$$

a procedure has been described for obtaining a controller-form realization of degree equal to $(\sum_{i=1}^{m} + \sum_{i=1}^{m} n_i + m)$ This realization can be different for MFDs that vary only trivially from $N(s)D^{-1}(s)$. Thus, let

$$H(s) = \tilde{N}(s)\tilde{D}^{-1}(s).$$

where

$$\tilde{N}(s) = N(s)U(s), \quad \tilde{D}(s) = D(s)U(s),$$

$U(s)$ unimodular. Then the before-mentioned procedure will yield a different controller-form realization $H(s)$. This lack of uniqueness is why those realizations are not called canonical.

VI.   IRREDUCIBLE MFDs AND MINIMAL REALIZATIONS

In Section III there have been developed, for scalar systems, relationships among the concepts of minimal realizations, jointly controllable and observable realizations, and irreducible MFDs. In Section V, multivariable analogs have been obtained between the first two concepts, and now the discussion is extended by showing the significance of irreducible MFDs.

The constructions of Section V show how to obtain, from an MFD $N(s) \times D^{-1}(s)$, a controllable realization. To obtain the minimal degree, it therefore seems reasonable to reduce the MFD to "lowest" terms by extracting a greatest common right divisor [29] of $N(s)$ and $D(s)$. This will be justified by proving the following theorem.

Theorem 9. Any realization of a generalized MFD with order equal to $(\sum_{i=1}^{m} n_i + \sum_{i=1}^{m} k_i + m)$ as in (39) and (45) will be minimal (equivalently, a c-controllable and c-observable) realization iff the MFD is irreducible.

This theorem is an obvious extension of Theorem 3 for scalar transfer functions and can be proved in a very similar way. Thus, the following are first established.

Lemma 6. If there exists one c-controllable and c-observable realization of $N(s)D^{-1}(s)$, with order $(\sum_{i=1}^{m} n_i + \sum_{i=1}^{m} k_i + m) = q$, then all realizations of the same order will also be c controllable and c observable.

Proof. Use S_1 and S_2 from Theorem 1, L_1 from Theorem 2, and L_2 from Definition 1. For the multivariable case the vectors b_1, b_2, c_1, c_2 are replaced by the matrices B_1, B_2, C_1, C_2. Use the obvious facts that

$$L_1(C_{11}, A_1)S_1(A_1, B_{11}) = L_1(C_{12}, A_2)S_1(A_2, B_{12}) \tag{73a}$$

and

$$L_2(C_{21}, K_1)S_2(K_1, B_{21}) = L_2(C_{22}, K_2)S_2(K_2, B_{22}). \tag{73b}$$

Now, since the realization

$$\begin{bmatrix} I & 0 \\ 0 & K_1 \end{bmatrix}, \begin{bmatrix} A_1 & 0 \\ 0 & I \end{bmatrix}, \begin{bmatrix} B_{11} \\ B_{21} \end{bmatrix}, \begin{bmatrix} C_{11} & C_{21} \end{bmatrix}$$

is minimal

$$\text{rank } L_1(C_{11}, A_1)S_1(A_1, B_{11})$$

$$= \text{rank } L_1(C_{12}, A_2)S_1(A_2, B_{12}) = \sum_{i=1}^{m} k_i$$

$$\text{rank } L_2(C_{21}, K_1)S_2(K_1, B_{21})$$

$$= \text{rank } L_2(C_{22}, K_2)S_2(K_2, B_{22}) = \sum_{i=1}^{m} n_i + m$$

and by using Sylvester's inequality

$$\text{rank } \left[L_1(C_{12}, A_2)S_1(A_2, B_{12}) \right]$$

$$\leq \min \text{rank } \left\{ L_1(C_{12}, A_2), \text{rank } S_1(A_2, B_{12}) \right\}$$

$$\text{rank } \left[L_2(C_{21}, K_1)S_2(K_1, B_{21}) \right]$$

$$\leq \min \operatorname{rank} \left\{ L_2(C_{22}, K_2), \operatorname{rank} S_2(K_2, B_{22}) \right\},$$

from which we have

$$\operatorname{rank} L_1(C_{12}, A_2) = \operatorname{rank} S_1(A_2, B_{12}) = \sum_{i=1}^{m} k_i = n$$

$$\operatorname{rank} L_2(C_{22}, K_2) = \operatorname{rank} S_2(K_2, B_{22}) = \sum_{i=1}^{m} n_i + m.$$

At this point a basic formula for polynomial matrices will be proved.

Lemma 7. Suppose $N(s)$ and $D(s)$ are two polynomial matrices $p \times m$ and $m \times m$, respectively, with $\det D(s) \equiv 0$. Then perform the division as in Theorem 8:

$$N(s)D^{-1}(s) = Q(s) + R(s)D^{-1}(s).$$

It is true that iff $N(s)$ and $D(s)$ are right coprime, then $R(s)$ and $D(s)$ are also right coprime.

Proof. Assume that $N(s)$ and $D(s)$ are right coprime and that $R(s)$ and $D(s)$ are not. Then there exist $R(s)$ and $D(s)$

$$R(s)D^{-1}(s) = \overline{R}(s)\overline{D}^{-1}(s) \tag{74}$$

and

$$\deg \det \overline{D}(s) < \deg \det D(s). \tag{75}$$

But then

$$N(s)D^{-1}(s) = \left[Q(s)\overline{D}(s) + \overline{R}(s) \right] \overline{D}^{-1}(s).$$

Write

$$Q(s)\overline{D}(s) + \overline{R}(s) = \overline{N}(s),$$

which is a polynomial matrix in s, and thus it has been shown that there exists an MFD for the pair $N(s)$, $D(s)$ such that (75) is true, which is a contradiction.

Conversely, assume that $R(s)$ and $D(s)$ are right coprime and $N(s)$ and $D(s)$ are not. Then

$$N(s)D^{-1}(s) = \overline{N}(s)\overline{D}^{-1}(s) \tag{76}$$

together with (75). But then

$$R(s)D^{-1}(s) = \left[\overline{N}(s) - Q(s)\overline{D}(s) \right] \overline{D}^{-1}(s),$$

which is a contradiction for the pair R(s), D(s).

Lemma 8. A controller-form realization of $N(s)D^{-1}(s)$, of order equal to q, will also be c observable iff the MFD is irreducible.

Proof. Use the division algorithm for

$$N(s)D^{-1}(s) = Q(s) + R(s)D^{-1}(s).$$

Then a well-known lemma [29] for regular systems states that the strictly proper part $R(s)D^{-1}(s)$ will be observable iff R(s) and D(s) are right coprime. This, together with Lemma 7, and the fact that L_2 is always of full rank, which will be proved below, prove Lemma 8.

Lemma 9. The matrix L_2 as in Definition 1, is of full rank for the controller-form realization.

Proof. Similar to the scalar case.

Theorem 9 then follows from the above two lemmas. It has been shown in the scalar case that any two minimal realizations can be related by a similarity transformation. The same happens with the multivariable case. Some important results similar to the regular case are given below.

Theorem 10. Suppose that $N_i(s)D_i^{-1}(s)$, i = 1, 2, are two irreducible generalized MFDs. Then there exists a unimodular matrix U(s) such that

$$D_1(s) = D_2(s)U(s), \quad N_1(s) = N_2(s)U(s)$$

Lemma 10. If N(s), D(s) is any generalized MFD of H(s) and N(s), D(s) is any irreducible MFD of H(s), then there exists a polynomial matrix R(s), not necessarily unimodular, such that N(s) = N(s)R(s) and D(s) = D(s)R(s).

The proof of Theorem 10 and of Lemma 10 is exactly similar to the regular case (see [29]).

VII. REALIZATION VIA MARKOV PARAMETERS

From the theory of "regular pencils" [15, 26], we recall that there exist nonsingular matrices M and N such that

$$M(sE - A)N = \begin{bmatrix} I_{n_1} - A & 0 \\ 0 & I_{n_2} - sK \end{bmatrix}, \tag{77}$$

where K is nilpotent (i.e., it has all its eigenvalues zero) and $n_1 = \deg \det (sE - A)$. Therefore, the matrix K can be chosen to have the Jordan canonical form, with all its entries zero except perhaps for entries of one in certain positions in the first superdiagonal. The matrix (77) is termed the "Kronecker form" of $sE - A$.

The Laplace transform of (1) yields

$$(sE - A)X(s) = \left[sEx(0) + BU(s) \right] \tag{78a}$$

$$Y(s) = CX(s), \tag{78b}$$

where $X(s)$, $U(s)$, $Y(s)$ denote the transforms of $x(t)$, $u(t)$, $y(t)$. If $x(0)$ is known and $u(t)$ is specified for $t \geq 0$, then the solution of (1) may be derived from (78).

System (78) may be written in the form

$$\begin{bmatrix} sE - A & -B \\ \hdashline C & 0 \end{bmatrix} \begin{bmatrix} X(s) \\ \hdashline U(s) \end{bmatrix} = \begin{bmatrix} sEx(0) \\ \hdashline Y(s) \end{bmatrix}, \tag{79}$$

where the coefficient matrix on the left is termed the "system matrix." System (79) is restricted system equivalent (RSE) [23] to the system, whose system matrix is the following:

$$\begin{bmatrix} M & 0 \\ 0 & I \end{bmatrix} \begin{bmatrix} sE - A & -B \\ \hdashline C & 0 \end{bmatrix} \begin{bmatrix} N & 0 \\ 0 & I \end{bmatrix} = \begin{bmatrix} M(sE - A)N & -MB \\ \hdashline CN & 0 \end{bmatrix}. \tag{80}$$

Now substituting (77) into (80) and using the transformation

$$X(s) = [X_1(s) \ X2(s)]T = N{-}1X(s),$$

we arrive at the following system, which is RSE to (79):

$$\begin{bmatrix} sI_{n_1} - A & 0 & -B_1 \\ 0 & I_{n_2} - sK & -B_2 \\ \hdashline C_1 & C_2 & 0 \end{bmatrix} \begin{bmatrix} X_1(s) \\ X_2(s) \\ \hdashline U(s) \end{bmatrix} = \begin{bmatrix} sx_1(0) \\ -sKx_2(0) \\ \hdashline Y(s) \end{bmatrix} \tag{81}$$

where

$$\overline{C} = CN = [C_1 \ C_2]$$

$$\overline{B} = MB = \begin{bmatrix} B_1 \\ B_2 \end{bmatrix}.$$

Now taking the inverse Laplace transform of (81), we arrive at the following decomposed form of system (1):

$$x_1(t) = \overline{A}x_1(t) + B_1 u(t) \tag{82a}$$

$$Kx_2(t) = x_2(t) + B_2 u(t) \tag{82b}$$

$$y(t) = \begin{bmatrix} C_1 & C_2 \end{bmatrix} \begin{bmatrix} x_1(t) \\ x_2(t) \end{bmatrix} \tag{82c}$$

System (82a) corresponds to the strictly proper part of the transfer-function matrix $H(s)$:

$$\overline{H}(s) = C_1 \left(sI_{n_1} - \overline{A} \right)^{-1} B_1 \tag{83a}$$

and system (82b) corresponds to the polynomial part $P(s)$ (since K is nilpotent)

$$P(s) = C_2 \left(sK - I_{n_2} \right)^{-1} B_2 \tag{83b}$$

The transfer function of (1) is the sum of (83a) and (83b), each having dimensions $p \times m$, as follows:

$$H(s) = \overline{H}(s) + P(s). \tag{84}$$

The power series representations of $H(s)$, $P(s)$ are given by

$$\overline{H}(s) = \sum_{i=0}^{\infty} R_i s^{-i-1} \tag{85a}$$

$$P(s) = -\sum_{i=0}^{\infty} Q_i z^{i}, \tag{85b}$$

where $\{R_i, i = 0, 1, \ldots\}$ are the Markov parameters of the strictly proper part given by (Gantmacher [26]; Ho and Kalman [16])

$$R_i = C_1 \overline{A}^{i} B_1 \tag{86a}$$

in terms of the matrices of the regular system, and $\{Q_i, i = 0, 1, \ldots\}$ are the Markov parameters of the polynomial part, given by

$$Q_i = C_2 K^{i} B_2 \tag{86b}$$

in terms of the matrices of the singular system.

The upper limit in the summation of (85b) is limited to $k - 1$, since K is nilpotent and $K^i = 0$, for $i \geq k$. This means that $k = \text{index}(K)$.

Now the realization problem that arises here may be formulated as follows: Given the Markov parameters $\{R_i, Q_i, i = 0, 1, \ldots\}$, compute a realization $\{E, A, B, C\}$ for system (1) that is minimal.

The Markov parameters R_i of the strictly proper part may be easily obtained by using well-known techniques. Thus, the realization problem is substantially reduced to the determination of the Markov parameters Q_i of the polynomial part (86b). It is known that the polynomial part makes the overall system noncausal. Therefore, in order to determine the Q_i's, we need to know the future behavior of our system, which is an impossible task in regular dynamical systems. However, it should be noted that this feature characterizes the mathematical description of the singular systems. Moreover, there are also other categories of systems where the future horizon is known; this may be seen, for example, in the case of two-dimensional systems, when we have spatial dimensions instead of time. Then the concept of causality is substituted by the concept of computability.

A realization is said to be minimal if the dimension of A satisfying (86a) together with the dimension of K satisfying (86b) are both as small as possible [1]. The dimension of the minimal realizations is denoted by n_0. If necessary, we will write $A = A_{min}$, $K = K_{min}$ to indicate the fact that (A, K) belong to a minimal realization.

We shall now describe the algorithm for the construction of a minimal realization. We assume implicitly that we know the degrees r_1, r_2 of the annihilating polynomials of A_{min}, K_{min}, respectively. For instance, if we are given the transfer-function matrix (84), then $r_1 \geq n_1, r_2 \geq n_2$.

Proposition 1. The sequences $\{R_i\}$, $\{Q_i\}$ have a finite-dimensional realization iff there are integers r_1, r_2 and constants $a_{1i}, i = 1, 2, \ldots, r_1$, and $a_{2i}, i = 1, 2, \ldots, r_2$, such that

$$R_{r_1 + j} = \sum_{i=1}^{r_1} a_{1i} R_{r_1 - i + j}, \quad \text{for all } j \geq 0 \tag{87a}$$

$$Q_{r_2 + j} = \sum_{i=1}^{r_2} a_{2i} Q_{r_2 - i + j}, \quad \text{for all } j \geq 0. \tag{87b}$$

Proof. a) Necessity: let

$$\Psi_1(s) = \beta_{01} s_1^{q_1} + \beta_{11} s_1^{q_1 - 1} + \ldots + \beta_{q_1, 1}, \beta_{01} = 1$$

$$\Psi_2(s) = \beta_{02}s_2^{q_2} + \beta_{12}s_2^{q_2-1} + \ldots + \beta_{q_2,2}, \beta_{02} = 1$$

be the minimal polynomials of some A_{min} and K_{min}, respectively. Then

$$0 = C_1 \overline{A}^{-j}\Psi_1(\overline{A})B_1 = \sum_{i=0}^{q_1} \beta_{i1}C_1\overline{A}^{-q_1-i+j}B_1 \tag{88a}$$

$$0 = C_2 K^j \Psi_2(K)B_2 = \sum_{i=0}^{q_2} \beta_{i2}C_2 K^{q_2-i+j}B_2. \tag{88b}$$

From (88a, b) and taking (86a, b) into account, it results that (87a, b) hold with $r_1 = q_1$, $r_2 = q_2$ and $a_{1i} = \beta_{1i}$, $a_{2i} = \beta_{2i}$. In fact, q_1 and q_2 defined above are the minimum values of r_1, r_2, respectively, for which (87a, b) hold.

b) Sufficiency: this follows from Theorem 1, which will be given later.

Proposition 2. If $\{R_i\}$, $\{Q_i\}$ have a finite-dimensional realization, then

$$n_0 = \text{rank } S_1 + \text{rank } S_2 = n_{01} + n_{02}, \tag{89}$$

where S_1, S_2 are the generalized Hankel matrices

$$S_1 = \begin{bmatrix} R_0 & R_1 & \cdots & R_{r_1-1} \\ R_1 & R_2 & \cdots & R_{r_1} \\ \vdots & \vdots & & \vdots \\ R_{r_1-1} & R_{r_1} & \cdots & R_{2r_1-2} \end{bmatrix} = [R_{i+j-2}] \tag{90a}$$

$$S_2 = \begin{bmatrix} Q_0 & Q_1 & & Q_{r_2-1} \\ Q_1 & Q_2 & & Q_{r_2} \\ \vdots & \vdots & & \vdots \\ Q_{r_2-1} & Q_{r_2} & \cdots & Q_{2r_2-2} \end{bmatrix} = [Q_{i+j-2}] \tag{90b}$$

Proof. Take a minimal realization $\{E, A, B, C\}$. The matrices S_1, S_2 may be written in the form

$$S_1 = V_1^T W_1 \tag{91a}$$

$$S_2 = V_2^T W_2, \tag{91b}$$

where T denotes transposition and

$$V_1 = \left[C_1^T \quad A^T C_1^T \quad ... \quad \left(A^T \right)^{r_1 - 1} \quad C_1^T \right]$$

$$V_2 = \left[C_2^T \quad K^t C_2^T \quad ... \quad \left(K^T \right)^{r_2 - 1} \quad C_2^T \right]$$

$$W_1 = \left[B_1 \quad \bar{A} B_1 \quad ... \quad (\bar{A})^{r_1 - 1} \quad B_1 \right]$$

$$W_2 = \left[B_2 \quad K B_2 \quad ... \quad (K)^{r_2 - 1} \quad B_2 \right]$$

Since A and K are $n_{01} \times n_{01}$, n_{02} square matrices, respectively, it follows that

rank V_1, rank $W_1 \leq n_{01}$

rank V_2, rank $W_2 \leq n_{02}$.

Hence, also, rank $S_1 \leq n_{01}$, rank $S_2 \leq n_{02}$. If rank $S_1 < n_{01}$ or rank $S_2 < n_{02}$, then a realization of dimension less than n_0 exists. This, however, contradicts the minimality of n_0.

Similar to the generalized Hankel matrices given by (90a, b), we write $\tau' S_1$, $\tau' S_2$ for the $r_1 \times r_1$, $r_2 \times r_2$ block matrices formed out of the translated sequences $\{R_k + 1\}$, $\{Q_{k+1}\}$, respectively, i.e.,

$$\tau' S_1 = \left[R_{i+j+1-2} \right] \tag{92a}$$

$$\tau' S_2 = \left[Q_{i+j+1-2} \right]. \tag{92b}$$

In the following the main theorem will be given, which provides a minimal realization of $\{R_i\}$, $\{Q_i\}$, whenever a finite realization exists. This theorem corresponds to that presented by Ho and Kalman [16] for regular state space systems.

Theorem 11. 1) Let S_1, S_2 be the $r_1 \times r_1$, $r_2 \times r_2$ block matrices given by (90a, b), where r_1, r_2 satisfy (87a, b).

2) Let (M_1, N_1), (M_2, N_2) be pairs of nonsingular matrices, such that

$$M_1 S_1 N_1 = \begin{bmatrix} I_{n_{01}} & 0 \\ 0 & 0 \end{bmatrix} = J_1 = U_{n_{01}}^T U_{n_{01}} \tag{93a}$$

$$M_2 S_2 N_2 = \begin{bmatrix} I_{n_{02}} & 0 \\ 0 & 0 \end{bmatrix} = J_2 = U_{n_{02}}^T U_{n_{02}}, \tag{93b}$$

where I_q is the $q \times q$ unit matrix, $U_q = [I_q \ 0]$, $n_{01} = \text{rank } S_1$, $n_{02} = \text{rank } S_2$ (according to Proposition 2), and J_1, J_2 are idempotent.

3) Let D_p be the block matrix $[I_p \ 0_p \ \dots \ 0_p]$. Then a minimal realization of $\{R_i\}$, $\{Q_i\}$ is given by

$$A = U_{n_0} \begin{bmatrix} J_1 M_1 (\tau S_1) N_1 J_1 & 0 \\ 0 & I_{r_2} \end{bmatrix} U_{n_0}^T \tag{94a}$$

$$E = U_{n_0} \begin{bmatrix} I_{r_1} & 0 \\ 0 & J_2 M_2 (\tau S_2) N_2 J_2 \end{bmatrix} U_{n_0}^T \tag{94b}$$

$$B = U_{n_0} \begin{bmatrix} J_1 M_1 S_1 \\ J_2 M_2 S_2 \end{bmatrix} D_m^T \tag{94c}$$

$$C = \begin{bmatrix} D_p S_1 N_1 J_1 & S_2 N_2 J_2 \end{bmatrix} U_{n_0}^T \tag{94d}$$

$$U_{n_0} = \begin{bmatrix} U_{n_0} & 0 \\ 0 & U_{n_0} \end{bmatrix}.$$

Proof. The proof of the above theorem is based on the decomposition of the above matrices $\{E, A, B, C\}$ into the two sets of matrices $\{\bar{A}, B_1, C_1\}$, $\{K, B_2, C_2\}$, which correspond to the regular system (82a) and the singular system (82b), both in conjunction with (82c), respectively. These matrices result from (94), as follows:

$$\overline{A} = U_{n_{01}}\left[J_1 M_1(\tau S_1)N_1 J_1\right] U_{n_{01}}^T \tag{95a}$$

$$B_1 = U_{n_{01}}\left[J_1 M_1 S_1 D_m^T\right] \tag{95b}$$

$$C_1 = \left[D_p S_1 N_1 J_1\right] U_{n_{01}}^T$$

and

$$K = U_{n_{02}}\left[J_2 M_2(\tau S_2)N_2 J_2\right] U_{n_{02}}^T \tag{96a}$$

$$B_2 = U_{n_{02}}\left[J_2 M_2 S_2 D_m^T\right] \tag{96b}$$

$$C = \left[D_p S_2 N_2 J_2\right] U_{n_{02}}^T.$$

Now the proof given by Ho and Kalman [16] may be used for each of the above two subsystems.

Proposition 3. Any two minimal realizations {E, A, B, C}, {E, A, B, C} of the same sequences {R_i}, {Q_i} are isomorphic.

This means that a nonsingular matrix T exists such that (10) holds.

Proposition 4. Every minimal realization may be derived by suitably choosing M_1, $M_2 N_1$, N_2 in the algorithm presented under Theorem 11.

For the proof of Propositions 3 and 4, we apply again the decomposition of the matrices {E, A, B, C} and use the results of Ho and Kalman [16].

VIII. REALIZATION VIA MARKOV PARAMETERS AND MOMENTS

We define the Markov parameters (R_i) and moments (F_i) for the strictly proper part (83a), by expansion of the various entries of the transfer function matrix about $s = \infty$ and $s = 0$, respectively, as follows:

$$\overline{H}(s) = R_0 s^{-1} + R_1 s^{-2} + R_2 s^{-3} + \ldots \tag{97a}$$

$$= -F_0 - F_1 s - F_2 s^2 - \ldots, \tag{97b}$$

where the ($p \times m$) matrices R_i and F_i are defined as

$$R_i = C_1 \overline{A}^{-i} B_1 \tag{98a}$$

$$F_i = C_1 \overline{A}^{-i-1} B_1. \tag{98b}$$

For the definition of the F_i's, it is assumed that A^{-1} exists. Similarly, we define the moments for the polynomial part (83b) by expansion around $s = 0$, as follows:

$$P(s) = Q_0 + Q_1 s + Q_2 s^2 + ..., \tag{99}$$

where

$$Q_i = -C_2 K^i B_2. \tag{100}$$

Here we cannot define Markov parameters, since the matrix K is not invertible (it is assumed nilpotent). Also, the upper limit in the summation of (99) is limited to $l - 1$, since K is nilpotent of index l. This means $K^i = 0$, for $i \geq l$. Now the realization problem may be formulated as follows: Given the Markov parameters R_i and moments F_i, Q_i, compute a realization $\{E, A, B, C\}$ for a system of the form (1) which is minimal.

The Markov parameters R_i of the strictly proper part and the moments F_i may be easily obtained by using well-known techniques. The realization problem is reduced to the determination of the moments of the polynomial part Q_i (100). It is well known that the polynomial part makes the overall system noncausal. Therefore, in order to determine the Q_i's we need to know the future behavior of (1), which is an impossible task in regular dynamical systems. However, it should be noted that this feature characterizes the mathematical description of the singular systems. Moreover, there are also other categories of systems where the future horizon is known; this may be seen, for example, in the case of two-dimensional systems, where we have spatial dimensions instead of time. In this case, the concept of causality is substituted by the concept of computability.

A realization is said to be minimal if the dimension of A satisfying (98a) together with the dimension of K satisfying (100) [or, analogously, A^{-1} (98b) with (100) are both the smallest possible]. The dimension of the minimal realization is denoted by n_0. We write $A = A_{min}$ and $K = K_{min}$ to indicate that (A, K) [equivalently, (A^{-1}, K)] belong to a minimal realization.

The algorithm is now described for the construction of a minimal realization. It is assumed that the degrees r_1, r_2 of the annihilating polynomials of A_{min}, K_{min} are known.

Proposition 5. The sequences $\{R_i\}$, $\{Q_i\}$ (analogously, $\{F_i\}$, $\{Q_i\}$) have a finite-dimensional realization iff there are integers r_1, r_2 and constants α_{1i} (α^*_{1j}), $i = 1, 2, ..., r_1$, and α_{2i}, $i = 1, 2, ..., r_2$, such that

$$R_{r_1+j} = \sum_{i=1}^{r_1} \alpha_{1i} R_{r_1-i+j}, \quad \text{for all } j \geq 0 \tag{101a}$$

$$Q_{r_2+j} = \sum_{i=1}^{r_2} \alpha_{2i} Q_{r_2-i+j}, \quad \text{for all } j \geq 0 \tag{101b}$$

or, analogously,

$$F_{r_1+j} = \sum_{i=1}^{r_1} \alpha^*_{1i} F_{r_1-i+j}, \quad \text{for all } j \geq 0 \tag{102a}$$

$$Q_{r_2+j} = \sum_{i=1}^{r_2} \alpha_{2i} Q_{r_2-i+j}, \text{ for all } j \geq 0. \tag{102b}$$

Proof. See Christodoulou and Mertzios [48].

Proposition 6. If $\{R_i\}$, $\{Q_i\}$ ($\{F_i\}$, $\{Q_i\}$) have a finite-dimensional realization, then

$$n_0 = \text{rank } S_1 + \text{rank } S_2 = n_{01} + n_{02} \tag{103}$$

or

$$n_0 = \text{rank } S_1^* + \text{rank } S_2 = n_{01} + n_{02}, \tag{104}$$

where S_1, S_1^*, S_2 are the Hankel matrices given below:

$$S_1 = \begin{bmatrix} R_0 & R_1 & \cdots & R_{r_1-1} \\ F_0 & R_0 & \cdots & R_{r_1-2} \\ F_1 & F_0 & \cdots & R_{r_1-3} \\ \vdots & & & \vdots \\ F_{r_1-2} & F_{r_1-3} & \cdots & R_0 \end{bmatrix}$$ (105)

$$S_1^* = \begin{bmatrix} R_0 & F_0 & \cdots & F_{r_1-2} \\ R_1 & R_0 & \cdots & F_{r_1-3} \\ R_2 & R_1 & \cdots & F_{r_1-4} \\ \vdots & & & \vdots \\ R_{r_1-1} & R_{r_1-2} & \cdots & R_0 \end{bmatrix}$$ (106)

$$S_2 = \begin{bmatrix} Q_0 & Q_1 & \cdots & Q_{r_2-1} \\ Q_1 & Q_2 & \cdots & Q_{r_2-1} \\ \vdots & \vdots & & \vdots \\ Q_{r_2-1} & Q_{r_2-2} & \cdots & Q_{2r_2-2} \end{bmatrix}.$$ (107)

Proof. a) Take a minimal realization of the form

$$\begin{bmatrix} I & 0 \\ 0 & K \end{bmatrix} \begin{bmatrix} \bar{A} & 0 \\ 0 & I \end{bmatrix} \begin{bmatrix} B_1 \\ B_2 \end{bmatrix} \begin{bmatrix} C_1 C_2 \end{bmatrix}.$$ (108)

The matrices S_1, S_2 may be written in the form

$$S_1 = V_1^T W_1$$ (109a)

$$S_2 = V_2^T W_2,$$ (109b)

where T denotes transposition and

$$V_1 = \left[C_1^T \ (\overline{A}^{-1})^T C_1^T \ \dots \ \{(\overline{A}^{-1})^T\}^{r_1-1} C_1^T \right]$$

$$V_2 = \left[C_2^T \ K^T C_2^T \ \dots \ (K^T)^{r_2-1} C_2^T \right]$$

$$W_1 = \left[B_1 \ AB_1 \ \dots \ (A)^{r_1-1} B_1 \right]$$

$$W_2 = \left[B_2 \ KB_2 \ \dots \ K^{r_2-1} B_2 \right]$$

Since A and K are $n_{01} \times n_{01}$, $n_{02} \times n_{02}$ square matrices, respectively, the result is that

rank V_1, rank $W_1 \le n_{01}$

rank V_2, rank $W_2 \le n_{02}$.

Hence also rank $S_1 \le n_{01}$, rank $S_2 \le n_{02}$. If rank $S_1 \le n_{01}$ or rank $S_2 \le n_{02}$, then a realization of dimension less than n_0 exists. This, however, contradicts the minimality of n_0.

b) Similarly, for the realization (108) we define

$$S_1^* = (V_1^*)W_1^*$$ (110a)

$$S_2 = V_2^T W_2,$$ (110b)

where

$$V_1^* = \left[C_1^T \ A^T C_1^T \ \dots \ (A^T)^{r_1-1} C_1^T \right]$$

$$W_1^* = \left[B_1 \ (A^{-1})B_1 \ \dots \ (A^{-1})^{r_1-1} B_1 \right]$$

and V_2, W_2 are as in a). Then an analogous reasoning, as in a), holds.

In the following the main theorem is given, which provides a minimal realization of $\{R_i\}$, $\{F_i\}$, $\{Q_i\}$, whenever a finite realization exists. The theorem corresponds to that presented by Eydgahi and Singh [20] for the regular state space systems.

Theorem 12.

1) Let S_1, $S_1{}^*$, S_2 be $r_1 \times r_1$, $r_1 \times r_1$, $r_2 \times r_2$ block matrices given by (105), (106), and (107), respectively, where r_1 and r_2 satisfy (101) and (102).

2) Let (M_1, N_1), $(M_1{}^*, N_1{}^*)$, (M_2, N_2) be pairs of nonsingular matrices such that

$$M_1 S_1 N_1 = \begin{bmatrix} I_{n_{01}} & 0 \\ 0 & 0 \end{bmatrix} = J_1 = U_{n_{01}}^T U_{n_{01}} \tag{111a}$$

$$M_1^* S_1^* N_1^* = \begin{bmatrix} I_{n_{01}} & 0 \\ 0 & 0 \end{bmatrix} = J_1 = U_{n_{01}}^T U_{n_{01}} \tag{111b}$$

$$M_2 S_2 N_2 = \begin{bmatrix} I_{n_{02}} & 0 \\ 0 & 0 \end{bmatrix} = J_2 = U_{n_{02}}^T U_{n_{02}}, \tag{111c}$$

where I_q is the $q \times q$ unit matrix, $U_q = [I_q \ 0]$, $n_{01} = \text{rank } S_1 = \text{rank } S_1{}^*$, $n_{02} = \text{rank } S_2$, and S_1, S_2 are idempotent.

3) Let D_p be the block matrix $[I_p \ 0 \ ... \ 0]$. Then minimal realizations of $\{R_i\}$, $\{F_i\}$, $\{Q_i\}$ are given accordingly:

a) Construction of the matrices E, A, B, and C are as follows:

$$E = U_{n_0} \begin{bmatrix} I_{r_1} & 0 \\ 0 & J_2 M_2(\tau S_2) N_2 J_2 \end{bmatrix} U_{n_0}^T \tag{112a}$$

$$A = U_{n_0} \begin{bmatrix} J_1 M_1(\tau S_1) N_1 J_1 & 0 \\ 0 & I_{r_2} \end{bmatrix} U_{n_0}^T \tag{112b}$$

$$B = U_{n_0} \begin{bmatrix} J_1 M_1 S_1 \\ J_2 M_2 S_2 \end{bmatrix} D_m^T \tag{112c}$$

$$C = D_p \begin{bmatrix} S_1 N_1 J_1 & S_2 N_2 J_2 \end{bmatrix} U_{n_0}^T, \tag{112d}$$

where (τS_i), $i = 1, 2$, is obtained by S_1 by deleting its first column and

$$U_{n_0} = \begin{bmatrix} U_{n_{01}} & 0 \\ 0 & U_{n_{02}} \end{bmatrix}.$$

b) The quadruple (E, A^{-1}, B, C) can be obtained using formulas similar to (113), where A is replaced by A^{-1} and both M_1, N_1 are replaced by M_1^*, N_1^*, respectively.

Proof. The proof of the theorem is based on the decomposition of the above matrices (E, A, B, C) [or (E, A^{-1}, B, C)] to the two sets of matrices (A, B_1, C_1) and (K, B_2, C_2) [or (A^{-1}, B_1, C_1) and (K, B_2, C_2)]. (See Christodoulou [49].)

IX. ILLUSTRATIVE EXAMPLES

Example 2. For a certain $H(s)$ which is not strictly proper, let

$$R(s) = \begin{bmatrix} s & 0 \\ -s & s^2 \end{bmatrix}$$

$$D(s) = \begin{bmatrix} 0 & -(s^3 + 4s^2 + 5s + 2) \\ (s + 2)^2 & s + 2 \end{bmatrix}$$

$$Q(s) = \begin{bmatrix} s + 1 & s^2 \\ 0 & s \end{bmatrix}.$$

Then, according to the above procedure, it can be shown that

$k_1 = 2$, $k_2 = 3$, $k_1 + k_2 = 5 = \deg \det D(s)$.

The highest-column-degree coefficient matrix is

$$D_{hc} = \begin{bmatrix} 0 & -1 \\ 1 & 0 \end{bmatrix},$$

with

$$D_{hc}^{-1} = \begin{bmatrix} 0 & 1 \\ -1 & 0 \end{bmatrix},$$

while

$$S(s) = \begin{bmatrix} s^2 & 0 \\ 0 & s^3 \end{bmatrix}$$

$$\Psi^T(s) = \begin{bmatrix} s & 1 & 0 & 0 & 0 \\ 0 & 0 & s^2 & s & 1 \end{bmatrix}$$

$$D_{lc} = \begin{bmatrix} 0 & 0 & -4 & -5 & -2 \\ 4 & 4 & 0 & 1 & 2 \end{bmatrix}$$

$$N_{lc} = \begin{bmatrix} 1 & 0 & 0 & 0 & 0 \\ -1 & 0 & 1 & 0 & 0 \end{bmatrix}$$

Therefore,

$$N_{lc} = \begin{bmatrix} 1 & 0 & 0 & 0 & 0 \\ -1 & 0 & 1 & 0 & 0 \end{bmatrix}$$

and by (49) and (51)

$$A_1 = \begin{bmatrix} -4 & -4 & 0 & -1 & -2 \\ 1 & 0 & 0 & 0 & 0 \\ \hdashline 0 & 0 & -4 & -5 & -2 \\ 0 & 0 & 1 & 0 & 0 \\ 0 & 0 & 0 & 1 & 0 \end{bmatrix}$$

$$B_1 = \begin{bmatrix} 0 & 1 \\ 0 & 0 \\ \hline -1 & 0 \\ 0 & 0 \\ 0 & 0 \end{bmatrix}, \ C_1 = N_{lc}.$$

Also,

$$n_1 = 1, \quad n_2 = 2, \quad n_1 - n_2 + m = 5.$$

Then

$$\Psi_p^T(s) = \begin{bmatrix} 1 & s & 0 & 0 & 0 \\ 0 & 0 & 1 & s & s^2 \end{bmatrix}$$

$$N_{hcp} = \begin{bmatrix} 1 & 1 & 0 & 0 & 1 \\ 0 & 0 & 0 & 1 & 0 \end{bmatrix}$$

and by (52)

$$K = \begin{bmatrix} 0 & 0 & 0 & 0 & 0 \\ 1 & 0 & 0 & 0 & 0 \\ \hline 0 & 0 & 0 & 0 & 0 \\ 0 & 0 & 1 & 0 & 0 \\ 0 & 0 & 0 & 1 & 0 \end{bmatrix},$$

$$
B_2 = \begin{bmatrix} 1 & 0 \\ 0 & 0 \\ \hline 0 & 1 \\ 0 & 0 \\ 0 & 0 \end{bmatrix}, \quad C_2 = -N_{hcp}.
$$

Thus the final controller-form realization as in (1) is

$$
E = \left[\begin{array}{ccccc|cc|ccc}
1 & 0 & 0 & 0 & 0 & 0 & 0 & 0 & 0 & 0 \\
0 & 1 & 0 & 0 & 0 & 0 & 0 & 0 & 0 & 0 \\
0 & 0 & 1 & 0 & 0 & 0 & 0 & 0 & 0 & 0 \\
0 & 0 & 0 & 1 & 0 & 0 & 0 & 0 & 0 & 0 \\
0 & 0 & 0 & 0 & 1 & 0 & 0 & 0 & 0 & 0 \\
\hline
0 & 0 & 0 & 0 & 0 & 0 & 0 & 0 & 0 & 0 \\
0 & 0 & 0 & 0 & 0 & 1 & 0 & 0 & 0 & 0 \\
\hline
0 & 0 & 0 & 0 & 0 & 0 & 0 & 0 & 0 & 0 \\
0 & 0 & 0 & 0 & 0 & 0 & 0 & 1 & 0 & 0 \\
0 & 0 & 0 & 0 & 0 & 0 & 0 & 0 & 1 & 0
\end{array}\right]
$$

$$
B = \begin{bmatrix}
0 & 1 \\
0 & 0 \\
\hline
-1 & 0 \\
0 & 0 \\
0 & 0 \\
\hline
1 & 0 \\
0 & 0 \\
\hline
0 & 1 \\
0 & 0 \\
0 & 0
\end{bmatrix}
$$

$$
A = \begin{bmatrix}
-4 & -4 & 0 & -1 & -2 & 0 & 0 & 0 & 0 & 0 \\
1 & 0 & 0 & 0 & 0 & 0 & 0 & 0 & 0 & 0 \\
\hline
0 & 0 & -4 & -5 & -2 & 0 & 0 & 0 & 0 & 0 \\
0 & 0 & 1 & 0 & 0 & 0 & 0 & 0 & 0 & 0 \\
0 & 0 & 0 & 1 & 0 & 0 & 0 & 0 & 0 & 0 \\
\hline
0 & 0 & 0 & 0 & 0 & 1 & 0 & 0 & 0 & 0 \\
0 & 0 & 0 & 0 & 0 & 0 & 1 & 0 & 0 & 0 \\
0 & 0 & 0 & 0 & 0 & 0 & 0 & 1 & 0 & 0 \\
0 & 0 & 0 & 0 & 0 & 0 & 0 & 0 & 1 & 0 \\
0 & 0 & 0 & 0 & 0 & 0 & 0 & 0 & 0 & 1
\end{bmatrix}
$$

$$
C = \begin{bmatrix}
1 & -1 \\
0 & 0 \\
0 & 1 \\
0 & 0 \\
0 & 0 \\
\hline
-1 & 0 \\
-1 & 0 \\
0 & 0 \\
0 & -1 \\
-1 & 0
\end{bmatrix}
$$

Example 3. Let the Markov parameters R_i, Q_i of a singular system of the form (1) have a finite-dimensional realization, i.e., (87a, b) hold. Furthermore, let the first seven Markov parameters of the regular (strictly proper) part be

$$R_0 = [1\ \ 0], \quad R_1 = [0\ \ 2], \quad R_2 = [0\ \ 0],$$

$$R_3 = [4\ \ 0] \quad R_4 = [4\ \ 8], \quad R_5 = [4\ \ 8], \quad R_6 = [20\ \ 8]$$

and the first four Markov parameters of the polynomial part be

$$Q_0 = [1\ \ 1], \quad Q_1 = [0\ \ 1], \quad Q_2 = Q_3 = [0\ \ 0].$$

Given the above values, it is found that the minimum values for which (87a, b) hold are $r_1 = 3, r_2 = 2$. Then we form the generalized Hankel matrices S_1, S_2 with minimum dimensions $n_{01} = 3$, $n_{02} = 2$, respectively, as follows:

$$S_1 = \begin{bmatrix} R_0 & R_1 & R_2 \\ R_1 & R_2 & R_3 \\ R_2 & R_3 & R_4 \end{bmatrix} = \begin{bmatrix} 1 & 0 & 0 & 2 & 0 & 0 \\ 0 & 2 & 0 & 0 & 4 & 0 \\ 0 & 0 & 4 & 0 & 4 & 8 \end{bmatrix}$$

$$S_2 = \begin{bmatrix} Q_0 & Q_1 \\ Q_1 & Q_2 \end{bmatrix} = \begin{bmatrix} 1 & 1 & 0 & 1 \\ 0 & 1 & 0 & 0 \end{bmatrix}.$$

Therefore, the minimal dimension of the whole system is $n_0 = n_{01} + n_{02} = 5$. Following the steps of Theorem 1, we select the matrices M_1, M_2, N_1, N_2 as follows:

$$M_1 = \begin{bmatrix} 1 & 0 & 0 \\ 0 & 0.5 & 0 \\ 0 & 0 & 0.25 \\ 0 & 0 & 0 \\ 0 & 0 & 0 \\ 0 & 0 & 0 \end{bmatrix}, \quad M_2 = \begin{bmatrix} 1 & 0 \\ 0 & 1 \\ 0 & 0 \\ 0 & 0 \end{bmatrix}$$

$$N_1 = \begin{bmatrix} 1 & 0 & 0 & -2 & 0 & 0 \\ 0 & 1 & 0 & 0 & -2 & 2 \\ 0 & 0 & 1 & 0 & -1 & -1 \\ 0 & 0 & 0 & 1 & 0 & 0 \\ 0 & 0 & 0 & 0 & 1 & -1 \\ 0 & 0 & 0 & 0 & 0 & 1 \end{bmatrix},$$

$$N_2 = \begin{bmatrix} 1 & -1 & 0 & -1 \\ 0 & 0 & 0 & 0 \\ 0 & 0 & 1 & 0 \\ 0 & 0 & 0 & 1 \end{bmatrix}.$$

Now the following minimal realization can be computed from (94):

$$A = \left[\begin{array}{ccc|cc} 0 & 2 & 0 & 0 & 0 \\ 0 & 0 & 2 & 0 & 0 \\ 1 & 0 & 1 & 0 & 0 \\ \hline 0 & 0 & 0 & 1 & 0 \\ 0 & 0 & 0 & 0 & 0 \end{array}\right],$$

$$E = \left[\begin{array}{ccc|cc} 1 & 0 & 0 & 0 & 0 \\ 0 & 1 & 0 & 0 & 0 \\ 0 & 0 & 1 & 0 & 0 \\ \hline 0 & 0 & 0 & 0 & 1 \\ 0 & 0 & 0 & 0 & 0 \end{array}\right]$$

$$B = \left[\begin{array}{cc} 1 & 0 \\ 0 & 1 \\ 0 & 0 \\ \hline 1 & 1 \\ 0 & 1 \end{array}\right], \quad C = \left[\begin{array}{ccc|cc} 1 & 0 & 0 & 1 & 0 \end{array}\right].$$

Example 4. Let the Markov parameters R_i and the moments F_i, Q_i of a singular system of the form (1) have a finite-dimensional realization. Furthermore, let the four Markov parameters and moments of the regular (strictly proper part) be

$$R_0 = [1 \ 0], \quad R_1 = [-1 \ 0], \quad R_2 = [1 \ -2], \quad R_3 = [-1 \ 3],$$

$$M_0 = [-1 \ -1], \quad M_1 = [1 \ 2], \quad M_2 = [-1 \ -3], \quad M_3 = [1 \ 4],$$

and the first four moments of the polynomial part be

$$Q_0 = [1 \ 0], \quad Q_1 = [-1 \ 0], \quad Q_2 = [0 \ 0], \quad Q_3 = [0 \ 0].$$

Given the above values, it is found that $r_1 = 2, r_2 = 2$. Then we form the generalized Hankel matrices S_1, S_2 with ranks equal to the minimum dimensions $n_{01} = 2$, $n_{02} = 2$, respectively, as follows:

$$S_1 = \begin{bmatrix} 1 & 0 & -1 & 1 \\ -1 & -1 & 1 & 0 \end{bmatrix}$$

$$S_2 = \begin{bmatrix} 1 & 0 & -1 & 0 \\ -1 & 0 & 0 & 0 \end{bmatrix}.$$

The minimal dimension of the system is $n_{01} + n_{02} = 4$. Following the steps of the theorem, the matrices M_1, M_2, N_1, N_2 are selected as follows:

$$M_1 = \begin{bmatrix} 1 & 0 \\ -1 & -1 \\ 0 & 0 \\ 0 & 0 \end{bmatrix},$$

$$M_2 = \begin{bmatrix} 1 & 0 \\ 1 & 1 \\ 0 & 0 \\ 0 & 0 \end{bmatrix}$$

$$N_1 = \begin{bmatrix} 1 & 0 & 1 & 1 \\ 0 & 1 & 0 & 1 \\ 0 & 0 & 1 & 0 \\ 0 & 0 & 0 & 1 \end{bmatrix},$$

$$N_2 = \begin{bmatrix} 1 & -1 & 0 & 0 \\ 0 & 0 & 1 & 0 \\ 0 & -1 & 0 & 0 \\ 0 & 0 & 0 & 1 \end{bmatrix}.$$

Now the following minimal realization can be computed from (113):

$$E = \begin{bmatrix} 1 & 0 & 0 & 0 \\ 0 & 1 & 0 & 0 \\ 0 & 0 & -1 & 1 \\ 0 & 0 & -1 & 1 \end{bmatrix},$$

$$A = \begin{bmatrix} -1 & 1 & 0 & 0 \\ 0 & -1 & 0 & 0 \\ 0 & 0 & 1 & 0 \\ 0 & 0 & 0 & 1 \end{bmatrix},$$

$$B = \begin{bmatrix} 1 & 0 \\ 0 & 1 \\ 1 & 0 \\ 0 & 0 \end{bmatrix}, \quad C = \begin{bmatrix} 1 & 0 & 1 & 0 \end{bmatrix}.$$

The transfer function of the above system is given by

$$H(s) = \left[\frac{s^2}{s+1} \quad \frac{1}{s^2 + 2s + 1} \right].$$

X. CONCLUSIONS

The main contribution of this article is the extension of the minimal realization theorem from regular to generalized transfer functions. The outcome is a satisfyingly consistent and useful framework for dealing with singular systems, and one that opens the door to interesting generalizations of results previously restricted to regular state space systems with strictly proper transfer functions.

There are several directions in which this work requires development. Note that to implement the realization actually the Kronecker form of $(sE - A)$ was used (see [26]). One may avoid this step by using some direct expansion. Nevertheless, the final conclusion must be the same. The way now is open to geometric state space representations, feedback design techniques, quadratic regulators with singular systems, and as an extension of the last case, linear quadratic differential games with singular system equations and with all matrices in the performance criteria positive semidefinite [50]. Finally, it should be mentioned that the stochastic case for the generalized systems is a new and open path for research.

REFERENCES

1. R. E. KALMAN, *SIAM J. Control 1*, 152–192 (1963).
2. D. G. LUENBERGER, *IEEE Trans. Autom. Control AC-11*, 190–197 (1966).
3. C. D. JOHNSON, *Int. J. Control 13*, 497–517 (1971).
4. M. HEYMANN, *Int. J. Control 12*, 913–927 (1970).
5. D. G. LUENBERGER, *IEEE Trans. Autom. Control AC-12*, 290–293 (1967).
6. V. M. POPOV, *SIAM J. Control 10*, 252–264 (1972).
7. J. RISSANEN, *Automatica 10*, 175–182 (1974).
8. J. ROMAN and T. E. BULLOCK, *IEEE Trans. Autom. Control AC-20*, 529–533 (1975).
9. L. M. SILVERMAN, *IEEE Trans. Autom. Control AC-16*, 559–567 (1971).
10. C. BONIVENTO, R. GUIDORIZI, and G. MARRO, *Int. J. Control 17*, 553–563 (1973).
11. M. J. DENHAM, *IEEE Trans. Autom. Control AC-19*, 646–656 (1974).
12. L. PANDOLFI, *J. Opt. Theor. Appl. 30*, 601–620 (1980).
13. E. L. YIP and R. F. SINCOVEC, *IEEE Trans. Autom. Control AC-26*, 39–147 (1981).
14. M. A. CHRISTODOULOU, "Analysis and Synthesis of Singular Systems," Ph.D. Dissertation in Electrical Engin., Univ. of Thrace, Greece, March 1984.
15. F. R. GANTMACHER, "The Theory of Matrices," Chelsea, New York, 1974.
16. B. L. HO and R. E. KALMAN, *Regelungstechnik 12*, 545–548 (1966).
17. S. PURI and H. TAKEDA, *IEEE Trans. Autom. Control AC-18*, 305–306 (1973).
18. R. PARTHASARATHY and H. SINGH, *Electron. Lett. 11*, 324–326 (1975).
19. Y. SHAMASH, *Int. J. Syst. Sci. 6*, 645–652 (1975).
20. A. M. EYDGAHI and H. SINGH, *IEEE Trans. Autom. Control AC-30*, 299–301 (1985).
21. S. L. CAMPBELL, "Singular Systems of Differential Equations," Pitman, London, 1980.

22. S. L. CAMPBELL, "Singular Systems of Differential Equations II," Pitman, San Francisco, 1982.
23. G. C. VERGHESE, B. G. LEVY, and T. KAILATH, *IEEE Trans. Autom. Control AC-26*, 811–830 (1981).
24. G. DOETSCH, "Introduction to the Theory and Application of the Laplace Transformation," Springer-Verlag, New York, 1974.
25. D. C. LUENBERGER, *IEEE Trans. Autom. Control AC-22*, 312–321 (1977).
26. F. R. GANTMACHER, "The Theory of Matrices," Vol. 2, Chelsea, New York, 1974.
27. C. A. DESOER, "Note for a Second Course on Linear Systems," Van Nostrand-Reinhold, New York, 1970.
28. C. T. CHEN, "Introduction to Linear System Theory," Rinehart & Winston, New York, 1970.
29. T. KAILATH, "Linear Systems," Prentice-Hall, Englewood Cliffs, New Jersey, 1980.
30. G. VERGHESE, "Infinite-Frequency Behavior in Generalized Dynamical Systems," Ph.D. Dissertation, Dept. Electrical Engineering, Stanford Univ., Dec. 1978.
31. G. VERGHESE and T. KAILATH, *Proc. 4th Int. Symp. Math. Theor. Networks Syst.* Delft, July (1979).
32. H. H. ROSENBROCK and A. C. PUCH, *Int. J. Control 19*, 845–867 (1974).
33. B. DJIURLA and R. NEWCOMB, *Proc. 4th Int. Symp. Math. Theor. Networks Syst.*, Delft, 283–289 (1979).
34. R. NEWCOMB, *IEEE Trans. Circuits Syst. CAS-28*, 62–71 (1981).
35. P. V. KOKOTOVIC, R. E. O'MALLEY, Jr., and P. SANNUTI, *Automatica 12*, 123–132 (1976).
36. D. G. LUENBERGER, *Proc. JACC*, San Francisco, 725–730 (1977).
37. D. KENDRICK, *Q. J. Econ. 86*, 693–696 (1972).
38. R. G. KREIJGER and H. NEUDECKER, *Q. J. Econ. 90*, 505–507 (1976).
39. W. LEONTIEFF et al., "Studies in the Structure of the American Economy," Oxford Univ. Press, New York, 1953.
40. W. LEONTIEFF, "Essays in Economics," Sharpe, New York, 1977.
41. D. A. LIVESEY, *Int. J. Syst. Sci. 4*, 437–440 (1973).
42. D. G. LUENBERGER and A. ARBEL, *Econometrica 45*, 991-995 (1977).
43. H. H. ROSENBROCK, *Int. J. Control 20*, 191–202 (1974).
44. E. GILBERT, *SIAM J. Control 1*, 121–151 (1963).
45. S. H. WANG, "Design of Linear Multivariable Systems," Memo. No. ERL-M309, Electronics Research Laboratory, University of California, Berkeley, 1971.
46. W. A. WOLOVICH, *Proc. 2nd IFAC Symp. Multivariable Tech. Control Syst.* Dusseldorf (1971).
47. W. A. WOLOVICH and P. L. F ALB, *SIAM J. Control 7*, 437–451 (1969).
48. M. A. CHRISTODOULOU and B. G. MERTZIOS, *Int. J. Control 42*, 1433–1441 (1985).
49. M. A. CHRISTODOULOU, *Int. J. Control 43* to appear (1986).
50. T. S. CHANG and Y. C. HO, *IEEE Trans. Autom. Control AC-28*, 477–488 (1983).

DISCRETE SYSTEMS
WITH MULTIPLE TIME SCALES*

MAGDI S. MAHMOUD

Department of Electrical and Computer Engineering
Kuwait University
Safat, Kuwait

I. INTRODUCTION

Many physical and engineering problems are appropriately described by large-scale dynamical models. The computational efforts required for control analysis and optimization of such models are quite excessive. It is therefore considered desirable to develop reduced-order models that approximate the dynamic behavior of large-scale systems [1, 16]. A lot of work is currently being done along this direction, including order-reduction techniques [16], singular perturbations [1], and multi-time-scale approaches [2–13]. With the recent developments in microprocessor technology, it becomes important to focus the analysis and design of feedback control systems on the use of digital equipment. This in turn motivates the study of discrete-time control systems, an important class of which is discrete multiple-time-scale systems [5, 13, 15]. Typical applications are found in the areas of power engineering, industrial processes, chemical plants, and managerial systems [1–17].

The objective of this article is to provide an overview of the available material on discrete systems with multiple time scales. It presents a comprehensive treatment of the modeling, analysis, feedback control, and optimization approaches that exploit the time-dichotomy properties in discrete models. For the purpose of simplicity in exposition, the article is organized into four sections. In Section II we cover the part of modeling and analysis of discrete multiple-time-scale systems. Each of the subsections is devoted to a particular aspect. The

---

* This work was supported by the Kuwait University Research Council under Grant No. RMU-EE-009 and Grant No. RMU-ECE-022.

developed results are then utilized in Section III when dealing with feedback control design. Here the feedback schemes include static-type controllers (by state or output feedback), observer-based controllers (full-order and reduced-order), and dynamic-type controllers. In all such schemes, two-stage procedures are emphasized using independent gains. Optimal control of linear discrete models and quadratic performance measures are presented in Section IV, where both approximate and reduced-order control profiles are derived in a standard form. Section V contains discussions of some interesting problems relevant to discrete systems with multiple time scales. Throughout the article several examples are worked out to illustrate the different concepts.

II.   DISCRETE MULTIPLE-TIME-SCALE SYSTEMS

Consider the linear, shift-invariant discrete system

$$x(k + 1) = A\underline{x}(k) + B\underline{x}(k) \tag{1}$$

$$\underline{y}(k) = C\underline{x}(k) \tag{2}$$

where $\underline{x}(k) \in R^n$, $\underline{u}(k) \in R^m$, and $\underline{y}(k) \in R^p$ are the state, control, and output vectors, respectively. Let $\lambda(A)$ denote the set of eigenvalues of A, V denote the modal matrix whose columns are the eigenvectors of A, and $W = V^{-1}$ denote the matrix of reciprocal basis vectors. In the following, we assume that the pair (A, B) is completely reachable and the pair (A, C^t) is completely reachable, that is [15],

$$\text{rank}\left[B \quad AB \quad A^2B \ldots A^{n-1}B \right] = n \tag{3}$$

$$\text{rank}\left[C^t \quad A^tC^t \quad (A^2)^tC^t \ldots (A^{n-1})^tC^t \right] = n. \tag{4}$$

Most of the results reported herein are for asymptotically stable systems, that is, $|\lambda(A)| < 1$. Of the various classes of discrete time systems having the foregoing properties, we are interested only in the class of systems that possess the mode-separation property [2–10]. This situation amounts to the existence of a gap in the eigenspectrum due to the interaction phenomena between clusters of modes in different physical models [5, 6]. A simple characterization of this property is when $\lambda(A)$ is separated by absolute value into two nonempty sets S_λ and F_λ so that:

$$|s_j| \ll |f_m|, \quad s_j \in S_\lambda \quad \text{and} \quad f_m \in F_\lambda. \tag{5}$$

Let the size of S_λ and F_λ be n_s and n_f, respectively, with $n_s = n_f = n$. Based on (5), the eigenvalue condition

$$\frac{\displaystyle \max_{j \in [n_s+1,\, n_s+n_f]} |\lambda_j|}{\displaystyle \min_{j \in [1,\, n_s]} |\lambda_j|} = \frac{\displaystyle \max_{F_\lambda} |f_m|}{\displaystyle \min_{S_\lambda} |s_j|} \ll 1 \tag{6}$$

is used in [2, 9, 11] to define a measure of the speed ratio of the slow versus fast modes. An alternative condition is derived in [17]

$$\frac{\displaystyle \max_{j \in [1,\, n_s]} |1 - s_j|}{\displaystyle \min_{m \in [n_s+1,\, n_s+n_f]} |1 - f_m|} \ll 1. \tag{7}$$

We note that condition (7) is more general than (6) in the sense that it can handle the class of discrete systems in which the set F_λ has unstable eigenvalues (on or outside the unit circle) or has stable but oscillatory eigenvalues [17]. It should be emphasized that either (6) or (7) is employed to identify the eigenvalue sets S_λ, F_λ such that $\lambda(A) = S_\lambda \cup F_\lambda$.

A. A GENERAL MODEL

In order to exhibit the mode-separation property (5), a suitable arrangement of the system (1) and (2) is often required. This can be done through permutation and/or scaling of states, which corresponds to "balancing" of a matrix and to transforming matrices to "block-order real schur form" in numerical analysis [19, 31]. The result is to cast (1) into the form of Model 1:

$$\underline{x}_1(k+1) = A_1 \underline{x}_1(k) + A_2 \underline{x}_2(k) + B_1 \underline{u}(k); \quad \underline{x}_1(0) = \underline{x}_{10} \tag{8}$$

$$\underline{x}_2(k+1) = A_3 \underline{x}_1(k) + A_4 \underline{x}_2(k) + B_2 \underline{u}(k); \quad \underline{x}_2(0) = \underline{x}_{20}, \tag{9}$$

where $\underline{x}_1(k) \in R^{n_s}$, $\underline{x}_2(k) \in R^{n_f}$, $\underline{x}^t(k) = [\underline{x}_1^t(k), \underline{x}_1^t(k)]$, $\lambda(A) = S_\lambda \cup F_\lambda = \{(\lambda_1, \dots , \lambda_{n_s}), (\lambda_{n_s+1}, \dots , \lambda_{n_s+n_f}\}$ such that the ordering $|\lambda_1| \geq \dots \geq |\lambda_{n_s}| \geq |\lambda_{n_s+1}| \geq \dots |\lambda_n|$ is obtained along with $V = [\underline{v}_1, \dots , \underline{v}_n]$ and $W = [\underline{w}_1, \dots , \underline{w}_n]$. We further consider that (2) is converted either into

$$\underline{y}(k) = C_1 \underline{x}_1(k) + C_2 \underline{x}_2(k) \tag{10}$$

or into

$$y(k) = [\underline{y}_1^t(k) \ \underline{y}_2^t(k)]^t$$

$$= \begin{bmatrix} C_1 & 0 \\ 0 & C_2 \end{bmatrix} \begin{bmatrix} \underline{x}_1(k) \\ \underline{x}_2(k) \end{bmatrix}, \tag{11}$$

where $\underline{y}_1(k) \in R^{p_s}$ and $\underline{y}_2(k) \in R^{p_f}$ with $p_s + p_f = p$. Note that coordinate transformation is usually a key step in partitioning the output matrix C of (2) into appropriate blocks as in (10) or (11).

The important feature of the two-time-scale model (8)–(11) is that the eigenvalue condition (5) signifies an intrinsic property; that is, there is no quantitative measure of the mode separation appearing explicitly in the model.

B.   OTHER MODELS

Starting from (1) under the eigenvalue condition (5), it has been shown in [11, 12] that a discrete two-time-scale system can be modeled as in Model II:

$$\begin{bmatrix} \underline{x}_1(k+1) \\ \underline{x}_2(k+1) \end{bmatrix} = \begin{bmatrix} A_{11} & \mu^{1-j}A_{12} \\ \mu^j A_{21} & \mu A_{22} \end{bmatrix} \begin{bmatrix} \underline{x}_1(k) \\ \underline{x}_2(k) \end{bmatrix} + \begin{bmatrix} B_1 \\ B_2 \end{bmatrix} \underline{u}(k), \tag{12}$$

where $\det[A_{11}] \neq 0$, $0 < j < 1$, and $\mu > 0$ is a small parameter given by the ratio $\|A_{22}\|/\|A_{11}\|$. The dimensions of $\underline{x}_1$, $\underline{x}_2$ are as those of (8) and (9). For the sake of comparison with Model I, we shall use the notation $A_1 = A_{11}$, $A_2 = \mu^{1-j}A_{21}$, $A_3 = \mu^j A_{21}$, $A_4 = \mu A_{22}$. It is thus obvious that the matrix blocks of (12) are implicit functions of μ.

Based on the asymptotic properties of difference equations with parameters [20, 24], an alternative model of discrete systems with the time-separation property can be described by [17, 18, 21] Model III:

$$\underline{x}_1(k+1) = (I_1 + \mu A_1)\underline{x}_1(k) + \mu A_2\underline{x}_2(k) + \mu B_1\underline{u}(k) \tag{13}$$

$$\underline{x}_2(k+1) = A_3\underline{x}_1(k) + A_4\underline{x}_2(k) + B_2\underline{u}(k) \tag{14}$$

where $\mu > 0$ is a small parameter and I_j is the $(n_j \times n_j)$ identity matrix.

C. BLOCK DIAGONALIZATION

We now discuss the properties of the three two-time-scale discrete models. For simplicity, we focus attention on systems without control $[\underline{u}(k) = \underline{0}]$. Define the explicitly invertible linear transformation:

$$T = \begin{bmatrix} I_1 + rML & rM \\ L & I_2 \end{bmatrix} \tag{15}$$

$$T^{-1} = \begin{bmatrix} I_1 & -rM \\ -L & I_2 + rLM \end{bmatrix} \tag{16}$$

where $r = 1$ for Models I and II and $r = \mu$ for Model III and the $(n_f \times n_s)$ matrix L and $(n_s \times n_f)$ matrix M are the real roots of[1]

$$A_4 L - L A_1 + L A_2 L - A_3 = 0 \tag{17}$$

$$rM(A_4 + LA_2) - r(A_1 - A_2 L)M + A_2 = 0. \tag{18}$$

It is easy to see that

$$\begin{bmatrix} \underline{x}_s(k) \\ \underline{x}_f(k) \end{bmatrix} = T \begin{bmatrix} \underline{x}_1(k) \\ \underline{x}_2(k) \end{bmatrix} \tag{19}$$

will convert any of the three two-time-scale models into the decoupled form:

$$\begin{bmatrix} \underline{x}_s(k + 1) \\ \underline{x}_f(k + 1) \end{bmatrix} = \begin{bmatrix} A_s & 0 \\ 0 & A_f \end{bmatrix} \begin{bmatrix} \underline{x}_s(k) \\ \underline{x}_f(k) \end{bmatrix} \tag{20}$$

where for Models I and II

$$A_s = A_1 - A_2 L \tag{21a}$$

$$A_f = A_4 + LA_2 \tag{21b}$$

and for Model III

$$A_s = I_1 + \mu(A_1 - A_2 L) \tag{22a}$$

---

[1] In the case of Model III, $A_1 \equiv A_1$, $A_2 \equiv A_2$, $A_3 \equiv A_3$, and $A_4 \equiv A_4$ in (17) and (18) to follow.

$$A_f = A_4 + \mu L A_2.$$ (22b)

By virtue of (8), (9), (15), and (20), it is readily evident that

$$\lambda(A) = \lambda(A_s) \quad \lambda(A_f),$$ (23)

which implies that the two-stage linear transformation (15), (16) decouples the eigenvalues of the discrete model (8), (9) into two disjoint sets: one is associated with the block matrix A_s and one is associated with the block matrix A_f. Due to the fact that the free response of linear discrete systems is determined by the form A^k, we call the $\underline{x}_s(k)$ the slow (dominant) variables and the $\underline{x}_f(k)$ the fast (nondominant) variables. By the same token, the n_s are the slow modes and the n_f the fast modes. Similar results have been obtained in [11] using other two-step procedures. It is important to note, in view of (15) and (19), that $\underline{x}_s(k)$ represents the exact dominant (slow) component of the $\underline{x}_1(k)$ variable. This will be explained later.

D.   APPROXIMATE ANALYSIS

It is evident from the foregoing development that the decoupled form (20) depends on the L and M matrices. There are two types of numerical methods: the dominant eigenspace method [11, 26] and the successive approximation method [9, 16, 27]. We discuss the latter method, in which the iterative scheme to solve (17) proceeds as follows:

1) Initial iteration (a = 0)

$$L_0 = -(I_2 - A_4)^{-1} A_3$$ (24a)

$$A_0 = A_1 - A_2 L_0$$ (24b)

$$= A_1 + A_2(I_2 - A_4)^{-1} A_3.$$

2) Subsequent iteration (a > 0)

$$L_{a+1} = L_0 + (A_4 + L_a A_2)(L_a - L_0) A_0^{-1},$$ (25)

where $\det[I_2 - A_4] \neq 0$ and $\det[A_0] \neq 0$, in view of the asymptotic stability of A.

Lemma 1. If the inequalities

$$(\|A_4\| + \|L_0\| \, \|A_2\|)^2 - 4(\|L_0\| \, \|A_2\| \, \|I_1 - A_0\|) \geq 0$$ (26)

$$\|A_0^{-1}\| < (\|A_4\| + \|L_0\| \|A_2\|)^{-1} \tag{27}$$

are satisfied, then the sequence L_a defined by (25) is monotonically decreasing. Moreover, L_0 is a first-order approximation of L, that is,[2]

$$L = L_0 + \mathcal{O}(\mu). \tag{28}$$

Also,

$$M = M_0 + \mathcal{O}(\mu)$$

$$\tag{29}$$

$$= A_0^{-1} A_2 + \mathcal{O}(\mu).$$

The proof is found in [9, 27] using a contraction mapping technique for Model I. An alternative procedure is employed in [11] for Model II based on eigenspace iterations.

Lemma 2. The set of eigenvalues $\lambda(A)$ is approximated to first order by

$$\lambda(A_s) = \lambda(A_0)[1 + \mathcal{O}(\mu)] \tag{30a}$$

$$\lambda(A_4) = \lambda(A_4)[1 + \mathcal{O}(\mu)]. \tag{30b}$$

A little algebra on block diagonalizing (8), (9) using (16) with L from (24a), (28) and M from (29) gives (30). The details are presented in [9]. An immediate result is that the system

$$\begin{bmatrix} \underline{x}_d(k+1) \\ \underline{x}_n(k+1) \end{bmatrix} = \begin{bmatrix} A_0 & 0 \\ 0 & A_4 \end{bmatrix} \begin{bmatrix} \underline{x}_d(k) \\ \underline{x}_n(k) \end{bmatrix} \tag{31}$$

is a "first-order approximation" to the system (8), (9), where $\underline{x}_d(k)$ and $\underline{x}_n(k)$ stand for the dominant (slow) and nondominant (fast) variables, respectively. It is readily evident that $\underline{x}_d(0) \cong \underline{x}_s(0)$ and $\underline{x}_n(0) \cong \underline{x}_f(0)$. More importantly, we can easily show [9], using (15), (26)–(29), that:

$$\underline{x}_1(k) = \underline{x}_d(k) - A_0^{-1} A_2 \underline{x}_n(k) + \mathcal{O}(\mu) \tag{32a}$$

$$\underline{x}_2(k) = (I_2 - A_4)^{-1} A_3 \underline{x}_d(k) + \underline{x}_n(k) + \mathcal{O}(\mu). \tag{32b}$$

---

[2] A vector or matrix function $\Pi(\mu)$ of a positive scalar μ is said to be $\mathcal{O}(\mu^m)$ if there exist positive constants d and μ^* such that $|\Pi(\mu)| \le d\mu^m$ for all $\mu \le \mu^*$.

The interpretation of (32) is significant on comparing the dynamic-free case [$\underline{u}$(k) = $\underline{0}$] of (8), (9) with

$$\begin{bmatrix} \underline{z}_1(k+1) \\ \underline{z}_2(k) \end{bmatrix} = \begin{bmatrix} A_1 & A_2 \\ A_3 & A_4 \end{bmatrix} \begin{bmatrix} \underline{z}_1(k) \\ \underline{z}_2(k) \end{bmatrix} \tag{33}$$

where $\underline{z}_1(k)$ and $\underline{z}_2(k)$ are the "discrete quasisteady states" [2, 7, 9]. Using (24), the system (33) reduces to

$$\underline{z}_1(k+1) = A_0 \underline{z}_1(k) \tag{34a}$$

$$\underline{z}_2(k) = (I_2 - A_4)^{-1} A_3 \underline{z}_1(k) \tag{34b}$$

Hence from (32)–(34) the components $\underline{x}_d(k)$, $(I_2 - A_4)^{-1} A_3 \underline{x}_d(k)$ can accordingly be interpreted as a "discrete quasisteady state" of $\underline{x}(k)$ after $\underline{x}_n(k)$ has decayed [2]. This discrete quasisteady state is varying slowly compared with the variation of $\underline{x}_n(k)$.

For discrete systems with control, the input matrix $B^t = [B_1^t \ B_2^t]$ under the transformation (15) becomes

$$\begin{bmatrix} B_s \\ B_f \end{bmatrix} = \begin{bmatrix} (I_1 + rML)B_1 + rMB_2 \\ LB_1 + B_2 \end{bmatrix} \tag{35}$$

whose first-order approximation using (28), (29) takes the form [7, 9]:

$$\begin{bmatrix} B_0 \\ B_2 \end{bmatrix} = \begin{bmatrix} r[B_1 + A_2(I_2 - A_4)^{-1}B_2] \\ B_2 \end{bmatrix} \tag{36}$$

where, again, $r = 1$ for Models I and II, and $r = \mu$ for Model III.

E.   TIME-SCALE DECOMPOSITION

Over the period [0, K] the dynamic behavior of system (8)–(10) is governed by the evolution of n_s slow modes (distributed near the unit circle of the complex plane) and n_f fast modes centered around the origin. In view of the eigenvalue condition (6) or (7), it is readily seen [3, 4] that for asymptotically stable systems, the fast modes are important only during a short initial period [0, K_f]. After that period they are negligible and the behavior of the system can be described by its slow modes. According to [3, 4], a reduced-order (slow) subsystem is defined by neglecting the fast modes, which is equivalent to replacing the dynamic equation (9) by its steady-state algebraic version

$$\bar{x}_1(k + 1) = A_1\bar{x}_1(k) + A_2\bar{x}_2(k) + B_1\bar{u}(k) \tag{37a}$$

$$\bar{x}_2(k) = A_3\bar{x}_1(k) + A_4\bar{x}_2(k) + B_2\bar{u}(k) \tag{37b}$$

$$\bar{y}(k) = C_1\bar{x}_1(k) + C_2\bar{x}_2(k), \tag{37c}$$

where a bar indicates a discrete quasisteady state [2, 9]. Since $[I_2 - A_4]$ is nonsingular, we express $\bar{x}_2(k)$ as

$$\bar{x}_2(k) = [I_2 - A_4]^{-1}[A_3\bar{x}_1(k) + B_2\bar{u}(k)], \tag{38}$$

and, substituting it into (37a), (37c) the slow subsystem of (8)–(10) is defined by:

$$\underline{x}_s(k + 1) = (A_1 + A_2[I_2 - A_4]^{-1}A_3)\underline{x}_s(k)$$

$$+ (B_1 + A_2[I_2 - A_4]^{-1}B_2)\underline{u}_s(k) \tag{39a}$$

$$= A_0\underline{x}_s(k) + B_0\underline{u}_s(k)$$

$$\underline{y}_s(k) = (C_1 + C_2[I_2 - A_4]^{-1}A_3)\underline{x}_s(k)$$

$$+ (C_2[I_2 - A_4]^{-1}B_2)\underline{u}_s(k) \tag{39b}$$

$$= C_0\underline{x}_s(k) + D_0\underline{u}_s(k).$$

Hence $\underline{x}_1(k) = \underline{x}_s(k)$, $\underline{y}(k) = \underline{y}_s(k)$, $\underline{x}_2(k)$ and $\underline{u}(k) = \underline{u}_s(k)$ are the slow components of the corresponding variables in system (8)–(10).

Form (39a) agrees with (34a) and (36). The fast subsystem is derived by making the assumptions that $\underline{x}_1(k) = \underline{x}_s(k) = $ constant, and $\underline{x}_2(k + 1) = \underline{x}_2(k)$. From (9), (10), and (38) we get

$$\underline{x}_f(k + 1) = \underline{x}_2(k + 1) - \bar{x}_2(k + 1)$$

$$\tag{40a}$$

$$= A_4\underline{x}_f(k) + B_2\underline{u}_f(k)$$

$$\underline{y}_f(k) = C_2\underline{x}_f(k) \tag{40b}$$

where $\underline{u}_f(k) = \underline{u}(k) - \underline{u}_s(k)$ and $\underline{y}_f(k) = \underline{y}(k) - \underline{y}_s(k)$. The initial conditions of (39), (40) are $\underline{x}_s(0) = \underline{x}_1(0)$, $\underline{x}_f(0) = \underline{x}_2(0) - \bar{x}_2(0)$, respectively.

The foregoing analysis of converting (8), (9) into (39), (40) reveals the two-time-scale nature of the system. More importantly, it is consistent with the decoupling procedure to a first-order approximation [2]. It should be evident that the condition $\underline{x}_2(k + 1) = \underline{x}_2(k)$ specifies the meaning of reduced-order modeling in discrete-time systems [16].

Following a parallel development, it has been shown [17] that the slow and fast subsystems of Model III given by (13), (14) are[3]

$$\underline{x}_s(k + 1) = (I_1 + \mu A_0)\underline{x}_s(k) + \mu B_0 \underline{u}_s(k) \tag{41}$$

$$\underline{x}_f(k + 1) = A_4 \underline{x}_f(k) + B_2 \underline{u}_f(k), \tag{42}$$

which, in turn, confirms the validity of quasi-steady-state analysis. It should be emphasized that the slow and fast subsystems are operating on different regions of the time horizon.

In [11, 12], state transformation and block diagonalization of the type (16) has been used for Model II to obtain a reduced-order (slow) subsystem. The result is

$$\underline{x}_s(k + 1) = A_s \underline{x}_s(k) + B_s \underline{u}_s(k). \tag{43}$$

In (12) as $\mu \to 0$ the fast state eigenvalue goes to zero and the fast system has a deadbeat response that responds instantaneously to changes in $\underline{x}_1(k)$ and $\underline{u}(k)$.

F.   SOME REMARKS

In light of the preceding analysis, Models I and II may be regarded as discrete systems in a slow time scale in the sense that the fast response to a control is quite rapid [deadbeat in the case of Model II and evoling on an $\mathcal{O}(\mu)$ scale in the case of Model I], and the slow state varies on an $\mathcal{O}(1)$ time scale. On the other hand, Model III is a fast-time-scale system. Here, rather than assuming the eigenvalues corresponding to the fast motion (the eigenvalues of $\hat{A}_4$) are $\mathcal{O}(\mu)$, it is assumed [17] that they are $\mathcal{O}(1)$ but within the unit circle of the complex plane. The eigenvalues corresponding to slow motion are assumed $\mathcal{O}(\mu)$ away from the point $z = 1$ in the z plane. Model III thus considers that the slow motion is so slow as to be almost constant while the fast motion is active and given by (42).

Going back to the linear transformation (16), in terms of the matrices V and $W = V^{-1}$, we express the system (8), (9) via the modal transformation $\underline{x}(k) = V\underline{z}(k)$ as

---

[3] $A_0 = A_1 + A_2(I_2 - A_4)^{-1}A_3; \ B_0 = B_1 + A_2 (I_2 - A_4)^{-1}B_2.$

$$\begin{bmatrix} A_1 & A_2 \\ A_3 & A_4 \end{bmatrix} = \begin{bmatrix} V_1 & V_2 \\ V_3 & V_4 \end{bmatrix} \begin{bmatrix} J_1 & 0 \\ 0 & J_2 \end{bmatrix} \begin{bmatrix} W_1 & W_2 \\ W_3 & W_4 \end{bmatrix} \tag{44}$$

where the matrix J_m is the Jordan block with dimension ($n_m \times n_m$) and the partitioning of V and W is made in accordance with that of A. Applying the linear transformation

$$g(k) = T_1 \underline{x}(k)$$

$$= \begin{bmatrix} I_1 & 0 \\ L & I_2 \end{bmatrix} \underline{x}(k) \tag{45}$$

to (44) yields [2, 29]

$$T_1 \begin{bmatrix} A_1 & A_2 \\ A_3 & A_4 \end{bmatrix} T_1^{-1} = \begin{bmatrix} A_s & A_2 \\ 0 & A_f \end{bmatrix}$$

$$= \begin{bmatrix} Q_1 & Q_2 \\ Q_3 & Q_4 \end{bmatrix} \tag{46}$$

where L satisfies (17) and

$$Q_1 = W_1 J_1 V_1 + W_2 J_2 V_3 - (W_1 J_1 V_2 + W_2 J_2 V_4)L$$

$$Q_2 = W_1 J_1 V_2 + W_2 J_2 V_4$$

$$Q_3 = (LW_1 + W_3)J_1 V_1 + (LW_2 + W_4)J_2 V_3 \tag{47}$$

$$- [(LW_1 + W_3)J_1 V_2 + (LW_2 + W_4)J_2 V_4]L$$

$$Q_4 = (LW_1 + W_3)J_1 V_2 + (LW_2 + W_4)J_2 V_4.$$

Using the fact that $W = V^{-1}$ and (21) reveals that $L = W_4^{-1}W_3 = -V_3 V_1^{-1}$, $Q_1 = V_1^{-1}J_1 V_1$, and $Q_4 = W_4 J_4 W_4^{-1}$. This emphasizes the result that the eigenvalues and eigenvectors of A_s and A_f are J_2, W_4^{-1}, respectively. We next apply the linear transformation

$\underline{h}(k) = T_2 \underline{g}(k)$

$$= \begin{bmatrix} I_1 & M \\ 0 & I_2 \end{bmatrix} \underline{g}(k) \tag{48}$$

to (46) and use (47) to result in

$$T_2 T_1 \begin{bmatrix} A_1 & A_2 \\ A_3 & A_4 \end{bmatrix} T_1^{-1} T_2^{-1} = \begin{bmatrix} A_s & 0 \\ 0 & A_f \end{bmatrix}$$

$$= \begin{bmatrix} Q_1 & 0 \\ 0 & Q_2 \end{bmatrix} \tag{49}$$

where M satisfies (18). A little algebra on (47)–(49) shows that $M = V_1 Q_2 = -V_2 W_4$. By virtue of the foregoing analysis, it follows from (16), (45), and (48) that

$$T = T_1 T_2 = \begin{bmatrix} V_1 W_1 & V_1 W_2 \\ -V_3 V_1^{-1} & I_2 \end{bmatrix} \tag{50}$$

which, in turn, recognizes the explicitly invertible linear transformation as a two-stage similarity relation that preserves the whole eigenspectrum of two-time-scale discrete systems [2–7].

A final remark related to Model II is that, for $j = 0$, another version discussed in [31] has the form

$$\begin{bmatrix} \underline{x}_1(k+1) \\ \underline{x}_2(k+1) \end{bmatrix} = \begin{bmatrix} A_{11} & \mu \hat{A}_{12} \\ \hat{A}_{21} & \mu \hat{A}_{22} \end{bmatrix} \begin{bmatrix} \underline{x}_1(k) \\ \underline{x}_2(k) \end{bmatrix} + \begin{bmatrix} B_1 \\ B_2 \end{bmatrix} \underline{u}(k).$$

It is simple to see [32] that the above model and (12) are related by $\underline{x}_2(k) = \mu^j \underline{x}_2(k)$. Further properties of both models and the underlying procedure for slow–fast grouping of states are presented in [32].

G.   SYSTEM PROPERTIES

Our purpose now is to examine the essential properties of the discrete system (8), (9) in relation to those of the slow system (39) and the fast system (40). We summarize the main results as derived in [4].

Lemma 3. If: 1) the discrete system (8), (9) with $\underline{u}(k) = \underline{0}$ satisfies the eigenvalues condition (6), 2) $|\lambda(A_4)| < 1$, 3) $|\lambda(A_0)| < 1$, then the discrete system (8), (9) is asymptotically stable.

A systematic procedure has been presented in [4] to prove Lemma 3 based on Lyapunov theory which gives bounds for perturbed solutions.

Lemma 4. Suppose that $\det[I_2 - A_4] \neq 0$. If

$$\text{rank}[B_0 A_0 B_0 A_0^2 B_0 \ldots A_0^{n_s-1} B_0] = n_s$$

and

$$\text{rank}[B_2 A_4 B_2 A_4^2 B_2 \ldots A_4^{n_f-1} B_2] = n_f$$

then the discrete system (8), (9) is completely reachable.

This result [4] establishes that the controllability properties of (8), (9) are determined by those of (39) and (40).

Lemma 5. Suppose that $\det[I_2 - A_4] \neq 0$. If

$$\text{rank}\left[C_0^t A_0^t (A^2)^t C_0^t \ldots (A^{n_s-1}) C_0^t \right] = n_s$$

and

$$\text{rank}\left[C_2 A_4^t C_2^t (A_4^2)^t C_2^t \ldots (A_4^{n_f-1}) C_2^t \right] = n_f,$$

then the discrete system (8)–(10) is completely observable.

This is obviously the dual of Lemma 4 and has been used ion [3] in the design of observers.

H.   ITERATIVE SEPARATION OF TIME SCALES

The underlying assumption of multi-time-scale theory [1, 38] is that during short-term studies the slow variables remain constant and that by the time their changes become noticeable, the fast transients have already reached their quasi-steady states. As pointed out in [38], the slow variables during transients are time-varying quantities, which implies that the true states $\underline{x}_1(k)$ and $\underline{x}_2(k)$ will differ from $\underline{x}_s(k)$ and $\underline{x}_f(k)$ mainly by their fast parts. Improving the approximate model requires careful treatment of the separation of variables.

In order to determine the fast part of $\underline{x}_2(k)$, we substitute

$$\underline{\beta}(k) = \underline{x}_2(k) + L\underline{x}_1(k) \tag{51}$$

into (9) to yield

$$\underline{\beta}(k + 1) = M\underline{x}_1(k) + [A_4LA_2]\underline{\beta}(k) + (B_2 + LB_1)\underline{u}(k), \tag{52}$$

where $M = A_3 - A_4L + LA_1 - LA_2L$. To completely decouple $\underline{x}_1(k)$ and $\underline{\beta}(k)$ in (51), the $(n_f \times n_s)$ matrix L is chosen such that $M = 0$. The iterative solution of $M = 0$ is given by [26]

$$L_{j+1} = L_j + \left(A_4L_j - L_jA_1 + L_jA_2L_j - A_3\right)$$

$$\times \left(A_1 - A_2L_j\right)^{-1}, \tag{53}$$

where $L_1 = -(I - A_4)^{-1}A_3$. The system (8), (9) after $j L$ iterations takes the form:

$$\underline{x}_1(k + 1) = F_j\underline{x}_1(k) + A_2\underline{\beta}_j(k) + B_1\underline{u}(k) \tag{54a}$$

$$\underline{\beta}_j(k + 1) = H_j\underline{x}_1(k) + P_j\underline{\beta}_j(k) + E_j\underline{u}(k), \tag{54b}$$

where

$$F_j = A_1 - A_2L_j \tag{55a}$$

$$H_j = A_3 - A_4L_j + L_jF_j \tag{55b}$$

$$P_j = A_4 + L_jA_2 \tag{55c}$$

$$E_j = B_2 + L_jB_1. \tag{55d}$$

In light of the time-separation property [2, 9], it is shown that H_1 is of order μ. After j iterations, H_j is reduced to $\mathcal{O}(\mu^j)$, but the model (54) still has the full fast input $A_2\underline{\beta}_j(k)$ into the slow subsystem. The substitution of

$$\underline{\lambda}(k) = \underline{x}_1(k) - K\underline{\beta}_j(k) \tag{56}$$

into (54a) yields

$$\underline{\lambda}(k + 1) = (F_j - KH_j)\underline{\lambda}(k) + N\underline{\beta}_j(k) + (B_1 - KE_j)\underline{u}(k), \tag{57}$$

and we set $N = A_2 - KP_j + (F_j - KH_j)K = 0$ to decouple $\underline{\beta}_j(k)$ from $\underline{\lambda}(k)$. Rearranging the expression $N = 0$ we obtain

$$K = -F_j^{-1}A_2 + F_j^{-1}K(P_j + H_jK) \tag{58a}$$

and solve for K iteratively as:

$$K_{ji+1} = -F_j^{-1} K_{ji}(P_j + H_j K_{ji})$$ (58b)

where $K_{j1} = -F_j^{-1} A_2$. The system (54a) and (54b) after i K iterations takes the form

$$\lambda_i(k + 1) = F_{ji}\lambda_i(k) + G_{ji}\beta_j(k) + R_{ji}\underline{u}(k)$$ (59a)

$$\beta_j(k + 1) = H_j\lambda_i(k) + P_{ji}\beta_j(k) + E_j\underline{u}(k),$$ (59b)

where

$$F_{ji} = F_j - K_{ji}H_j$$ (60a)

$$G_{ji} = A_2 - K_{ji}P_j + F_{ji}K_{ji}$$ (60b)

$$P_{ji} = P_j + H_j K_{ji}$$ (60c)

$$R_{ji} = (I - K_{ji}L_j)B_1 - K_{ji}B_2.$$ (60d)

It should be noted that the slow and fast subsystems of the discrete system (59) are very weakly coupled since G_{ji} is $\mathscr{O}(\mu^i + \varphi)$ and H_j is $\mathscr{O}(\mu^j)$. It is also evident that F_{ji} and P_{ji} are $\mathscr{O}(\mu^{j+i})$ approximations of the slow and fast modes, respectively. As an important special case, setting $j = 1$ and $i = 0$ in (54), (55), (59), and (60) results in the lower-order models (39) and (40). Interpretations of the L, K iterations are that they provide for a succession of quasi-steady-state assumptions.

To recover $\underline{x}_2(k)$ from $\beta_j(k)$ and $\underline{x}_1(k)$ we observe that the j-th iteration of (51) gives

$$\beta_j - \underline{x}_2(k) = L_j\underline{x}_1(k).$$ (61)

Similarly, to recover $\underline{x}_1(k)$ from $\lambda_i(k)$ and $\beta_\varphi(k)$ we use the i-th iteration of (56) to obtain:

$$\lambda_i(k) - \underline{x}_1(k) = -K_{ji}\beta_j(k).$$ (62)

Expressions (61) and (62) emphasize that $\lambda_i(k)$ and $\beta_j(k)$ have the same physical meaning as $\underline{x}_1(k)$ and $\underline{x}_2(k)$, respectively.

The above analysis shows clearly how to reduce a discrete system with coupled slow and fast parts. In the transformed system (59a) and (59b) the coupling terms G_{ji} and H_j are weak and can be neglected. Instead of the original full-order system (59a), (59b), we will use the separate lower-order approximate subsystems:

$$\lambda_i^a(k + 1) = F_{ji}\lambda_i^a(k) + R_{ji}\underline{u}(k) \tag{63a}$$

$$\beta_j^a(k + 1) = P_{ji}\beta_j^a(k) + E_j\underline{u}(k) \tag{63b}$$

with the initial value $\beta_j^0(k)$ obtained from $\underline{x}_1^0(k)$ and $x_2^0(k)$ using (61 and $\lambda_i^0(k)$ obtained from $\underline{x}_1^0(k)$ and $\underline{\beta}_j^0(k)$ via (62). The error $\lambda_i(k) - \lambda_i^a(k)$ is $\mathcal{O}(\mu^i)$, while the error $\beta_j(k) - \beta_j^a(k)$ is $\mathcal{O}(\mu^j)$. Note that in long- or short-term studies, a further simplification is obtained by keeping only model (63a) or (63b). In general, we need to compute four matrices F_{ji}, P_{ji}, R_{ji}, and E_j by using (55a)–(55d) and (60a)–(60b). The foregoing analysis generalizes the results of]2–4, 11, 12] and extends the available material on continuous models [1, 38] to the discrete case.

I.   EXAMPLES

We now provide some examples to demonstrate the various concepts developed in this section.

Example 1. Consider a seventh-order model of a single machine-infinite bus power system [39] discretized with sampling period T = 0.25 sec. It has the rotor angle, rotor speed, field flux linkage, flux linkage of armature direct and quadrature axes and flux linkage of damper direct, and quadrature axes as the state variables. The control variables are the input torque and field voltage.

The system state transition matrix after permutation and scaling is given by

$$
\begin{bmatrix}
0.9949 & 0.2444 & -0.0062 & -0.0011 & -0.0006 & -0.0001 & 0.0001 \\
-0.0384 & 0.9542 & -0.0495 & -0.0056 & -0.0027 & -0.0004 & 0.0003 \\
-0.1029 & -0.0126 & 0.7994 & 0.0348 & 0.0012 & 0.0001 & 0.0014 \\
-0.2114 & -0.0386 & 0.6330 & 0.0278 & 0.0011 & 0.0001 & 0.0011 \\
-0.2321 & -0.0468 & -0.0409 & -0.0018 & 0.0014 & -0.0001 & -0.0001 \\
-0.4944 & -0.1148 & 0.3781 & 0.0168 & 0.0009 & 0.0001 & 0.0006 \\
-0.3087 & -0.0734 & -0.0532 & -0.0021 & 0.0006 & 0 & -0.0001
\end{bmatrix}
$$

It is estimated that this system has three slow variables and four fast variables. Evaluating the spectral norms of the subsystem matrices, we obtain

$\|A_1\| = 1.1014, \quad \|A_2\| = 0.0353$

$\|A_3\| = 0.8933, \quad \|A_4\| = 0.0326$

$\|A_0\| = 1.1055, \quad \|A_0^{-1}\| = 1.2381$

$\|L_0\| = 0.991$

It is easy to see that conditions (26), (27) are satisfied, which implies that the system possesses the two-time-scale property. For an input matrix in the form

$$B = \begin{bmatrix} -11.3888 & 2.2860 \\ 0.9949 & -0.0049 \\ 7.2007 & -1.4505 \\ 7.1947 & -1.4475 \\ 2.3474 & -0.4686 \\ 8.4932 & -1.7071 \\ 3.1212 & -0.6256 \end{bmatrix}$$

the slow and fast subsystems are specified by

$$A_0 = \begin{bmatrix} 0.99530 & 0.24451 & -0.00687 \\ -0.03646 & 0.95456 & -0.05317 \\ -0.11036 & -0.01416 & 0.82194 \end{bmatrix}$$

$$B_0 = \begin{bmatrix} -0.00114 & 2.28796 \\ 0.94498 & 0.00519 \\ 7.46618 & -1.50390 \end{bmatrix}$$

$$A_4 = \begin{bmatrix} 0.02777 & 0.00106 & 0.00007 & 0.00106 \\ -0.00175 & 0.00138 & -0.00005 & -0.00009 \\ 0.01684 & 0.00089 & 0.00008 & 0.00059 \\ -0.00213 & 0.00056 & 0 & -0.00012 \end{bmatrix}$$

$$B_2 = \begin{bmatrix} 7.1947 & -1.4475 \\ 2.3474 & -0.4696 \\ 8.4932 & -1.7071 \\ 3.1212 & -0.62565 \end{bmatrix}$$

Example 2. The discrete model of an eighth-order power system [11] has the state transition matrix:

$$\begin{bmatrix}
0.835 & 0 & 0 & 0 & 0 & 0 & 0 & 0 \\
0.096 & 0.861 & 0 & 0 & 0 & 0 & 0 & 0.029 \\
-0.002 & -0.005 & 0.882 & -0.253 & 0.041 & -0.003 & -0.025 & -0.001 \\
0.007 & 0.014 & -0.029 & 0.928 & 0 & 0.006 & 0.059 & 0.002 \\
0.03 & 0.061 & 2.028 & 2.303 & 0.088 & -0.021 & -0.224 & -0.008 \\
0.048 & 0.758 & 0 & 0 & 0 & 0.165 & 0 & 0.023 \\
-0.012 & -0.027 & 1.209 & -1.4 & 0.161 & -0.013 & 0.156 & 0.006 \\
0.815 & 0 & 0 & 0 & 0 & 0 & 0 & 0.011
\end{bmatrix}$$

To put this matrix in two-time-scale form, we use the permutation matrix $P = \{e_4, e_3, e_2, e_1, e_7, e_5, e_6, e_8\}$, where e_i is the elementary column vector whose i-th entry is 1 and the scaling matrix $S = \text{diag}\{1, 1, 0.5, 0.22, 0.1, 0.055, 0.075, 0.05\}$ to obtain

$$A = \begin{bmatrix}
0.928 & -0.029 & 0.028 & 0.0212 & 0.06 & 1.0727 & 0 & 0.04 \\
-0.253 & 0.882 & -0.01 & 0.061 & -0.03 & -0.4545 & 0.5464 & -0.02 \\
0 & 0 & 0.861 & 0.1454 & 0 & 0 & 0 & 0.29 \\
0 & 0 & 0 & 0.835 & 0 & 0 & 0 & 0 \\
0 & 0 & 0.1516 & 0.0145 & 0.165 & 0 & 0 & 0.046 \\
-0.077 & 0.0665 & -0.003 & -0.002 & -0.0072 & 0.156 & 0.1181 & 0.0066 \\
-0.1727 & 0.1521 & -0.0092 & 0.0068 & -0.0158 & -0.3055 & 0.088 & -0.012 \\
0 & 0 & 0 & 0.1235 & 0 & 0 & 0 & 0.011
\end{bmatrix}$$

The eigenspectrum of A {0.8745 ± j, 0.1696, 0.861, 0.835, 0.2866, 0.165, 0.0184, 0.011} suggests that the eight-order model has four slow and four fast variables. Computation of the spectral norm of the different matrices gives

$\|A_1\| = 1.057, \qquad \|A_2\| = 1.1914$

$\|A_3\| = 0.2521,$ $\|A_4\| = 0.3446$

$\|A_0\| = 1.0011,$ $\|A_0^{-1}\| = 1.3167$

$\|L_0\| = 0.2523,$ $\|I_1 - A_0\| = 0.3455$

$\|M_0\| = 1.3451,$

It is evident that condition (26) has the value 0.0023; and the ratio of the left- to the right-hand side of inequality (27) is (1/1.177). Using the algorithm (25), the transformation matrix L after four iterations is given by

$$
L = \begin{bmatrix}
0 & 0 & -0.2178 & 0.0293 \\
0.0843 & -0.1238 & -0.0012 & 0.0037 \\
0.1358 & -0.1561 & 0.0053 & 0.0033 \\
0 & 0 & 0 & -0.1499
\end{bmatrix}
$$

with $\|L\| = 0.2551$. The sixth iterate of the numerical solution of (18) yields:

$$
M = \begin{bmatrix}
0.0947 & 1.9788 & 0.0421 & 0.0573 \\
-0.0058 & 0.1009 & 0.6207 & 0.0039 \\
0 & 0 & 0 & 0.3412 \\
0 & 0 & 0 & 0
\end{bmatrix}
$$

with $\|M\| = 1.9860$.

These results show that we can use L_0 and M_0 as first-order approximations to L and M, respectively.

Example 3. A fifth-order model of a steam power system, considered in [15], has the system matrix

$$
\begin{bmatrix}
-0.1125 & 0.02333 & 0.035 & 0 & 0.025 \\
0 & -0.167 & 0 & 0 & 0.167 \\
0 & 2.0 & -2.0 & 0 & 0 \\
-4.0 & 0 & 0 & -2.0 & 0
\end{bmatrix}
$$

This model has been discretized using $T = 0.7$ sec and scaled by the matrix $S = \text{diag}\{3.0, 1.5, 1.0, 1.5, 0.4\}$ to give

$$\begin{bmatrix} 0.9147 & 0.0506 & 0.0375 & 0.0150 & 0.0385 \\ -0.0301 & 0.8893 & -0.0005 & 0.0456 & 0.1107 \\ -0.0065 & 0.4677 & 0.2465 & 0.0139 & 0.0480 \\ -0.715 & -0.0219 & -0.0207 & 0.2399 & -0.0236 \end{bmatrix}$$

This system possesses the time separation property with $n_1 = 2$ and $n_2 = 3$.

The discretized model has the eigenvalue $\gamma(A) = \{0.8928 \pm j, 0.0937, 0.2506 \pm j, 0.0252, 0.0295\}$. For the subsystem matrices, the respective norms are

$$\|A_1\| = 0.9193, \qquad \|A_2\| = 0.1272$$

$$\|A_3\| = 0.7306, \qquad \|A_4\| = 0.2597$$

$$\|A_0\| = 0.9054, \qquad \|A_0^{-1}\| = 1.138$$

$$\|L_0\| = 0.9635, \quad \|I_1 - A_0\| = 0.1545$$

$$\|M_0\| = 0.1442.$$

Simple calculation shows that condition (26) has the value 0.0176 and the ratio of the left- to the right-hand side of inequality (27) is $(1/2.2988)$. The transformation L after five iterations is

$$\begin{bmatrix} -0.0685 & -0.7161 \\ 1.0787 & -0.0740 \\ 0.2812 & 0.0267 \end{bmatrix}$$

with $\|L\| = 1.1177$.

The matrix M, after five iterations, is given by

$$M = \begin{bmatrix} 0.0573 & 0.0146 & 0.0305 \\ 0.0132 & 0.0924 & 0.1329 \end{bmatrix}$$

Here $\|M\| = 0.1673$.

The above results indicate that we can use L_0 and M_0 as first-order approximations to L and M.

Example 4. To illustrate Lemma 2, the eigenvalues of the eighth-order power system in Example 2 are $\{0.8745 \pm j, 0.1696, 0.861, 0.835, 0.2866, 0.165, 0.0184, 0.011\}$, whereas the eigenvalues of the approximate system (31) are $\lambda(A_0) = \{0.8592 \pm j, 0.1373, 0.861, 0.835\}$ and $\lambda(A_4) = \{0.\lambda22 \pm j, 0.1868, 0.165, 0.011\}$. Thus the eigenvalues of the approximate model (31) compare favorably with the actual ones.

The eigenvalues of the steam power system in Example 3 are $\{0.8928 \pm j, 0.0937, 0.\lambda506 \pm j, 0.0252, 0.0295\}$, while $\lambda(A_0) = \{0.8879 \pm j, 0.0848\}$ and $\lambda(A_4) = \{0.2387 \pm j, 0.0258, 0.035\}$. It is readily seen that the set of eigenvalues $\lambda(A_0) \text{ ú } \lambda(A_4)$ is close to that of the complete system. Consequently, (30) is verified.

III. FEEDBACK CONTROL DESIGN

In this section, we focus our attention on the design of feedback controllers for discrete systems of the type (8)–(11) by exploiting the eigenvalue condition (7). It has been shown in Section II that, as a consequence of (7), the model (8)–(11) can be broken into (20) and (21) using block diagonalization or approximated to a first order by (39) and (40) via quasi-steady-state analysis. We will use approaches in feedback control design [2, 15, 16].

A. STATIC-TYPE CONTROLLERS

The problem is to find a feedback gain matrix G such that the eigenvalues of the feedback control systems are arbitrarily positioned within the unit circle. It is desirable, in view of the slow–fast separation phenomena, to carry out the design in two stages. We assume that (3) and (4) are satisfied or, equivalently, that Lemmas 4 and 5 are satisfied. There are two ways to solve this problem: the first is based on state-variable information and the second is based on output measurements.

1. Using State Information

Consider the eigenvalue placement problem for system (8) and (9) using a linear state feedback control of the form

$$\underline{u}(k) = G\underline{x}(k), \tag{64}$$

where G is the $(m \times n_s + n_f)$ gain matrix of design parameters. As mentioned earlier, the design procedure is implemented in two stages. In the first stage we use the transformation (16) to convert (8) and (9) into the decoupled form (20) and design an $(m \times n_s)$ feedback matrix K_s to place the eigenvalues of $(A_s + B_s K_s)$ at n_s desired locations, where (35) has been used. Define

$$\underline{u}(k) = \underline{u}_1(k) + \underline{u}_2(k)$$

$$= [K_s \; 0]g(k) + \underline{u}_2(k).$$

(65)

The substitution of (65) into (20), (35) yields:

$$g(k+1) = \begin{bmatrix} A_s + B_s K_s & 0 \\ B_f K_s & A_f \end{bmatrix} g(k) + \begin{bmatrix} B_s \\ B_f \end{bmatrix} \underline{u}_2(k),$$

(66)

where $g^t(k) = [\underline{x}_s{}^t(k) \; \underline{x}_f{}^t(k)]$. Since (66) is a lower triangular, we use the transformation

$$T_s = \begin{bmatrix} I_1 & 0 \\ L_s & I_2 \end{bmatrix}; \quad T_s^{-1} \begin{bmatrix} I_1 & 0 \\ -L_s & I_2 \end{bmatrix}$$

(67)

which is of the type (45) and a special case of (15) by setting $M = 0$, $L_s = L$. In this regard, with $A_f = A_4$, $B_f K_s = A_3$, $A_2 = 0$, and $(A_s + B_s K_s) = A_1$ in (17), it becomes

$$L_s(A_s + B_s K_s) - A_f L_s + B_f K_s = 0,$$

(68)

which defines L_s. The transformation $\underline{h}(k) = T_s g(k)$ gives

$$\underline{h}(k+1) = \begin{bmatrix} A_s + B_s K_s & 0 \\ 0 & A_f \end{bmatrix} \underline{h}(k) + \begin{bmatrix} B_s \\ B_f + L_s B_s \end{bmatrix} \underline{u}_2(k).$$

(69)

It can be easily seen [40] that the pair $(A_f, B_f + L_s B_s)$ is reachable since the pair (A_f, B_f) is reachable. We design an $(m \times n_f)$ feedback matrix K_f in the second stage to place the eigenvalues of $(A_f, B_f + L_s B_s)B_f$ at n_f desired locations. Then, the substitution of the state feedback control

$$\underline{u}_2(k) = [0 \; K_f]\underline{h}(k)$$

(70)

into 65) with the aid of (16) and (67) results in the overall gain matrix G in (64):

$$G = \left[K_s + K_f(L + L_s)(I_1 + M_L) + K_sML : \right.$$

$$\left. K_f + (K_fL_s + K_s)M \right],$$
(71)

which obviously requires the computation of L, M, and L_s as defined by (17), (18), and (68), respectively.

Had we reversed the order in the two-stage eigenvalue placement, we would arrive at [11, 12]:

$$G = \left[K_s + K_s(M + M_s)L + K_fL : K_f + K_s(M + M_s) \right],$$
(72)

where now K_s and K_f are designed to place the eigenvalues of $[A_s + (B_s + M_sG_f)K_s]$, (A_f, B_fK_f) at n_s, n_f desired positions. M_s is a solution of

$$M_s(A_f + B_fK_f) - A_sM_s + B_sK_f = 0.$$
(73)

This completes the two-stage state feedback design using block diagonalization. In [41], suitable algorithms for eigenvalue assignment are discussed.

A different route to the design problem addressed above is via quasi-steady-state analysis in which (39) and (40) are the slow and fast subsystems, respectively. The linear state feedback control $\underline{u}(k)$ is sought of the form $\underline{u}(k) = \underline{u}_s(k) + \underline{u}_f(k)$ with

$$\underline{u}_s(k) = K_0\underline{x}_s(k), \quad \underline{u}_f(k) = K_f\underline{x}_f(k),$$
(74)

where K_0 and K_f are the design parameters. By virtue of

$$\overline{\underline{x}}_2(k) = [I_2 - A_4]^{-1}[A_3 + B_2K_0 \, \underline{x}_s(k)],$$
(75)

which follows from (38), the composite control

$$\underline{u}(k) = \underline{u}_s(k) + \underline{u}_f(k)$$

$$= K_0\underline{u}_s(k) + K_f\underline{x}_f(k)$$

$$= \left\{ \left(I_m - K_f[I_2 - A_4]^{-1}B_2 \right)K_0 \right.$$

$$\left. - K_f[I_2 - A_4]^{-1}A_3 \right\}\underline{x}_s(k)$$

$$+ K_f\left\{ [I_2 - A_4]^{-1}(A_3 + B_2K_0)\underline{x}_s(k) + \underline{x}_f(k) \right\}.$$
(76)

The following lemma [2] summarizes the main result:

Lemma 6. If the controls $\underline{u}_s(k)$, $\underline{u}_f(k)$ in (74) and

$$\underline{u}(k) = \left\{ \left(I_m - K_f[I_2 - A_4]^{-1}B_2 \right) K_0 \right. \tag{77}$$

$$\left. - K_f[I_2 - A_4]^{-1}A_3 \right\} \underline{x}_1(k) + K_f \underline{x}_2(k)$$

are applied to the systems given by (39) and (40) and the original system (8) and (9), respectively, and if $\lambda |(A_f + B_2 K_f)| < 1$, then

$$\underline{x}_1(k) = \underline{x}_s(k) + \mathcal{O}(\mu) \tag{78a}$$

$$\underline{x}_2(k) = [I_2 - A_4]^{-1}(A_3 + B_2 K_0)\underline{x}_s)(1) + \underline{x}f(k) + (\mu) \tag{78b}$$

hold for all finite $k \geq 0$. If also $\lambda |(A_0 + B_0 K_0)| < 1$, then (78) holds for all $k \in [0, \infty])$.

Proof. The feedback system given by (8), (9), and (77) is

$$\begin{bmatrix} x_1(k+1) \\ x_2(k+1) \end{bmatrix} = \begin{bmatrix} F_1 & F_2 \\ F_3 & F_4 \end{bmatrix} \begin{bmatrix} x_1(k) \\ x_2(k) \end{bmatrix} \tag{79}$$

where

$$F_1 = A_1 + B_1 \left(I_m - K_f[I_2 - A_4]^{-1}B_2 \right) K_0 \tag{80a}$$

$$- B_1 K_f[I_2 - A_4]^{-1}A_3$$

$$F_2 = A_2 + B_1 K_2 \tag{80b}$$

$$F_3 = (I_2 - A_4 - B_2 K_f)[I_2 - I_4]^{-1}(A_3 + B_2 K_0) \tag{80c}$$

$$F_4 = A_4 + B_2 K_f \tag{80d}$$

Following [7, 9] we construct a transformation

$$H = \begin{bmatrix} I_1 + NK & N \\ K & K_2 \end{bmatrix}, \quad H^{-1} = \begin{bmatrix} I_1 & N \\ -K & I_2 + KN \end{bmatrix} \tag{81}$$

where

$$K = -(I_1 - A_4)^{-1}(A_3 + B_2 K_0) + \mathcal{O}(\mu) \tag{82a}$$

$$N = (A_0 + B_0 K_0)^{-1}(A_2 + B_1 K_f) + \mathscr{O}(\mu). \tag{82b}$$

Combining (79)–(82) and using the time-separation property (27), we obtain

$$H = \begin{bmatrix} F_1 & F_2 \\ F_3 & F_4 \end{bmatrix}, \quad H^{-1} = \begin{bmatrix} F_0 & 0 \\ 0 & F_f \end{bmatrix} \tag{83}$$

where

$$F_0 = A_0 + B_0 K_0 + \mathscr{O}(\mu) \tag{84a}$$

$$F_f = A_4 + B_2 K_f + \mathscr{O}(\mu). \tag{84b}$$

Now, if $(A_4 + B_2 K_f)$ is stable, the solution of (79) is approximated for all finite $k \geq 0$ by

$$x_1(k) = (A_0 + B_0 K_0)^k x_s(0) + \mathscr{O}(\mu) \tag{85a}$$

$$x_2(k) = (I_2 - A_4)^{-1}(A_3 + B_2 K_0)(A_0 + B_0 K_0)^k x_s(0) \tag{85b}$$

$$+ (A_4 + B_2 K_f)^k x_f(0) + \mathscr{O}(\mu),$$

where $\underline{x}_s(0)$, $\underline{x}_f(0)$ are given in (39) and (40). If, in addition, $|\lambda(A_0 + B_0 K_0)| < 1$, then (75) holds for all $k \in [0, \infty)$. Finally, (78) follows directly from (39), (40), and (85). Lemma 6 suggests that K_0 and K_f be separately designed according to slow- and fast-mode performance specifications. It is readily evident that K_f is designed to place the eigenvalues of $(A_4 + B_2 K_f)$ at n_f desired locations.

Corollary 1. If $|\lambda(A_4)| < 1$, then the lower-order control $\underline{u}(k) = K_0 \underline{x}_1(k)$ stabilizes the system (8) and (9).

It has been shown in [2] that in this case the fast dynamics can be neglected and that the slow subsystem becomes $\underline{x}_s(k + 1) = (A_0 + B_0 K_0)\underline{x}_s(k)$, which can be stabilized by appropriate design of K_0.

Corollary 2. Any reduced-order state-feedback control keeps the nondominant eigenvalues unaltered. This result has been proved in [2] using modal analysis and aggregation.

Consider the fast feedback control

$$\underline{u}(k) = \underline{f}(k) + S\underline{x}_2(k), \tag{86}$$

where $\|S\| = \mathscr{O}(1)$ and $\det[A_4 + B_2 S] \neq 0$. The following lemma establishes properties of system (8) and (9) under feedback control of the type (86).

Lemma 7. If $\det[I_2 - (A_4 + B_2S)] \neq 0$, then the slow subsystem of (8) and (9) under the control (86) is reachable if and only if (39) is reachable. Also, the slow subsystem reachability is invariant to fast controls of the class (86).

Proof. We follow the procedure of [4]. For the slow subsystem (39) we construct a nonsingular transformation T_1 of the control $\underline{u}_s(k)$, such that the new control $\underline{r}(k) = T_1^{-1}\underline{u}_s(k)$. Then we introduce a partial feedback $\underline{r}(k) = \underline{v}_s(k) + T_2\underline{x}_s(k)$, such that the slow subsystem (39) becomes

$$\underline{x}_s(k + 1) = A_s - B_sT_1T_2\underline{x}_s(k) + B_sT_1\underline{v}_s(k). \tag{87}$$

Define

$$T_1 = I_2 + S\left[I_2 - (A_4 + B_2)\right]^{-1}B_2$$

and consider the matrix B_sT_1:

$$B_sT_1 = \left[B_1 + A_2(I_2 - A_4)^{-1}B_2\right]T_1$$

$$= B_1 + A_2(I_2 - A_4)^{-1}B_2\left\{I_2 + S\left[I_2 - (A_4 + B_2S)\right]^{-1}B_2\right\}$$

$$+ B_1S\left[I_2 - (A_4 + B_2S)\right]^{-1}B_2$$

$$= B_1 + B_1S\left[I_2 - (A_4 + B_2S)\right]^{-1}B_2$$

$$+ A_2(I_2 - A_4)^{-1}\left\{I_2 + B_2S\left[I_2 - (A_4 + B_2S)\right]^{-1}\right\}B_2. \tag{88}$$

Making use of the matrix identity

$$I_2 - (A_4 + B_2S)^{-1} = (I_2 - A_4)^{-1}\left\{I_2 + B_2S\left[I_2 - (A_4 + B_2S)\right]^{-1}\right\},$$

(88) reduces to

$$B_sT_1 = B_1 + (B_1S + A_2)\left[I_2 - (A_4 + B_2S)\right]^{-1}B_2 \equiv B_c. \tag{89}$$

Define $T_2 = S[I_2 - A_4]^{-1}A_3$ and consider the matrix $A_s + B_sT_1T_2$:

$$A_s + B_sT_1T_2 = A_s + B_cT_2$$

$$= A_1 - A_2(I_2 - A_4)^{-1}A_3 + \left\{ B_1 + (A_2 + B_1S)\left[I_2 - (A_4 + B_2S)\right]^{-1}B_2 \right\}T_2$$

$$= A_1 + (A_2 + B_1S)(I_2 - A_4)^{-1}A_3$$

$$+ (A_2 + B_1S)\left[I_2 - (A_4 + B_2S)\right]^{-1}B_2S(I_2 - A_4)^{-1}A_3$$

$$= A_1 + (A_2 + B_1S)\left\{ I_2 + \left[I_2 - (A_4 + B_2S)\right]^{-1}B_2S \right\}(I_2 - A_4)^{-1}A_3. \tag{90}$$

Using the matrix identity

$$\left[I_2 - (A_4 + B_2S)\right]^{-1} = \left\{ I_2 + \left[I_2 - (A_4 + B_2S)\right]^{-1}B_2S \right\}(I_2 - A_4)^{-1}.$$

(90) becomes

$$A_s + B_sT_1T_2 = A_1 + (A_2 + B_1S)\left[I_2 - (A_4 + B_2S)\right]^{-1}A_3 \equiv A_c. \tag{91}$$

Now (89) and (91) show that the use of the control $\underline{u}_s(k) = T_1\underline{v}_s(k) + T_1T_2\underline{x}_1(k)$ reduces system (87) to the system

$$\underline{x}_s(k + 1) = A_c\underline{x}_s(k) + B_c\underline{v}_s(k).$$

Since the transformation $\underline{r}(k) = T_1^{-1}\underline{u}_s(k)$ and the partial feedback control $\underline{r}(k) = \underline{v}_s(k) + T_2\underline{x}_s(k)$ do not change the controllability subspace of system (38), the columns of $[B_0, A_0B_0, \ldots, A_0^{n_1-1}B_0]$ and $[B_c, A_cB_c, \ldots, A_c^{n_1-1}B_c]$ span the same subspace, and thus the first part of Lemma 7 is proved.

Furthermore, if $\|S\| = \mathcal{O}(1)$, then system (87) is the slow subsystem of the discrete two-time-scale system (8) and (9) under the fast control (86), and hence its reachability is preserved.

Lemma 7 indicates that to determine whether the slow subsystem of (1) is reachable or not, we only have to test the controllability of the pair (A_c, B_c) for a single value of S. Moreover, the eigenvalues of the fast subsystem $(A_4 + B_2S)$ can be arbitrarily positioned without affecting the reachability of the slow subsystem.

Simple comparison of the feedback gain in (71) or (72) obtained by block diagonalization, with that of (77) derived by quasi-steady-state analysis, shows that the latter is easier to compute and implement than the former; however, at the expense of yielding first-order approximate results. Parallel results can be obtained

for Model III defined by (13) and (14), as discussed in [17, 18]. Other approaches
have been developed in {33–35] using asymptotic expansion methods.

2. Using Output Measurements

We now consider the situation in which a limited number of state variables
can be measured; that is, the discrete system is modeled by (1) and (2). Using appropriate coordinate transformation with the eigenvalue condition (6) or (7), the
system is put in the form (8), (9), and (11). The main reason for using (11) is to
facilitate the design of a two-stage output feedback scheme [6, 14]. It is further
assumed that

$$\text{rank}[C_1] = p_s, \quad \text{rank}[C_2] = p_f \tag{92}$$

$$A_3 = PC_1. \tag{93}$$

The interpretation of (93) is [14] that the effect of the slow part on the fast part,
which is known to be weak [7, 9], is linearly related to the output of the slow
part. In view of (92), a least-squares estimate of P is given by

$$P = A_3 C_1^t (C_1 C_1^t)^{-1}. \tag{94}$$

To develop the slow and fast subsystems of (8) and (9) with output (11), we adopt
the time-scale decomposition procedure. We know that neglecting the effect of the
fast modes is equivalent to letting $\underline{x}_2(k + 1) = \underline{x}_2(k)$. Without the fast modes, system (8), (9), and (11) reduces to:

$$\bar{\underline{x}}_1(k + 1) = A_1\bar{\underline{x}}_1(k) + A_2\bar{\underline{x}}_2(k) + B_1\bar{\underline{x}}(k); \tag{95a}$$

$$\bar{\underline{x}}_1(0) = \underline{x}_{10}$$

$$\bar{\underline{x}}_2(k) = A_3\bar{\underline{x}}_1(k) + A_4\bar{\underline{x}}_2(k) + B_2\bar{\underline{x}}(k); \tag{95b}$$

$$\bar{\underline{x}}_2(0) = \underline{x}_{20}$$

$$\bar{\underline{y}}_1(k) = C_1\bar{\underline{x}}_1(k) \tag{95c}$$

$$\bar{\underline{y}}_2(k) = C_2\bar{\underline{x}}_2(k), \tag{95d}$$

where a bar indicates a quasi-steady state [2, 9]. Assuming that $(I_2 - A_4)^{-1}$ exists,
where I_j is the $n_j \times n_j$ identity matrix, we can write $\underline{x}_2(k)$ as:

$$\bar{x}_2(k) = (I_2 - A_4)^{-1} A_3 \bar{x}_1(k) + B_2 \bar{u}(k) \tag{96}$$

and, substituting it into (95) with the aid of (93), the slow subsystem is defined by:

$$\underline{u}_s(k + 1) = A_0 \underline{x}_s(k) + B_0 \underline{u}_s(k); \tag{97a}$$

$$\underline{x}_s(0) = \underline{x}_{10}$$

$$\underline{y}_s(k) = C_0 \underline{x}_s(k) + D_0 \underline{u}_s(k) \tag{97b}$$

$$= \left[\underline{y}_{1s}^t(k) \quad \underline{y}_{2s}^t(k) \right],$$

where

$$A_0 = A_1 + A_2 (I_2 - A_4)^{-1} PC_1 \tag{98a}$$

$$B_0 = B_1 + A_2 (I_2 - A_4)^{-1} B_2 \tag{98b}$$

$$C_0 = \begin{bmatrix} C_1 \\ C_2 (I_2 - A_4)^{-1} PC_1 \end{bmatrix} \tag{98c}$$

$$D_0 = \begin{bmatrix} 0 \\ C_2 (I_2 - A_4)^{-1} B_2 \end{bmatrix} \tag{98d}$$

Hence, $\underline{x}_1(k) = \underline{x}_s(k)$, $\underline{x}_2(k), \underline{y}(k) = \underline{y}_s(k)$, $\underline{u}(k) = \underline{u}_s(k)$ are the slow components of the corresponding variables in system (8), (9), and (11).

The fast subsystem is derived by making the assumption [2, 9] that $\underline{x}_1(k) = \underline{x}_s(k) = $ constant and $\underline{x}_2(k + 1) = \underline{x}_2(k)$. From (9) and (96) we then obtain:

$$\underline{x}_2(k + 1) - \bar{x}_2(k + 1) = A_4 \left[\underline{x}_2(k) - \bar{x}_2(k) \right] + B_2 \left[\underline{u}(k) - \underline{u}_s(k) \right] \tag{99}$$

Letting $\underline{x}_f(k) = \underline{x}_2(k) - \underline{x}_2(k)$, $\underline{u}_f(k) = \underline{u}(k) - \underline{u}_s(k)$, and $\underline{y}_f(k) = \underline{y}(k) - \underline{y}_s(k)$, the fast subsystem is defined as:

$$\underline{x}_f(k + 1) = A_4 \underline{x}_f(k) + B_2 \underline{u}_f(k); \tag{100a}$$

$$\underline{x}_f(0) = \underline{x}_2(0) - \bar{\underline{x}}_2(0)$$

$$\underline{y}_f(k) = \begin{bmatrix} 0 \\ C_2 \end{bmatrix} \underline{x}_f(k)$$

(100b)

$$= \begin{bmatrix} \underline{y}_{1f}^t(k) & \underline{y}_{2f}^t(k) \end{bmatrix}^t.$$

Suppose now that $\underline{u}_s(k) = G_1 \underline{y}_{1s}(k)$ and $\underline{u}_f(k) = G_2 \underline{y}_{2f}(k)$ are designed subject to some specifications. In view of

$$\bar{\underline{x}}_2(k) = (I_2 - A_4)^{-1}(P + B_2 G_1)\underline{y}_{1s}(k),$$

(101)

which follows from (96) and (98), the composite control

$$\underline{u}_s(k) + \underline{u}_f(k) = G_1 \underline{y}_{1s}(k) + G_2 \underline{y}_{2f}(k)$$

(102)

can be rewritten as:

$$\underline{u}(k) = \underline{u}_s(k) + \underline{u}_f(k)$$

$$= \left\{ \left[I_m - G_2 - C_2(I_2 - A_4)^{-1} B_2 \right] - G_2 C_2(I_2 - A_4)^{-1} \right\} \underline{y}_{1s}(k)$$

$$+ G_2 \left[\underline{y}_{2f}(k) + C_2(I_2 - A_4)^{-1}(P + B_2 G_1)\underline{y}_{1s}(k) \right].$$

(103)

The following lemma establishes properties of the feedback system (8), (9), and (11) with a composite control of the form, but with $\underline{y}_1(k)$ replacing $\underline{y}_{1s}(k)$ and $\underline{y}_2(k)$ replacing $\underline{y}_{2f}(k) + \underline{y}_2(k)$.

Lemma 8. If the output feedback controls

$$\underline{u}_s(k) = G_1 \underline{y}_{1s}(k), \quad \underline{u}_f = G_2 \underline{y}_{2f}(k)$$

(104)

$$\underline{u}(k) = \left\{ \left[I_m - G_2 C_2(I_2 - A_4)^{-1} B_2 \right] G_1 \right.$$

(105)

$$\left. - G_2 C_2(I_2 - A_4)^{-1} P \right\} \underline{y}_1(k) + G_2 \underline{y}_2(k)$$

are applied to systems (97) and (100) and (8)–(11), respectively, and if $(A_4 + B_2 G_2 C_2)$ is stable, then

$$\underline{y}_1(k) = \underline{y}_{1s}(k) + \mathcal{O}(\mu)$$

(106a)

$$\underline{y}_2(k) = C_2(I_2 - A_4)^{-1}(P + B_2G_1)\underline{y}_{1s}(k) + \underline{y}_{2s}(k) + \mathcal{O}(\mu) \tag{106b}$$

$$\underline{u}(k) = \underline{u}_s(k) + \underline{u}_f(k) + \mathcal{O}(\mu) \tag{106c}$$

holds for all finite $k \geq 0$. If $(A_s + B_sG_1C_1)$ is also stable, then (97) and (98) hold for all $k \in [0, \infty]$.

Proof. System (8), (9), and (11) with the output feedback control (105) becomes:

$$\begin{bmatrix} \underline{x}_1(k+1) \\ \underline{x}_2(k+1) \end{bmatrix} = \begin{bmatrix} F_1 & F_2 \\ F_3 & F_4 \end{bmatrix} \begin{bmatrix} \underline{x}_1(k) \\ \underline{x}_2(k) \end{bmatrix} \tag{107}$$

where

$$F_1 = A_1 + B_1\left[I_m - G_2C_2(I_2 - A_4)^{-1}B_2\right]G_1C_1 \tag{108a}$$

$$- B_1G_2C_2(I_2 - A_4)^{-1}PC_1$$

$$F_2 = A_2 + B_1G_2C_2 \tag{108b}$$

$$F_3 = (I_2 - A_4 - B_2G_2C_2)(I_2 - A_4)^{-1}(P + B_2G_1)C_1 \tag{108c}$$

$$F_4 = A_4 + B_2G_2C_2 \tag{108d}$$

Following [6, 9], we construct a linear transformation:

$$T_0 = \begin{bmatrix} I_1 + RQ & R \\ Q & I_2 \end{bmatrix} \tag{109}$$

$$T_0^{-1} = \begin{bmatrix} I_1 & -R \\ -Q & I_2 + QR \end{bmatrix}$$

with

$$Q = -(I_2 - A_4)^{-1}(P + B_2G_1)C_1 + \mathcal{O}(\mu) \tag{110a}$$

$$R = (A_0 + B_0G_1C_1)^{-1}(A_2 + B_2G_2C_2) + \mathcal{O}(\mu). \tag{110b}$$

Retaining first-order perturbation terms, we obtain:

$$T_0 = \begin{bmatrix} F_1 & F_2 \\ F_3 & F_4 \end{bmatrix} \tag{111}$$

$$T_0^{-1} = \begin{bmatrix} I_1 & -R \\ -Q & I_2 + QR \end{bmatrix}$$

where

$$D_1 = (A_0 + B_0 G_1 C_1) + \mathcal{O}(\mu) \tag{112a}$$

$$D_4 = (A_4 + B_2 G_2 C_2) + \mathcal{O}(\mu). \tag{112b}$$

If $(A_4 + B_2 G_2 C_2)$ is stable, the solution of (107) and (108) is approximated for all finite $k \geq 0$ by

$$\underline{x}_1(k) = (A_0 + B_0 G_1 C_1)^k \underline{x}_s(0) + \sigma(\mu) \tag{113a}$$

$$\underline{u}_2(k) = (I_2 - A_4)^{-1}(P + B_2 G_1)C_1(A_0 + B_0 G_1 C_1)^k \underline{x}_s(0) \tag{113b}$$

$$+ (A_4 + B_2 G_2 C_2)^k \underline{x}_f(0) + \mathcal{O}(\mu),$$

where $\underline{x}_s(0)$, $\underline{x}_f(0)$ are given by (97a) and (100a). If, in addition, $(A_0 + B_0 G_1 C_1)$ is also stable, (113) holds for all $k \in [0, \infty]$. In light of (11), (97), (98), (100), and (113), (105) follows directly.

Corollary. Setting $C_1 = I_1$ and $C_2 = I_2$ in (106), we obtain the state feedback control (77).

The above lemma suggests that G_1 and G_2 be separately designed according to the slow- and fast-mode performance specification, and implemented as the composite control defined by (105). Using pole assignment techniques, the gain matrices G_1 and G_2 can be designed to place $\min(n_s, p_s)$ and $\min(n_f, p_f)$ eigenvalues arbitrarily close to their desired locations [40].

B.   OBSERVER-BASED CONTROLLERS

Our purpose here is to study the problem of constructing observers (state reconstructors or asymptotic estimators) in order to estimate the slow and fast states. These observers employ only the available directly measurable input and output signals. We assume that there is a one-step delay between measuring and processing the information records. Thus, a full-order observer for system (8)–(10) is given by:

$$\hat{x}_1(k + 1) = A_1 \hat{x}_1(k) + A_2 \hat{x}(k) + B_1 u(k)$$

$$+ K_1 \left[y(k) - C_1 \hat{x}_1(k) - C_2 \hat{x}_2(k) \right]$$

(114a)

$$\hat{x}_2(k + 1) = A_3 \hat{x}_1(k) + A_4 \hat{x}_2(k) + B_2 u(k)$$

$$+ K_2 \left[y(k_- - C_1 \hat{x}_1(k) - C_2 \hat{x}_2(k) \right]$$

(114b)

where $\hat{x}_1(k) \in R^{ns}$ is the estimate of $x_1(k)$, $\hat{x}_2(k) \in R^{nf}$ is the estimate of $x_2(k)$, and K_1, K_2 are the design parameters that may be suitably selected to ensure any desired degree of convergence of the observation scheme. The purpose is to use the time-separation property in order to establish the conditions under which the full-order observer (114) can be designed so as to reconstruct the state vectors of system (8)–(10). In terms of the observation error vectors $\underline{x}_1(k) = \hat{x}_1(k) - \underline{x}_1(k)$ and $\underline{x}_2(k) = \hat{x}_2(k) - \underline{x}_2(k)$, it follows from (8)–(10) and (114) that:

$$\begin{bmatrix} \underline{x}_1(k + 1) \\ \underline{x}_2(k + 1) \end{bmatrix} = \begin{bmatrix} A_1 - K_1 C_1 & A_2 - K_1 C_2 \\ A_3 - K_2 C_1 & A_4 - K_2 C_2 \end{bmatrix} \begin{bmatrix} \underline{x}_1(k) \\ \underline{x}_2(k) \end{bmatrix}$$

(115)

System (115) will function as an observer for system (8)–(10) if the $(n_s \times p)$ matrix K_1 and the $(n_f \times p)$ matrix K_2 can be chosen such that system (114) is asymptotically stable. The following lemma establishes the main result.

Lemma 9. Suppose that $(I_2 - A_4)^{-1}$ exists. If (A_0, C_0) and (A_4, C_2) are observable pairs, then system (115) is asymptotically stable. The gain matrix K_1 is given by

$$K_1 = K_0 \left[I + C_2(I_2 - A_4)^{-1} K_2 \right] - A_2(I_2 - A_4)^{-1} K_2,$$

(116)

where K_0 and K_2 are any matrices for which $(A_0 - K_0 C_0)$ and $(A_4 - K_2 C_2)$, respectively, have spectral norms less than one.

Proof. The time-separation property entails that system (115) has slow and fast subsystems given by

$$\tilde{x}_s(k + 1) = H_s \tilde{x}_s(k)$$

(117a)

$$\tilde{x}_f(k + 1) = H_f \tilde{x}_f(k),$$

(117b)

where

$$H_s = (A_1 - K_1C_1) + (A_2 - K_1C_2)(I_2 - A_4 + K_2C_2)^{-1}(A_3 - K_2C_1) \qquad (118a)$$

$$H_f = (A_4 - K_2C_2). \qquad (118b)$$

The gain matrix K_2 can be chosen so that $(A_4 - K_2C_2)$ has spectral norm less than one, since (A_4, C_2) is an observable pair by hypothesis. This means that the fast subsystem (117b) and (118b) is asymptotically stable.

Consider the slow subsystem. Using the matrix identities

$$(F + GH)^{-1} = F^{-1}(I + GHF^{-1})^{-1}$$

$$= F^{-1}\left[I - G(I + HF^{-1}G)^{-1}HF^{-1}\right]$$

with $F = (I_2 - A_4)$, $G = K_2$, $H = C_2$, and manipulating (118a) along with (39), it follows that

$$H_s = A_0 - K_0C_0, \qquad (119a)$$

where

$$K_0 = K_1 + (A_2 - K_1C_2)(I_2 - A_4)^{-1}K_2 \qquad (119b)$$

$$\times \left[I + C_2(I_2 - A_4)^{-1}K_2\right]^{-1}.$$

The $(n_s \times p)$ matrix K_0 can be chosen so that $(A_0 - K_0C_0)$ has spectral norm less than one, since (A_0, C_0) is an observable pair by hypothesis. Hence, the slow subsystem ((117a) and (118a) is asymptotically stable. From (119b) and the matrix identity, one immediately obtains (116). By virtue of Lemma 3, the asymptotic stability of (114) is guaranteed, which completes the proof.

Corollary. If $|\lambda(A_4)| < 1$, then (114) reduces to

$$\hat{x}_1(k + 1) = A_1\hat{x}_1(k) + A_2\hat{x}_2(k) + B_1u(k)$$

$$+ K_0\left[y(k) - C_1\hat{x}_1(k) - C_2\hat{x}_2(k)\right]$$

This is obvious since $K_2 = 0$ is an admissible choice for K_2 [3].

In light of the results of sections II,F and III, it is readily evident that for stable plants one can drop out the fast modes, and hence a reduced-order observer of the slow subsystem of the form of (39) is given by

$$\hat{\underline{x}}_s(k + 1) = A_0\hat{\underline{x}}_s(k) + B_0\underline{u}(k) + K_0\left[\underline{y}(k) - C_0\hat{\underline{x}}(k) - D_0\underline{u}(k)\right] \quad (120)$$

an observer-based controller is described by [3]

$$\underline{u}(k) = G_0\hat{\underline{x}}_s(k) \quad (121)$$

where the $(n_s \times p)$ matrix K_0 and the $(m \times n_s)$ matrix G_0 are unknown gains to be determined. The composite system of (8)–(10), (120), and (121) is expressed as

$$\begin{bmatrix} \underline{x}_1(k + 1) \\ \hat{\underline{x}}_s(k + 1) \end{bmatrix} = \begin{bmatrix} A_1 & B_1G_0 \\ K_0C_1 & A_0 + B_0G_0 - K_0C_0 - K_0D_0G_0 \end{bmatrix}$$

$$\times \begin{bmatrix} \underline{x}_1(k) \\ \hat{\underline{x}}_s(k) \end{bmatrix} + \begin{bmatrix} A_2 \\ K_0C_2 \end{bmatrix}\underline{x}_2(k) \quad (122a)$$

$$\underline{x}_2(k + 1) = [A_3 - B_2G_0]\begin{bmatrix} \underline{x}_1(k) \\ \hat{\underline{x}}_s(k) \end{bmatrix} + A_4\underline{x}_2(k). \quad (122b)$$

The fast subsystem of (122) is [3]

$$\underline{x}_f(k + 1) = A_4\underline{x}_f(k) \quad (123a)$$

and the slow subsystem is given by

$$\hat{\underline{x}}_s(k + 1) = F_0\hat{\underline{x}}_s \quad (123b)$$

where

$$F_0 = \begin{bmatrix} A_1 & B_1G_0 \\ K_0C_1 & A_0 + B_0G_0 - K_0C_0 - K_0D_0G_0 \end{bmatrix}$$

$$+ \begin{bmatrix} A_2 \\ K_0C_2 \end{bmatrix}[I_2 - A_4]^{-1}[A_3 - B_2G_0]. \quad (123c)$$

Lemma 10. If $|\lambda(A_4)| < 1$ and (A_0, B_0, C_0) is completely reachable and completely observable, then the control (121) is a stabilizing controller. The gains G_0 and K_0 are any matrices for which $(A_0 + B_0G_0)$ and $(A_0 - K_0C_0)$, respectively, are stable matrices.

Proof. We follow [3]. Since $|\lambda(A_4)| < 1$, (123a) can be neglected because the subsystem (123b) and (123c) can be controlled against any fast disturbances. In view of (39), F_0 in (123c) reduces to

$$F_0 = \begin{bmatrix} A_0 & B_0G_0 \\ K_0C_0 & A_0 + B_0G_0 - K_0C_0 \end{bmatrix}$$

which under the equivalent transformation becomes

$$\begin{bmatrix} I & 0 \\ I & -I \end{bmatrix} F_0 \begin{bmatrix} I & 0 \\ I & -I \end{bmatrix} = \begin{bmatrix} A_0 + B_0G_0 & -B_0G_0 \\ 0 & A_0 - K_0C_0 \end{bmatrix}$$

so that

$$\lambda(F_0) = \lambda(A_0 + B_0G_0) \cup \lambda(A_0 - K_0C_0).$$

Since (A_0, B_0) and (A_0, C_0) are reachable and observable pairs by hypothesis, it follows that matrices G_0 and K_0 exist such that F_0 is a stable matrix. Thus (121) is a stabilizing feedback controller for the composite system (122).

We note from Lemma 10 that a two-stage eigenvalue assignment algorithm can be used to place n_s observer eigenvalues at arbitrary positions (thus determining K_0) and then to position n_s control eigenvalues at desired locations (and thus determine G_0).

Parallel development has been presented in [35] for Model II given by (12) and using different measurement schemes. However, the design algorithm is more involved than the foregoing one.

C.   DYNAMIC-TYPE CONTROLLERS

A common feature of the foregoing feedback design methods for discrete two-time scale systems has been to ensure that the closed-loop system of the form

$$z_1(k + 1) = H_1 z_1(k) + H_2 z_2(k) \tag{124a}$$

$$z_2(k + 1) = H_3 z_1(k) + H_4 z_2(k) \tag{124b}$$

is asymptotically stable. In view of the time-separation property, necessary and sufficient conditions for (124) to be asymptotically stable are

$$|\lambda(H_4)| < 1 \tag{125a}$$

$$\left| \lambda \left(H_1 + H_2 (I_2 - H_4)^{-1} H_3 \right) \right| < 1. \tag{125b}$$

These conditions need to be satisfied for reliable control design.

A dynamic output feedback scheme based on the reduced (slow) model (39) is generated by [10].

$$\underline{f}(k + 1) = E_1 \underline{f}(k) + E_2 \underline{y}(k) + E_3 \underline{u}(k) \tag{126a}$$

$$\underline{u}(k) = E_4 \underline{f}(k) + E_5 \underline{y}(k), \tag{126b}$$

where $\underline{f}(k) \in R^r$; $0 \le r \le n$, and the matrices E_1 through E_5 contain the design parameters. The application of (126) to the reduced model (39) results in:

$$\begin{bmatrix} \underline{x}_s(k + 1) \\ \underline{f}(k + 1) \end{bmatrix} = \begin{bmatrix} V_1^0 & V_2^0 \\ V_3^0 & V_4^0 \end{bmatrix} \begin{bmatrix} \underline{x}_s(k) \\ \underline{f}(k) \end{bmatrix} \tag{127a,b}$$

where

$$V_1^0 = A_0 + B_0 (I_m - E_5 D_0)^{-1} E_5 C_0 \tag{128a}$$

$$V_2^0 = B_0 (I_m - E_5 D_0)^{-1} E_4 \tag{128b}$$

$$V_3^0 = \left[E_2 + (E_2 D_0 + E_3)(I_m - E_5 D_0)^{-1} E_5 \right] C_0 \tag{128c}$$

$$V_4^0 = E_1 + (E_2 D_0 + E_3)(I_m - E_5 D_0)^{-1} E_4 \tag{128d}$$

and I_m is the $(m \times m)$ identity matrix. The matrix $(I_m - E_5 D_0)$ is assumed invertible to ensure that $\underline{u}(k)$ as given by (126b) is uniquely defined. For proper control design, the matrices $E_1, \dots, E_5$ need to be selected such that the system (127) is asymptotically stable.

It should be remarked that:

1) It is interesting to observe that upon comparing (126) with (120) and (121), we find that $E_5 = 0$, and

$$E_1 = A_0 - G_0 C_0; \quad E_2 = G_0;$$

$$E_3 = B_0 - G_0 D_0; \quad E_4 = K_0.$$

With the substitution of the above conditions into (128), it can be easily seen that the system (127) can be stabilized by the choice of G_0 and K_0, where $\underline{x}_s(k) = \underline{f}(k)$.

2) For the static output feedback scheme (104), one can readily see that it is a special case of (126) with $E_4 = 0$ and $E_5 = [G_1 \ G_2]$. Given the choice of G_1 and G_2 that meets the design specifications, it has been shown [16] that the resulting closed-loop system is asymptotically stable when C_1 in (11) is of full rank.

Next we consider the application of the feedback control (126) to the original system (8)–(10). The resulting closed-loop system takes the form (124) with:

$$H_1 = \begin{bmatrix} (A_1 + B_1 E_s C_1) & B_1 E_4 \\ \\ (E_2 + E_3 E_5) C_1 & (E_1 + E_3 E_4) \end{bmatrix} \tag{129a}$$

$$H_2 = \begin{bmatrix} (A_2 + B_1 E_5 C_2) \\ \\ (E_2 + E_3 E_5) C_2 \end{bmatrix} \tag{129b}$$

$$H_3 = \begin{bmatrix} (A_3 + B_2 E_5 C_1) B_2 E_4 \end{bmatrix} \tag{129c}$$

$$H_4 = (A_4 + B_2 E_5 C_2), \tag{129d}$$

where $z_1(k) = [x_1{}^t(k) \ f^t(k)]^t$ is the combined dominant state and $z_2(k) = x_2(k)$ is the nondominant state. It is now required to validate conditions (125a) and (125b). We first demonstrate the existence of $(I_2 - H_4)^{-1}$. Since (8)–(10) is asymptotically stable, the matrix $(I_2 - A_4)$ is invertible. Using the matrix identities

$$(R - ST)^{-1} = R^{-1} \left[I - STR^{-1} \right]^{-1}$$

$$= R^{-1} \left[I + S \{ I - TR^{-1} S \}^{-1} TR^{-1} \right]$$

with $R = (I_2 - A_4)$, $S = B_2$, $T = E_5 C_2$; it follows that

$$(I_2 - A_4 - B_2 E_5 C_2)^{-1} = (I_2 - A_4)^{-1} \Big[I_2 + B_2 \tag{130}$$

$$\times \left\{ I_m - E_5 C_2 (I_2 - A_4)^{-1} B_2 \right\}^{-1} E_5 C_2 (I_2 - A_4)^{-1} \Big].$$

Since the matrix

$$\left\{ I_m - E_5 D_0 \right\} = \left\{ I_m - E_5 C_2 (I_2 - A_4)^{-1} B_2 \right\}$$

is assumed invertible, (130) therefore shows that $(I_2 - H_4)^{-1}$ exists. Using (129) and (13), and after some algebraic manipulations, we arrive at:

$$H_1 + H_2(I_2 - H_4)^{-1}H_3 = \begin{bmatrix} V_1^0 & V_2^0 \\ V_3^0 & V_4^0 \end{bmatrix} \qquad (131)$$

which indicates that once the design parameters $(E_1, \ldots, E_5)$ are selected to ensure the asymptotic stability of the augmented reduced model (127), then condition (125b) is satisfied. We now turn to condition (125a). It is clear from (129d) that H_4 depends mainly on the matrices describing the neglected nondominant modes, and in general there is no guarantee that (125a) can be satisfied. Recall that system (8)–(11) being asymptotically stable implies that [4]:

$$|\lambda(A_4)| < 1. \qquad (132)$$

Based on this, we can identify classes of discrete two-time-scale systems for which (125a) can be satisfied:

1) The nondominant states are not affected by the input $\underline{u}(k)$; that is, $B_2 = 0$. In view of (132), this means that the nondominant modes are stabilizable, and it is evident that (132a) can be satisfied for arbitrary E_5.

2) The nondominant states are not directly measurable at the output; that is, $C_2 = 0$. This implies that the nondominant modes are detectable. Once again (125a) can be satisfied for arbitrary E_5 by virtue of (132).

3) The particular case in which $E_5 = 0$ is an admissible choice to stabilize (127) since it obviously satisfies (125a). The dynamic output feedback reduces to the observer-based controller structure.

4) Another class of systems can be identified by evaluating the eigenvalues of the matrix H_4 under negative static feedback.

$$\det\left[\lambda I_2 - A_4 + B_2 E_5 C_2\right] = \det\left[(\lambda I_2 - A_4)\right.$$
$$\times \left.\left(I_2 + (\lambda I_2 - A_4)^{-1}B_2 E_5 C_2\right)\right]$$
$$= \det\left[(\lambda_2 - A_4)\right]$$
$$\times \det\left[\left(I_2 + (\lambda I_2 - A_4)^{-1}E_2 E_5 C_2\right)\right]. \qquad (133)$$

Using the determinant identity

$$\det\left[\left(I_2 + (\lambda I_2 - A_4)^{-1}B_2 E_5 C_2\right)\right]$$
$$= \det\left\{\left[I_m + E_5 C_2(\lambda I_2 - A_4)^{-1}B_2\right]\right\}$$

in (133), it becomes

$$\det\left[\lambda I_2 - A_4 + B_2 E_5 C_2\right] = \Delta(\lambda)\det\left[I_m + E_5 \psi(\lambda)\right], \tag{134}$$

where

$$\Delta(\lambda) = \det\left[(\lambda I_2 - A_4)\right] \tag{135a}$$

$$\phi(\lambda) = (\lambda I_2 - A_4)^{-1} \tag{135b}$$

$$\psi(\lambda) = C_2 \phi(\lambda) B_2. \tag{135c}$$

Now to satisfy (125a) it is required that the columns of $\psi(\lambda)$ be linearly independent. It is known that the above requirement implies that the asymptotically stable nondominant modes must be output controllable [42]. An equivalent statement is that

$$\text{rank}\left[B_2 A_4 B_2 A_4^2 B_2 \ldots A_4^{n_f - 1} B_2\right] = n_f \tag{136a}$$

$$\text{rank}[C_2] = p. \tag{136b}$$

We note that once (3) is satisfied, then (136a) follows immediately. It therefore remains to satisfy (136b) under negative static feedback, which is quite restrictive.

The preceding discussions indicate that neglecting the nondominant modes in designing output feedback control schemes generally provides unsatisfactory results unless the original system is in one of the four classes identified above.

D.   EXAMPLES

Some examples are worked out to illustrate the control design techniques.

Example 5. Consider the fifth-order model of Example 3, Section II, in which the matrices L and M were computed. The slow-subsystem dynamic is described by

$$A_s = \begin{bmatrix} 0.8904 & 0.0804 \\ -0.111 & 0.895 \end{bmatrix}$$

$$\lambda(A_s) = \{0.8928 \pm j\,0.0937\},$$

By inspection, we see that (30a) is verified. The fast-subsystem dynamic is described by

$$A_f = \begin{bmatrix} 0.2487 & 0.0479 & 0.1301 \\ -0.0617 & 0.2271 & -0.0564 \\ -0.0142 & 0.0874 & 0.0182 \end{bmatrix}$$

$\lambda(A_f) = \{0.2506 \pm j0.0252, 0.0295\}$,

whereas its first-order perturbation is given by

$$A_4 = \begin{bmatrix} 0.2465 & 0.0139 & 0.048 \\ -0.0207 & 0.2399 & -0.0236 \\ -0.0035 & 0.0904 & 0.0259 \end{bmatrix}$$

$\lambda(A_4) = \{0.2387 \pm j0.0258, 0.035\}$.

Once again, we can see that (30b) is satisfied.

With an input matrix $B^t = [0.0098 \; 0.122 \; 0.036 \; 0.562 \; 0.115]$, for state feedback control design, the input matrices of the slow and fast subsystems are given by

$$B_0 = \begin{bmatrix} 0.0306 \\ 0.1761 \end{bmatrix}$$

$$B_2 = \begin{bmatrix} 0.0359 \\ 0.5619 \\ 0.11543 \end{bmatrix}.$$

The pair (A_0, B_0) is controllable, and, for the slow-subsystem eigenvalues to be placed at 0.893 and 0.825, the feedback gain is

$K_0 = [-0.5465 \; 0.0402]$.

For the eigenvalues of the fast subsystem to be placed at 0.251, 0.25, and 0.0295, the feedback gain is

$K_f = [-0.0365 \; -0.0195 \; -0.0509] = K_2$,

From (77), the slow feedback gain K_1 takes the form

$K_1 = [-0.5679 \; 0.0432]$.

The closed-loop eigenvalues of the fifth-order model using the composite control

$$u(k) \; K_1 x_1(k) + K_2 x_2(k)$$

are $\{0.8891, 0.8890, 0.243, 0.242, 0.0342\}$, which are close to the desired locations. Since A_4 is asymptotically stable, we can use $\underline{u}(k) = K_0 \underline{x}_1(k)$ as a feedback control. In this case, the eigenvalues of the closed-loop system are $\{0.8915 \pm j0.1306, 0.2526 \pm j0.0341, 0.0277\}$, from which one finds that Corollary 1 is verified; i.e., the first two eigenvalues (slow modes) are close to the desired ones and the remaining three eigenvalues are those of the fast modes of the open-loop system.

Example 6. A model of a petrol engine, representative of the type used to power medium-sized passenger cars, has as the state variables [43] the dynamometer rotor speed, shaft torque, engine speed, and current amplifier states, and the control signals are the input voltages to the throttle servo system and to the dynamometer field-current amplifier. In terms of (8)–(11), the model matrices are [6]:

$$A = \begin{bmatrix} 0.8070 & 0 & 0 & 0.0092 & 0 \\ -0.0267 & 0.5527 & 0.0171 & -0.0002 & 0.0012 \\ -0.1998 & 5.9560 & 0.1599 & -0.0018 & -0.2576 \\ -5.0795 & 0 & 0 & -0.0381 & 0 \\ 0.0243 & -6.8493 & 0.2311 & 0.0003 & -0.3805 \end{bmatrix}$$

$$B = \begin{bmatrix} 0 & 0.8511 \\ 0.0766 & -0.0106 \\ 0.7019 & -0.0832 \\ 0 & 22.3995 \\ 0.1418 & 0.0257 \end{bmatrix}$$

$$C = \begin{bmatrix} 0 & 1.0 & 0 & 0 & 0 \\ 0 & 0 & 0 & 0 & 1.0 \end{bmatrix}$$

The open-loop eigenvalues are $0.7487, 0.7476, -0.2083 \pm j0.2274, 0.0213$, which shows that the static separation ratio has the value of 0.4125. It is readily seen that this model has two slow states ($n_s = 2$) and three fast states ($n_f = 3$). Direct calculation gives the slow-subsystem matrices as

$$A_0 = \begin{bmatrix} 0.7621 & 0 \\ -0.0294 & 0.6885 \end{bmatrix}$$

$$B_0 = \begin{bmatrix} 0 & 1.0492 \\ 0.0899 & -0.0179 \end{bmatrix}$$

$$C_0 = \begin{bmatrix} 0 & 1.8 \\ -0.2213 & 8.191 \end{bmatrix}$$

$$D_0 = \begin{bmatrix} 0 & 0 \\ 0.7648 & -0.1439 \end{bmatrix}$$

and the fast-subsystem matrices as:

$$A_4 = \begin{bmatrix} 0.1599 & -0.0018 & -0.2576 \\ 0 & -0.0381 & 0 \\ 0.2311 & 0.0003 & -0.3805 \end{bmatrix}$$

$$B_2 = \begin{bmatrix} 0.7019 & -0.0832 \\ 0 & 22.3995 \\ 0.1418 & 0.0257 \end{bmatrix}$$

$C_2 = [0 \quad 0 \quad 1.0]$.

Through the use of auxiliary devices, we can consider that all the state variables become available for generating feedback signals, and proceed to apply the state feedback design scheme. The desired eigenvalues are to be placed at $\{0.8, 0.7, 0.0999, -0.2026, -0.2173\}$ to eliminate system oscillation. The gain matrix K_0 is computed as:

$$K_0 = \begin{bmatrix} 0.0076 & -0.0913 \\ 0.0076 & -0.0913 \end{bmatrix}$$

whereas the fast gain K_f takes the form:

$$K_f = \begin{bmatrix} -0.2861 & 0.0011 & -0.0787 \\ -0.2861 & 0.0011 & -0.0787 \end{bmatrix}$$

From (77), the composite control law is given by:

$$\underline{u}(k) = \begin{bmatrix} 0.0541 & 0.0301 & -0.2877 & 0.0012 & -0.0784 \\ 0.0541 & 0.0301 & -0.2877 & 0.0012 & -0.0784 \end{bmatrix}\underline{x}(k).$$

This state-feedback control yields the closed-loop eigenvalues as $\{0.8, 0.7001, 0.0998, -0.2179, -0.2021\}$, which are very close to the desired ones.

In the case of an output feedback design scheme, we place the desired slow eigenvalue at 0.88 and obtain the gain matrix:

$$G_1 = \begin{bmatrix} 3.7690 \\ 0.5276 \end{bmatrix}$$

For the desired fast eigenvalues to be positioned at $(-0.16 \pm j0.16)$, we obtain the gain matrix:

$$G_2 = \begin{bmatrix} -0.2614 \\ -0.2932 \end{bmatrix}$$

From (105), the output feedback control law takes the form:

$$\underline{u}(k) = \begin{bmatrix} 0.664 & -0.2614 \\ -0.2697 & 0.2932 \end{bmatrix}\underline{y}(k)$$

and yields the closed-loop eigenvalues $(0.9069, 0.9038, -0.1864 \pm j0.1356, -0.0076)$. It is interesting to note that these eigenvalues are close to the desired ones.

Example 7. This example demonstrates the design procedure of dynamic-type controllers.

A fourth-order discrete two-time-scale system, arranged according to (8)–(11), is described by:

$$A_1 = \begin{bmatrix} 0.9 & 0 \\ 0.1 & 0.8 \end{bmatrix}; \quad A_2 = \begin{bmatrix} 0 & 0.1 \\ 0.05 & -0.1 \end{bmatrix};$$

$$A_3 = \begin{bmatrix} -0.1 & 0 \\ 0.12 & 0.003 \end{bmatrix}; \quad A_4 = \begin{bmatrix} 0.15 & 0 \\ 0 & 0.1 \end{bmatrix};$$

$$B_1 = \begin{bmatrix} 1 & 0 \\ 0 & 1 \end{bmatrix}; \quad B_2 = \begin{bmatrix} 1 & 0.5 \\ 0.5 & 0 \end{bmatrix};$$

$$C_1 = \begin{bmatrix} 0.1 & 0 \\ 0 & 0.1 \end{bmatrix}; \quad C_2 = \begin{bmatrix} 0 & 0.1 \\ 0.2 & 0 \end{bmatrix}$$

This system has $n_s = n_f = 2$. A reduced model of order 2 can therefore be constructed as:

$$x_s(k + 1) = \begin{bmatrix} 0.9133 & 0.0033 \\ -0.0192 & 0.8033 \end{bmatrix} x_s(k)$$

$$+ \begin{bmatrix} 1.0556 & 0 \\ 0.0032 & 0.0294 \end{bmatrix} \underline{u}(k);$$

$$\underline{y}(k) = \begin{bmatrix} 0.1133 & 0.0033 \\ -0.0235 & 0.1 \end{bmatrix} x_s(k)$$

$$+ \begin{bmatrix} 0.0556 & 0 \\ 0.2353 & 0.1177 \end{bmatrix} \underline{u}(k).$$

We note that neither B_2 nor C_2 is equal to zero; hence $D_0 \neq 0$. However, it is easy to check that the condition (136) is satisfied. Thus, we can design E_5 to place the eigenvalues of H_4 at desired locations. Let $\lambda_1 = 0.5$, $\lambda_5 = 0.5$ be the desired eigenvalues. The output controllability matrix $\psi(\lambda)$ is first computed as:

$$\psi(\lambda) - \begin{bmatrix} \dfrac{0.05}{\lambda - 0.1} & 0 \\ \dfrac{0.2}{\lambda - 0.15} & \dfrac{0.1}{\lambda - 0.15} \end{bmatrix}$$

Following the design procedure given by Brogen [40], the matrix E_5 is obtained from:

$$E_5 = - \begin{bmatrix} 1 & 0 \\ 0 & 1 \end{bmatrix} \begin{bmatrix} 0.125 & 0 \\ 0.5714 & 0.4 \end{bmatrix}^{-1}$$

$$= \begin{bmatrix} -8 & 0 \\ 11.428 & -2.5 \end{bmatrix}$$

If we select

$$E_1 = \begin{bmatrix} 0.6 & 0 \\ 0 & 0.6 \end{bmatrix}; \quad E_2 = \begin{bmatrix} 0.1 & 0 \\ 0 & -0.1 \end{bmatrix};$$

$$E_3 = \begin{bmatrix} 0.3 & 0 \\ 0 & 0.3 \end{bmatrix}; \quad E_4 = \begin{bmatrix} -0.1 & 0 \\ 0 & -0.1 \end{bmatrix};$$

then by direct substitution we obtain the augmented system matrix:

$$V^0 = \begin{bmatrix} 0.2511 & -0.016 & -0.0731 & 0 \\ 0.0089 & 0.7984 & -0.0003 & -0.0023 \\ -0.1804 & -0.0053 & 0.5789 & 0 \\ 0.312 & -0.057 & 0.0009 & 0.5777 \end{bmatrix}$$

which is clearly asymptotically stable since all of its eigenvalues (0.7988, 0.615, 0.577, 0.2151) have moduli strictly less than one. Thus the dynamic output feedback scheme

$$\underline{f}(k+1) = \begin{bmatrix} 0.6 & 0 \\ 0 & 0.6 \end{bmatrix} \underline{f}(k) + \begin{bmatrix} 0.1 & 0 \\ 0 & -0.1 \end{bmatrix} \underline{y}(k)$$

$$+ \begin{bmatrix} 0.3 & 0 \\ 0 & 0.3 \end{bmatrix} \underline{u}(k)$$

$$\underline{u}(k) = \begin{bmatrix} -0.1 & 0 \\ 0 & -0.1 \end{bmatrix} \underline{f}(k) + \begin{bmatrix} -8 & 0 \\ 11.428 & -2.5 \end{bmatrix} \underline{y}(k)$$

is a stabilizing controller for the original fourth-order discrete system. Now, suppose that

$$C_2 = \begin{bmatrix} 0.1 & 0.1 \\ 0.2 & 0.2 \end{bmatrix}$$

with all other matrices remaining unchanged.

From (135) we have

$$\psi(\lambda) = \begin{bmatrix} 0.1 & 0.1 \\ 0.2 & 0.2 \end{bmatrix} \begin{bmatrix} \lambda - 0.15 & 0 \\ 0 & \lambda - 0.1 \end{bmatrix}^{-1} \begin{bmatrix} 1 & 0.5 \\ 0.5 & 0 \end{bmatrix}$$

$$= \begin{bmatrix} \dfrac{0.15\lambda - 0.0175}{(\lambda - 0.1)(\lambda - 0.15)} & \dfrac{0.05}{\lambda - 0.15} \\ \dfrac{0.3\lambda - 0.035}{(\lambda - 0.1)(\lambda - 0.15)} & \dfrac{0.1}{\lambda - 0.15} \end{bmatrix}$$

It is readily evident that $\det[\psi(\lambda)] = 0$ for all values of λ. This is expected since rank$[C_2] = 1 \neq p$ and, consequently, the design matrix E_5 cannot be determined.

IV. LINEAR QUADRATIC REGULATORS

Here we discuss the development of optimal controllers of discrete systems that can be implemented in two stages using lower-order subsystems. There are three main approaches to tackling this problem. The first [8] is based on extending the separable feedback design procedure presented in Section III using Model I given by (8)–(10). In the second approach [18, 21], slow–fast decompositions of singularly perturbed difference equations of the type (13) and (14) and Model III are derived. Asymptotic expansion methods constitute the third approach [33, 36, 37, 51] utilizing Model II defined by (12). In the first and second approaches compact expressions for the near-optimal control were obtained, whereas in the third approach an iterative procedure was used to improve the suboptimal control. Our focus therefore will be mainly on the first and second approaches.

A.   TWO-TIME-SCALE REGULATORS

Recall that Model I of discrete systems with mode separation was described by (8)–(10) and had (39) and (40) as the slow and fast subsystems, respectively. A linear feedback scheme of the type (74) can be put in the composite form (77) with independent gains K_0 and K_f. Building on this fundamental idea, we consider the linear system (8)–(10) and the associated performance measure to be minimized:

$$J = \frac{1}{2} \sum_{j=0}^{\infty} \left[\underline{y}^t(j)\underline{y}(j) + \underline{u}^t(j)R\underline{u}(j) \right],$$
$$R > 0 \qquad \qquad (137)$$

Instead of tackling the regulator problem (8)–(10) and (137) directly, we decompose it [8] appropriately into two discrete regulators. The first (slow) regulator consists of the slow subsystem (39) and a quadratic performance measure J_s. The second (fast) regulator consists of the fast subsystem (40) and a quadratic performance measure J_f. We emphasize that the construction of the subsystem measure is done such that $J = J_s + J_f$. By solving the fast- and slow-regulator problems independently, we obtain the slow and fast controls $\underline{u}_s(k)$ and $\underline{u}_f(k)$. Then we recompose these controls, which are subsystem optimal, to form the control $\underline{u}_c(k)$ to be implemented on the system (8)–(11).

1. Slow Regulator

The problem is to find $\underline{u}_s(k)$ to minimize

$$J_s = \frac{1}{2} \sum_{j=0}^{\infty} \left[\underline{y}_s^t(j)\underline{y}_s(j) + \underline{u}_s^t(j)R\underline{u}_s(j) \right] \qquad (138)$$

for the slow subsystem (39). Using (39b), we rewrite (138) as:

$$J_s = \frac{1}{2} \sum_{j=0}^{\infty} \left[\underline{x}_s^t(j)C_0^t C_0 \underline{x}_s(j) \right.$$
$$\left. + 2\underline{u}_s^t(j)D_0^t C_0 \underline{x}_s(j) + \underline{u}_s^t(j)R_s\underline{u}_s(j) \right], \qquad (139)$$

where

$$R_s = R + D_0^t D_0.$$

Recall from [45] that if the triple (A_0, B_0, C_0) is stabilizable-detectable, then there exists a positive semidefinite stabilizing solution K_s for the algebraic Riccati equation

$$K_s = \left(A_0^t K_s A_0 + C_0^t C_0 \right) - \left(B_0^t K_s A_0 + D_0^t C_0 \right)^t \qquad (140)$$
$$\times \left(R_s + B_0^t K_s B_0 \right)^{-1} \left(B_0^t K_s A_0 + D_0^t C_0 \right).$$

The corresponding linear optimal control law is given by

$$\underline{u}_s(k) = -\left(R_s + B_0^t K_s B_0\right)^{-1}\left(B_0^t K_s A_0 + D_0^t C_0\right)\underline{x}_s(k). \tag{141}$$

2. Fast Regulator

The problem is to find $\underline{u}_f(k)$ to minimize

$$J_f = \frac{1}{2}\sum_{j=0}^{\cdot}\left[\underline{y}_f^t(j)\underline{y}_f(j) + \underline{u}_f^t(j)R\underline{u}_f(j)\right] \tag{142}$$

for the fast subsystem (40). The substitution of (40b) into (142) yields:

$$J_f = \frac{1}{2}\sum_{j=0}^{\infty}\left[\underline{x}_f(t)(j)C_2^t C_2\underline{x}_f(j)\right.$$

$$\left. + \underline{u}_f^t(j)R\underline{u}_f(j)\right]. \tag{143}$$

From [45] it is known that if the triple (A_4, B_2, C_2) is stabilizable-detectable, then there exists a positive semidefinite stabilizing solution K_f which satisfies the algebraic Riccati equation

$$K_f = \left(A_4^t K_f A_4 + C_2^t C_2\right) - A_4^t K_f B_2\left(R + B_2^t K_f B_2\right)^{-1}B_2^t K_f A_4. \tag{144}$$

The optimal control $\underline{u}_f(k)$ is given by

$$\underline{u}_f(k) = -\left(R + B_2^t K_f B_2\right)^{-1}B_2^t K_f A_4\underline{x}_f(k). \tag{145}$$

Note that the stabilizability-detectability conditions of the triples (A_0, B_0, C_0) and (A_4, B_4, C_4) are eventually independent, and they are equivalent to that of (A, B, C) of system (8)–(11) where $B^t = [B_1^t \ B_2^t]$.

3. Approximate Control

By comparing (139) and (145) with (74), we can identify the gains

$$G_0 = -\left(R_s + B_0^t K_s B_0\right)^{-1}\left(B_0^t K_s A_0 + D_0^t C_0\right) \tag{146a}$$

$$G_f = -\left(R + B_2^t K_f B_2\right)^{-1} B_2^t K_f A_4, \tag{146b}$$

which enables us to obtain the composite control $\underline{u}_c(k)$ from (76) as:

$$\underline{u}_c(k) = -\Big\{ \Big[I_m + \left(R + B_2^t K_f B_2\right)^{-1} B_2^t K_f A_4 \left(I_2 - A_4\right)^{-1}$$

$$\times\, B_2 \Big]\left(R_s + B_0^t K_s B_0\right)^{-1}\left(B_0^t K_s A_0 + D_0^t C_0\right)$$

$$-\left(R + B_2^t K_f B_2\right)^{-1} B_2^t K_f A_4 \left(I_2 - A_4\right)^{-1} A_3 \Big\}$$

$$\times\, \underline{x}_1(k) - \left(R + B_2^t K_f B_2\right) B_2^t K_f A_4 \underline{x}_2(k). \tag{147}$$

It should be evident that the state feedback control (147) is an approximate one. However, it possesses the separation property since the unique matrices K_s and K_f are mutually independent. To express $\underline{u}_c(k)$ in a compact form, we define the following quantities:

$$R_2 = R + B_2^t K_f B_2 \tag{148a}$$

$$K_m^t = K_s A_2 \left(I_2 - A_4\right)^{-1} \tag{148b}$$

$$A_b = -B_1 G_f \tag{148c}$$

$$S = (B_0 - B_1)G_0 + B_1 G_f (I_2 - A_4)^{-1}(B_2 G_0 + A_3) \tag{148d}$$

$$A_d = A_3 - \left(I_2 - A\right)^{-1}\left(B_2 G_0 + A_3\right) + B_2\left(B_2^t K_f B_2\right)^{-1} B_1^t K_s S$$

$$+ K_f^{-1}\Big[K_m S + \left(I_2 - A_4^t\right)^{-1} C_2^t\left(C_0 + D_0 G_0\right)\Big]. \tag{148e}$$

The next lemma summarizes the desired result [8].

Lemma 11. The approximate control $\underline{u}_c(k)$ can be put in the form

$$\underline{u}_c(k) = L\underline{x}(k) = -\left(R + B^t K_c B\right)^{-1} B^t K_c A_c \underline{x}(k), \tag{149}$$

where

$$K_c = \begin{bmatrix} K_s & 0 \\ K_m & K_f \end{bmatrix}; \quad A_c = \begin{bmatrix} A_0 & A_b \\ A_d & A_4 \end{bmatrix}. \tag{150}$$

It is significant to observe that (nnn) is in the standard form of optimal discrete regulator theory [45]. To evaluate the suboptimality of control (76), we recall that the exact optimal control for the complete dynamic problem (8)–(11) and (137) is given by [45]:

$$\underline{u}_c(k) = -\left(R + B^t P_0 B\right)^{-1} B^t P_0 A \underline{x}(k) = -G^0 \underline{x}(k), \tag{151a}$$

where P_0 is the stabilizing solution of the algebraic Riccati equation

$$P_0 = A^t P_0 A - A^t P_0 B \left(R + B^t P_0 B\right)^{-1} B^t P_0 A + C^t C \tag{151b}$$

and the associated optimal performance measure is $J_0 = 1/2 \underline{x}_0{}^t P_0 x_0$, where $\underline{x}_0$ is the initial state. By virtue of (149), the approximated closed-loop system takes the form

$$\underline{x}(k + 1) = (A - BL)\underline{x}(k). \tag{152}$$

From [45], we know that minimizing (137) subject to (152) results in the suboptimal performance measure $J_c = 1/2 \underline{x}_0{}^t P_c \underline{x}_0$, where P_c is the positive definite solution of the discrete Lyapunov equation

$$P_c = (A - BL)^t P_c (A - BL) + C^t C + L^t RL. \tag{153a}$$

Let the suboptimality index ε be defined by

$$P_c - P_0 = \varepsilon P_0, \tag{153b}$$

which, in light of J_0 and J_c, expresses the relative performance degradation; that is, $\varepsilon = (J_c - J_0)/J_0$. The following lemma holds [8].

Lemma 12. An upper bound on the suboptimality index ε is given by

$$\varepsilon \le \left(\|A^t P_0 A\| + \|P_c\|\right)/\|C^t C\| - 1. \tag{154}$$

It is important to observe that the relative performance degradation ε depends on the subsystem information.

4. Reduced-Order Control

We consider that the fast modes are asymptotically stable. With $G_f = 0$ in (77), the reduced-order control becomes:

$$\underline{u}_r(k) = -\left(R_s + B_0^t K_s B_0\right)^{-1}\left(B_0^t K_s A^0 + D_0^t C_0\right)\underline{x}_1(k)$$

$$= -V_r^{-1}\left(B_0^t K_s A_0 + D_0^t C_0\right)\underline{x}_1(k) = -L_r^{\cdot}\underline{x}(k). \tag{155}$$

In terms of

$$W = D_0^t D_0 + B_2^t\left(I_2 - A_4^t\right)^{-1} A_2^t K_m^t B_2 \tag{156a}$$

$$A_e = K_m B_1\left(B_1^t K_m^t K_m B_1\right)^{-1} D_0^t C_0 - W V^r\left(B_0^t K_s A_0 + D_0^t C_0\right) \tag{156b}$$

$$K_r = \begin{bmatrix} K_s & K_m^t \\ K_m & 0 \end{bmatrix}; \quad A_r = \begin{bmatrix} A_0 & 0 \\ A_e & 0 \end{bmatrix} \tag{156c}$$

we have the following result [8]:

Lemma 13. The reduced-order control (155) can be expressed as

$$\underline{u}_r(k) = -\left(R + B^t K_r B\right)^{-1} B^t K_r A_r \underline{x}(k), \tag{157a}$$

which produced performance degradation bounded by

$$\varepsilon \leq \varepsilon_r \leq \|A^t P_r A\| + \|P_r\|/\|C^t\| - 1, \tag{157b}$$

where

$$P_r = \left(A - BL_r\right)^t P_r\left(A - BL_r\right) + C^t C + L_r^t RL_r. \tag{157c}$$

From Lemmas 12 and 13 we conclude that

$$J_0 \leq J_c \leq J_r.$$

A similar approach has been worked out in [44, 46] but with a zero-sum performance criterion; that is, $J_s + J_f = 0$.

B.   SINGULARLY PERTURBED REGULATORS

In [18, 21] the linear shift-invariant system

$$\underline{x}_1(k+1) = \left(I_1 + \lambda \hat{A}_1\right)\underline{x}_1(k) + \mu \hat{A}_2 \underline{x}_2(k) + \lambda B_1 \underline{u}(k) \tag{158a}$$

$$\underline{x}_2(k+1) = \hat{A}_3 \underline{x}_1(k) + \hat{A}_4 \underline{x}_2(k) + B_2 \underline{u}(k) \tag{158b}$$

$$\underline{y}(k) = C_1 \underline{x}_1(k) + C_2 \underline{x}_2(k) + C_3 \underline{u}(k) \tag{158c}$$

was considered. With $C_3 = 0$, (158c) reduces to (10), (13), and (14). The finite-time performance index

$$J = \mu \sum_{k=0}^{N} \left[\underline{y}^t(k)\underline{y}(k) + \underline{u}^t(k)R\underline{u}(k) \right]; \tag{159}$$

$$R = R^t > 0$$

was studied in [18] and extended to the infinite-time case $N \to \infty$ in [21]. Under certain stabilizability-detectability conditions, it has been shown [21] that the infinite-time singularly perturbed regulator (158), 159) has a unique positive-semidefinite stabilizing solution and the associated Riccati matrix has a power-series expansion at $\mu = 0$.

1.   Slow–Fast Decomposition

Following the work in [18–21], the slow variables of (85) are considered to evolve in a slow-time scale (μk) satisfying the outer solution

$$\underline{x}_1(\mu k + \mu) - \underline{x}_1(\mu k) = \mu \hat{A}_1 \underline{x}_1(\mu k) + \mu \hat{A}_2 \underline{x}_2(\mu k) + \mu B_1 \underline{u}(\mu k) \tag{160a}$$

$$\underline{x}_2(\mu k) = \hat{A}_3 \underline{x}_1(\mu k) + \hat{A}_4 \underline{x}_2(\mu k) + B_2 \underline{u}(\mu k) \tag{160b}$$

$$\underline{y}(\mu k) = C_1 \underline{x}_1(\mu k) + C_2 \underline{x}_2(\mu k) + C_3 \underline{u}(\mu k). \tag{160c}$$

In the limit $\mu \to 0$, (160) can be put in the form

$$d\underline{x}_s/dt = \hat{A}_0 \underline{x}_s(k) + \hat{B}_0 \underline{u}_s(k) \tag{161a}$$

$$y_s(k) = C_0 \underline{x}_s(k) + \hat{D}_0 \underline{u}_s(k) \tag{161b}$$

where

$$\widehat{A}_0 = \widehat{A}_1 + \widehat{A}_2\left(I_2 - \widehat{A}_4\right)^{-1}\widehat{A}_3 \tag{162a}$$

$$\widehat{B}_0 = B_1 + \widehat{A}_2\left(I_2 - \widehat{A}_4\right)^{-1}B_2$$

$$\widehat{C}_0 = C_1 + C_2\left(I_2 - \widehat{A}_4\right)^{-1}\widehat{A}_3 \tag{162b}$$

$$\widehat{D}_0 = C_3 + C_2\left(I_2 - \widehat{A}_4\right)^{-1}\widehat{A}_3$$

Being a continuous-time model, an integral type of performance is introduced [21] in the form

$$J_s = \int_0^\infty \left[\underline{y}_s^t(t)\underline{y}_s(t) + \underline{u}_s^t(t)R\underline{u}_s(t)\right]dt. \tag{163}$$

Assuming that the triple (A_0, B_0, C_0) is stabilizable-detectable in the continuous sense [21], the solution of the regulator problem (161)–(163) is given by

$$\underline{u}_s(t) = -\left[R + \widehat{D}_0^t\widehat{D}_0\right]^{-1}\left[\widehat{D}_0^t\widehat{C}_0 + \widehat{B}_0^t P_s\right]\underline{x}_s(t) \tag{164a}$$

$$= -F_s x_s(t)$$

$$0 = P_s\left(\widehat{A}_0 - \widehat{B}_0\left[R + \widehat{D}_0^t\widehat{D}_0\right]^{-1}\widehat{D}_0^t\widehat{C}_0\right)$$

$$+ \left(\widehat{A}_0 - \widehat{B}_0\left[R + \widehat{D}_0^t\widehat{D}_0\right]^{-1}\widehat{D}_0^t\widehat{C}_0\right)^t P_s$$

$$- P_s\widehat{B}_0\left(\left[R + \widehat{D}_0^t\right]^{-1}\widehat{B}_0^t P_s\right)$$

$$+ \widehat{C}_s^t\left(I - \widehat{D}_0\left[R + \widehat{D}_0^t\widehat{D}_0\right]^{-1}\widehat{D}_0^t\right)\widehat{C}_0. \tag{164b}$$

On considering the fast variables as the difference between the original variables in (158) and the corresponding slow variables in (161), the fast model is shown [21] to be

$$\underline{x}_f(k + 1) = \hat{A}_4 \underline{x}_f(k) + B_2 \underline{u}_f(k) \tag{165a}$$

$$\underline{y}_f = C_2 \underline{x}_f(k) + C_3 \underline{u}_f(k). \tag{165b}$$

The fast-performance index J_f is defined by

$$J_f = \sum_{k=0}^{\infty} \left[\underline{y}_f^t(k) \underline{y}_f(k) + \underline{u}_f^t(k) R \underline{u}_f(k) \right]. \tag{166}$$

If the triple (A_4, B_2, C_2) is stabilizable and detectable, the optimal solution of the fast regulator (165) and (166) is summarized by

$$\underline{u}_f(k) = -\left[R + C_3^t C_3 + B_2^t P_f B_2 \right]^{-1}$$

$$\times \left[B_2^t P_f \hat{A}_4 + C_3^t C_2 \right] \underline{x}_f(k) \tag{167a}$$

$$= -F_f \underline{u}_f(k)$$

$$P_f = C_2^t C_2 + \hat{A}_4^t P_f \hat{A}_4$$

$$- \left[B_2^t P_f \hat{A}_4 + C_3^t C_2 \right]^t \left[R + C_3^t C_3 + B_2^t P_f B_2 \right]^{-1}$$

$$\times \left[B_2^t P_f \hat{A}_4 + C_3^t C_2 \right]. \tag{167b}$$

A composite feedback control is formed as [21]

$$\underline{u}_c = \underline{u}_s + \underline{u}_f = -F_s \underline{x}_s(t) - F_f \underline{x}_f(k),$$

which can be manipulated to yield

$$\underline{u}_c = -\left[F_s - F_f \left(I_2 - \hat{A}_4 \right)^{-1} \left(\hat{A}_3 - B_2 F_s \right) \right] \underline{x}_1(k)$$

$$- F_f \underline{x}_2(k). \tag{168}$$

It is important to observe that $\underline{u}_c$ yields $\mathcal{O}(\mu^2)$ the near-optimal cost; that is, $J_c - J^0 = \mathcal{O}(\mu^2)$.

C.   EXAMPLE

The eighth-order model of Example 2, Section II, is arranged in the form (8)–(11) with

$$A_1 = \begin{bmatrix} 0.928 & -0.029 & 0.028 & 0.0318 \\ -0.253 & 0.882 & -0.09 & -0.0091 \\ 0 & 0 & 0.861 & 0.218 \\ 0 & 0 & 0 & 0.835 \end{bmatrix}$$

$$A_2 = \begin{bmatrix} 0.06 & 1.073 & 0 & 0.04 \\ -0.03 & -0.455 & 0.5467 & -0.02 \\ 0 & 0 & 0 & 0.29 \\ 0 & 0 & 0 & 0 \end{bmatrix}$$

$$A_3 = \begin{bmatrix} 0 & 0 & 0.1516 & 0.0218 \\ -0.077 & 0.0665 & -0.003 & -0.003 \\ -0.1727 & 0.152 & 0.152 & -0.0102 \\ 0 & 0 & 0 & 0.185 \end{bmatrix}$$

$$A_4 = \begin{bmatrix} 0.165 & 0 & 0 & 0.046 \\ -0.007 & 0.156 & 0.118 & 0.007 \\ -0.016 & -0.31 & 0.088 & -0.012 \\ 0 & 0 & 0 & 0.011 \end{bmatrix}$$

$$B_1^t = \begin{bmatrix} -0.038 & 0.294 & 0 & 0 \\ 0.01 & -0.003 & 0.076 & 0.725 \end{bmatrix}$$

$$B_2^t = \begin{bmatrix} 0 & 0.081 & 0.207 & 0 \\ 0.006 & -0.0008 & -0.004 & 0.124 \end{bmatrix}$$

$$C_1 = \begin{bmatrix} 0 & 0 & 0 & 4.545 \\ 0 & 1 & 0 & 0 \\ 0 & 0 & 0 & 0 \\ 0 & 0 & 0 & 0 \end{bmatrix}$$

$$C_2 = \begin{bmatrix} 0 & 0 & 0 & 0 \\ 0 & 0 & 0 & 0 \\ 0 & 0 & 13.333 & 0 \\ 0 & 18.182 & 0 & 0 \end{bmatrix}$$

With $R = I_2$, direct computation of the two-time-scale regulators yields the gain matrices

$$G^0 = \begin{bmatrix} 0.818 & -0.744 & 0.038 & 0.026 & 0.075 & 0.685 & -0.635 & -0.025 \\ -0.019 & 0.005 & -0.006 & -1.061 & -0.002 & -0.037 & -0.0014 & -0.0031 \end{bmatrix}$$

$$L = \begin{bmatrix} 0.813 & -0.743 & 0.039 & 0.0259 & 0.072 & 0.615 & -0.608 & -0.023 \\ -0.021 & 0.0061 & -0.005 & -1.061 & -0.001 & -0.075 & -0.011 & -0.003 \end{bmatrix}$$

$$L_r = \begin{bmatrix} 0.806 & -0.736 & 0.0523 & 0.03 & 0 & 0 & 0 & 0 \\ -0.02 & 0.006 & -0.006 & -1.061 & 0 & 0 & 0 & 0 \end{bmatrix}$$

together with $J_0 = T_r(P_0) = 567.4224$, $J_c = T_r(P_c) = 567.5176$, and $J_r = T_r(P_r) = 578.861$. The index ε in (153b) has the value 0.0168, whereas its bound in (154) is 0.19845. Also, $\varepsilon_r = 0.0202$, whereas its upper bound in (157b) is 0.22232. It is clearly evident that the composite control produces good performance results.

V.   DISCUSSION AND
CONCLUDING REMARKS

So far we have been concerned with the analysis, control design, and optimization of linear, discrete systems with time-scale separation which can be described by implicit-type models (e.g., Model I) or explicit-type models (e.g., Models II and III) having single, singular-perturbation parameter. A natural extension of the latter category of models is to deal with situations which have multiparameter singular perturbations. Some preliminary results have been obtained in [47], where Model III has been generalized to include several parameters expressing ratios of speeds of clusters of eigenvalues. An important control design problem is that of output feedback using Models II and III, which has not been resolved completely despite the initial attempts in [35].

One of the attractive areas of contemporary research is that of adaptive control. Thus, discrete plants for which the dominant part can be analyzed and controlled, whereas the nondominant part is unknown (due to the presence of parasitics or unmodeled dynamics), represent good examples calling for adaptive techniques. Fortunately, this class of plants can be treated in the frame of discrete multiple-time-scale systems as well (see Section II). Therefore, combining adaptive control methodology with discrete multiple-time-scale systems would reveal ample interesting technical problems that require much research effort. Again, some work has been performed in this direction, and the results are compiled in [48–50].

A description of discrete systems with slow–fast decomposition in stochastic environments is by far the most challenging problem for which no single result has been reported up to now. Although the problem is technically sound, it requires a different mathematical analysis more profound than that pursued in the deterministic case.

It should be noted that our starting point was the model in (1) and (2) under the eigenvalue condition (7). A more realistic approach would start from a physical model of the singularly perturbed continuous-time system [1] of the form

$$\underline{x}(t) = A_c(\mu)\underline{x}(t) + B_c(\mu)\underline{u}(t) \tag{169}$$

$$\underline{y}(t) = C_c(\mu)\underline{x}(t) + D_c(\mu)\underline{u}(t), \tag{170}$$

then by employing suitable discretization scheme, one would obtain the general form

$$\underline{x}(k+1) = A_d(T, \mu)\underline{x}(k) + B_d(T, \mu)\underline{u}(k) \tag{171}$$

$$\underline{y}(k) = C_d(T, \mu)\underline{x}(k) + D_d(T, \mu)\underline{u}(k), \tag{172}$$

where $\mu > 0$ is a singular perturbation parameter and T is the sampling period. Several questions arise related to the selection of T to preserve the properties of (169) and (170) and whether or not there is a link between T and μ for (171) and (172) to exhibit the fast–slow separation.

These are some of the interesting problems that deserve future investigation.

REFERENCES

1. V. R. SAKSENA, J. O'REILLY, and P. V. KAKOTOVIC, "Singular Perturbations and Time-Scale Methods in Control Theory: Survey 1976–1983," *Automatica 20*, 273–293 (1984).
2. M. S. MAHMOUD, "Order Reduction and Control of Discrete Systems," *Proc. IEE Part D 129*, 129–135 (1982).
3. M. S. MAHMOUD, "Design of Observer-Based Controllers for a Class of Discrete Systems," *Automatica 18*, 323–328 (1982).
4. M. S. MAHMOUD, "Structural Properties of Discrete Systems with Slow and Fast Modes," *Large Scale Syst. 3*, 227–236 (1982).
5. M. S. MAHMOUD, "Multi-Time-Scale Analysis in Discrete Systems," *J. Eng. Appl. Sci. 2*, 301–315 (1983).
6. M. S. MAHMOUD and Y. CHEN, "Design of Feedback Controllers by Two-Stage Methods," *Appl. Math. Model. 7*, 163–168 (1983).
7. M. S. MAHMOUD, Y. CHEN, and M. G. SINGH, "On the Eigenvalue Assignment in Discrete Systems with Fast and Slow Modes," *Int. J. Syst. Sci. 16*, 61–70 (1985).
8. H. A. OTHMAN, N. M. KHRAISHI, and M. S. MAHMOUD, "Discrete Regulators with Time-Scale Separation," *IEEE Trans. Autom. Control AC-30*, 293–297 (1985).
9. M. S. MAHMOUD, Y. CHEN, and M. G. SINGH, "Discrete Two-Time-Scale Systems," *UMIST Control Syst. Centre Rep. No. 497*, Dec. 1980.
10. M. S. MAHMOUD and M. G. SINGH, "On the Use of Reduced-Order Models in Output Feedback Design of Discrete Systems," *Automatica 21* (1985).
11. R. G. PHILLIPS, "Reduced Order Modeling and Control of Two-Time-Scale Discrete Systems," *Int. J. Control 31*, 765–780 (1980).
12. R. G. PHILLIPS, "The Equivalence of Time-Scale Decomposition Techniques Used in the Analysis and Design of Linear Systems," *Int. J. Control 37*, 1239-1259 (1983).
13. S. H. JAVID, "Multi-Time Methods in Order Reduction and Control of Discrete Systems," *Proc. Asilomar Conf.* 375–379 (1979).
14. M. S. MAHMOUD, Y. CHEN, and M. G. SINGH, "A Two-Stage Output Feedback Design," *Proc. IEE* (1985).
15. M. S. MAHMOUD and M. G. SINGH, "*Discrete Systems: Analysis, Optimization and Control,*" Springer-Verlag, Berlin, 1984.
16. M. S. MAHMOUD and M. G. SINGH, "*Large-Scale Systems Modeling,*" Pergamon, Oxford, 1981.
17. H. K. KHALIL (Ed.), "Singular Perturbation Methods and Multimodel Control," *Tech. Rep. No. DE-ACO1-80RA50425*, pp. 134–160, Michigan State University, 1983.
18. B. LITKOUHI and H. K. KHALIL, "Infinite-Time Regulators for Singularly Perturbed Difference Equations," *Int. J. Control 39*, 587–598 (1981).
19. G. DAHLQUIST and A. BJORK, "Numerical Methods," Prentice Hall, Englewood Cliffs, New Jersey, 1974.

20.   F. C. HOPPENSTEADT and W. L. MIRANKER, "Multitime Methods for Systems of Dif-
       ference Equations," *Stud. Appl. Math.* 56, 273–289 (1977).
21.   G. BLANKENSHIP, "Singularly Perturbed Difference Equations in Optimal Control
       Problems," *IEEE TRANS. AUTOM. CONTROL AC-26*, 911–917 (1981).
22.   M. T. TRAN and M. E. SAWAN, "Reduced Order Discrete-Time Models," *Int. J. Syst.
       Sci.* 14, 745-752 (1983).
23.   A. LOCATELLI and N. SCHIAVONI, "Two-Time-Scale Discrete Systems," *Proc. 2st Int.
       Conf. Inf. Sci. Syst.*, Patras, 421425 (1976).
24.   C. COMSTOCK and G. C. HSIAO, "Singular Perturbations for Difference Equations,"
       Rocky Mountain J. Math. 6, 561–567 (1976).
25.   P. K. RAJAGOPALAN and D. S. NAIDU, "A Singular Perturbation Method for Discrete
       Control Systems," *Int. J. Control 32*, 925-936 (1980).
26.   M. S. MAHMOUD, "Discrete Singular Perturbations Technique," *World Conf. Syst.*,
       Caracas, Paper No. XI-3-1 (1983).
27.   B. AVRAMOVIC, "Subspace Iterations Approach to the Time Scale Separation," *Proc.
       18th IEEE Conf. Decision Control*, Florida, 684687 (1976).
28.   M. T. EL-HADIDI and M. H. TAWFIK, "A New Iterative Algorithm for Block-Diagonal-
       ization of Discrete-Time Systems," *Syst. Control Lett.* 4 (1984).
29.   G. C. HSIAO and K. E. JORDAN, Solutions to the Difference Equations of Singular Per-
       turbation Problems, *in "Numerical Analysis of Singular Perturbation Problems"*
       (Hemker and Miller, Eds.), pp. 433–440. Academic Press, London, 1979.
30.   M. S. MAHMOUD and Y. CHEN, "Feedback Design of Discrete Two-Time-Scale Sys-
       tems," *UMIST Control Syst. Centre Rep.* No. 512, April (1981).
31.   B. N. PARLETT and C. REINSCH, "Balancing a Matrix for Calculation of Eigenvalues
       and Eigenvectors," *Num. Math.* 13, 293–304 (1969).
32.   G. P. SYRCOS and P. SANNUTI, "Singular Perturbation Modelling of Continuous and
       Discrete Physical Systems," *In. J. Control 37*, 1007–1022 (1983).
33.   H. KANDO and T. IWAZUMI, "Sub-optimal Control of Discrete Regulator Problems via
       Time-Scale Decomposition," *Int. J. Control 37*, 1323–1347 (1983).
34.   H. KANDO and T. IWAZUMI, "Stabilizing Feedback Controllers for Singularly Perturbed
       Discrete Systems," *IEEE Trans. Syst. Man Cybernet. SMC-14*, 903–911 (1984).
35.   H. KANDO and T. IWAZUMI, "Design of Observers and Stabilizing Feedback Con-
       trollers for Singularly Perturbed Discrete Systems," *Proc. IEE 132*, 1–10 (1985).
36.   P. K. RAJAGOPALAN and D. S. NAIDU, "Singular Perturbation Method for Discrete
       Models of Continuous Systems in Optimal Control," *Proc. IEE 128*, 142–148 (1981).
37.   M. S. MAHMOUD, "Comment on Singular Perturbation Method for Discrete Models of
       Continuous Systems in Optimal Control," *Proc. IEE 130*, 136 (1983).
38.   P. V. KOKOTOVIC, J. J. ALLEMONG, J. R. WINKELMAN, and J. H. CHOW, "Singular
       Perturbation and Iterative Separation of Time Scales," *Automatica 16*, 23–32 (1980).
39.   M. ARUMUGAM and M. RAMAMOORTY, "A Method for Simplifying Large Dynamic
       Systems," *Int. J. Control 17*, 1129–1135 (1973).
40.   BROGAN, *"Modern Control Theory,"* Quantum Publ., New York, 1974.
41.   N. MUNRO, "Pole Assignment," *Proc. IEE 126*, 549–554 (1979).
42.   C. T. CHEN, "Introduction to Linear System Theory," Holt, New York, 1970.
43.   J. MONK and J. COMFORT, "Mathematical Model of an Internal Combustion Engine
       and Dynamometer Test Rig," *Measure. Control 3*, T93–T100 (1970).
44.   M. T. TRAN and M. E. SWAN, "On the Well-Posedness of Discrete-Time Systems with
       Slow and Fast Modes," *Int. J. Syst. Sci. 15*, 1289–1294 (1984).
45.   Y. BAR-NESS, "Solution of the Discrete Infinite-Time, Time-Invariant Regulator by the
       Euler Equation," *Int. J. Control 22*, 49–66 (1975).
46.   M. T. TRAN and M. E. SWAN, "Decentralized Control of Two-Time-Scale Discrete-Time
       Systems," *Int. J. Syst. Sci. 15*, 1295–1300 (1984).
47.   M. S. MAHMOUD, "Stabilization of Discrete Systems with Multiple Time Scales," *IEEE
       Trans. Autom. Control* to appear (1986).

48. N. M. KHRAISHI, H. A. OTHMAN, and M. S. MAHMOUD, "Reduced-Order Modeling and Control in Adaptive Discrete Systems," *Tech. Rep.* No. ECE-CS-84-10-7, Kuwait University, 1984.

49. N. M. KHRAISHI, H. A. OTHMAN, and M. S. MAHMOUD, "Discrete Adaptive Systems with Reduced Models," *Tech. Rep.* No. ECE-CS-84-10-8, Kuwait University, 1984.

50. M. S. MAHMOUD, H. A. OTHMAN, and N. M. KHRAISHI, "Reduced-Order Performance of Adaptive Control Systems," *Tech. Rep.* No. 84-10-9, Kuwait University, 1984.

51. A. K. RAO and D. S. NAIDU, "Singular Perturbation Method Applied to the Open-Loop Discrete Optimal Control Problem," *Optimal Control Appl. Methods 3*, 121–131 (1982).

INDEX